ALZHEIMER'S AND THE LAW

Counseling Clients with Dementia and Their Families

Kerry Peck and Rick L. Law
with Brandon Peck and Diana Law

ALZHEIMER'S AND THE LAW

Counseling Clients with Dementia and Their Families

Foreword by Scott Turow

AMERICAN BAR ASSOCIATION
Senior Lawyers
Division

Cover by Andrew O. Alcala/ABA Publishing.

The materials contained herein represent the opinions of the authors and editors, and should not be construed to be the views or opinions of the law firms or companies with whom such persons are in partnership with, associated with, or employed by, nor of the American Bar Association or the Senior Lawyers Division unless adopted pursuant to the bylaws of the Association.

Nothing contained in this book is to be considered as the rendering of legal advice for specific cases, and readers are responsible for obtaining such advice from their own legal counsel. This book is intended for educational and informational purposes only.

Printed in the United States of America

17 16 15 14 13   5 4 3 2

Library of Congress Cataloging-in-Publication Data

Alzheimer's and the law : counseling clients with dementia and their families / Edited by Kerry Peck and Rick Law, with Brandon Peck and Diana Law.
    pages cm
Includes bibliographical references and index.
    ISBN 978-1-62722-240-2 (print : alk. paper)
    1. Alzheimer's disease—Patients—Legal status, laws, etc.—United States 2. Practice of law—United States. I. Peck, Kerry, editor. II. Peck, Brandon, editor. III. Law, Diana, editor.
    KF3803.A56A49 2013
    344.7303'2196831—dc23

                                                                                    2013025541

Discounts are available for books ordered in bulk. Special consideration is given to state bars, CLE programs, and other bar-related organizations. Inquire at Book Publishing, ABA Publishing, American Bar Association, 321 North Clark Street, Chicago, Illinois 60654-7598.

www.ShopABA.org

FOREWORD

In my new novel, *Identical*, Tim Brodie, an elderly private investigator who hopes to unravel the mysteries of a murder that took place nearly three decades before visits a nursing home so he can interview Lidia Gianis, 87, a woman Tim has known for years but who is now deeply in the grip of dementia:

"Is he my husband?" Lidia asked Eloise, her attendant, as Tim entered.

"Oh no, honey. He just a friend." Eloise propped Lidia up in the leatherette recliner. "You all go head and visit. I'm just outside, case you need me."

Tim sat down in a wooden-armed chair a few feet from Lidia.

"Do I know you?" she asked Tim.

"Tim Brodie, Lidia. We met a million years ago at St. D's."

"I don't know you," she said. "I had a stroke and my memory is not so good."

"Yeah, well, my memory isn't what it once was either. "

In thirty years on the police force, and twenty five since then as a P.I., Tim had done lots of interviews under daunting circumstances, questioning children and the mentally handicapped, and naturally enough, the desperately bereaved. But this would be a new chapter and Tim had no idea how to start.

On Lidia's bedside table, there were photographs of her two daughters and of her twin sons and a passel of kids.

"Now who are all these folks?" he asked her.

"I don't know. The girl just put them there. But they're all nice people."

Tim picked up one photograph, a group shot of Lidia's grandchildren.

"Now these grandkids of yours, they're a good-looking bunch." Tim meant it. The Gianises were always a handsome family.

Lidia was frowning. "Is that who they are?" she asked.

"Beautiful," Tim said, "All of them."

"Yes, I think they're all nice people. I have a son, did you know that?"

"Two, I believe." He tapped the picture beside her of her identical boys.

"My sons come here all the time. One of them is a big deal, too. Is he an actor? she asked Tim, referring to Paul who was now running for Mayor. "People just love him. They tell me so all the time. Everyone here knows who he is."

Tim said he knew Paul too, then asked about Cass, hoping for any information about the other twin.

Lidia pondered a second and shook her head. "I had a stroke and my memory's not so good." She raised her hand again to stare at her bracelet, which, by whatever logic was left to her, once more brought her attention to Tim. "Who are you?" she asked. "Do I know you?"

This dialogue, unfortunately, is based more on experience than imagination. My mother, who passed in 2011 at the age of 91, spent her last six years increasingly confused by dementia. The perseveration and repetitions that characterize Lidia's conversation became familiar to me, as did the fact that my mom could have unpredictable flashes of amazing lucidity. Caring for her was always a challenge, even though I had the complete support of my sister, Vicki, who shared the responsibility with me, and the heroic assistance of two wonderful cousins, Joy and Sy Dordick, who spent time with my mom and often stood in for me when I was travelling. Nonetheless, when my mom lay dying, I felt compelled to ask her whether she wanted to go on with her life. That was simply not a decision any of us felt we could make for her.

"Are you ready to quit?" I asked my mother.

She shook her head no. I doubt that she understood the full implications of the question, but she got the basic point and, Alzheimer's or not, my sister and I abided by her decision that she was not ready to die. The medical interventions continued, although she was gone days later, notwithstanding.

The complexity of that moment and of entrusting such a profound question to someone whose capacities were so compromised makes for intense family drama. But the legal implications of such situations are in many ways even more difficult to unravel.

That is why this is such a fascinating and important book. It is not the usual ponderous legal treatise. It is a practical quick start guide so that you, as a professional, can be a beacon to a client, a friend, a loved one, or even a colleague who has been affected by the darkness of dementia.

When it comes to understanding Alzheimer's disease, lawyers are laypeople. Every one of us knows someone who has been affected, but the disease is so pervasive and frightening that many of us try to block it from our minds. When someone asks us what to should do now that a loved one has been diagnosed, we don't even know how to begin to find the right answers. This book will be your starting point and a trustworthy guide. It is written by practicing lawyers who are on the front lines fighting to serve clients with Alzheimer's disease and their families. In this book they share with you their practice pointers, their wisdom, and the uncommon knowledge that comes from years of multiple client experiences.

You are about to meet some great storytellers and many deeply admirable people. The authors know that no matter how well attorneys fulfill their legal role, when it comes to Alzheimer's disease, dementia sufferers and their families need help from a team of capable and concerned professionals. Within these pages you will hear from nurses, legal guardians, advocates for elder-abuse victims, hospice personnel, Alzheimer's Association leaders, technology visionaries, geriatric psychiatrists, police officers specializing in scam prevention, family caregivers, forensic experts, and even prosecutors. Each one has an important story to tell that will provide you and your client with the gift of deeper understanding.

Alzheimer's disease is one of the scourges of our time, and one whose toll on the country will only deepen with the aging of the Baby Boomers and the inevitability of increased life spans. Curing Alzheimer's would probably do more than any single step to reduce health care expenses and—far more important—improve the quality of life of the elderly here and around the world. But until there is a cure, you'll be grateful to have this book at your side.

—Scott Turow
July 2013

CONTENTS

Foreword   v

Acknowledgments   xv

Introduction   xix

Expert View: I Have Become My Wife's Parent   xxiii

CHAPTER ONE: WHAT IS ALZHEIMER'S DISEASE?   1

The Alzheimer's Journey   2

Memory Loss Ignored   4

Memory Loss Masked/Denied   6

Unsafe Alone   8

Aid Needed, But Fights Back   10

Assisted Living   11

Nursing Home   13

Hospice/Death   15

Statistical Projections   18

**Expert View: Client Confabulation: The Attorney's
    Consternation   21**

CHAPTER TWO: ETHICS AND THE ALZHEIMER'S CLIENT   25

Rule 1.14   26

Client-Lawyer Relationship   27

Rule 1.4   39

Client-Lawyer Relationship   39

Rule 1.6   40
   Client-Lawyer Relationship   40
Rule 1.7   42
   Client-Lawyer Relationship   42

CHAPTER THREE: LIFE, DEATH, AND CARE INSTRUCTIONS   51
Advance Directives   53
   What Can Happen Without an Advance Directive?   54
   The Importance of an Advance Directive in the Context of Alzheimer's
      Disease   57
Living Wills   60
   Both Federal and State Law Regulate Advance Directives   61
Power of Attorney   68
   Powerful Versus Powerless Power of Attorney   69
   Illinois   75
   California   77
   Florida   77
   New York   79
   Power of Attorney for Property (Financial Decisions)   80
   Powerful or Powerless Power of Attorney for Property?   81
Do Not Resuscitate Order   84
Choosing an Agent   85
POLST   87
**Appendix: Health-Care Power of Attorney and Combined
   Advance Directive Legislation   89**
Expert View: Surprising Truths Within Hospice Care   144
Expert View: 10 Tips for Caregivers   147

CHAPTER 4: SPECIAL-NEEDS TRUSTS AND POOLED TRUSTS   151
Trusts Background   155
   Special-Needs Trusts   155
OBRA 93   157
Revocable Trusts   159
Irrevocable Trusts   159
D4A: Self-Settled Medicaid Payback Trust   160
D4B: Miller Trust   160

D4C: Charitable Pooled Trust   160
How to Take Care of the Spouse   164
    Testamentary Trusts   164
    Common Mistakes When Creating a Spousal Special-Needs Trust   167
How to Provide for an Adult Child with Disabilities   169
    Non-Spouse Third-Party Trustor   172
    Third-Party Trust Created for a Public Benefits Recipient   172
    Third-Party Trust Created for Another Where the Grantor Seeks
       Public Benefits   172
Appendix A: Declaration of Trust (Excerpt)   175
Appendix B: Will of John Pourback   176
Expert View: The Marriage of Technology and Alzheimer's
  Caregiving: Staying Safely at Home Longer   182

CHAPTER 5: GOVERNMENT BENEFITS   185
Winning the Diagnosis Lottery   185
Medicare Versus Medicaid   187
Medicare   188
    Hospital Insurance (Part A)   189
    Medical Insurance (Part B)   191
    Medicare Advantage Plans (Part C)   192
    Medicare Prescription Drug Plans (Part D)   192
    Medigap Policies   193
Medicaid   195
    Eligibility   199
    Principal Place of Residence   200
    Spending Down   203
    Caregiver Contracts   209
    State Examples of Medicaid   212
Veterans Affairs Benefits   219
    Non-Service-Connected Disability Pension   219
    Income/Net Worth Requirements   221
    Possible Medicaid Trap   222
    DIC Benefits   222
Expert View: The Red Flag of Alzheimer's: A Change
  of Character   225

CHAPTER 6: GUARDIANSHIPS AND CONSERVATORSHIPS 229
Guardianship to the Rescue 231
Guardian Defined 232
Current Estate Plan 235
Mental Capacity 235
Substituted Judgment Standard 236
Conflict 237
Types of Guardianships 238
   Guardian of Person 239
   Surrogate Decision Maker 240
   Guardian of the Estate 240
   Short-Term Guardian 241
   Temporary Guardian 242
   Limited Guardianship 246
   Contested 252
   Hearing 255
Reporting Requirements 258
   Guardian of Person 258
   Guardian of Estate 259
Termination/Removal of the Guardian 260
   California 261
   Florida 262
   New York 265
Adult Guardianship and Protective Proceedings
   Jurisdiction Act 268
Divorce and Guardianship Issues for Individuals
   with Alzheimer's Disease 270
   Illinois and the "Best Interests" Hearing 270
**Expert View: Even Experienced Lawyers Make These
   Mistakes 278**

CHAPTER 7: FINANCIAL EXPLOITATION 283
Financial Exploitation 285
Forensic Accounting 291
Stranger Danger 292
Grandma Scam 293
Lottery Scam 294
Spoofing 294

Ruse Entry   295
Drive-By Contractors   295
Vulnerability   297
Wolf in Sheep's Clothing   301
Defenses Against Financial Exploitation   303
    Probate/Citations   303
Fiduciary Relationship   307
Seniors Tolerate Lesser of Two Evils   309
Going Forward   310
**Expert View: When the Indispensable Caregiver Is the
    Abuser   312**

**CHAPTER 8: PERSONAL-CARE AGREEMENTS AND NURSING
HOME CONTRACTS   315**
Adult Children Providing Care   319
Perfect World Versus Real World   321
How to Draft a Powerful Personal-Care Agreement   323
Burden on Caretaker   327
Employment Taxes   329
The Invisible Opponents: The Backstory of Cultural and Religious
    Tradition, Judicial Bias, Elder Abuse Statutes, and the State
    Medicaid Department   330
    Medicaid Issues with Personal Care Contracts   332
    Avoiding the Hidden Traps of Nursing Home Contracts   337
    Arbitration Clauses: The Bane of the Litigator and Clients   342
    Residents' Rights   343
    Patient Transfers/Discharges   345
**Expert View: The Hope of Vanquishing Alzheimer's
    Disease   348**

GLOSSARY   351
INDEX   365

DON'T SKIP THIS! PRAISE FOR THE PRACTICING LAWYER AND THOSE TO WHOM CREDIT IS DUE

We are very excited to share this book with you. We had you in mind from the beginning. Our primary goal was to create a book that will be read by, be applied by, and be helpful to attorneys working with persons with dementia and their families. That is why we, as your fellow practicing attorneys, agreed to fit this project into our lives.

We acknowledge you! You are the counselors at law who spend 60 to 80 hours working per week. You have a spouse or significant other who wishes that you would just say no to the endless lists of things that you agree to do. You are the leaders who must meet a payroll; woo clients; go to court; attend funerals, weddings and bar mitzvahs—and still see your kids' or grandkids' soccer games.

We, Kerry and Rick, really want to thank our own devoted sweethearts, Hillary Peck and Rose Law. They have put up with us for a long time. We know we do a lot of things that make you roll your eyes, but we admit that you bring out the best in us!

This book would not be possible without the sacrifices of the legal teams at both Peck Bloom, LLC and Law ElderLaw, LLP. Our teams supported us both personally and financially in the creation of this book.

This book idea originated with the American Bar Association. ABA editor Erin Nevius brought the concept to Kerry Peck. Once Kerry got inspired, he asked Rick Law to "help out." As lawyers who practice law alongside our adult lawyer children, we did use a little parental encouragement to enlist Brandon Peck, Esq. and Diana Law, Esq. to become contributors. Together we got the project rolling.

From the start, we knew that you should hear from the many voices of insight and wisdom that are outside of the law. These are the voices of caregivers, health care professionals, and others who need to be heard, so that your clients with dementia and their families can find not only legal solutions but also care and peace of mind.

Katherine Motley, an experienced member of the Law ElderLaw team, is a gifted writer, storyteller, and teacher. She has the title of Executive VP of Operations, but that underestimates her client-centered experiences within the elder law firm. She is an author in her own right of a book entitled 7 *Secrets to Success in Your Law Firm* and the co-author with Rick Law of a book entitled *Cruising Through Retirement—Avoiding the Potholes*. Many of this book's practice pointers and client stories were written by Kathy. It would not be too much of a stretch for us to call her a co-author of this book.

Anything that Jessica Bannister of Law ElderLaw decides to do, she does extremely well. We often refer to her as "VP of Special Projects." For this project she was the organizational hub of operations. She coordinated the diverse interviews, research assignments, editorial deadlines, and administrative details. Without Jessica, we could not have delivered this project on time.

Special thanks needs to be extended to Kerry Peck's dear friend and colleague Sanford I. Finkel, M.D. Over the years they have both been involved with intriguing cases and discussions involving testamentary capacity as it may be influenced by dementia, depression, psychosis, medication, and end-of-life issues. They enjoy being both friends and neighbors.

As lawyers we know when to call in expert help. For the chapter on special needs trusts, we reached out to nationally recognized attorney Timothy L. Takacs of Hendersonville, Tennessee. Tim has been an especially close friend of Rick and Diana Law. We have deeply appreciated his mentorship in guiding us in the development of our own elder law practice.

Our chapter on financial exploitation is a treasure, thanks in part to the contributions of attorney Charles (Chuck) Golbert, Deputy Public

Guardian of the Office of the Cook County Public Guardian of Chicago, Illinois. He is responsible for overseeing the operation of the office's guardianship services for its 800 adult wards with disabilities, including legal and social services and management of more than $100 million in collected ward assets. He has been lead counsel in numerous financial exploitation lawsuits that have achieved the recovery of tens of millions of dollars in assets stolen from persons with Alzheimer's disease and other disabilities.

Another voice that we deeply appreciate is that of our friend Shay Jacobson. Shay is the President and CEO of Life Care Innovations, Inc., the largest home healthcare agency in the Chicago metropolitan area. Her operation focuses on disputed guardianships as well as complex care management for persons with substantial disabling conditions. She is an able storyteller and a consummate professional. Her compelling stories provide lead-ins for our chapters on guardianship and financial exploitation.

We still needed even more help to put together the various puzzle pieces of research, interviews, and stories. That role was filled by attorney Robert Wilson. Bob's day job involves editing several legal and tax journals. For the year and a half that we spent working on this project, he helped us provide you, the reader, with a beautifully put together piece of work—as opposed to having a lot of random puzzle pieces lying on the table after we each threw in our disparate contributions.

We want to thank the wonderful people we interviewed who generously allowed us to use their stories within this book. You will find the interviews between the chapters or woven into the fabric of the text.

- Cherie Aschenbrenner, Crime Prevention Specialist and Elderly Service Officer, City of Elgin, Illinois Police Department
- Dr. Dean Bryson, educational psychologist
- Scott Ewing, Chief Operating Officer at The Oaks, Orangeburg, South Carolina
- Dr. Sanford Finkel, clinical professor of psychiatry at the University of Chicago Medical School *and* an active clinician
- Amy Flynn, Elder Abuse Supervisor, Senior Services, Kane and Kendall Counties, Illinois
- Charles (Chuck) P. Golbert, Deputy Public Guardian and Supervisor of Adult Guardian Division, Office of the Cook County, Illinois Public Guardian

- Jo Huey, Licensed Nursing Home Administrator, Alzheimer's caregiving trainer, and author
- Shay Jacobson, RN, Bachelor and Masters degrees, Master Guardian, founder and president of Lifecare Innovations, Lifecare Solutions, and Lifecare Guardianship in the Chicago metropolitan area
- Harry Johns, President & CEO, Alzheimer's Association
- Rev. James McGee, CEO of the Oaks, a Continuous Care Retirement Community, Orangeburg, South Carolina
- Dr. Sara F. Mosey, Au.D., Doctor of Audiology, San Diego, California
- Dr. Nishad (Nick) Nadkarni, licensed physician and surgeon in Wisconsin and Illinois, board certified general and forensic psychiatrist
- Caroline Peterson, R.N. with a special certificate in hospice and palliative care
- Stacie Pierce, COTA (Certified Occupational Therapy Assistant), CSA (Certified Senior Advisor), ATP (Assistive Technology Practitioner) CAPS (Certified Aging in Place Specialist), from The Oaks, Orangeburg, South Carolina
- Dr. William Theis, Senior Scientist in Residence, Alzheimer's Association
- Linda Voirin, Victim's Advocate, Seniors & Persons with Disabilities Unit, Office of Joseph H. McMahon, Kane County, Illinois State's Attorney

Our research assistants included law students from two Chicago area colleges of law. From John Marshall College of Law, we were assisted by Amanda C. Wyzykowski and Brittany Bergstrom. From Northern Illinois University College of Law, we were assisted by Bryant Storm, Brandon Ayers, and Colby Hathaway.

It is not an exaggeration to say that working on this book has substantially expanded our own lives and taught us more than we had ever imagined. We are very proud to have been the team captains on this project. We truly hope we can help you, the reader, make a positive difference for persons with dementia and those who love them.

Kerry Peck
Peck Bloom, LLC
www.PeckBloom.com

Rick Law
Law ElderLaw, LLP
www.lawelderlaw.com

INTRODUCTION

Rick Law's Story

How and Why I Became an Elder Law Attorney

It all started with a phone call to my law office in the year 2000. I was 50 years old and my practice was primarily focused on taxation, real estate investments, and traditional estate planning. I received a call from my dear friend, Luise. With panic in her voice she cried: "Bob has just been diagnosed with Alzheimer's. What are we going to do? Am I going to lose my home? Are we going to lose everything?"

I had to respond, "Luise, I have no idea. I have never been asked those questions before. I don't know, but I will find the answers for you." Unknowingly, I had been launched on a new life path that would lead me to the creation of a new law firm. The firm is known as Law Elderlaw, LLP, which has a regional presence in the Chicago metropolitan area.

The caller, Luise, was a woman in her 60s whose husband, Bob, was 72 years old. Due to receiving a dreaded diagnosis, they had suddenly lost a comfortable retirement. They also lost their hope of a long and fulfilling retirement marriage. Even though only one of them had been diagnosed with Alzheimer's disease, they both became victims. Both husband and wife were smashed by the wrecking ball of dementia.

Bob was a former amateur chess champion, so he was well aware that he was mentally declining. He was also a tough guy. He had fought in the Korean War, walked the beat as a cop, and had survived everything up until his diagnosis. Now he felt helpless and dreaded sliding into the dark abyss of his doctor's diagnosis of Alzheimer's disease. Luise was panicked with the fear of losing her husband, her home and her hard-earned financial security. Would she be able to continue to live in the same neighborhood? They were both scared, yet they were walled apart from each other by their own individual fears.

Bob and Luise are typical of millions of aging American citizens. Most of them have lived frugally, played by the rules, and planned on enjoying a modest and pleasant retirement. But now, after the diagnosis of a long-term disability, they're overwhelmed by the staggering emotional, physical, and financial cost. They fear the diagnosis may destroy their marriage, finances, and dreams.

Luise had many questions:

1. What was going to happen to Bob?
2. How was he going to get the health care that he needed?
3. How are we going to plan to help both me and Bob live through the years that may go by between the time of his diagnosis and his eventual death?
4. How will we protect the home so that I can continue to live in the community, despite Bob's multiyear care needs?
5. Will my husband's health-care needs totally impoverish me while stealing his health and life?
6. Prior to Bob's eventual death, how are we going to access, find, and obtain quality long-term care?
7. What would be left for me to live on after the disease has run its course?

When Luise initially called me, my mind had immediately searched through my mental list of items I had in my legal professional tool kit. Here is what I found that I was prepared to provide an estate-planning client:

1. Reduce and eliminate estate tax.
2. Protect the survivor spouse while protecting the estate tax credit for residuary beneficiaries.

3. Avoid probate and keep administrative costs low.
4. Avoid any problems with distribution at the death of the client.

Looking at the questions that Luise and Bob's situation presented, they wanted nontraditional solutions for which my training was inadequate.

I have learned to distinguish between those who desire traditional estate planning versus those who desire or need eldercare estate planning or longevity planning. The traditional estate plan is triggered into action by the death of an individual. An eldercare estate plan, while being fashioned in accordance with traditional estate plan concepts, is initially triggered into implementation by a long-term illness diagnosis.

The "eldercare journey" is a concept and accompanying graphic (below) that I created in 2007 to make it easier for clients to understand the distinctive focus of eldercare estate planning. In its simplest form, it looks at the fact that a senior citizen often starts out as a healthy, vigorous senior whose only health-care needs are for acute care. Obviously, anyone can die a sudden death anywhere along life's trajectory, but if

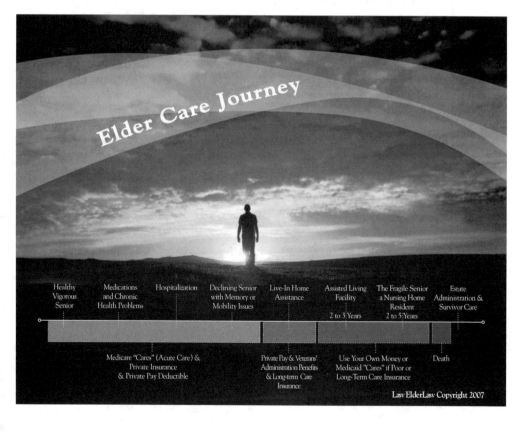

Elder Care Journey

Healthy Vigorous Senior	Medications and Chronic Health Problems	Hospitalization	Declining Senior with Memory or Mobility Issues	Live-In Home Assistance	Assisted Living Facility	The Fragile Senior a Nursing Home Resident	Estate Administration & Survivor Care
					2 to 3 Years	2 to 5 Years	

| | Medicare "Cares" (Acute Care) & Private Insurance & Private Pay Deductible | | | Private Pay & Veterans' Administration Benefits & Long-term Care Insurance | Use Your Own Money or Medicaid "Cares" if Poor or Long-Term Care Insurance | Death | |

Law ElderLaw Copyright 2007

the person remains alive and well during the healthy vigorous senior stage, that person may eventually become a declining senior who has memory or mobility issues. Declining seniors with memory or mobility issues have to change health-care needs. They move from having an acute illness to having a long-term health-care condition. This causes them to start paying out-of-pocket for numerous health-care expenses.

Almost all health-care insurance policies and Medicare are designed to pay for acute-care illness and injury and do not pay for long-term-care expenses. Most declining seniors (90 percent) survive to become what we call a "fragile senior" who needs full-time nursing home care. Of course, death eventually comes to us all. At that point in time, there may very well be estate administration and the triggering of the traditional portion of the estate plan and the fulfillment of that plan in avoiding probate, avoiding problems relative to distribution of assets through heirs, and, of course, protecting the survivor and any other vulnerable loved ones.

Over the years, Law Elderlaw has developed a complementary practice track by comparison to that of the Peck Bloom Law Firm. Our colleagues and good friends at Peck Bloom in downtown Chicago are focused on contested litigation of estates, elder abuse, special-needs trusts, and high-net-worth estate planning.

Law Elderlaw serves people who need crisis planning, such as those who

1. have been residing in a long-term-care facility, such as a nursing home or assisted/supported living facility;
2. have an immediate need to go to a long-term care facility or assisted/supported living facility;
3. have been living at home alone or with relatives and are paying for full-time care;
4. have been living at home or with a child and the child has been providing a majority of the care; or
5. wish to continue to live at home and need to access governmental benefits to pay for care from the community.

Another area of focus of Law Elderlaw has been veterans' benefits related to wartime veterans who are entitled to receive a special monthly pension after they turn 65 and are paying a substantial portion of their income for unreimbursed medical expenses.

A primary focus of our clients is that they are dealing with a long-term care condition and/or diagnosis of illnesses that have a multiple-year trajectory, such as dementia.

Since beginning the firm, it has grown from being a law practice that was focused around me, Rick L. Law, with an initial staff of three to today's practice wherein I share the partnership with my daughter, attorney Diana Law. The law firm now includes five attorneys and an overall professional staff, including attorneys as well as our support colleagues, of 20 individuals. Diana was recently chosen by the governor of the state of Illinois to become the Kane County Public Guardian and Administrator. The Kane County Public Guardian and Administrator is typically a private attorney who has become certified to provide guardianship services in addition to their active services in the practice of law. She has been recognized for excellence at both the county and state levels.

KERRY PECK'S STORY

How I Became the Warrior Lawyer of Elder Law in Cook County and Illinois

My role as an advocate of older adults, in large measure, stems from my exposure to watching older adults being exploited. Older adults, who are really the crux of our society in the context of wisdom, experience, and viability, are unfortunately the frequent victims of unscrupulous individuals who financially exploit them due to their vulnerability. Often that vulnerability relates to cognitive impairments. It might be Alzheimer's disease or it might be a cognitive impairment as a result of a different type of illness, perhaps vascular dementia. I became enamored with the notion of representing and defending older adults when I became aware many decades ago that older adults were constantly being victimized by money grabs, being taken advantage of by their children, and being abused by contractors and, frequently, by those providing them with care. Older adults need a strong, zealous advocate to defend them, and I am happy to wear that hat.

As an elder law attorney who focuses primarily on the litigation of trust and estate cases, I frequently spend many hours in the courthouse—Cook County Courthouse, Lake County Courthouse, Kane County Courthouse—representing older adults or representing family members in the context of trust and estate disputes. Those would include contested guardianships, wills, and trusts, as well as citation proceedings in an effort to bring back funds into an estate that may have been stolen from it. I'm frequently involved in continuing education programs and am a frequent presenter to various organizations: Illinois Institute of Continuing Legal Education, the Chicago Bar, the Illinois State Bar, National Academy of Elder Law Attorneys (NAELA), and the American Bar Association. My week typically involves a lot of courtroom time, time meeting with clients regarding their cases, and time meeting with other lawyers in my firm to develop litigation strategy.

In the context of probate and estate litigation, Peck Bloom Law Firm has probably been involved in at least a dozen litigation matters that have gone to the appellate court and several that have gone to the Supreme Court during the course of my practice. Appellate work, in conjunction with trust and estate litigation, is very interesting. We have an opportunity to make a major impact in terms of interpretation of the law and expansion of the law.

I became involved in drafting legislation in the probate arena very early on in my career. I joined the Chicago Bar Association Probate Practice Committee and was promptly assigned to a subcommittee addressing the terminology of illegitimates on whether, for example, siblings would be half brothers or illegitimates, and ultimately that legislation changed the manner in which half siblings now inherit under the law.

Seniors are often vulnerable and need advocates. I have been actively involved in lobbying and the drafting of legislation to protect seniors. My endeavors have included being engaged by the City of Chicago Department of Aging as a Special Assistant Corporation Counsel to draft amendments to the Illinois Elder Abuse and Neglect Act. I was engaged to lobby the legislature and testify before the legislative body hearings in Springfield, and did so to the goal of passing amendments, which were major changes to the Elder Abuse and Neglect Act. Those included the self-neglect amendment. During my presidency of the Chicago Bar Association, we proposed changing the power of attorney for property requirements in which we required that the witnesses to the document acknowledge under oath that an individual is of sound mind and memory. I had previously seen circumstances in which a power of attorney for property was used to exploit individuals when it was not necessary to have two witnesses plus a notary legislation, and so we shepherded power of attorney reform legislation through the Illinois House and the Senate and obtained the governor's signature. Now two witnesses are required to acknowledge that the individual is of sound mind and memory and not under duress. I have been involved in the passage of legislation at the federal level through the NAELA. I have been involved in many attempts to better our legislative books to protect older adults, and will continue to do so with a strong advocacy fashion.

My involvement in the political process includes taking two groups of NAELA lawyers to Washington and meeting with members of the president's staff, as well as members of Congress and members of the Senate, as we advocate for adults. I've had an opportunity to testify before the Illinois House and the Illinois Senate. I testified before the Illinois House as a witness on a special task force against elder abuse. I was appointed many years ago by Governor Ryan to his Elder Abuse Task Force. I currently chair the Cook County State's Attorney Anita Alvarez's task force on elder abuse, and I've had an opportunity to testify before the Chicago City Counsel, Health Committee, and Finance Committee on power of attorney–related matters. I've been called upon in many instances to assist the passage of legislation, and I've been called upon by elected officials to advise them as to viability of legislation, which I'm honored to say is an important role since our elected officials have to rely on other individuals from time to time.

As we move forward, I think the typical practitioner is going to be overrun with questions from clients and from family members of clients regarding the sudden onset, or even the slow onset, of Alzheimer's disease in the lives of older adults. Today we are seeing more and more circumstances in which families are calling and saying, "Mom's cognitive impairment has now impacted her ability to manage her affairs. She has done no advanced planning, has no powers of attorney in place, and has no successor trustee and revocable living trust in place. What's the remedy for solving this problem?" Of course, in that case, it's guardianship.

Individuals clearly are living far longer than anybody anticipated, and as a result, the projections on cognitively impaired individuals are a very large number. I think that the average practitioner is going to encounter these circumstances with a cognitively impaired client on a regular basis.

The Peck Bloom Law Firm focuses on litigation and estate/tax planning. On the litigation side of the firm, we litigate trust and estate matters, primarily, as well as contested guardianships and wills, financial exploitation cases, trust construction cases, and the like. We have seven lawyers devoted to that side of our practice. I lead the law firm as a managing member, and I lead the litigation side of the law firm. My son, Brandon Peck, is also on the litigation side. He practices in the areas of trust litigation, probate litigation, fiduciary defense litigation, elder law, and estate administration, with an emphasis on contested trusts and estates.

Brandon has been an active member of the Chicago Bar Association's Young Lawyer's Section, on which he currently serves as a director. Previously, he served as cochair of its Estate Planning Committee from 2011 to 2012. Brandon is also a junior member of the Alzheimer's Association's Greater Illinois Chapter Junior Board.

We have three lawyers that are devoted to the estate/tax planning, asset protection, and transactional side of our law firm. Asset-protection planning relates in large measure to representations of individuals that may be exposed to continuing liability and relates from matters as simple as creating serial limited liability companies to asset protection, domestic trust protection, and offshore trust protection. The transactional work that those three lawyers do generally arises out of the estate litigation matters, such as the sale of real estate in an estate administration case. We do estate administration and trust administration as well.

 **EXPERT VIEW**

I Have Become My Wife's Parent

Dr. Dean Bryson has a PhD in educational psychology from the University of Nebraska. During his professional career, he has worked with numerous individuals, primarily in the family setting, but also dealing with crisis situations involving hostage taking. In addition, he has worked in cross-cultural relationships with the Sioux Nation. One of his proudest moments is having been inducted into the Sioux tribe and given a Sioux name. Dr. Bryson says, "I love elderly people. There's no other way I can say that. They're sometimes frustrating, but so am I. They are sometimes confused, but so am I. I love them. They are a challenge."

Q: Dr. Bryson, give me some information about yourself and your qualifications to speak to attorneys about dealing with elderly people.

A: Last July, I turned 75, and I'm married to a 75-year-old. I started working with elderly people when I was in graduate school at the University of Nebraska in 1963, and I've been working with them ever since. I have lived in senior citizen centers; I've lived in dementia centers; I've lived in assisted-living centers. And my wife with dementia is living in a rehab center and will soon go into a dementia center.

Q: Could you tell me about your journey with your wife? Could you explain a little about what it means to be a psychologist married to a person with Alzheimer's?

A: I first became a parent to my wife eight years ago. That's when I first started noticing changes; perhaps it's an occupational hazard of being a psychologist. We know that the loss of short-term memory is the single most common symptom of any form of dementia—and there are 71 forms of dementia. Fifty percent of them will be a type of Alzheimer's and the other 50 percent will be spread among the other 70 types.

For us, it was the little things. She started to develop aphasia—looking for the right word. She was a teacher and she started to stumble—wanting to say something, but the right word wouldn't come. We've all done that, but in normal forgetting, it will come back in a few minutes, or in an hour. But with my wife and so many others, it doesn't come back. What so many people do is try to reason with the person with dementia and say, "Just relax. Take a couple of minutes." To try to reason with someone who is losing the ability to reason is pointless. It isn't going to happen.

Then it became forgetting more and more common, everyday activities. She loved to cook, but now was forgetting many of her recipes. Then it got to not answering the phone, then to not knowing how to use the phone. And then it progressed to forgetting how to read, then forgetting how to write. . . . Then it progressed to forgetting how to eat, how to bathe, and how to take medications. And then the wandering began, which is very common. So there were times when at night—and I typically go to bed around midnight and get up around five—that within the five hours that I tried to sleep, I would be up as many as 16 times with her, night after night.

That became too much after a while. I put alarms on every door so that if she opened the door, the alarm went off, but it got to the point where there was just no way I could take care of her and keep her safe. She was a threat to herself, whether it was wandering or it was something in the house. So we sold everything—our house and everything—and moved to a facility where I could live in the independent living area and she could live in the Alzheimer's unit and be taken care of 24 hours a day. So now she's in a facility and she needs help with everything—dressing, brushing her teeth, combing her hair. Physically, she's still incredibly healthy. She's still fully ambulatory. No other illnesses, no other diseases, no disabilities.

Q: That gives us the perspective of what you've gone through. As a psychologist, think about what you wish lawyers of all disciplines knew about Alzheimer's disease and its impact upon individuals and families. Imagine that someone comes to us who might be in one of those early stages. How can you help us be better lawyers in that situation?

A: I'm going to be blunt: For attorneys to be more effective, one of the first things is that they have to be comfortable with the fact that they are not going to have all the answers. The attorney is not going to know if this person has some sort of dementia. If a person has MS and they're in a wheelchair, it just takes a pair of eyes. But when it comes to dementia, an attorney is not going to know.

Number two, they need to plan ahead as to whom they can make a referral to get an evaluation. Is there a psychiatrist or other type of physician who is qualified? The attorney needs to know an appropriate person for the referral, or there are going to be all kinds of other problems.

The answer to whether or not a person is having difficulty doesn't come from the mind, it comes from the gut. The attorney should think to themselves: "Oh my goodness, that person never elaborates on their answers. They give very few words when I ask questions." A lot of times, people with dementia will just sit and look at you and not talk. They want *you* to indicate what they need to say. Or they'll say, "I know what I want to say, but I just can't find the words." Or they might not even call their son or daughter by their right name.

The attorney has to trust that gut feeling that says, "This conversation isn't flowing right. I don't know why, but it just isn't." The attorney doesn't have to be able to use the jargon of aphasia and agraphia—you only have to know that there's something that's out of focus. While talking with the client, it's 45 minutes of them twisting the pen around, or playing with their glasses, or playing with an earring—well, your gut should tell you there's something not right.

Once in a while, that kind of behavior comes about because of the anxiety of being with an attorney. Being with an attorney is a very high-stress situation for most people and even more so with seniors. But the attorney needs to listen to that little voice that should be saying right now, "It seems like this is not quite right; it doesn't feel right!" I know that may sound ambiguous and evasive, but that's how it is. We don't have a test that's going to measure all of it, but when you see it, you need to take action to protect yourself and to protect your client and get an evaluation by an experienced health-care professional.

CHAPTER ONE

WHAT IS ALZHEIMER'S DISEASE?

ALZHEIMER'S DISEASE IS A FORM of dementia characterized by the loss of memory and other intellectual abilities to the point that the disease interferes with daily life. It is the most common form of dementia, accounting for 50 to 80 percent of all dementia cases.[1]

"Dementia" is a term used to describe a multitude of diseases or conditions that develop as a result of damage to the brain's nerve cells (neurons). The damage to or destruction of the neurons creates changes in an individual's memory and behavior and affects the person's ability to think clearly.

As Alzheimer's runs its course, it ultimately impairs basic bodily functions, like walking and swallowing, and finally results in death.[2]

A person can have dementia but not have Alzheimer's disease. However, a person cannot have Alzheimer's and not have dementia.

---

1. *What Is Alzheimer's?*, ALZHEIMER'S ASS'N, http://www.alz.org/alzheimers_disease_what _is_alzheimers.asp (last visited May 27, 2012).
2. *2012 Alzheimer's Disease Facts and Figures*, 8 ALZHEIMER'S & DEMENTIA: J. OF THE ALZHEIMER'S ASS'N 131 (2012), *available at* http://www.alzheimersanddementia.com /article/S1552-5260(12)00032-5/fulltext.

The term "Alzheimer's disease" comes from German physician Dr. Alois Alzheimer. Dr. Alzheimer presented a case history of a 51-year-old woman suffering from a rare brain disorder at a medical meeting in 1906. An autopsy of the woman's brain revealed the plaques and tangles that characterize Alzheimer's disease.[3]

THE ALZHEIMER'S JOURNEY

Lawyers need to be aware of the many questions that must be addressed when a client or a client's loved one has Alzheimer's disease. These questions should include the following:

- How do we get health care for the patient?
- What options are available for health care?
- How are these options going to affect the patient and the family/spouse?
- What is the long-term outlook for everyone?
- How can we protect the family assets?

(Foremost on lawyers' minds may also be the ethics of working with clients with Alzheimer's and how to protect themselves; this is discussed in detail in chapter 2.)

Most lawyers are not accustomed to dealing with a client with Alzheimer's and probably are not prepared to answer these types of questions. This book is designed to educate lawyers so that they will have the knowledge needed to answer these questions and guide their client through the arduous journey of dealing with Alzheimer's disease.

Before the questions can be answered, lawyers have to be able to identify the signs signifying the onset of Alzheimer's or dementia. Unfortunately, the initial signs of Alzheimer's or dementia are usually the most difficult to spot. It may be months or longer before family members realize that a loved one is forgetting a few too many things or is confused too frequently. Often, these first signs are dismissed as "natural aging." However, neither Alzheimer's nor dementia is a natural part of growing old.

---

3. William G. Hammond, Rick L. Law, Karen Hays Weber & Mary Helen Gautreaux, The Alzheimer's Legal Survival Guide: Action Guide 10 (2009).

One of the first signs of dementia is also one of the most dangerous—a growing inability to understand and control financial matters. In the oldest American generation, those who saw World War II and the Korean War, most couples' finances have been controlled by the husband; it is not unusual for the wife to have no idea of the family's financial situation. That can be particularly problematic since men, on average, decline and die earlier than their wives.

It is very important that the healthy spouse and their children be alert for signs of memory loss, which can lead to both financial vulnerability and folly. The sooner these signs are identified and reported to the family doctor and lawyer to be dealt with, the better off everyone will be. Once a lawyer suspects that a client has some form of dementia, he or she should take extra care to protect the financial assets.

There is no legal standard for "vulnerability," but vulnerable individuals are more likely to make poor financial decisions and are prime targets for scam artists and criminals. Many so-called charities send direct mailings to senior citizens that are actually solicitations for donations but, to the untrained eye, appear to be bills. Some of the less scrupulous charities are hoping that these solicitations will result in donations from recipients who are confused and think that they must owe this amount since they are receiving a "bill" from a charity. Other organizations prey on the fears of senior citizens and send out mailings promising a dire future or political upheaval that is unavoidable without contributions from good people like the recipient.

The lawyer needs to make the client's family aware of these dangers and to warn the client's relatives of the possibilities that their loved one could become the victim of financial foul play.

Criminal enterprises and scam artists are not the only financial threat to clients with dementia. Online shopping, infomercials, and the lottery can be just as dangerous to a person with Alzheimer's.

Senior citizens afflicted with Alzheimer's on a fixed income may choose to spend thousands of dollars buying gifts for their relatives on their computer, or they may buy what they see on an infomercial because the commercial convinces them that they need something that they do not really need and quite possibly cannot afford.

Who does not enjoy playing the lottery occasionally? Legitimate lotteries are incredibly popular and, when the jackpots grow, the television and radio news coverage can be very exciting. Most people are able to play the lottery without going overboard and spending more on tickets than they can afford. However, one of the effects of dementia is the lessening of healthy cynicism. Most people "know" they are not really going to win the lottery and may buy a ticket here and there and daydream about winning, but deep down they do not expect to really win. Individuals with dementia may not understand that they are not going to win or that they are spending more money on tickets than they can afford. Individuals with dementia lose their capacity to understand financial meaning and to appreciate the consequences of their own actions.

People on the Alzheimer's journey often progress through this trajectory:

- memory loss ignored
- memory loss masked/denied
- unsafe alone
- aid needed
- assisted living required
- nursing home required
- hospice care required/death

The family of a loved one with Alzheimer's often progresses through a complementary trajectory that may have some of these components:

- memory loss ignored
- memory loss masked/denied/facilitated
- memory loss assistance needed by loved one, but hidden from "outsiders"

Family members need to be extremely proactive in carefully investigating a loved one's change in behavior. It is equally important for lawyers to be aware of these stages so that they may identify the stages themselves or assist the family in identifying or coming to terms with the symptoms of Alzheimer's disease.

Memory Loss Ignored

It is difficult to determine when memory loss is the first step of Alzheimer's or just normal aging. As people age, they forget things. However, forgetting what they had for lunch last Saturday is different from forgetting that they do not have unlimited financial assets.

Lawyers often need to rely on the client's family members when dealing with a client with Alzheimer's disease. Lawyers must be able to determine which relatives the client believes are honest and reliable, and who may be able to safeguard family finances and provide ongoing care and attention to the situation. Familiarity with multiple family members gives more options if signs of dementia do start to appear, and an atmosphere of open communication can go a long way toward preventing suspicion, family fights, and claims against the lawyer by disgruntled family members later on.

Once a lawyer has discussed options for the future with the client's family members and determined who might be the best person to take control of the client's finances in the event that the client is unable, the lawyer can assist the family with the development of appropriate legal documents and power of attorney for financial decision making. These documents give a nominated agent the power to make financial decisions for the affected loved one. The time to work on these plans is while the client with Alzheimer's still has sufficient capacity to make a will, trust, power of attorney for health care, power of attorney for property, and any other estate protection plans. Lawyers trained in this area of planning work to make sure that the healthy spouse is not excessively impoverished by long-term care expenses. (More on estate planning in chapter 4.)

There is no single factor that can provide a clear sign that an adult is functioning with diminished capacity, but there are clues that, when taken together, may indicate that professional medical tests should be conducted. For a lawyer, the potential signs of incapacity focus on decisional abilities rather than a person's cooperativeness or friendliness. Therefore, the lawyer will have to rely on the client's family to provide much of the information. Knowing the factors to look for allows the lawyer to ask the client's family the correct questions.

Some of the factors include

- change in the client's typical manner of behavior (these changes may take place over a long period of time and may not be instantly recognizable);
- unusually poor grooming or hygiene;
- short-term memory loss;
- comprehension problems;

- lack of mental flexibility;
- calculation problems;
- emotional signs of incapacity, such as emotional distress or emotional inappropriateness; and
- behavior incapacity, such as delusions or disorientation.

Do not assume that the normal aging process is the same as diminished capacity.

Memory Loss Masked/Denied

One good way to help determine if a client has diminished mental capacity is to observe the "15-minute reset." Look at a watch to note the beginning of a conversation with a person suspected of being affected by Alzheimer's or a related disorder. Often, people with excellent social skills (still common in women in their 80s and 90s) are able to hold a conversation that includes all the correct words and head nods. They are so adept at making conversation that it seems certain that there is nothing wrong with them. However, after about 13 or 14 minutes, they will start the conversation over again, almost as if they were playing a tape. Once again, they are so masterful with the skill that it makes people question their own memory of the conversation—as if they might have misremembered—or at the very least it makes people look around to see if someone else has entered the room to create the "reset."

In addition to the "15-minute reset," even when the client has excellent "small talk" skills and what seem to be appropriate interactive skills, the client may neither understand nor remember anything that the lawyer has said, either then or during any subsequent conversations. Seemingly appropriate questions and head nodding may imply understanding, but do not expect actual understanding on the part of people with disability or impairment. They often do not understand, and even if they do, they do not remember what was said. In reality, they have difficulty remembering new information and/or retrieving that information later. Lawyers should test for understanding by asking individuals to summarize their understanding of what the lawyers have told them.

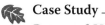

Case Study

Peter and Helen

"Peter" and his wife "Helen" came to their lawyer to deal with Helen's failing physical and mental health. They were very fortunate to have a loving and healthy adult caregiver daughter (something lawyers may encounter quite often). This daughter was sacrificially serving in a way that allowed Peter and Helen to continue living in their home. She was reaching the end of her ability to care for Helen, so they needed a lawyer's advice. Peter was a successful businessman in the community and had a reputation for frugality and integrity. He was in the role of the caregiver spouse and the focus of concern was about Helen and her need for long-term care.

Over the next two years, their lawyer received a number of calls from their daughter, who was distressed at Peter's financial decision making. One day, she called after she learned that her father had called a private ambulance service to take Helen to her hairdresser. Peter was deeply devoted to Helen, but he could not afford to spend $800 to have Helen transported to and from her hairdresser.

Peter and his daughter saw their lawyer the next week. At that appointment, the lawyer met with Peter alone and reviewed his finances with him. Peter seemed capable and intelligent at the meeting. He was able to add and subtract and respond appropriately to the questions. Nonetheless, one week later, Peter called another ambulance to take Helen to her hair appointment. The lawyer was dumbfounded—he did not realize at the time that Peter was suffering from his own rising level of dementia.

A person with dementia may be able to answer questions correctly, but completely fail to appreciate the consequences of the answer that he or she has given. In other words, Peter was able to say what his income was and what his assets were, but he no longer understood the difference in the effect upon him of spending $8 or $800.

If family members live far away, some of the first people likely to notice these signs of dementia are the person's own advisors—their doctor, lawyer, or financial planner. Unfortunately, these advisors often do not always have the ability to take action. Doctors and lawyers are bound by patient or client privilege, and even if they want to inform the family of their suspicions, they may not be able to do so. Recent changes to Illinois State Bar Association code of ethics do allow a lawyer to take action to protect a client when there is a reasonable belief that the client has become incapacitated and is in danger—check the state's code for similar allowances.[4] The American Medical Association is also sensitive to this issue, and has guidelines for dealing with patients who show signs of incapacity.[5]

Unfortunately, doctors are under pressure to spend minimal amounts of time with patients. Many people are able to "fake it" during a short interview by doctors, lawyers, or financial advisors.

Lawyers will sometimes need to step in and help provide guidance when there is memory loss and assistance is required but is being refused. Alzheimer's is a progressive disease, and the memory loss will eventually rise to the level that the afflicted individual is no longer safe living alone.

Unsafe Alone

People with Alzheimer's living alone—quick facts:

An estimated 800,000 individuals with Alzheimer's (or one in seven) live alone. People with Alzheimer's and other dementias who live alone are exposed to higher risks, including inadequate self-care, malnutrition, untreated medical conditions, falls, wandering from home unattended, and accidental deaths, compared with those who do not live alone.[6] Of those who have Alzheimer's and live alone, up to half of them do not have an identifiable caregiver.[7]

One of the signs of early-onset Alzheimer's is the tendency to wander off or to become lost.[8] This is especially dangerous because people with Alzheimer's do not act, or react, in the manner that a typical lost person would. Wanderers with dementia typically will not cry out for help or respond to calls to them, nor will they leave many physical clues to lead

---

4. MODEL RULES OF PROF'L CONDUCT R. 1.14 (2002).
5. AMA CODE OF MEDICAL ETHICS: OPINION 2.191 (2011), *available at* http://www.ama-assn.org/ama/pub/physician-resources/medical-ethics/code-medical-ethics/opinion2191.page?.
6. *2012 Alzheimer's Disease Facts and Figures, supra* note 2, n.198.
7. *Id.*
8. *Id.* at n.178.

people to them. More than likely, a wanderer will go to an old place of residence or a favorite location from the past.

Advise clients to register their loved ones in the Safe Return program run by the Alzheimer's Association. Members of the Safe Return program are issued a bracelet or other form of jewelry with the association's logo on one side and the individual's identification number on the other side to aid in identification.[9]

Lawyers can also suggest that adult children living with a parent suffering from dementia put a baby monitor in the parent's bedroom so that they can hear them get up in the middle of the night. It is also a good idea to put safety devices in the home and warn the neighbors of the possibility of wandering and ask them to keep an eye out.[10]

Another danger is falling. Many elderly adults suffer falls as they age, but falls are more likely and can be more dangerous when the individual has Alzheimer's disease.[11] Because clients with Alzheimer's or other dementias commonly suffer from impaired judgment and disorientation, and a decrease in problem-solving abilities, visual perception, and spatial perception, the risk of falls is significantly increased.[12]

People caring for a loved one with Alzheimer's should also be warned about hallucinations or delusions. It is hard to tell if these are brought on by the disease or if they are side effects from a medication, but individuals with Alzheimer's have been known to suffer from one or both. Of course, some people will never suffer from either.[13]

If the client suspects that the hallucinations or delusions are being caused by a drug the patient is taking to treat a condition, it is advisable to contact the patient's doctor. If the hallucinations do not upset or frighten the patient, it may be best for the caregiver to just go along with the hallucination. In fact, validating the hallucinations is important and even healthy.[14] However, if the hallucinations upset the patient, advise clients to consult the patient's doctor.[15]

---

9. Rick L. Law, Everything You Always Wanted to Know About Alzheimer's but Were Afraid to Ask 5 (2009).
10. *Id.*
11. *2012 Alzheimer's Disease Facts and Figures, supra* note 2, nn.196–97.
12. *Id.* at nn.194, 195.
13. Law, *supra* note 9, at 6.
14. *Id.*
15. *Id.*

Aid Needed, But Fights Back

When an individual with Alzheimer's needs aid but is fighting back, it can be very hard on that person's family. Caring for a loved one with Alzheimer's can be draining, and at a certain point additional help is needed.

Lawyers who know their elder law can make a couple of helpful suggestions to their clients at this point of the journey. One option is to take advantage of a respite care program. These programs offer substitute caregivers and are designed to provide temporary relief for the primary caregiver from day-to-day responsibilities. Some respite programs are offered by paid health aides, while others involve volunteers from churches or other groups.[16]

If more intensive help is required, the lawyer can suggest home-based care. This involves having a health aide provide custodial care in the home of the patient. This can be a good option when the primary caregiver is also elderly.[17] This type of care allows patients to keep their independence for as long as possible and continue to live in their home.

Unfortunately, Medicare does not cover home health aides who provide custodial care, which is the type of care an individual with Alzheimer's needs. Custodial care involves bathing, dressing, help with the housekeeping and grocery shopping, and occasionally staying overnight when needed.[18]

Medicaid may cover portions of custodial services through a waiver program. Because the services available through the waiver program vary greatly state by state, lawyers should advise interested clients to contact their state office on aging to schedule a medical assessment to determine the level of service necessary to keep their loved one at home.

Another option lawyers should be aware of is adult day care. This option is great for situations in which the primary caregiver (perhaps an adult child) still works, but wants to keep the individual suffering from Alzheimer's in the home. Adult day care programs provide socialization and therapeutic activities that may slow the mental decline brought on by Alzheimer's.[19] Often these programs offer different levels of care

---

16. HAMMOND ET AL., *supra* note 3, at 34.
17. *Id.* at 35.
18. *Id.*
19. *Id.* at 36.

ranging from one half day per week to full-time care Monday through Friday.[20]

Adult day care is considered to be a stage between independent living and living in a nursing home. Lawyers should suggest that clients and their family decision makers visit a few facilities prior to picking one to ensure the program offered is what their loved one requires at this stage of the Alzheimer's journey. Clients' family members and/or decision makers should look for the following:

- Is the program licensed? State regulations vary, so lawyers should be aware of state regulations so that they can educate their clients.
- Is the atmosphere friendly? They will want their loved one to be as comfortable as possible.
- What medical care is available?
- Are the activities aimed at socialization and mental stimulation?
- What is the staffing level? Generally, it's good to aim for one staff member per four adults in adult day care.
- Is the program exclusively for people suffering from dementia?
- Is a contract necessary? Alzheimer's progresses at unpredictable rates, so avoid contracts longer than 30 days in case they need to switch to a nursing home sooner.[21]

Assisted Living

There comes a point in time when the client will need to be placed in an assisted-living facility. The lawyer can play an important role in this very personal decision by identifying the signs when a client has reached this stage of the Alzheimer's journey and by counseling the family members and advising them of the many available options.

> As mentioned earlier in this chapter, individuals in the beginning stages of Alzheimer's disease often wander off and can become lost. When a client has begun to wander off, it is time for the lawyer to suggest that the family consider assisted-living options.

Lawyers need to be aware that older people with dementia who live alone are more likely to need emergency medical services because

---

20. *Id.*
21. *Id.* at 38.

of self-neglect.[22] Overall, people with dementia who live alone are at a greater risk of accidental death than those living with others. This increased risk may be due to lack of recognition of harm and delays in seeking medical help.[23]

When lawyers are aware of these facts, they are in a position to counsel the family of the afflicted client and ultimately help both the client and the family. Assisted-living facilities can be the right choice for people suffering from Alzheimer's when skilled nursing is not yet needed—a step before a nursing home.[24] Moving a loved one into one of these facilities often allows the healthy spouse to better cope with the difficulties of caretaking for the spouse with the disease.

Lawyers with clients considering moving a loved one to an assisted-living facility should ask their clients the following questions about the facility to ensure they are making an informed choice:

- Is the facility licensed? Check with the state's guidelines to see what kind of licensing is required.
- What is the environment like? What are the common areas like? Is there an enclosed yard or patio that is a safe area that an Alzheimer's patient could not wander away from?
- What kinds of activities are offered? Ask to see the activities calendar. Is there a full-time activities director? It is important to find a place that offers a wide variety of activities to provide social interaction and mental stimulation.
- What is the staff to patient ratio? Generally, look for one certified nurse's aide (CNA) per five residents during the day, and a ratio of 1:10 at night.
- How well trained are the staff? Look for a facility where staff instruction includes interaction with an instructor, group discussions, and role-playing activities to ensure a quality staff that is ready to help a loved one.
- Does the facility have a special Alzheimer's unit? Some facilities have residents with a variety of needs, while others have a unit for people with dementia, and others are completely dedicated to residents with dementia. The best choice may be a facility with a special care unit devoted to residents suffering from dementia.

---

22. *2012 Alzheimer's Disease Facts and Figures, supra* note 2, at nn.189, 192.
23. *Id.* at n.197.
24. HAMMOND ET AL., *supra* note 3, at 40.

In these facilities, the staff is more experienced in handling people with dementia and more extensive care can be provided. Integrated units that have residents with dementia mixed in with otherwise healthy residents can cause problems for the residents with dementia because they may be excluded from group activities due to disruptions just when they need socialization and mental stimulation the most.[25]

By helping clients work their way through this list of questions, lawyers can help the clients make the best choice for their loved one.

Assisted-living facility contracts are very similar to apartment leases. However, lawyers need to be aware that the common yearlong contract can be problematic for someone with Alzheimer's disease. As previously mentioned, the progression of dementia is different for everyone and can be incredibly fast. A client could be in the early stages of Alzheimer's at the beginning of the contract term but need more extensive care, such as a nursing home, well before the year is over.

Ensure there is an escape clause in the contract allowing the resident to move out with reasonable notice in the event a higher level of care is needed.[26] By doing this, lawyers can save clients a lot of money and heartache.

Nursing Home

When clients reach the point where they have to put a loved one in a nursing home, it can be one of the hardest decisions they ever have to make. When Alzheimer's disease has progressed to the point where the afflicted person can no longer live alone or when the primary caregiver cannot provide the needed level or expertise of care, a move to a nursing home becomes necessary.

There are ways lawyers can help their clients through this difficult time. As always, having a plan and knowing the right questions to ask beforehand will allow lawyers to provide invaluable help to their clients.

Counsel clients to visit several different nursing homes before narrowing down their choices. Once they have found a few facilities that stand out, they should visit each one several times, preferably at different

---

25. *Id.* at 41.
26. *Id.* at 42.

times in the day and at least once during a meal.[27] It is important to find a nursing home with an Alzheimer's special care unit.[28]

As discussed earlier, people with Alzheimer's disease have a tendency to wander off and can easily get lost, confused, and scared. Some special care units accommodate this behavior by providing a safe area to wander in, in the form of a walled-in garden or yard.[29]

Just like when a client is looking at an assisted-living facility, staff training is an important area to examine. Staff in special care units should take specialized training courses in order to be able to encourage the residents' independence and help them realize the maximum potential of their mental and physical abilities as their dementia progresses.[30] Lawyers need to advise their clients that the special units often come at an added price. Some states have established guidelines for these units, but there are no federal guidelines. Lawyers wishing to practice elder law should become familiar with their state's guidelines.

Advise clients to look for the following qualities from a nursing home with a special unit before agreeing to pay the higher rate:

- Does the facility confirm all incoming residents' Alzheimer's diagnosis?
- Is the staff aware of the progressive nature of Alzheimer's disease, and how do they address the expected changes in the mental and physical abilities of the residents?
- Are all of the employees in the special unit (the housekeepers, maintenance workers, etc.) given some training regarding Alzheimer's?
- Are the buildings and grounds designed for people suffering from Alzheimer's disease?
- Are the resident activities appropriate for people with Alzheimer's?[31]

It is important to advise clients early on in the nursing home search that this type of care is expensive. Fees average around $45,000 a year nationwide, and can be as expensive as $100,000 or more. Most insurance plans do not cover this type of long-term care and neither does Medicare.

---

27. *Id.*
28. *Id.*
29. *Id.* at 43.
30. *Id.*
31. *Id.*

Fortunately, Medicaid is available for qualified individuals. Medicaid is a federally funded, state-administered medical assistance program that is explained in detail in chapter 5.

Hospice/Death

Hospice care is a team approach to caring for an individual in the final stages of a terminal illness, such as Alzheimer's. The goal of hospice care is to provide comfort, reassurance, and support for dying patients and their families and friends.[32]

Qualifications for hospice care require a physician's prognosis that the patient only has a life expectancy of six months. The point of hospice care is not to attempt to cure the illness, but to comfort the patient, lessen the pain, and help all involved deal with the inevitable death. Hospice care focuses on "dying well."[33] Medicare usually covers charges for hospice services for qualified patients, and most hospice program requirements conform to Medicare and National Hospice Association Guidelines.[34]

Because the lawyer does not have the emotional attachment that the family members have, it may be easier for the lawyer to identify (or admit) when it is time for hospice care. It is a good idea for lawyers to counsel clients to explore the possibility of hospice care before it is needed so that the clients do not have to deal with this at the most emotional point of the journey. The client should be advised to discuss hospice criteria with the patient's doctor to see how willing the doctor is to certify a patient for a hospice program. If the doctor seems unwilling, lawyers should advise their clients to consider finding another doctor.[35] Alzheimer's is terminal, and all sufferers reach the point where the only thing left to do is to comfort and prepare them as best as possible for death.

Jo Huey, the owner of the Alzheimer's Caregiver Institute, warns us that the symptoms that signify that a patient is in the final stages of Alzheimer's disease can be as varied as the individuals and their personalities and may be affected by other unrelated health conditions.

---

32. *Id.* at 38.
33. *Id.*
34. *Id.* at 39.
35. *Id.*

With that fact in mind, Huey notes that there have to be some guidelines to follow.

According to Huey, only about 6 percent of people with Alzheimer's (and related disorders) actually make it to the end stage of the disease. The most easily identifiable sign that someone is dying from Alzheimer's and related disorders is when he or she can no longer swallow safely (without aspiration) and has chosen not to use a feeding tube (often a legal issue, discussed further in chapter 3). If clients are not allowed to take oral nutrition or hydration safely, they are unlikely to survive for a long period of time. Lawyers should be aware that it is advisable, at the very least, to have a speech therapist make this determination.

Huey says the second most common qualifier for hospice is when there is a significant weight loss even though the person is eating meals regularly. She notes that the majority of people with Alzheimer's and related disorders actually die from infection. Common examples are

1. sepsis from undiagnosed urinary tract infection or other infection (abscessed tooth, etc.) that creates an infection in the blood and can't be stopped if it has progressed too far; and
2. pneumonia, sometimes from aspiration or an illness or virus; because the clients cannot communicate their illness, it goes undetected until it has progressed too far.

 Case Study

Jo Huey, Owner of the Alzheimer's Caregiver Institute

Jo Huey's mother was 84 years old and had vascular dementia. She hated going to the hospital ER, which was the legal procedure required if she became ill in the assisted-living community where she lived. When she went to the ER, Jo would hurry there from out of state, and, in the meantime, one of the relatives (sometimes Jo's sister who also had medical POA) would accompany her. They would have the "doctor/attending ER physician/ medical residency student" call and talk to Jo because the family did not want her mother to have an MRI, CAT scan, and any extensive diagnostic procedures that terrified her.

An angry physician in August 2006 told Jo that he was trained to "treat" people in the ER and if Jo wanted to decline treatment for her mother, then she should put her mother in hospice and stop bringing her to the ER. Jo called hospice and learned that her mother qualified for the service. Her doctor was willing to sign for it and she was recertified again in six months. She happened to be doing quite well in August of 2007 when the recertification came up again. Although she still qualified, a physician's signature was required for recertification. The physician declined to recertify her because "she could live another 10 years."

Jo called her physician, who just happened to be someone with whom Jo had grown up, and asked him why he wouldn't recertify, and he gave her the same answer. Jo asked what to do about ER and extensive diagnostic procedures and he said something to the effect of, "You can just come here and stop those things or tell the community not to send her to the ER (he was unfamiliar with the community's regulations or didn't care). When Jo told him her mother qualified for hospice and that Jo wanted her recertified, he angrily accused Jo of "using the system" (Jo's mother was in a private pay community and had insurance that supplemented her Medicare). Jo retorted, "Even if we were using the system, it was none of his business that I wanted her to have hospice." He asked Jo how she was going to do that without his signature and Jo told him that she would call another physician in the same town "whom we both knew" and change doctors. He said, "You wouldn't really do that." Jo said, "Without a signature you will be getting a fax to transfer records in the next 15 minutes." He was furious and signed the hospice certification.

Just 19 days later, Jo's mother died in her sleep following a massive stroke and four days of being comatose. She died in her own bed in the assisted-living community where she had been dancing and smiling less than a week prior.

Huey stresses the importance of making certain that lawyers individualize situations to meet the specific needs and desires of the person with Alzheimer's disease and the loved ones who are responsible for the decisions when the person can no longer make them alone.

Alzheimer's Association—quick facts:

Alzheimer's is the sixth-leading cause of death in the United States and the only cause of death among the top 10 that cannot be prevented, cured, or even slowed. Based on final mortality data from 2000 to 2008, death rates have declined for most major diseases—heart disease (-13 percent), breast cancer (-3 percent), prostate cancer (-8 percent), stroke (-20 percent), and HIV/AIDS (-29 percent)—while deaths from Alzheimer's disease have risen 66 percent during the same period.[36]

---

36. *2012 Alzheimer's Disease Facts and Figures, supra* note 2.

It is not uncommon for people in the final stages of Alzheimer's to reach the point where they do not want to go to the hospital again— they're ready, and hospice can help them achieve a "wonderful death." According to one hospice nurse: "The three essential elements to providing a wonderful death are the collaborative efforts of the family, the assisted-living staff, and the hospice personnel—which then allows our residents to stay in their home environment with friends and familiar caregivers and peacefully live out the end of their lives. I have been part of several end-of-life decisions with our residents. I am richer for it and tremendously grateful to have shared with the resident and his or her family some wonderful deaths."

STATISTICAL PROJECTIONS

The Alzheimer's Association estimates 5.4 million people are currently afflicted with the disease.[37] Because Alzheimer's disease is underdiagnosed and many people with Alzheimer's may think that they are just experiencing the normal issues associated with growing older, many of the afflicted are unaware that they have the disease. Current estimates are that one in eight Americans 65 or older has Alzheimer's.[38]

As our population ages and people live longer, it is only natural to assume that the numbers of Americans with Alzheimer's disease will grow. In fact, the Alzheimer's Association predicts that the annual incidence of Alzheimer's disease and other dementias will double by the year 2050.[39]

The baby boomers, who make up a large part of our population, are entering the age brackets where they will be in greater danger of Alzheimer's and other forms of dementia. The first baby boomers turned 65 in 2011. It is estimated that the population of those 65 years old and older will double to 71 million by 2030. Those senior citizens will make up 20 percent of the total population at that time.[40] When the first baby boomers turn 85 years old in 2031, the number of people 85 years old and older is expected to reach 3.5 million, up from 2.5 million in 2012.[41]

---

37. *Id.*
38. *Id.* at nn.A2, A3.
39. *Id.* at n.76.
40. *Id.* at n.81.
41. *Id.* at n.47.

Alzheimer's breakdown by age:

    under 65 years old = 4 percent
    65 to 74 years old = 6 percent
    75 to 84 years old = 44 percent
    85 years old and older = 46 percent[42]

Every 68 seconds a new case of Alzheimer's develops in America.[43] However, that rate is estimated to double by mid-century, with a new case developing every 33 seconds.[44] The time to become educated about Alzheimer's is now. If the Alzheimer's Association's future projections are even close to accurate, we are about to witness an explosion of new cases of the disease. The number of Alzheimer's sufferers will soon be too high for the current elder law practitioners, and more expertise will be needed.

There were an estimated 411,000 new cases of Alzheimer's disease in 2000. That number was estimated to increase by 10 percent to 454,000 by 2010. By 2030, it is projected that there will be 615,000 new cases, a 50 percent increase from 2000. By 2050, it is believed that there will be 959,000 new cases, a 130 percent increase from 2000.[45]

By 2025, the number of people 65 years old and older with Alzheimer's is estimated to reach 6.7 million, nearly a 30 percent increase in just 15 years.[46] By 2050, the number of people 65 years old and older with Alzheimer's may double or triple to a projected 11 million to 16 million, unless a medical breakthrough is developed to prevent, slow, or stop the disease.[47]

By 2050, it is estimated that the number of Americans 85 years old and older will nearly quadruple to 21 million.[48] In fact, between 2010 and 2050, Americans 85 years old and up are expected to increase from 15 percent of all older people in the United States to 24 percent.[49]

---

42. *Id.*
43. *Id.* at n.A7.
44. *Id.*
45. *Id.* at n.76.
46. *Id.* at n.47.
47. *Id.*
48. *Id.* at n.80.
49. *Id.*

With all of these new victims of Alzheimer's disease, more lawyers will need to be versed in elder law.

The more educated a lawyer is in elder law issues, the quicker the lawyer can act. Acting early allows those afflicted a better opportunity to have their wishes honored and puts the lawyer in the best position to help the client and the family, and decreases the chances of claims arising that the client's best interests were not followed.[50] Getting the appropriate legal documents in place early, while the client is still able to take part in the decision-making process, is a crucial step.[51]

---

50. Hammond et al., *supra* note 3.
51. *Id.*

 **EXPERT VIEW**

Client Confabulation: The Attorney's Consternation

Dr. Nishad "Nick" Nadkarni is a licensed physician and surgeon in Wisconsin and Illinois. In addition, he is certified as a general and forensic psychiatrist. His professional experience includes working in private practice and, starting in 2004, working full time for the Circuit Court of Cook County, Forensic Clinical Services. The Forensic Clinical Services are primarily charged with determining clinical competencies, like fitness to stand trial and fitness for medications, for people indicted or charged with criminal offenses. Part of the training is learning to understand the different levels of capacity from the standpoint of legal definitions of capacity; for example, testamentary capacity, contractual capacity, donative capacity, and other criminal and civil competencies.

Q: Would you say based on your experience that it's common for someone to admit to their dementia or their memory issues?

A: I would say it is *not* common, and almost always it is outright denied, even in the face of tremendous contradictory evidence.

Q: Despite short-term memory issues, can people develop a masking technique?

A: Yes. One of the techniques is confabulation—the insertion of details to fill in holes in the memory. For example, if I really couldn't remember what happened this morning, I might give you what sounds like a reasonable explanation. You could ask me, "Dr. Nick, what did you do this morning?" and I could say, very convincingly, "I ate breakfast—I had two eggs, bacon, and toast," and even with that I may be confabulating. I really can't remember what I did—but I'm going to fill in the detail and not even be aware that I'm telling you something that is confabulated or made up. It's very possible that someone can give you a complete rundown of what they did even though they have absolutely no actual remembrance. People will tell you what meets social expectations and what you would expect to hear.

Whatever that person may be consulting you about, it may have absolutely no basis in truth. Without reliable collateral information, you, the attorney, would not know that. So when you hear about a person's activities of daily living and independence, it's important to receive collateral information to back up what someone who is confabulating is telling you. The only way that you would know that there were problems is by doing some formal testing, some mini mental status exam testing, which would not be appropriate for your role as an attorney.

With all due respect, I don't believe that attorneys are trained or competent in doing those kinds of tests. I think it brings about a bigger issue philosophically, ethically, about the responsibility you take on. If an attorney decides to try to do these kinds of workups, you'd better be competent and you'd better do it right, because if you make a mistake, you're going to be held liable for that.

Q: Over the years as a forensic psychiatrist, have you had the opportunity to observe a large number of lawyers?

A: Yes, several hundred.

Q: You have had the opportunity to observe attorneys in the civil and criminal arenas. What do you wish lawyers knew about dementia?

A: There is an old saying in medicine: get consultation, get consultation, and then get consultation. Whenever there is a question about mental capacity, to protect everyone's interests—primarily the client's—I wish more attorneys would seek consultation from mental health professionals before drafting and filing complaints.

The other thing that concerns me is attorneys' basic understanding of dementia, even attorneys who focus in elder law. It can be very difficult to assess. For example, early-onset Parkinson's disease has a dementia component. These types of dementias will present themselves very atypically and might affect a 58-year-old man who is having a bizarre complex of symptoms that may not be understood unless professionally evaluated. They are not necessarily affecting the short-term memory of the individual.

Also, there are certain things that cause *reversible* memory impairment, like major depressive disorder—what's called the pseudodementia of depression. If the depression is bad enough, the thinking can be so slow that they're unable to take in and retain information, and in a sense it dissipates. But antidepressants can reverse that. This is a very common phenomenon in the elderly. In addition, many older people are affected by hypothyroidism, which can increase the appearance of dementia.

Attorneys need to be aware of more than just memory impairment. An attorney should look for clusters of problems with cognitive processing, memory processing, behavioral processing and control, emotional problems, emotional control, impulsivity, activities of daily living, sequencing and arranging, what we call executive functioning, ability to communicate, ability to feel secure with familiar people. All of these things may deteriorate in dementia and some may be subtle. If an attorney has a bona fide doubt about a person's capacity, they should make a referral to an appropriate healthcare professional for an evaluation.

On the other hand, just because a person is on a certain medication doesn't mean that they have incapacity. A person may be taking Aricept, Namenda, or some other medicine often prescribed for dementia—but they may still have testamentary or contractual or donative capacity. A medicine doesn't equate a diagnosis, and a diagnosis does not equate a capacity issue.

Q: Describe a typical evaluation.

A: When I do an examination I break it up into three phases. First I like to see the person in their own home. I am able to look at safety issues. I then spend 30–45 minutes asking people what they think is important. I then go through a formal evaluation of psychiatric history, any history of psychiatric symptoms, memory problems, history of substance abuse, current medications, allergies, medical problems, and their understanding of why they're taking their medications. We'll often go through a brief legal history as well.

Secondly, I would make an examination called a Mini Mental Status Exam, or MMSE, which is a screening tool for the grossest levels of dementia. At that point I have a quantitative number that may or may not mean something, but courts seem to appreciate an ability to quantify. I personally think that the mental status observations on the person's thought flow are more significant, but I do a Mini Mental Status Exam.

The third phase involves understanding of one's finances. I go through a series of questions to ascertain someone's general knowledge about how much they make in a year, how much their home costs, how much their car costs, etc. Then I address areas of insight, judgment, and impulse control regarding safety issues. What should you do if the house smells like gas? When is it appropriate to call emergency services? When should you go to an emergency room?

I'm interested in looking at whether they're jumping from one time frame to another without any logical connection. That tells me whether the person is confused regarding significant key events in their life and whether or not they're able to identify or tag certain areas and build a story around those areas.

So I do much more than just asking somebody to add two plus two. It is a comprehensive evaluation that allows me to see *how* people are thinking, in addition to *what* they're thinking.

CHAPTER TWO

ETHICS AND THE
ALZHEIMER'S CLIENT

THIS CHAPTER ANALYZES THE ABA model rules regarding representation of a client with compromised mental status and focuses on how to properly represent such clients. However, sometimes the best thing a lawyer can do is decline representation.

Mrs. Margaret Sundowner

555 Main St.

Springfield, IL 50050

Re: Our decision to not accept representation

Dear Margaret,

On two occasions we have met with you and adult members of your family. The purpose of the meetings was to explore the possibility of doing some estate planning and Medicaid-related asset protection. The Rules of

Professional Responsibility require that we assess the capacity of prospective clients to engage us as their attorney and to determine if they have testamentary capacity [estate planning].

After two extensive meetings, it is my legal concern that your capacity to do estate planning may be impaired. We would like to refer you to a geriatric psychiatrist or neurologist. Their evaluation would be necessary for us to determine your ability to engage in estate planning.

At this time, we are unable to be of assistance to you, and we decline to represent you to do the estate planning that your adult children seem to believe is in your best interests.

Sincerely,

Rick L. Law

RULE 1.14

As the graying of America continues, lawyers are much more likely to find themselves representing clients with cognitive impairments such as Alzheimer's disease. These impairments are often hidden or difficult to identify in their early stages. Thus, it is extremely important that any lawyer interacting with a client or potential client who is, or may be, impaired consult ABA Model Rule 1.14 as a starting point.

Model Rule 1.14 is a joint effort of the American Bar Association Commission on Law and Aging and the American Psychological Association. It is designed to give lawyers direction and guidance on how to actually take such action. The rule addresses a lawyer's professional obligations when dealing with a client with diminished capacity.

This guidance is more important now than ever as the entire country is experiencing an unprecedented transfer of wealth from the WWII generation through the baby boomer generation.

The ABA Commission on Law and Aging states that its mission is to strengthen and secure the legal rights, dignity, autonomy, quality of life, and quality of care of elders. Its mission is carried out through research, policy development, technical assistance, advocacy, education, and training.

Specifically, there is a three-part test that a lawyer must apply to clients in order to have the option to take proactive action: first, clients must have diminished capacity; then, there must be a risk of substantial harm; and lastly, clients must have an inability to protect their own interest.[1]

The rule is set out below.

Client-Lawyer Relationship
ABA Rule 1.14 Client with Diminished Capacity

(a) When a client's capacity to make adequately considered decisions in connection with a representation is diminished, whether because of minority, mental impairment or for some other reason, the lawyer shall, as far as reasonably possible, maintain a normal client-lawyer relationship with the client.

(b) When the lawyer reasonably believes that the client has diminished capacity, is at risk of substantial physical, financial or other harm unless action is taken and cannot adequately act in the client's own interest, the lawyer *may* take reasonably necessary protective action, including consulting with individuals or entities that have the ability to take action to protect the client and, in appropriate cases, seeking the appointment of a guardian ad litem, conservator or guardian.

(c) Information relating to the representation of a client with diminished capacity is protected by Rule 1.6. When taking protective action pursuant to paragraph (b), the lawyer is impliedly authorized under Rule 1.6(a) to reveal information about the client, but only to the extent reasonably necessary to protect the client's interests.[2]

Practice Pointer:

It is critical to note that Rule 1.14(b), by using the term "may" in the phrase "the lawyer may take reasonable necessary protective action," is giving the lawyer an option rather than creating a duty. Were the term "shall" or "must" used in place of "may," a duty would be created, but as the rule is written, no duty is being forced upon lawyers.

This is a key choice of words used by the ABA, and the rule is often misinterpreted as creating a duty when, in fact, that is not the case at all.

---

1. ABA Comm'n on L. & Aging & Am. Psychological Ass'n, Assessment of Older Adults with Diminished Capacity: A Handbook for Lawyers 2 (2005), *available at* http://www.apa.org/pi/aging/resources/guides/diminished-capacity.pdf.
2. Model Rules of Prof'l Conduct R. 1.6 (2002) (emphasis added).

Succinctly, the rule states that lawyers are supposed to treat a client with diminished capacity in the same manner as they would treat any other client. Unfortunately, it is not quite that simple in the real world.

The reality is that the burden of trying to determine capacity of an individual can be very daunting for lawyers.

> **Practice Pointer:**
>
> Dr. Nishad "Nick" Nadkarni, who is board certified in both general psychiatry and forensic psychiatry, recognizes the difficult task lawyers face in complying with Rule 1.14.
>
> "I think that this [Rule 1.14] would be, as written, extremely difficult to implement competently by an average attorney," he says. "Let me explain that by saying that I believe that these guidelines, or these structured considerations, are created with the best intent, but without formal training in medicine would be very difficult to implement.
>
> "It's very difficult, and I'm thinking both in the civil and criminal arenas, for a non-trained individual to be able to identify those issues and then seek consultation. People that don't have the proper training in that area don't know what to look for, as we (psychiatrists) would know. The protective action that attorneys may take is very similar to actions physicians who have questions about somebody's specialty medical problem should take.
>
> "For example, if I had somebody on the psychiatric floor that I was treating who had end-stage renal disease, I would consult with a nephrologist (kidney specialist) even though I'm trained and licensed to undertake these issues—I would not want to, since I am not a specialist. Instead, I would consult a nephrologist to come in for the dialysis set-up."

It is important to note that while estate-planning and elder-law lawyers must be focused on the assessment of older adults with diminished capacity, Model Rule 1.14 applies to all lawyers. It applies to lawyers that go to traffic court, it applies to lawyers that handle personal injury cases, it applies to lawyers that do contract law, and it applies to lawyers that do real estate closings. The rule applies to everyone, and most lawyers probably don't even know that this rule exists.

The rule suggests that lawyers should try to maintain a normal client–lawyer relationship with a client with diminished capacity to the extent that is possible. However, as noted in ABA Formal Ethics Opinion 96-404, treating a client normally is not always possible in the face of the unfortunate reality of Alzheimer's. "When the client's ability to communicate, to comprehend and assess information, and to make reasoned decisions is partially or completely diminished, maintaining the ordinary relationship in all respects may be difficult or impossible."[3]

In these instances, the lawyer has a responsibility to the client to change the relationship accordingly.

One way to alter the relationship is to seek help from the client's family. Going to the client's family for assistance generally does not affect the applicability of the attorney-client evidentiary privilege.[4] However, lawyers need to be vigilant in not forgetting whom they are representing. The client's interests must be kept foremost and the lawyer is required, to the extent possible, to look to the client and not the family members to make decisions on behalf of the client.[5]

The comments to the rule also provide that the lawyer may consult a diagnostician to help determine whether the client has sufficient capacity to make informed decisions.[6]

Rule 1.14(b) permits the lawyer to take reasonable necessary protective action in instances where a client with diminished capacity is at risk of substantial physical, financial, or other harm unless action is taken and it is determined that the client is incapable of acting for him/herself.

 **Case Study**

The Abduction and Taking of a Senior Citizen to Another State by One Family Member

One of the authors of the book has noticed a disturbing trend of abduction of seniors by their family members. Recently, he had a client come into his office for some estate planning and he applied Rule 1.14 to the engagement with the client. The client engagement agreement was signed by the elderly client and her adult son with a power of attorney for property. The author's firm went through its capacity determination process and determined that she had more than mild problems and that, per Rule 1.14, the firm needed to refer her for evaluation. So the author, recognizing that he may have a client with diminished capacity, told the family members who accompanied the client to the office that the firm was going to require that she be evaluated by a geriatric psychiatrist. The author's firm scheduled her to be interviewed by a geriatric psychiatrist before having her sign any documents.

---

3. ABA Comm. on Ethics & Professional Responsibility, Formal Op. 96-404 (1996).
4. MODEL RULES OF PROF'L CONDUCT R. 1.14 cmt. 3.
5. *Id.*
6. MODEL RULES OF PROF'L CONDUCT R. 1.14 cmt. 6.

Prior to the capacity evaluation, one of the client's sons, who did not accompany her on the initial consultation, "abducted" his mother and took her to his out-of-state home. Then he called and demanded the return of his mother's retainer to him on her behalf. Obviously, if a professional evaluation had determined that the client did not have the capacity to do estate planning, the author's firm would not go forward and would return the retainer to the client's original power of attorney for property. The author responded to the abductor-son:

> Dear out-of-state son of client, it is our understanding that your mother is with you, but there are questions about whether or not you're exercising undue influence over her. We would like to have our client, your mother, returned to our office. At the time that she is with us, we will interview your mother privately so that we can find out what her wishes are and also to go further in assessing her level of mental capacity. No monies can be released to anyone prior to that time.

This case study highlights some of the uncertainties lawyers are faced with when dealing with Rule 1.14.

Rick Law as lead attorney of Law ElderLaw, LLP:

> We went through our capacity determination process and determined that we did have questions about the client's capacity. We, as lawyers, were really unable to determine whether our client had sufficient capacity to contract with us, so we were unsure if we had a valid engagement agreement. Our client was scheduled for a full psychiatric exam, but she was abducted prior to that appointment. So, if we don't have a valid contract, obviously we need to return all of the money regardless of what the contract says. But, to whom should we return the money?

> We could tell that there were some limitations on capacity, but we did not have the ability to really know whether she had the capacity to contract or whether she had the capacity to do estate planning, and, therefore, we took the risk of doing work pending having the client's family hire the psychiatrist to determine the woman's capacity prior to actually signing the new estate plan. We did this recognizing that if it turned out that she didn't have capacity, then perhaps we would have to recommend that a guardianship needed to be done. I made the decision to go to court and file an interpleader to determine the proper party to whom the retainer should be disbursed.

It is important to remember, though, that ABA Opinion 96-404 makes it clear that Rule 1.14(b) is not authorizing the lawyer to take protective action simply because the client is not acting in what the lawyer deems to be the client's best interest. The authorization is only given when the client cannot adequately act in the client's own interest.[7] Thus the lawyer may not seek protective action simply to protect the client from perceived errors in judgment. The lawyer may, and is encouraged to, offer a candid assessment of the client's behavior and the possible consequences and offer alternative options, but ultimately must defer to the client's wishes.

Hypothetical A:

Larry Lawyer represents Carla Client, who is of limited means and is a defendant in a contract dispute. Client has a complete defense to the action based on the creditor's fraudulent conduct. However, Client instructs Lawyer to pay the disputed bill, despite Lawyer's advice to the contrary and the disastrous impact on Client's financial well-being, because Client has always paid her bills in the past.

Resolution to Hypothetical A:

If Lawyer believes that Client has sufficient mental capacity to make an informed decision about the resolution of the contract dispute, he should respect Client's decision even if he thinks it contrary to her interest.

However, if Lawyer believes that Client's mental capacity is so diminished that it limits her ability to make an informed decision, Lawyer may have Client's family participate in discussions to assist Client in her decision making. Alternatively, Lawyer may decide to take action to protect Carla Client, including seeking the appointment of a guardian.

The comments to Rule 1.14 provide a lawyer with factors to balance in determining the extent of diminished capacity.[8] The factors are

- the client's ability to articulate reasoning leading to a decision, variability of state of mind, and ability to appreciate the consequences of a decision;

---

7. ABA Comm'n on L. & Aging & Am. Psychological Ass'n, *supra* note 1.
8. Model Rules of Prof'l Conduct R. 1.14 cmt. 6.

- the substantive fairness of a decision; and
- the consistency of a decision with the known long-term commitments and values of the client.

Hypothetical B:

Lawyer has also represented Sam Senior for many years and has been engaged to represent him in the sale of his home to obtain funds to move into an assisted-living facility—a move that Lawyer and Senior agree is in Senior's best interest in light of his failing health and increasing memory problems. Shortly before the scheduled closing, Senior suffers a stroke and is unable to communicate with Lawyer or attend the closing.

Resolution to Hypothetical B:

Given the substantial impact of Senior's stroke on his ability to adequately act in his own interest, Lawyer may take reasonable protective actions under Rule 1.14(b) and obtain the appointment of a legal representative to complete the transaction on Senior's behalf.

Furthermore, in situations where the client with diminished capacity has substantial property that should be sold for the client's benefit, it may be necessary to appoint a legal representative for effective completion of the transaction. Additionally, rules of procedure in litigation often state that people with diminished capacity must be represented by a guardian or next friend if they do not have a general guardian.[9] (Chapter 6 covers guardianship issues in great detail.)

However, lawyers need to be aware of the caveat in Comment 7 warning that in many circumstances, the appointment of a legal representative may be more expensive or traumatic for the client than circumstances require. Evaluation of such circumstances is a matter entrusted to the professional judgment of the lawyer. In considering alternatives, the lawyer should be aware of any law that requires the lawyer to advocate the least restrictive action on behalf of the client.

Rule 1.14(c) Avoiding Inappropriate Disclosure

Rule 1.14(c) reminds lawyers that information relating to the representation of a client with diminished capacity is protected by Rule 1.6. In

---

9.   Model Rules of Prof'l Conduct R. 1.14 cmt. 7.

fact, when lawyers take protective action under Rule 1.14(b), they are impliedly authorized by Rule 1.6(a) to reveal information about the client *only to the extent reasonably necessary* to protect the interests of the client.

Comment 8 warns lawyers that by disclosing the client's diminished capacity, they could be adversely affecting the client's interests. For example, by disclosing this information, a lawyer could set in motion circumstances that may lead to proceedings for the involuntary commitment of the client. Thus, lawyers may not disclose such information unless authorized to do so.

The comment goes on to state:

> When taking protective action pursuant to paragraph (b), the lawyer is impliedly authorized to make the necessary disclosures, even when the client directs the lawyer to the contrary. Nevertheless, given the risks of disclosure, paragraph (c) limits what the lawyer may disclose in consulting with other individuals or entities or seeking the appointment of a legal representative. At the very least, the lawyer should determine whether it is likely that the person or entity consulted with will act adversely to the client's interests before discussing matters related to the client. The lawyer's position in such cases is an unavoidably difficult one.[10]

 Case Study
Caregiver Child

Dr. Nadkarni states that the cases in which there is a "caregiver" child involved in helping the parent with diminished capacity provide an excellent example of the complexity of Rule 1.14 and how difficult it can be to tell if a client is impaired.

"In these cases, we often have an individual whose dementia is progressing in the early stages where these paranoid ideations can come about even without the presence of a severely impaired working memory," he says. "The individual may approach the lawyer and state, 'My daughter is putting poison in my food and my medications, and so I'm not taking those medicines, and I don't want her around my money. I don't want her around my house. Mr. Lawyer, I'd like you to take my will and change it so that the bulk of my estate goes to my nephew, because my daughter is really out to get me. She's got listening devices placed in my house.'"

It is difficult to tell if this person is being truthful or if she is suffering from delusions due to dementia. When a client and comes in and says, for

---

10. Model Rules of Prof'l Conduct R. 1.14 cmt. 8.

example, that Martians are communicating with the client and the client wants to change her will based on these communications, even a person with absolutely no training in the mental health field could see and identify that the person is suffering from dementia. That would be obvious to anybody. But when a client comes in and says that her daughter is actually withholding medications and poisoning medicines and food, there may or may not be some truth to that—and that is not so easy to ascertain. Now it's time to consult with a medical professional to determine capacity.

Unfortunately, there are no special training secrets to comply with Rule 1.14; much is simply based on experience. It can certainly help to attend continuing legal education in the elder law niche of practice to keep abreast of any new developments. Lawyers should speak to a local state-appointed public guardian and public administrator who deals constantly with dementia and its manifestations—hoarding, wandering, and a wide variety of other aberrations—to learn more about that person's experiences and training. And, if possible, lawyers may want to work with an outside psychiatric consultant.

Fortunately for those lawyers who do not focus solely on elder law, but are still affected by Rule 1.14, the ABA does provide guidance.

ABA Handbook

Assessment of Older Adults with Diminished Capacity: A Handbook for Lawyers is a wonderful tool that the ABA has put out, but many lawyers probably have never read it, much less worked to actually apply it to their practice.[11]

The handbook is another joint effort of the American Bar Association Commission on Law and Aging and the American Psychological Association. The goal of this particular handbook is to provide an approach that lawyers may find useful in understanding, assessing, and responding to clients and potential clients with diminished capacity.

The handbook, and by corollary, the rule itself, offers a way—and even a duty—for lawyers to deal with a possibility that more and more of the clients that they're sitting across the table from are having anywhere

---

11. ABA Comm'n on L. & Aging & Am. Psychological Ass'n, *supra* note 1.

from subtle decisional problems and perhaps questionable judgments to perhaps very obvious capacity-related problems.

Understanding how to apply Rule 1.14 is important, because we have, for really the first time in human history, millions of people who are aging beyond 60 years of age, and this is an evolutionary change. This has never confronted lawyers before, and the practice of law has never had to really grapple with a sheer voluminous number of people who are in the older adult category.

Capacity Worksheet

Of special import is the capacity worksheet found within the handbook. This worksheet is a checklist of sorts aimed at helping lawyers to be able to assess their clients and determine whether or not a client has diminished capacity.

While the handbook has some wonderful case examples, the closest thing to a guide of how to implement the rule is the "Capacity Worksheet for Lawyers" on pages 23 through 26.

The capacity worksheet is a great tool, but it seems as though it would be necessary to have the worksheet present while interviewing clients, and that could be problematic. The last page of this worksheet is entitled "Preliminary Conclusions About Client Capacity" and has the following choices to check—each with directions on how to proceed: intact, mild problems, more than mild problems, and severe problems.

One of the book's authors notes, "It is a really wonderful worksheet, and I think it is fine as a guide for me, but I cannot imagine having this in front of me while I have clients with me. It would be offensive to them and any loved ones if they saw it."

A good way to get around this issue is to create a worksheet using the ABA's worksheet as a template.

One of the book's authors has done just that. The author's worksheet is entitled "Script for Key Points to Discuss" (included later in this chapter). So if the client or someone else was looking down at the big print, all it says is "Key Points to Discuss."

Next, this worksheet uses codes or abbreviations, such as TC. The lawyer interviewer knows that TC means "testamentary capacity," but it doesn't scream out that the lawyer is evaluating their testamentary capacity. Under TC are several questions or prompts: "Where do you live?" "Do you own your home?" "What do you think it is worth?" "Tell me about your income." The script reminds the interviewer to ask the clients to describe their children using words such as "honest," "reliable," "caring," "loving," "shopaholic," "irresponsible," or "dishonest."

Clients that come in for estate planning would not be surprised by these questions and would not jump to the conclusion that their mental capacity was being tested. However, these types of questions serve to assess clients in the same manner as the ABA's capacity worksheet. These types of questions allow the interviewer to determine the client's ability.

On page 25 of the ABA worksheet, under "Capacity, General Legal Elements of Capacity for Common Tasks, Testamentary Capacity," "testamentary capacity" is defined as the ability to appreciate the following elements in relation to each other:

1. Understands the nature of the act of making a will.
2. Generally understands the nature and extent of his/her property.
3. Generally recognizes those persons who are the natural objects of his/her bounty.
4. Has/understands a distribution scheme.[12]

The author's script is designed in such a way to determine that if a person has enough capacity to answer those questions about understanding the nature and the extent of property and recognition of the people who are the natural objects of their bounty, the interviewer will be able to determine that the client has testamentary capacity.

According to interviews with Dr. Dean Bryson, a psychologist; Dr. Sanford Finkel, a geriatric psychiatrist; Dr. Nick Nadkarni, geriatric psychiatrist; and Dr. Sara Mosey, a doctor of audiology, people have a tendency to answer "yes" to almost any question because they want to humor people and keep the conversation moving. So if lawyers ask only yes/no questions, they are going to get a "yes" most of the time. The clients may not hear the question, but they are going to answer "yes." The clients may not understand, but they are going to answer "yes." So the most important thing to do, whether the person has mental incapacity or hearing incapacity, is to ask open-ended questions. For example: "Okay, tell me why you are here today. What did you hope we could

---

12. *Id.* at 25.

accomplish? What did you hope we could do for you?" Then sit back, keep quiet, and don't lead them in the answer.

Another good question is, "Do you have any specific legal questions for me regarding your estate plan or your estate?"

It is also useful to ask older clients and prospective clients what medications they are taking. If they cannot answer, then chances are there's a problem, because they are almost all on some sort of medication and many of them are taking several types multiple times a day.

At the end of the client interview, the interviewing lawyer notes any educational or cultural barriers to the interview. Did the client have any cognitive issues, i.e., memory problems, repeating disorientation, or trouble comprehending? The lawyer describes the client's hygiene and grooming. Were there any mitigating factors such as vision or hearing impairment, stress, or grief or other emotional practice? Finally, the interviewing attorney assigns a rating: intact, mild, more than mild, or possible undue influence.

While the capacity worksheet covers a variety of issues, Rule 1.14 can seem daunting to some lawyers.

Practice Pointer:

"I don't think anything is impossible; however, I do think that the worksheet places a significant or substantial burden on lawyers to be able to comply with it. The problem I see is that the rule [1.14] is asking you to go outside of your profession. I'm used to having some interaction with the law, but if you ask me not only to treat geriatric patients but to assist them with their estate planning, I would not know where to start."—Dr. Nick Nadkarni

---

While Dr. Nadkarni's point is certainly valid, Rule 1.14 can also be read as giving lawyers a duty to engage in a process of discovering legal capacity concerns that would put a reasonable layperson on alert that something is not right.

Rule 1.14 is based on the concept that lawyers must make a systematic good-faith effort to determine the legal capacity of older adult clients and prospective clients. Lawyers are charged with the responsibility to understand the legal elements of capacity for the legal action to be taken.

After legal evaluation, if lawyers have a bona fide doubt as to the capacity of an individual, they would then seek medical consultation, refer the client for evaluation, and/or consider any necessary steps to protect the person from harm.

The Model Rule 1.14 capacity worksheet for lawyers provides a needed framework to determine the existence of diminished capacity. While lawyers cannot be expected to unerringly detect the presence of incapacity, use of the capacity worksheet should be the foundation of lawyers' determination process. Familiarity with the Model Rule 1.14 and the capacity worksheet will help alert lawyers to behaviors that trigger a bona fide doubt about a client's legal capacity.

The intent of the rule is to protect the public and the legal profession in the uniquely new environment wherein millions of people are aging with physically healthy bodies but are imperiled by dementia, which affects their decision making.

The capacity worksheet is a great tool, and an example of how a firm can create its own worksheet to fit its particular practice needs; it's just one illustration of how to use the tools provided by the ABA and the APA to ensure lawyers are applying Rule 1.14 correctly.

Practice Pointer:

Follow up meetings with a letter. One of the book's authors met with a prospective senior citizen client who was interested in having some estate planning done and sent a follow-up letter to confirm the prospective agreement. A few days later, the author received a call from the prospective client who was short of breath because she thought she had hired them for $900, but the author thought she had hired the firm for $9,900.

Once the prospective client calmed down, the lawyer told the prospective client not to worry, since the next meeting was what they call the "design meeting" and the first meeting was just the "intake meeting." The lawyer told her to come to the next meeting and bring her adult son, and if it doesn't make sense for her to go forward, then don't worry about it and no monies would be owed.

That is an example of how important it is to follow up with a written document that memorializes what happened during the meeting, though it may not be what the client thought happened during the meeting.

RULE 1.4

ABA Model Rule 1.4 deals with communications. There is some interplay between Rules 1.14 and 1.4, because lawyers who suspect their client may have diminished capacity due to dementia or Alzheimer's disease may need to disclose some communications. Rule 1.4 follows:

Client-Lawyer Relationship
Rule 1.4 Communication

(a) A lawyer shall:

> (1) promptly inform the client of any decision or circumstance with respect to which the client's informed consent, as defined in Rule 1.0(e), is required by these Rules;

> (2) reasonably consult with the client about the means by which the client's objectives are to be accomplished;

> (3) keep the client reasonably informed about the status of the matter;

> (4) promptly comply with reasonable requests for information; and

> (5) consult with the client about any relevant limitation on the lawyer's conduct when the lawyer knows that the client expects assistance not permitted by the Rules of Professional Conduct or other law.

(b) A lawyer shall explain a matter to the extent reasonably necessary to permit the client to make informed decisions regarding the representation.

Rule 1.4(b) brings up some interesting questions when a client has Alzheimer's. Lawyers must ensure that their client is not suffering from diminished capacity and that the client can make an informed decision. If the client is capable of informed consent, to what extent must the lawyer explain the matter? Depending on the level of Alzheimer's, the level of explanation could vary.

Comment 5 requires that clients should have sufficient information to participate intelligently in decisions concerning the objectives of the representation and the means by which they are to be pursued—to the extent the clients are willing and able to do so.[13] This can be tricky when

---

13. MODEL RULES OF PROF'L CONDUCT R. 1.4 cmt. 5.

the client suffers from Alzheimer's, and may require the lawyer to go through the capacity worksheet checklist or consult Rule 1.14 to make sure the client is not suffering from diminished capacity.

The comments also note that, ordinarily, the information to be provided is appropriate for a client who is a comprehending and responsible adult. However, fully informing the client according to this standard may be impracticable, for example, when the client is a child or suffers from diminished capacity. In these instances, the lawyer is advised to consult Rule 1.14.[14]

RULE 1.6

Although it may be necessary to consult with the client's family in cases where the client has Alzheimer's, lawyers may face potential issues pertaining to privileged information. ABA Model Rule 1.6 explains what a privileged communication is. The rule is provided below.

Client-Lawyer Relationship
Rule 1.6 Confidentiality of Information

(a) A lawyer shall not reveal information relating to the representation of a client unless the client gives informed consent, the disclosure is impliedly authorized in order to carry out the representation or the disclosure is permitted by paragraph (b).

(b) A lawyer may reveal information relating to the representation of a client to the extent the lawyer reasonably believes necessary:

(1) to prevent reasonably certain death or substantial bodily harm;

(2) to prevent the client from committing a crime or fraud that is reasonably certain to result in substantial injury to the financial interests or property of another and in furtherance of which the client has used or is using the lawyer's services;

(3) to prevent, mitigate or rectify substantial injury to the financial interests or property of another that is reasonably certain to result or has resulted from the client's commission of a crime or fraud in furtherance of which the client has used the lawyer's services;

---

14. MODEL RULES OF PROF'L CONDUCT R. 1.4 cmt. 6.

(4) to secure legal advice about the lawyer's compliance with these Rules;

(5) to establish a claim or defense on behalf of the lawyer in a controversy between the lawyer and the client, to establish a defense to a criminal charge or civil claim against the lawyer based upon conduct in which the client was involved, or to respond to allegations in any proceeding concerning the lawyer's representation of the client; or

(6) to comply with other law or a court order.

Hypothetical C:

Constance Counselor prepares "mirror wills" for John and Jennifer Couple. The wills stipulate that each leaves one's assets to the other. Several months later, John visits Counselor alone and asks her to prepare a new will leaving a substantial portion of his estate to a much younger woman and instructs Counselor to not disclose the change to Jennifer.

Resolution to Hypothetical C:

Unless there was a prior agreement by both John and Jennifer to the contrary, John's communication with Counselor would not be privileged. If Counselor changes John's will and keeps it from Jennifer, Counselor will be disciplined.

A fundamental principle of the client-lawyer relationship is that, in the absence of the client's informed consent, the lawyer must not reveal information relating to the representation.[15] This can become complicated when the client has Alzheimer's disease. Lawyers in this position will need to look to Rule 1.14 to determine if their client is capable of providing informed consent.

A lawyer is impliedly authorized to make disclosures about a client when appropriate in carrying out the representation, except in situations where the client's instructions or special circumstances limit that authority.[16] This issue can arise when dealing with clients with Alzheimer's disease.

---

15. MODEL RULES OF PROF'L CONDUCT R. 1.6 cmt. 2.
16. MODEL RULES OF PROF'L CONDUCT R. 1.6 cmt. 5.

Lawyers with clients that may have diminished capacity should be aware of comment 12 to Rule 1.6. This comment clarifies that a lawyer may be required by other law to disclose information about a client. Whether such a law supersedes Rule 1.6 is a question of law beyond the scope of these rules. When disclosure of information relating to the representation appears to be required by other law, the lawyer must discuss the matter with the client to the extent required by Rule 1.4. If, however, the other law supersedes this rule and requires disclosure, paragraph (b)(6) permits the lawyer to make such disclosures as are necessary to comply with the law.[17]

RULE 1.7

As all lawyers know, identifying the client and establishing the scope of representation at the outset of the client-lawyer relationship is a crucial step. This is even more important when dealing with clients suffering from Alzheimer's, because the need to seek help from the client's family may arise.

Issues can crop up when a lawyer attempts to represent a family instead of individual members of the family. These issues must be addressed at the inception of the relationship. ABA Model Rule 1.7 lays out this groundwork:

Client-Lawyer Relationship
Rule 1.7 Conflict of Interest: Current Clients

(a) Except as provided in paragraph (b), a lawyer shall not represent a client if the representation involves a concurrent conflict of interest. A concurrent conflict of interest exists if:

(1) the representation of one client will be directly adverse to another client; or

(2) there is a significant risk that the representation of one or more clients will be materially limited by the lawyer's

---

17. MODEL RULES OF PROF'L CONDUCT R. 1.6 cmt. 12.

responsibilities to another client, a former client or a third person or by a personal interest of the lawyer.

(b) Notwithstanding the existence of a concurrent conflict of interest under paragraph (a), a lawyer may represent a client if:

(1) the lawyer reasonably believes that the lawyer will be able to provide competent and diligent representation to each affected client;

(2) the representation is not prohibited by law;

(3) the representation does not involve the assertion of a claim by one client against another client represented by the lawyer in the same litigation or other proceeding before a tribunal; and

(4) each affected client gives informed consent, confirmed in writing.

Competing interests may compromise the joint representation. Comment 8 explains that a conflict of interest exists "if there is a significant risk that a lawyer's ability to consider, recommend or carry out an appropriate course of action for the client will be materially limited as a result of the lawyer's other responsibilities or interests."[18] The comment further notes that the issue is whether it is possible that clients could eventually have competing interests that could materially interfere with the lawyer's independent professional judgment.

When debating about whether one should represent multiple clients in the same matter, a lawyer must be aware that if the common representation fails because the potentially adverse interests cannot be reconciled, the result can be additional cost, embarrassment, and recrimination.[19] Normally if the common representation fails, the lawyer will be forced to withdraw from representing all of the clients. In some situations, the risk of failure is so great that multiple representation is plainly impossible. Lawyers with clients suffering from Alzheimer's should be wary of the many dangers highlighted by Rule 1.7 and need to carefully consider all the issues before representing multiple family members.

---

18. MODEL RULES OF PROF'L CONDUCT R. 1.7 cmt. 8.
19. MODEL RULES OF PROF'L CONDUCT R. 1.7 cmt. 29.

Hypothetical D:

Amy Attorney is visited by two adult children of Wendy Widow. Widow's children are worried about her ability to care for her basic needs and ask Attorney to help get Widow to explore available options. Widow has considerable assets, and the children, who are her beneficiaries, express their concern that the assets might be dissipated before she dies. The children offer to pay Attorney's fee for consulting with Widow.

Attorney meets with Widow, who asks Attorney to draw up a new will leaving her estate to her church.

Resolution to Hypothetical D:

To avoid the possible conflict of interest that might otherwise arise, Attorney must clarify whom she is representing at the outset of her discussion with Widow's children. If Attorney is representing Widow, she should advise the children that she is obligated to represent Widow's interests, not theirs. This would include pointing out to the children that just because they are paying her fee does not affect her duty to render independent professional judgment on Widow's behalf and maintain the confidentiality of her information pertaining to the representation.

If Attorney is representing both the Widow and the children, she has a duty to advise all of them that conflicts of interest may arise that could affect her ability to represent their respective interests and maintain confidentiality. In this case, if she were to implement Widow's request to change her will, she may find herself in violation of Rule 1.7's conflict of interest provisions.

Situations arise where a lawyer may be paid from a source other than the client, including a co-client. The client must be informed of and consent to the arrangement and the arrangement cannot compromise the lawyer's duty of loyalty or independent judgment to the client. (See Rule 1.8(f).)[20]

It is important to remember when considering representing multiple family members that the prevailing rule is that, as between commonly represented clients, the privilege does not attach. Therefore, it must be assumed that if litigation eventuates between the clients, the privilege

---

20. Model Rules of Prof'l Conduct R. 1.8 cmt. 12.

will not protect any such communications, and the clients should be so advised.[21]

Comment 31 to Rule 1.7 notes that continued common representation will almost certainly be inadequate as to the duty of confidentiality if one client asks the lawyer not to disclose to the other client information relevant to the common representation. The lawyer has an equal duty of loyalty to each client, and each client has the right to be informed of anything bearing on the representation that might affect that client's interests and the right to expect that the lawyer will use that information to that client's benefit. (See Rule 1.4.) In these situations, the lawyer must, at the outset of the common representation and as part of the process of obtaining each client's informed consent, advise each client that information will be shared and that the lawyer will have to withdraw if one client decides that some matter material to the representation should be kept from the other.

In limited circumstances, it may be appropriate for the lawyer to proceed with the representation when the clients have agreed, after being properly informed, that the lawyer will keep certain information confidential. For example, the lawyer may reasonably conclude that failure to disclose one client's trade secrets to another client will not adversely affect representation involving a joint venture between the clients and agree to keep that information confidential with the informed consent of both clients.

Loyalty to a current client prohibits lawyers from undertaking representation directly adverse to that client, without that client's informed consent. Thus, absent consent, a lawyer may not act as an advocate in one matter against a person the lawyer represents in some other matter, even when the matters are wholly unrelated. While this seems simple enough, it is an issue that lawyers need to be thinking about when they consult the family of their client in situations where the client has Alzheimer's and is unable to consent.[22]

The comments to Rule 1.7 also point out that there are certain circumstances in which it may be impossible to make the disclosure necessary to obtain consent. For example, when the lawyer represents different clients in related matters and one of the clients refuses to consent to the disclosure necessary to permit the other client to make an

21. MODEL RULES OF PROF'L CONDUCT R. 1.7 cmt. 30.
22. MODEL RULES OF PROF'L CONDUCT R. 1.7 cmt. 6.

informed decision, the lawyer cannot properly ask the latter to consent. In some cases, the alternative to common representation can be that each party may have to obtain separate representation with the possibility of incurring additional costs. These costs, along with the benefits of securing separate representation, are factors that may be considered by the affected client in determining whether common representation is in the client's interests.[23] Lawyers with clients suffering from Alzheimer's disease need to keep this in mind.

> **Hypothetical E:**
>
> Bob and Jessica Goldenyears own a small but successful family business. They and their two children meet with Attorney and ask her to help them sell their business to their children to finance their move into an assisted-living facility due to Bob suffering from Alzheimer's.
>
> **Resolution to Hypothetical E:**
>
> At the very outset of her discussions with the Goldenyears and their children, Attorney is required to discuss the conflicts that could come about in the representation of both parties in the sale of the business. Because of the obvious differing interests that will arise, Attorney should assume the joint representation of seller and buyer is prohibited under Rule 1.7. Attorney may represent one party and advise the other party to obtain separate counsel.

The chart located at http://www.americanbar.org/content/dam/aba/administrative/professional_responsibility/mrpc_1_14.authcheckdam.pdf is a state-by-state breakdown created by the ABA describing the various alternations that states have made to Model Rule 1.14. It breaks down the changes in terminology, additions, and deletions.

The following is a capacity worksheet created by Rick Law for use in his law practice.

CAPACITY EVALUATION PROCESS OVERVIEW

This is a summary overview and practical guide prepared from information found in *Assessment of Older Adults with Diminished Capacity: A*

---

23. MODEL RULES OF PROF'L CONDUCT R. 1.7 cmt. 19.

Handbook for Lawyers, by the American Bar Association Commission on Law and Aging and American Psychological Association.

What is dementia? Decline in memory, decline in other cognitive abilities, judgment, and abstract thinking and personality change.

Situation-Specific Standards of Capacity: See capacity abbreviations above each section of the interview that apply to that level.

Testamentary Capacity (TC): Natural objects of a person's bounty; nature and extent of property.

Donative Capacity (DC): Includes knowing the above as well as the nature and purpose of the gift.

Contractual Capacity (CC): The person's ability to understand the business being transacted.

Capacity to Convey Real Property (CCRP): The person's ability to understand the nature and effect of the act at the time of conveyance.

Capacity to Execute a Durable POA for Property (C-POA-P): Testamentary plus contractual.

Capacity to Execute a Health Care POA (C-POA-HC): Ability to understand benefits, risks and alternatives to proposed health care and to make and communicate a health-care decision.

Capacity Conclusion Codes: Use these abbreviations in interviews while going through the script for each section.

I   INTACT: No evidence or very minimal evidence of DC.

MP   MILD PROBLEMS: Some evidence of DC, but insufficient to preclude representation or proposed planning.

MMP   MORE THAN MILD PROBLEMS: Refer client for evaluation.

SP   SEVERE PROBLEMS: Client lacks capacity to proceed with planning unless agent or guardian represents the client. No change in any current estate planning should be done.

PUI   POSSIBLE UNDUE INFLUENCE: Someone may be influencing the client to make changes; the person may be berating other family members who are heirs. Someone is trying to "run" the meeting and speak for the senior.

Script for Key Points to Discuss in Client Review

"In the process of assisting you with your planning, it is my job to do everything that I possibly can to make sure that your actions are not challenged now or at a later time. So I will be asking you some questions and discussing with you some issues that will help us establish that you have legal capacity to go forward with your estate planning today. The likelihood of someone challenging your plan is greater if you disinherit someone or distribute in unequal shares. When someone gets less than he or she anticipated, there is a great risk for challenging your capacity at the time you made the plan. It is our practice to interview our client alone so that no one could assert any undue influence by the individuals who are with you today." **(Ask others to wait in the lobby while speaking with the client alone.)**

"I want you to understand that the things we talk about today, and any other day for that matter, are confidential. The more you share with me, the better I will be able to understand your goals and concerns and to design your plan according to your wishes. After having said the things regarding capacity, possible challenges to your planning and confidentiality, do you have any questions for me?" (Allow client to ask any questions. This will also help in assessing capacity.) **THEN SAY: "Okay, let's talk about you."**

TC

Where do you live? How long have you lived there? Do you own your home? What do you think it is worth? Do you owe anything on your house?

Tell me about your income. Social Security? Pension? Annuity or interest income?

Okay, besides your home, what other assets do you have, such as bank, investment accounts, bonds?

Do you have any debts such as car loan, credit card debt?

Okay, so your net worth is approximately . . . $____. Does that sound about right?

Let's talk about your family? Spouse? (If deceased, when?) Children (how many, names, where they live)? Grandkids (how many, any other things they want to tell you)?

(Client Name), if I gave you some descriptive words and asked which best describe each of your children, would you do that for me? Okay, let's take (Child's Name #1). Here are the words: honest, reliable, caring, loving, shopaholic, irresponsible, dishonest—what key word might you use to describe (Child's Name #1)? **Then move on through each child (and even grandchildren if they might be included as a decision maker in documents).**

DC/CC

What about gifts to your family? Have you made any gifts or loans to your children or grandchildren? What about charitable giving?

Okay, let's talk about why you are here today. What would you hope our firm could help you with?

Do you have any specific legal questions for me regarding your estate plan?

We would be entering into an engagement agreement with you regarding the fee to be paid and the work to be done, and I will be reviewing that with you and answering any questions you might have regarding the agreement. **(Later when reviewing this, lawyers will be able to test the client's capacity regarding contracts.)**

C-POA-P/POA HC

So, (Client Name), tell me if you were unable to make your financial decisions or handle your own financial transactions such as banking or bill paying, who would you want to handle those things for you? And would you want them to carry out planning to help preserve your assets, or would you want them to simply pay your bills and your care needs until such time that you died?

Okay, that makes sense based on what you told me about your children and grandchildren when you were describing them.

How would you describe your current health? Any concerns? Are you on any medications? If you were unable to make your health-care decisions, such as speak with your doctors, make decisions regarding procedures and care, whom would you want to make those decisions for you?

It would be important for that person to know your wishes with regards to end of life decisions. Do you want to talk about your thoughts on certain life support issues?

[Thank the client for taking the time to share. Ask if the client has any other questions or concerns. Ask if it is okay now to bring the family back in.]

In your assessment please note any educational or cultural barriers to the interview? Did the client have any cognitive issues such as memory problems, repeating, disorientation, trouble comprehending? Note the client's hygiene and grooming. Note if there were any mitigating factors such as vision or hearing impairment, stress, grief, other emotional factors.[24]

---

24. Katherine D. Motley, Client Capacity Evaluation Guide for Lawyers (on file with Law ElderLaw, LLP).

CHAPTER THREE

LIFE, DEATH, AND CARE INSTRUCTIONS

ELDER LAW LAWYERS FACILITATE discussions about life, death, and disability. This is not an easy task, because nobody really wants to talk about his or her own death.

People know that they are going to die—someday. But in their heart of hearts, most people cannot believe that they are actually going to die. How else can we explain the fact that 85 percent of the adult population does not have a simple will, power of attorney, or health-care directive? The most obvious answer is that they must not truly believe that they are going to die. Even more importantly, most people do not plan for their incapacity because they do not believe that they will reach a point where they will not have the mental ability to be in control of their own finances or of their own decision making about their health care.

Most couples can expect that their health will track alongside of each other pretty much the same way from the ages of 20 to 60. They can expect to be primarily healthy and only experience acute care problems.

However, during the period from 60 to 80 years old, there is a good chance that one of the two is going to become incapacitated and one spouse is going to end up taking care of the other.

Practice Pointer: Incapacity Defined

An elder care lawyer commented that he has learned through presenting health-care power of attorney language to several thousand people that when he uses the word "incapacity," they don't know what he's talking about. Whatever the typical layperson believes incapacity is, it is not what the lawyer is talking about. When the lawyer asks a layperson who's doing estate planning, "Do you know what it means to be incapacitated?" the layperson gets a fuzzy look on his or her face, and when trying to describe it, more or less describes being unconscious.

So, when lawyers advise a client that they need to do planning in case the client is incapacitated, there is a good chance the client is not thinking of being in a state where he or she is potentially conscious, but unable to properly respond to making health-care and/or financial decisions. The word "incapacity" does not communicate to the client what the lawyer is thinking. Lawyers are talking about a person who cannot appreciate and understand the consequences of a decision or an act.

The general public, typically, does not understand incapacity in that manner. Therefore, when lawyers try to talk to them about making a power of attorney that would deal with their incapacity, they have a hard time imagining anything but the rarest of occurrences that could possibly happen to them that would cause them to be unconscious.

Therefore, it's very important for the lawyer who's working with clients to take the time and effort to explain that, legally, the idea of mental incapacity means being unable to properly control assets and/or health-care decision making, and that the situation can come up through an accident, an illness, or a long-term degenerative disease, such as any of the many types of dementia, which includes, of course, Alzheimer's disease.

It is really up to the lawyer to educate the client when going through a power of attorney form, because most clients actually think that the possibility of being incapacitated is rare, but the incidents of incapacity are, of course, much higher than they imagine.

ADVANCE DIRECTIVES

Advance directives are documents such as the living will, power of attorney for health care, power of attorney for property, and the do not resuscitate order (DNR). People primarily sign these forms because they want to avoid unwanted resuscitation and other "heroic measures" when there is no hope of recovery and returning to an enjoyable life.

These are very important documents when dealing with Alzheimer's disease because they are documents that allow people to communicate health-care preferences ahead of time so that when they lose the capacity to make or communicate their own decisions, their wishes can still be communicated.

It is important to remember that an advance directive has to be signed while a person still has the mental capacity to sign legal documents.[1]

Simply filling out an advance directive is not enough, though. Later in this chapter, there will be a discussion about the difference between a powerful health-care power of attorney and a powerless health-care power of attorney.

For example, even if a client has a standard health-care power of attorney or a living will and gets to the point where he cannot swallow, the medical professional will tell the client's family that the condition is not terminal, but "he is going to die if you don't feed him." This puts a tremendous amount of guilt on the family if they don't know the client's wishes, and they will probably say, "Well, I guess we should put in the feeding tube." Now, because the client doesn't have a qualifying condition in his advance directive, even if he signed the normal statutory power of attorney or living will, no one is going to take action to stop the doctors from putting in a feeding tube. Even if the client never wanted to have a feeding tube in that situation, he will end up with one because he does not have a qualifying condition.

> **Practice Pointer: No One Knows It All**
>
> Rick Law admitted in the book's introduction that when his clients Luise and Bob came into his office dealing with dementia issues, he was not prepared to help them. He did not yet possess the tools to deal with their issues.

---

1. RICK L. LAW, EVERYTHING YOU ALWAYS WANTED TO KNOW ABOUT ALZHEIMER'S BUT WERE AFRAID TO ASK 93 (2009).

Practice Pointer: Be Familiar with Statutory Definitions

Very few lawyers know it all within the context of health-care powers of attorney. Most people, including the majority of lawyers, take advance directives for granted.

Every phrase and many words used within a health-care power of attorney are legal terms of art for which many paragraphs of defining language can be found within the empowering state legislation. Lawyers should read and be familiar with the statutory definitions of the words and phrases within any form of health-care power of attorney provided to clients.

The goal of this chapter is to teach lawyers how to get the right advance directive in place for clients so that when the Alzheimer's disease advances, clients will get the end-life treatment that they desire.

What Can Happen Without an Advance Directive?

If a client does not have a living will and has not created a power of attorney and the Alzheimer's disease has progressed to the point where the client is no longer competent, lawyers will find themselves in court attempting to convince a judge who the proper people are to represent the client. The client could face a lengthy, expensive, and embarrassing court hearing to determine competency.[2]

Worse yet, if the client is determined to be incompetent, another hearing will be held and the court will appoint a conservator to handle the client's financial affairs, and/or a guardian will be appointed to tend to the client's personal and health-care needs.[3] (Conservator and guardians are discussed in more detail in chapter 6.)

While most states' laws encourage the courts to appoint family members as conservators and guardians, court involvement can be expensive and may impose cumbersome supervision on the client and the conservator and guardian.

In some cases where the incapacitated patient is in the hospital and does not have a living will or a power of attorney, the attending physician may appoint a surrogate decision maker who would then be authorized to make health-care decisions for the patient. These decisions include

---

2. William G. Hammond, Rick L. Law, Karen Hays Weber & Mary Helen Gautreaux, The Alzheimer's Legal Survival Guide: Action Guide 15 (2009).
3. *Id.*

whether to forgo life-sustaining treatment. The order of priority for being appointed a surrogate decision maker varies from state to state, but is generally similar to the example below from Illinois:

(1) the patient's guardian of the person;
(2) the patient's spouse;
(3) any adult son or daughter of the patient;
(4) either parent of the patient;
(5) any adult brother or sister of the patient;
(6) any adult grandchild of the patient;
(7) a close friend of the patient;
(8) the patient's guardian of the estate.[4]

The Illinois statute states that health-care providers have the right to rely on any of the above surrogates if the provider believes after reasonable inquiry that neither a health-care agent under the Powers of Attorney for Health Care Law nor a surrogate of higher priority is available.[5]

Many older adults have told their lawyers stories of doctors and/ or hospital staff that have ignored the refusal of life-prolonging care wishes of a now-deceased loved one. These individuals stated that they had insisted that their loved one did not want life-prolonging treatment, but nonetheless a doctor ordered feeding tubes, ventilators, and other life-prolonging measures. Recent studies confirm this lack of regard for patients' preferences in life-sustaining treatment decisions by doctors and hospital staff.[6]

A 2008 study reviewed life-sustaining-treatment decisions that occurred between hospital medical staff and their patients and/or their health-care agents under advance directives.[7] The conclusion of the study is frightening. "Despite patients' wishes, the indiscriminate use of technology and the lack of communication between patients and health care providers have been shown to result in unnecessary pain

---

4. *See* 755 ILL. COMP. STAT. 40/25 (2012).
5. See *id.*
6. NAT'L QUALITY FORUM, SAFE PRACTICES FOR BETTER HEALTHCARE: 2009 UPDATE (2009), *available at* http://www.qualityforum.org/Publications/2009/03/Safe_Practices_for_Better_Healthcare%e2%80%932009_Update.aspx.
7. FM PIERACCI, PROSPECTIVE ANALYSIS OF LIFE-SUSTAINING THERAPY DISCUSSIONS IN THE SURGICAL INTENSIVE CARE UNIT: A HOUSESTAFF PERSPECTIVE (2008).

and suffering for patients."[8] Additionally, according to the study, the medical costs of prolonging a dying patient's life via artificial ventilation and intensive care often range between $11,000 and $36,000.[9]

Fortunately, there are ways to prevent "wrongful resuscitation" from happening. To avoid wrongful resuscitation, lawyers should do the following:

- Create a written advance directive such as a health-care power of attorney, living will, and/or a DNR in appropriate circumstances;
- Insist that the client's advance directives are placed in all of his or her medical records and that the physician is well aware of the existence of such documents;
- Advise the client to have "the talk" with family and the doctor to make sure that everyone is very aware of the client's feelings regarding life-sustaining treatment in the event there is no hope of recovery; and
- Have the client choose an "advocate" as his or her health-care power of attorney and/or surrogate decision maker.

An advocate is someone who can look a medical professional in the eye and insist that certain wishes be carried out. It is recommended that the client look through his or her family and friends and choose someone who can insist that the client's desire regarding life-prolonging treatment be respected by the medical profession.

It's important to know that there is substantial legal authority for health-care directives to be followed. In fact, it is now considered to be a "sentinel incident" when a hospital performs a wrongful resuscitation. The Centers for Medicare and Medicaid Services (CMS) has emphasized that patients have the right to make decisions regarding their long-term health care and that those decisions should be respected by physicians and hospitals.[10]

When lawyers begin speaking with clients and their families about advance directives, they should be prepared to encounter resistance. Seniors (even terminally ill seniors) often say, "I do not care. Funerals are for the living, so do whatever you want." But families really want to

---

8. *Id.*
9. *Id.*
10. CTRS. FOR MEDICARE & MEDICAID SERVS., http://www.cms.gov/.

know how their loved ones feel about these issues. When seniors choose to talk about it, they often find it very meaningful to share their expectations. Once we overcome this conversational taboo, the discussion almost always ends with a hug.

When lawyers are dealing with clients with Alzheimer's it is even more important to have the Final Arrangement Conversation sooner rather than later. Alzheimer's is a terminal disease, and it is in everyone's best interest to find out how the person suffering from the disease feels about life-prolonging treatment.

The Importance of an Advance Directive in the Context of Alzheimer's Disease

Clients with Alzheimer's that are in the early or mild stage of dementia may retain their mental faculties for months or even years. At this stage they may only experience short episodes of impaired mental function and can still receive, understand, and evaluate information. More importantly, for purposes of advance directives, these clients can still use that information to make rational decisions and evaluate legal documents.[11]

Unfortunately, Alzheimer's progresses and does so at a different rate for everyone. As the disease advances, episodes of dementia may become more frequent and may last longer. Eventually, the disease will reach the point where the individual may no longer meet a state's legal test for "capacity" and will no longer be able to execute a valid and enforceable legal document, such as an advance directive. The requirements vary from state to state, but "capacity" generally is defined as the mental ability to perceive and appreciate relevant facts and make rational decisions.[12]

In the case of Alzheimer's disease, advance planning should begin at diagnosis so that the person with dementia can participate as much as possible. Advance planning also avoids the issue of family members having to make important decisions during a crisis on behalf of the individual suffering from Alzheimer's.

---

11. HAMMOND ET AL., *supra* note 2, at 13.
12. *Id.* at 13, 14.

If lawyers do not advise their clients to act quickly, the clients run the risk of not being deemed "competent" and a court will have to step in and appoint a guardian. (See chapter 6 for more coverage of guardians.)

It is very important for lawyers to be involved as early as possible when a client is diagnosed with Alzheimer's. Lawyers are needed to

- identify and complete legal documents such as wills, trusts, and deeds;
- interpret state laws;
- make plans for medical and treatment decisions;
- make plans for finance and property; and
- help to name another person to make decisions on his or her behalf when the client no longer is able to do so.

There are several important questions that every lawyer should ask when clients have been diagnosed with dementia. Some of these questions include

- Describe the current stage of the illness.
- What needs are being met?
- How well can they care for themselves?
- To what extent can they understand the financial affairs?
- Will they qualify for any federal or state benefits? If so, which ones?
- Who, if anyone, is available and able to act as the primary caregiver?

There are two general levels of legal (mental) capacity. Testamentary capacity is necessary for the execution of a valid will and/or testamentary trust and is defined as "sound mind and memory." (Capacity is discussed further in chapter 2.)

To be of sound mind and memory, people must

- know they are making a will;
- know and remember the natural objects of their bounty;
- comprehend the character and extent of their property; and
- make the disposition of their property according to a plan formed in their mind.

The other level of capacity is termed "contractual capacity" and is required for the execution of inter vivos trusts, deeds, and nondurable powers of attorney. Contractual capacity is defined as the ability to comprehend and understand the terms and effect of the contract.

Practice Pointer:

Very few doctors, nurses, and other health-care personnel understand the interplay between the Illinois statutory advance directives such as the living will, power of attorney for health care, and DNR. When a person lacks effective advance directives, a physician can trigger the Illinois Health Care Surrogate Act to designate a decision maker.[13]

Unfortunately, many lawyers consider the health-care power of attorney as a "throw-in" document in an estate plan. In reality, it is important to consider the hidden definitions for terms used in the statutory advance directives and the Health Care Surrogate Act.

For example, a principal should be very careful when naming both primary agent and successor agents. Many clients seem to be willing to vest life-and-death authority in people they know are inappropriate. Individuals will put fear of upsetting family members above their own welfare.

These issues are not unique to Illinois, and lawyers should check the statutes in their states to avoid similar problems.

It is the job of the lawyer to point out that even successor agents may come to hold a person's life in their hands if the best agent is "unavailable." Even if an individual is a third or a fourth successor agent, if the higher-priority agents are unavailable, then whichever agent is available will make the final decision. An agent is considered "unavailable" if "the person's existence is not known; the person has not been able to be contacted by telephone or mail."[14]

Lawyers need to add the full contact information of agents into the power of attorney. This simple act makes it easier for health-care providers to communicate with the highest-priority agent during a time of crisis.

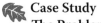 **Case Study** ────────────────────────────
The Problem of Doing It Yourself

In this Internet age when seemingly everything is available online, many people may be tempted to download their own living will or health-care power of attorney instead of consulting a lawyer. The forms seem to be self-explanatory, but are actually more complex than they look.

---

13. *See* 755 Ill. Comp. Stat. 40/25 (2012).
14. See *id.*

An elder law lawyer had a client who had actually initialed all three choices in regard to end-of-life decisions rather than simply choosing one. Another client brought in a form on which the person named as the principal had not signed the form. Rather, the daughter (the client's agent) had signed it where the principal was supposed to sign. Often, clients bring in forms that are not witnessed or are witnessed by interested parties (very interested, in some instances). If one can imagine an error that could be made on these forms—there is an individual who will make that error if not helped by a capable lawyer. In the arena of advance directives, the do-it-yourself approach can be a waste of time or can lead to disastrous results.

Living Wills

One of the first things a lawyer with a client diagnosed with Alzheimer's should do is make sure the client has a living will. This document sets forth the Alzheimer's patient's choices for future medical decisions, such as the use of artificial life support, and is used to instruct medical personnel of the principal's wishes. A living will only takes effect when two doctors certify in writing that the person is irreversibly ill or critically injured and near death.

It is important to be aware of the defined terms and to advise clients of their meanings in filling out a living will. For example, many people may not be aware that when they say they want "sustenance" they are *actually demanding* to have a feeding tube and hydration. Elder law lawyers are probably aware of the ramifications of agreeing to sustenance, but most laypersons are not.

It is extremely important to advise clients that if they do not want a feeding tube, they need to put that in their advance directive in writing. Not only will that help ensure their wishes are met, but it will also remove the guilt from the family by taking the decision-making process out of their hands.

 Case Study _____

Terri Schiavo Case

One of the leading cases dealing with advance directives is the Terri Schiavo case, in which Terri Schiavo had no advance directives of any kind. Her parents and her estranged husband were in disagreement about whether to keep her on life support, and a long and contentious legal battle ensued. If she had had a living will in place, it would have served as a written expression of her intent and could have put an end to the controversy.

Certainly, the expression of intent regarding removal of life support in writing is a circumstance that will put a family's mind at ease. However, it is preferable that a family, an Alzheimer's patient, or a client use a durable power of attorney for health care rather than a living will. There is always the danger that a living will may end up in front of an ethics committee regarding the terminal condition of the patient.

Both Federal and State Law Regulate Advance Directives

The federal regulations for living wills and power of attorney for health care are the same because they are both under the umbrella category of advance directives. This section will briefly summarize the federal regulations for advance directives.

Advance directives are covered in 42 C.F.R. 489. Section 489.100 defines the term: "For purposes of this part, *advance directive* means a written instruction, such as a living will or durable power of attorney for health care, recognized under State law (whether statutory or as recognized by the courts of the State), relating to the provision of health care when the individual is incapacitated."[15]

Section 489.200 sets out what are essentially limitations on healthcare providers. That section requires that hospitals (and other providers) provide patients with information regarding their rights to advance directives under the relevant state's law. Additionally, it requires that a provider give a patient support for a limitation on the use of advance directives, and it requires that the support be established in state law.[16]

While most states have similar requirements for living wills, there are some differences, so it is important for lawyers to be familiar with the laws of the state(s) they practice in. Below are the general requirements for Illinois, California, Florida, and New York.

(The appendix includes a chart produced by the ABA that provides basic information regarding advance directives for all 50 states.)

---

15. Advance Directives, 42 C.F.R. § 489.100 (2011), *available at* http://www.gpo.gov/fdsys /pkg/CFR-2011-title42-vol5/xml/CFR-2011-title42-vol5-part489.xml.
16. *Id.* § 489.200.

Illinois

The Illinois Department of Public Health (IDPH) website contains a statement of Illinois law on advance directives.[17]

In terms of procedural requirements, the IDPH website provides the following:

> Clients can use a standard living-will form or a customized form. Clients may write specific directions about the death-delaying procedures that they do or do not want.
>
> Two people must witness the signing of the living will. The health-care professional cannot be a witness. It is the client's responsibility to tell the health-care professional about a living will if able to do so. Clients can cancel their living will at any time, either by telling someone or by canceling it in writing.[18]

The website also has a link to a uniform advance directive form that can be easily filled out and serves as a functional advance directive, satisfying the few procedural requirements.[19] This would be a good website for lawyers interested in practicing elder law to become familiar with.

Illinois also has a living-will act.[20] Section 3 of that act sets out the following requirements for execution of a living will:[21]

1. The declarant must be of sound mind and either an adult or an emancipated minor.
2. The declarant must be suffering from a terminal condition (and it is under those circumstances that he is requesting to have death delaying procedures not utilized for the prolongation of life).
3. The declaration must be signed by the declarant.
4. A declaration of a pregnant woman, whose fetus could be delivered by live birth, is not valid if the life prolonging procedures would have the result of a successful live birth.
5. The patient if able must notify their attending physician of the declaration. The patient if able should seek a transfer of physician if the physician is unwilling to carry out the declaration.

---

17. *See Advance Directives*, ILL. DEP'T OF PUB. HEALTH, http://www.idph.state.il.us/public/books/advin.htm (last visited June 4, 2012).
18. See *id.*
19. *See Living Will*, ILL. DEP'T OF PUB. HEALTH, http://www.idph.state.il.us/public/books/Livin.PDF (last visited June 4, 2012).
20. *See* 755 ILL. COMP. STAT. 35 (2012).
21. *See* 755 ILL. COMP. STAT. 35/3.

The section also includes a sample form and indicates that "[t]he declaration may, but need not, be" in the form that is provided.[22]

The act also sets out the circumstances under which a declaration (living will) can be revoked.[23] Section 6 provides that "[a] declaration may be revoked at any time by the declarant, without regard to declarant's mental or physical condition, by any of the following methods":

1. By physically destroying it,
2. By a written revocation that is signed and dated,
3. By an oral revocation that was witnessed by a person 18 or older who signs a statement confirming the revocation.[24]

In Illinois, a revocation is effective upon communication to the attending physician.[25]

A separate section of the same statute indicates that a declaration executed in another state in compliance with the law of that state or of Illinois is considered validly executed for purposes of the Illinois Act.[26]

California

The California attorney general's website contains information on advance directives.[27] An advance directive form is made available by the California government as a PDF.[28]

California's Probate Code contains a Uniform Health Care Decisions Act, which contains a section on advance health-care directives.[29] California does not have separate statutes for living wills because, for California purposes, both living wills and powers of attorney for health care fall under the umbrella category of advance directive.

However, the advance directive form found in section 4701 of California's Probate Code describes how to create "individual instructions," which effectively serve as a living will. In California, if a person wants an advance directive, that person can choose from a power of attorney

---

22. *Id.*
23. *See* 755 ILL. COMP. STAT. 35/5.
24. *Id.*
25. *Id.*
26. *See* 755 ILL. COMP. STAT. 35/9.
27. *See Advance Health Care Directive: What's Important to You*, CAL. OFFICE OF THE ATT'Y GEN., http://oag.ca.gov/consumers/general/adv_hc_dir (last visited June 4, 2012).
28. *See Advance Health Care Directive Form*, CAL. OFFICE OF THE ATT'Y GEN., http://ag.ca .gov/consumers/pdf/AHCDS1.pdf (last visited June 4, 2012).
29. *See* CAL. PROB. CODE § 4670 (West 2000).

for health care or an individual instruction. The instructions for the individual instructions come in the second part of the form after the power of attorney, and that part does not need to be filled out if an individual does not want to give such specific instructions. As far as the legal requirements are concerned, the entire statutory form must be signed by two witnesses or a notary.[30]

In terms of the general requirements for health-care instruction, the statute provides that an adult can give an individual health-care instruction in written or oral form.[31]

The procedural requirements for an advance directive are broken down into two sections: written and electronic. To create a valid advance directive will in California, the advance directive must

1. contain the date of execution;
2. be signed by the patient or by someone in the patient's presence at the patient's direction; and
3. be notarized or witnessed by two witnesses.[32]

If the advance directive is an electronic one, it must satisfy all of the criteria of a written advance directive plus the following additional criteria:

1. The digital signature must meet either the requirements of section 16.5 of the Government Code and chapter 10 (commencing with section 22000) of division 7 of title 2 of the California Code of Regulations or the digital signature uses an algorithm approved by the National Institute of Standards and Technology.
2. The digital signature is unique to the person using it.
3. The digital signature is capable of verification.
4. The digital signature is under the sole control of the person using it.
5. The digital signature is linked to data in such a manner that if the data are changed, the digital signature is invalidated.
6. The digital signature persists with the document and not by association in separate files.
7. The digital signature is bound to a digital certificate.[33]

---

30. See id. § 4701.
31. See id. § 4670.
32. See id. § 4673(a).
33. See id. § 4673(b).

The code provides that a written advance health-care directive or similar instrument executed in another state or jurisdiction in compliance with the laws of that state or jurisdiction or in compliance with California law is valid and enforceable in California to the same extent as a written advance directive validly executed in California.[34]

A California advance directive can include in its terms the nomination of a conservator of the person or estate, or both.[35]

The statute indicates that a "patient having capacity" can revoke all or part of an advance directive at any time "and in any manner that communicates intent to revoke."[36] However, in California, "a patient having capacity may revoke the designation of an agent only by a signed writing or by personally informing the supervising health care provider."[37]

An advance directive can be revoked by virtue of the existence of a more recent advance directive that conflicts with the earlier one.[38]

Additionally, dissolution of marriage causes an automatic revocation of the spouse as a principal's agent regarding a health-care power of attorney.[39]

Florida

The Florida Agency for Health Care Administration's website has a PDF document that explains advance directives and provides a form to fill out.[40] This particular document suggests, but does not expressly state, that the only procedural requirement is that two people witness an oral or written directive.[41]

Florida's civil rights statute contains a section that sets out the procedures for the construction of a living will as follows:[42]

> Any competent adult may, at any time, make a living will or written declaration and direct the providing, withholding, or withdrawal of

---

34. *See id.* § 4676.
35. *See id.* § 4672.
36. *Id.* § 4695(b).
37. *Id.* § 4695(a).
38. *Id.* § 4698.
39. *Id.* § 4697(a).
40. *See Health Care Advance Directives, The Patient's Right to Decide*, Agency for Health Care Administration, https://floridahealthfinderstore.blob.core.windows.net/documents /reports-guides/documents/English-Health%20Care%20Advance%20Dir%202006 .pdf (last visited June 4, 2012).
41. See *id.*
42. Fla. Stat. Ann. § 765.302 (West 2012).

life-prolonging procedures in the event that such person has a terminal condition, has an end-stage condition, or is in a persistent vegetative state. A living will must be signed by the principal in the presence of two subscribing witnesses, one of whom is neither a spouse nor a blood relative of the principal. If the principal is physically unable to sign the living will, one of the witnesses must subscribe the principal's signature in the principal's presence and at the principal's direction.[43]

Thus, a valid living will in Florida essentially requires that the declarant be a competent adult and that the living will be signed in the presence of two subscribing witnesses.[44] It should also be noted that the procedural section of the statute indicates that it is the responsibility of the principal (patient) to notify the attending physician of the advance directive.[45]

Additionally, the attending physician and an additional consulting physician must make the determination as to whether a patient has a "terminal condition, has an end-stage condition, or is in a persistent vegetative state."[46]

A competent principal may revoke any advance directive (living will or health-care power of attorney):

1. by a signed, dated writing;
2. by means of the physical cancellation or destruction of the advance directive by the principal or by another in the principal's presence and at the principal's direction;
3. by means of an oral expression of intent to amend or revoke; or
4. by means of a subsequently executed advance directive that is materially different from a previously executed advance directive.

Also, the dissolution or annulment of marriage of the principal revokes the designation of the principal's former spouse as a surrogate, unless otherwise specifically provided in the advance directive or in an order of dissolution or annulment of marriage.[47]

---

43. *Id.*
44. *Id.* § 765.302(a).
45. *Id.* § 765.302(b).
46. *Id.* § 765.306.
47. *Id.* § 765.104.

New York

There is no statute in New York that governs living wills. Nor is there a standard form for a living will in New York that is interpreted in a uniform way. Therefore, even a well-drafted living will is ultimately open to interpretation by those who need to determine the principal's wishes.

However, the New York State Bar Association website contains a form for filling out a New York living will.[48] This form requires that the declarant be of sound mind and direct the attending physician and other medical personnel to withhold or withdraw treatment that serves only to prolong the process of dying, if the declarant should be in an incurable or irreversible mental or physical condition with no reasonable expectation of recovery.

The form further states that the instructions apply if the declarant is

- in a terminal condition;
- permanently unconscious; or
- conscious, but has irreversible brain damage and will never regain the ability to make decisions and express any wishes.

The New York State Department of Health has some information on its website including an "advance care planning booklet," which does set out some of the procedural requirements for living wills in New York.[49]

The booklet states that the living will becomes effective if the principal becomes

- terminally ill,
- permanently unconscious, or
- minimally conscious due to brain damage and will never regain the ability to make decisions.[50]

---

48. *See* Living Will Form, N.Y. State Bar Ass'n, http://www.nysba.org/Content/Navigation Menu/PublicResources/LivingWillHealthCareProxyForms/LivingWillEnglish.pdf (last visited June 5, 2012).

49. *Who Will Speak for You?*, N.Y. Dep't of Health, http://www.health.ny.gov/professionals /patients/health_care_proxy/index.htm (last visited June 5, 2012); *Advance Care Planning*, N.Y. State Bar Ass'n 4 (2011), *available at* http://www.nysba.org/AM/Template .cfm?Section=Mitchell_Rabbino_National_Healthcare_Decisions_Day&Template= /CM/ContentDisplay.cfm&ContentID=150801 (last visited May 14, 2013).

50. *Advance Care Planning, supra* note 49, at 4.

It also indicates that while notarization is *not* necessary, a legally binding living will requires a signature, date, and a witness.[51]

POWER OF ATTORNEY

The most important documents to put in place when dealing with individuals with Alzheimer's are durable powers of attorney for financial matters and health-care decisions.[52] These documents are important because they allow a family member or trusted friend to have legal authority to carry out the wishes of people suffering from Alzheimer's once they are no longer able to speak or act for themselves.

Powers of attorney are relatively simple, inexpensive legal documents that essentially allow another person to act for the person signing the documents.[53] The person granting the authority by signing the documents is referred to as the principal and the person being granted the authority is the agent or attorney of fact. This person stands in for the principal and is authorized to take almost any action for the principal so long as that action is included in the powers of attorney document.[54]

A power of attorney can be described as a legal document that grants the authority to another person to become the lawyer's "legal clone."[55] A "durable" power of attorney continues in effect after the principal becomes incapacitated and is unable to supervise and direct the agent.[56]

Lawyers should go over the following questions with their clients before granting powers of attorney:

- Can they trust the person they grant powers of attorney to carry out their wishes and/or act in their best interest?
- Are there any unresolved family conflicts that have not been addressed? Lawyers should be sure to communicate with all family members when making end-of-life planning decisions because implementing these choices can cause conflict.[57]

---

51. *Id.* at 3.
52. HAMMOND ET AL., *supra* note 2, at 14.
53. *Id.* at 15.
54. *Id.*
55. KERRY PECK, LEGAL GUIDANCE FOR PEOPLE WITH EARLY STATE DEMENTIA & THEIR FAMILIES 9 (2011).
56. *Id.* at 10.
57. *Id.* at 9, 11.

The mental capacity required for appointment of a power of attorney agent is different from the capacity required to manage one's own affairs. It is possible to be capable of appointing an agent yet lack the capacity to make certain types of personal decisions. Individuals appointing an agent must be able to comprehend that they have a choice whether or not to appoint an agent and are capable of making that choice.[58]

Powerful Versus Powerless Power of Attorney

While it is true that powers of attorney are important documents to have when dealing with clients with Alzheimer's; it is only as powerful as the powers included by the lawyer drafting it.

Even though a power may be legally available and necessary, if it is not in the power of attorney document, agents are powerless to avail themselves of that missing tool.

Most lawyers, when they need to draft a power of attorney, just pull out the form and place it in front of the client, and then they quickly go over it, if they do at all. Typically there's no really deep thinking going on during the process.

The standard health-care powers of attorney that are available, for the most part, are typical examples of what legislators have written. They are statutory documents that reflect the political forces that were exerted upon them. They are compromised documents cobbled together by various political factions, religious organizations, disability lobbyists, and medical groups. But for the most part, statutory forms are written by lawyers, and lawyers primarily think about the law and cases and the difficulty of administering these kinds of forms.

Very few health-care powers of attorney are written by health-care providers or social workers or those who deal with more of the emotional side of human beings as they're going through their final life decision making. The closest thing to a health-care power of attorney that deals with the emotional aspect is the document referred to as Five Wishes.[59]

---

58. *Id.* at 12.
59. *See* AGING WITH DIGNITY, http://www.agingwithdignity.org/five-wishes.php (last visited Aug. 4, 2012).

Practice Pointer: Five Wishes

Almost every state legislature has a statutory power of attorney written by lawyers that many times is only good within the boundaries of that state and doesn't work well in another state. Five Wishes, on the other hand, is the most accepted form power of attorney in the country. There are 42 states plus the District of Columbia that recognize Five Wishes. There is no other health-care power of attorney that's been promulgated by any state legislature that is as nationally recognized as Five Wishes.[60]

Five Wishes was written with the help of the ABA's Commission on Law and Aging and national leading experts in end-of-life care and with a religious background. The creator of the document was inspired by working with Mother Teresa and wanted to create a way for patients and their families to plan for and cope with the worst. In fact, the document is the first living will that talks about personal, emotional, and spiritual needs, as well as medical wishes.

Five Wishes lets clients explain exactly how they wish to be treated if they get seriously ill, including things like having their hand held or having relatives pray with them. Five Wishes also provides signees the chance to express their wishes toward life support or other medical options as seen in a standard living will. The document is very easy to use—all a person has to do is check a box, circle a direction, or write a few sentences to express any wishes. Five Wishes is produced by Aging with Dignity, a national nonprofit organization with a mission to affirm and safeguard the human dignity of individuals as they age and to promote better care for those near the end of life.[61]

Lawyers should take a look to see if Five Wishes meets the statutory requirements of their state. If so, this is a great document to be aware of and to utilize.

An important fact to keep in mind when looking at the statutory health-care power of attorney (or the living will) is that the terms and concepts that are used are defined in a manner that would surprise most laypersons. For example, in Illinois the definition of terminal illness is quite detailed, yet does not apply to many issues with dementia that

60. *Id.*
61. *Id.*

the average person might assume would fall under the definition of terminal.[62]

However, we already know that no doctor is going to say that a person with Alzheimer's is terminal—even if that person cannot swallow and requires a feeding tube to stay alive.

When most people hear that "death is imminent," they probably think that death is days or perhaps a week or two away. Not too many people would consider six months to be imminent. However, in medical terms, an "imminent death" means a determination made by the attending physician according to accepted medical standards that death will occur in a relatively short period of time, even if life-sustaining treatment is initiated or continued.[63] One becomes qualified for hospice if death is imminent, meaning that the person will die within the next six months.

"Life-sustaining treatment" is defined as any medical treatment, procedure, or intervention that in the judgment of the attending physician, when applied to a patient with a qualifying condition, would not be effective to remove the qualifying condition or would serve only to prolong the dying process. Those procedures can include, but are not limited to, assisted ventilation, renal dialysis, surgical procedures, blood transfusions, and the administration of drugs, antibiotics, and artificial nutrition and hydration.[64]

Qualifying conditions are the conditions that trigger a living will to come into effect. They typically trigger a doctor to talk to a family with a health-care power of attorney about making an end-of-life decision or cause an attending physician to recommend no further life treatment or to make a referral to hospice.

In Illinois, "qualifying condition" means the existence of one or more of the following conditions in a patient certified in writing in the patient's medical record by the attending physician and by at least one other qualified physician:

> (1) "Terminal condition," means an illness or injury for which there is no reasonable prospect of cure or recovery, death is imminent, and the application of life sustaining treatments would only prolong the dying process. (2) "Permanent unconsciousness" is a condition that, in a high degree of medical certainty, [i] will last permanently, without

---

62. 755 Ill. Comp. Stat. 40/10 (2012).
63. *Id.*
64. *Id.*

improvement, [ii] in which thought, sensation, purposeful action, social interaction, and awareness of self and environment are absent, and [iii] for which initiating or continuing life sustaining treatment, in light of the patient's medical condition, provides only minimal medical benefit and (3) "incurable or irreversible condition" means an illness or injury [i] for which there is no reasonable prospect of cure or recovery, [ii] that ultimately would cause the patient's death even if life sustaining treatment is initiated or continued, [iii] that imposes severe pain or otherwise imposes an inhumane burden on the patient and [iv] for which initiating and continuing life sustaining treatment in light of the patient's medical condition provides only minimal medical benefits.[65]

Practice Pointer:

Notice that in the qualifying conditions above there is no mention of a condition in which a person has Alzheimer's or dementia and gets to the point of not being able to swallow.

It doesn't say what to do, because a person with Alzheimer's or dementia is not likely to be diagnosed as being terminally ill.

A terminal illness or condition is most often defined by state law as the triggering event for the use of a living will and/or end-of-life decision making by an agent under a health-care power of attorney. It is common for a "terminal illness or condition" to indicate that a person will die "imminently," as that term is defined in state law.

Physicians do understand that Alzheimer's is progressive and fatal, but they often do not call it a terminal illness that puts the patient in a condition in which they will die "imminently." This distinction causes great confusion among agents under a health-care power of attorney and family members, as it is unclear to them what decisions the principal would want regarding life-prolonging health care.

The majority of those who are affected with Alzheimer's do not die of Alzheimer's disease, but from other causes prior to Alzheimer's disease running to the end of its progressive, degenerative, and fatal trajectory.

That is why it is so important to have a powerful power of attorney with qualifying conditions that are suited to the desires of the signee and clearly describe the principal's desires.

---

65. *Id.*

An example of a powerful power of attorney is one that includes language that clients can choose to elect, if they wish, so that they can tell their families what to do in situations, even though they may not be diagnosed as being terminally ill. Most living wills and health-care power of attorney statutory forms include instructions regarding life-prolonging treatment. The triggering event for the decision to withhold or withdraw life-prolonging treatment is usually a diagnosis by the principal's attending physician that the principal suffers from a terminal condition, injury, or illness from which death is imminent.

Many physicians do not diagnose either Alzheimer's-type dementia or other dementias as a "terminal condition, injury, or illness from which death is imminent." Lawyers may wish to discuss with clients their feelings about life-prolonging treatment when and if clients reach late stages of dementia.

It is very common for doctors to recommend a feeding tube when a person with late stage dementia is no longer able to swallow. Clients' opinions on life-prolonging treatment when and if they have dementia and need a feeding tube should be customized and added into their health-care power of attorney.

A lawyer can take the guilt off the family by asking the client to say either "No, I don't want that" or "Yes, I want my life prolonged."

 Case Study ────────────────────────────

Life Support Decisions

One afternoon a client who was diagnosed with Parkinson's disease entered his attorney's office with his wife of many years and a caring adult daughter. His lawyer told him that they needed to discuss one of the most difficult questions that a lawyer has to ask a client—they needed to talk about feeding tubes, hydration/water, ventilators, and other life-prolonging treatment.

These things are all the more difficult to deal with when looking at a man who has a high probability of being alive, incapable, and subject to the life-and-death decision making of his loved ones.

The lawyer took a breath and then looked into the client's eyes. The client met his lawyer's gaze, and then the lawyer placed his hand over the client's hand and said, "Your family needs to hear from you how you feel about life-prolonging treatment. I understand that you have been diagnosed with Parkinson's disease. One of the things that may happen with Parkinson's is that you may get to the point where you won't be able to make your own life-and-death decisions. You may not actually die from Parkinson's disease—but you have a high probability of dying from a complication of Parkinson's. You may get to the point where the doctor comes to your family and says that you are unable to make a decision about life support, and they must decide whether or not you should have a feeding tube or hydration or a ventilator. What do you want your family to do? Do you want these things?"

The client looked at his lawyer, and then he looked at his family. He answered firmly, "I do not want that! Just keep me comfortable."

The lawyer turned to his wife and his daughter and asked them if they understood his wishes and if they would be able to make sure that his wishes were respected when other family members show up and insist that "we have to do everything we can for Dad!" They were given a chance to talk, and after that the daughter said, "Dad, I am so grateful that I know what you want. It gives me such peace of mind to be sure about what you would want us to do."

Once the client's wishes are clear, it is essential to get them down in writing.

Discussing end-of-life decisions with clients and their families can be difficult, but it will give them clarity and peace of mind when these life-support issues arise.

Another example of a powerful Power of Attorney is to give clients the opportunity to say, "You know what? I don't want antibiotics either." Everyone has a constitutional right to refuse medical treatments. But if lawyers never ask clients because they don't know to ask them, the clients may be given antibiotics against their will.

Lawyers need to sit down with their clients and ask them what kind of treatment they want if they don't have a terminal illness, but they do have dementia. We now know that if a person lives to be 85 years old, that person has close to a 50 percent chance of having dementia.

Lawyers owe it to their clients to look them in the eyes when they start to see signs under Rule 1.14 (see chapter 2) and say, "Let's do some decision making here about what to tell your family in the event that you get Alzheimer's or another dementia and you are to the point that you can't make your own decisions, but you're not necessarily diagnosed as terminally ill. What do you want?"

> **Practice Pointer:**
>
> If lawyers do not create a powerful power of attorney, for 50 percent of the people who wind up with dementia, the typical health-care power of attorney is powerless to help them. If they sign a living will, it's powerless to help them too. Lawyers have to deal with the fact that the world has changed and that they need to ask clients these kinds of questions.
>
> The typical client has these wishes: (1) to have quality care; (2) to protect the spouse as much as possible while balancing the client's own needs for quality care; and (3) to make sure that the surviving spouse, who the majority of the time is the wife, is able to continue to live in the home and has sufficient assets to not have to sell the home and move out of the neighborhood.
>
> Unfortunately, the traditional view of completing the health-care power of attorney does not accomplish the job. The general principle to take away here is that regardless of whether the use of a power is legal, or available through common financial processes, if the power is not listed in the power of attorney, the agent does not have it.

As previously mentioned, federal regulations do not differentiate between living wills and powers of attorney for health care in their treatment of advance directives. Therefore, this discussion will jump right into state coverage of power of attorney for health care for Illinois, California, Florida, and New York.

Illinois

In Illinois, there is a short form for a power of attorney that is provided by statute.[66] Use of that statutory form will constitute sufficient substance and procedure to create a legally enforceable health-care power of attorney.[67]

There are several limitations that Illinois has put on health-care agencies. For example, neither the attending physician nor any other health-care provider may act as agent under a health-care agency.[68]

---

66. *See* 755 Ill. Comp. Stat. 45/4-10.
67. *See* 755 Ill. Comp. Stat. 45/4-3.
68. *See* 755 Ill. Comp. Stat. 45/4-5.

Additionally, a health-care agency in Illinois requires a signing and a witness to that signing.[69]

Although there is a provided form, the statute indicates that the form of health-care agency in the law is not intended to be exclusive. Other forms of powers of attorney may be chosen by the principal to provide powers and protection similar to the statutory short-form power of attorney for health care.[70] In other words, although the statute is clearly advising use of its own form, it also generally states that other forms, without direction as to what that would entail, will suffice.

The power of attorney declaration needs to be signed and witnessed by at least one witness.[71] The form clarifies that the purpose of the power of attorney is to give the principals' designated agent broad powers to make health-care decisions for them, including the power to require, consent to, or withdraw from treatment for any physical or mental condition and to admit or discharge the principal from any hospital, home, or other institution.

The principal may name successor agents under this form, but not co-agents. It is important to note that the form does not impose a duty upon the agent to make such health-care decisions, so it is important to select an agent who will agree to make those decisions as the principal would wish.

The form also states that any agent who is acting for the principal has a duty to act in good faith for the principal's benefit and to use due care, competence, and diligence. The agent must also act in accordance with the law and with the statements in this form. The agent is required to keep a record of all significant actions taken as agent.

Unless the principal specifically limits the period of time that the power of attorney will be in effect, the agent may exercise the powers throughout the principal's lifetime, even after the principal becomes disabled. The form explains that a court can take away the powers of the agent if it finds that the agent is not acting properly.

A power of attorney for health care may be revoked by the principal at any time, without regard to the principal's mental or physical condition, by any of the following methods:[72]

---

69. *See* 755 ILL. COMP. STAT. 45/4-5.1.
70. *See* 755 ILL. COMP. STAT. 45/4-1.
71. *See* 755 ILL. COMP. STAT. 45/4-5.1.
72. *See* 755 ILL. COMP. STAT. 45/4-6.

1. by being obliterated, burnt, torn, or otherwise destroyed or defaced in a manner indicating intention to revoke;
2. by a written revocation of the document signed and dated by the principal or person acting at the direction of the principal; or
3. by an oral or any other expression of the intent to revoke the document in the presence of a witness 18 years of age or older who signs and dates a writing confirming that such expression of intent was made.

Every power of attorney for health care may be amended at any time by a written amendment signed and dated by the principal or person acting at the direction of the principal.

Any person, other than the agent, to whom a revocation or amendment is communicated or delivered, must make all reasonable efforts to inform the agent of that fact as promptly as possible.[73]

California

As noted above, California does not have a separate living-wills statute, but it has basic requirements that cover living wills and powers of attorney as advance directives.

The attorney general's website contains a link to an advance directive form that has a health-care power of attorney component.[74] That form requires the signing of the declarant and two witnesses. The probate code also has an advance directive form that covers powers of attorney.

Thus, the requirements for a California health-care power of attorney are the same as those listed above under the living wills section since California refers to both instruments as advance directives.

Florida

It should be noted that Florida uses the term "health care surrogate designation" rather than "health care power of attorney." The procedural requirements for the appointment of a health-care surrogate are set out in statute as follows:[75]

1. A written document designating a surrogate to make health care decisions for a principal shall be signed by the principal

---

73. *See* 755 ILL. COMP. STAT. 45/4-6.
74. *See Advance Health Care Directive: What's Important to You, supra* note 27.
75. FLA. STAT. ANN. § 765.202 (West 2012).

in the presence of two subscribing adult witnesses. A principal
unable to sign the instrument may, in the presence of witnesses,
direct that another person sign the principal's name as required
herein. An exact copy of the instrument shall be provided to the
surrogate.

2. The person designated as surrogate shall not act as witness
    to the execution of the document designating the health care
    surrogate. At least one person who acts as a witness shall be
    neither the principal's spouse nor blood relative.

3. A document designating a health care surrogate may also
    designate an alternate surrogate provided the designation
    is explicit. The alternate surrogate may assume his or her
    duties as surrogate for the principal if the original surrogate
    is unwilling or unable to perform his or her duties. The
    principal's failure to designate an alternate surrogate shall not
    invalidate the designation.

4. Unless the document states a time of termination, the
    designation shall remain in effect until revoked by the
    principal.

5. A written designation of a health care surrogate executed
    pursuant to this section establishes a rebuttable presumption of
    clear and convincing evidence of the principal's designation of
    the surrogate.[76]

The statute provides a suggested form for the health-care power of
attorney, which can be found in section 765.203.[77]

The statute also states that a principal is presumed to be capable of
making health-care decisions unless the principal is ruled to be incapacitated. Incapacity may not be inferred from the person's voluntary or
involuntary hospitalization for mental illness.[78]

The Florida statutes set out requirements for revoking any advance
directive (living will or health-care power of attorney) rather than having separate revocation requirements for each document.[79] The requirements are set forth above in the living wills section.

---

76. *Id.*
77. *Id.* § 765.203.
78. *See id.* § 765.204.
79. *Id.* § 765.104.

New York

New York uses the term "health care proxy" to refer to a "document delegating the authority to make health care decisions."[80]

New York statute provides that a competent adult may appoint a health-care agent.[81] The statute provides some general requirements for such an appointment, stating that the proxy must be

> [s]igned and dated by the adult in the presence of two adult witnesses who shall also sign the proxy. Another person may sign and date the health care proxy for the adult if the adult is unable to do so, at the adult's direction and in the adult's presence, and in the presence of two adult witnesses who shall sign the proxy. The witnesses shall state that the principal appeared to execute the proxy willingly and free from duress. The person appointed as agent shall not act as witness to execution of the health care proxy.[82]

There are some restrictions on who may be appointed as a health-care agent. For example, an operator, administrator, or employee of a hospital may not be appointed as a health-care agent by any person who, at the time of the appointment, is a patient or resident of, or has applied for admission to, such hospital.[83]

The statute also sets out the necessary form of the proxy, stating that it must

- identify the principal and agent; and
- indicate that the principal intends the agent to have authority to make health-care decisions on the principal's behalf.

The statute notes that health-care proxy may include the principal's wishes or instructions about health-care decisions and limitations upon the agent's authority.

The health-care proxy may provide that it expires upon a specified date or upon the occurrence of a certain condition. If no such date or condition is set forth in the proxy, the proxy will remain in effect until revoked. If, prior to the expiration of a proxy, the authority of the agent

---

80. *See* N.Y. Pub. Health Law § 2980(8) (McKinney 2010).
81. *See id.* § 2980(8).
82. *Id.* § 2981.
83. *Id.*

has commenced, the proxy will not expire while the principal lacks capacity.[84]

A health-care proxy can be, but does not necessarily have to be, in the provided form at section 2981.[85]

Power of Attorney for Property (Financial Decisions)

Lawyers can draft a power of attorney for property (financial decisions) to include one or more specific documents, such as for paying bills; documents can also be all encompassing. All-encompassing documents include the authority to cash checks, withdraw funds from bank accounts, pay taxes, trade stock, buy or sell property, take out loans, or take other actions. The all-encompassing document is best for clients with Alzheimer's, provided that they have an agent that they fully trust.[86]

Lawyers should consider including the following items when drafting the power of attorney for financial decisions:

- the power to apply for public benefits entitlements like Medicaid
- the power to make gifts from the client to specified loved ones such as a spouse and/or disabled child
- the power to do Medicaid-related asset protection
- if the client has a trust, the power to remove and/or add assets to the trust

Lawyers can draft financial powers of attorney to be "durable," and it is strongly recommended that this be done for clients with Alzheimer's. A durable power of attorney remains valid and in effect even after the client becomes incapacitated.[87]

A durable power of attorney may be drafted to be immediate or springing, depending on the state law and the time and manner in which the powers become effective. An immediate power of attorney takes effect upon signing—as one would expect; a springing power of attorney does not take effect until the principal becomes incapacitated.[88]

Generally, durable powers of attorney are effective immediately upon signing in most states and will remain effective after the principal

---

84. *Id.*
85. *See id.* § 2981(5).
86. HAMMOND ET AL., *supra* note 2, at 16.
87. *Id.*
88. *Id.* at 17.

becomes incompetent. However, it is advisable that lawyers be familiar with state requirements to discuss the requirements with their clients.

A springing power of attorney is a poor choice for someone suffering from Alzheimer's, because in the early and middle stages of the disease people may move in and out of a demented state, creating confusion as to whether the principal has become incapacitated. A court may rule that only an immediate durable financial power of attorney, and not a springing type, will substitute for conservatorship court proceedings to determine when the principal has reached incapacity.[89]

Practice Pointer:

The power of attorney for property, when used appropriately, is a wonderful device. It can be used when an individual is cognitively impaired and no longer capable of making decisions or when an individual is mildly impaired and needs assistance from an agent.

Unfortunately, when a durable power of attorney for property is used inappropriately, it can be used on a regular basis to exploit individuals.

People no longer use guns to rob banks; today they use a durable power of attorney. A durable power of attorney, when presented to an unsuspecting teller of a bank, will be used to withdraw massive sums of money.

Sadly, there are many cases in which individuals have signed durable powers of attorney under duress or having been defrauded into signing the document and have no idea what they've signed. However, the documents have been witnessed and notarized as required and, therefore, are valid. (Chapter 7 deals with financial exploitation in greater depth.)

Today—certainly in Illinois—the document requires the inclusion of an attestation clause, which provides that the witnesses believe the principal is of sound mind and memory. However, durable powers of attorney are frequently used to transfer assets, which are then used by an agent to award gifts to themselves.

Powerful or Powerless Power of Attorney for Property?

When dealing with a client with Alzheimer's, it is a good idea for clients to include the power to gift the interest in a couples' home to the healthy spouse. Unfortunately, that power won't be found in the typical power of attorney for property.

89. *Id.*

Case Study

A lawyer has a client whose husband has Alzheimer's and is incapacitated. So the lawyer looks at their documents—he had previously drafted a traditional power of attorney for property. The lawyer looks for a power that says "power to gift my interest in my home to my wife," but it does not exist. It's not in the statutory powers of attorney forms. Even when gifting is mentioned, it's usually limited to tax-related gifting power. Those traditional tax-related gifting powers are insufficient to empower a transfer of the incapacitated principal's interest in the marital residence to the healthy spouse.

Now the lawyer finds out that the estate plan, the will and/or a trust, and the powers of attorney are totally powerless to help people with long-term-care problems. The client is forced to file a guardianship at great expense. The spouse sues for guardianship, goes before a judge, and gets on her knees and pleads with the judge, "Your Honor, please, please, please, my husband would have intended for his portion of the home to be transferred to me."

The spouse is going to win 50 percent of the time because a judge is going to say, "You're right," because the judge feels that it's right and lets it happen. The other 50 percent of the time the judge is going to say, "Not all of your husband's assets must be used for his health-care needs."

The nightmare scenario above can be avoided with some careful drafting that can change a powerless power of attorney for property into a powerful one.

What follows is an example of just a few of the powers that a lawyer might add to create a more powerful power of attorney for property. These are powers that, even though nontraditional, people who are going through long-term care may need. While there are many family situations in which one would never use the following powers, in the majority of couples with long-term relationships, these concepts may be properly provided.

a. My agent shall have the power to change beneficiary designations *or ownership* on life insurance policies, annuities, or individual retirement accounts or other retirement-plan accounts owned by me.

b. My agent shall also have the power to sever any joint tenancies or tenancies by the entirety on my behalf.

c. In addition to the power contained herein, my agent shall have the power to create, alter, amend, fund, or revoke any inter vivos trust, including, but not limited to, any account held as a Totten trust where I am the trustee or cotrustee, and/or to create and fund a special-needs trust to benefit a member of my family.

d. My agent shall have the power to change the ownership of any asset owned by me to my spouse or a trust created for the benefit of my spouse.

e. My agent shall have the power to change the ownership of any assets owned by me to a child of mine who is legally disabled or to a trust for that child's benefit.

These are examples of the types of powers that will make a powerful power of attorney for property, and lawyers dealing with clients going through the aging process need to consider these types of powers instead of just pulling out the standard form and creating a powerless form.

Lawyers need to also be aware that the power to do gifting is fraught with dangers and they should consider the power to do a pooled trust. Some states allow this and some do not, so lawyers should check their state statutes. (Pooled trusts are covered in chapter 4.)

Practice Pointer: Don't Create a Powerless Power of Attorney

This is what lawyers need to know about powers of attorney for a 60-year-old or older adult. Lawyers who focus their practice in elder law and estate planning know how to add nursing home, Medicaid-specific powers to empower a trusted spouse or agent, under the guidance of legal counsel, to be able to

- use gifting powers, consistent with the estate plan, to effectuate appropriate asset protection;
- take all reasonable and prudent actions allowable under Medicaid law to qualify the ill person for care, but also avoid doing anything that would make the ill person ineligible for benefits;
- if appropriate, encourage an adult child to move into the home as a caretaker;
- allow a caretaker child to be paid a market rate for care;
- create and fund a special-needs trust to provide dignity and supplemental monies, even if receiving nursing home Medicaid; and
- much more, subject to each client's circumstances and the law.

If power of attorney for property lacks these powers—and 99.99 percent of the time a person's power of attorney does lack these powers—get a more powerful power of attorney!

DO NOT RESUSCITATE ORDER

Another example of an advance directive is the DNR.

The Supreme Court held in *Cruzan v. Director of Missouri Department of Health*, that individuals have a constitutional right to refuse any medical treatment, including ventilators and feeding tubes.[90]

A DNR instructs health-care professionals not to perform cardiopulmonary resuscitation if a person's heart stops or the person stops breathing. DNRs are signed by a doctor and put in the individual's medical chart.

It is important to point out that the DNR is the only advance directive that is also a doctor's order or a physician's order for medical care. It is only a two-page document, and the only thing that's important is what's on page one. So, if there's absolutely nothing on page two, but page one is filled out correctly, that's a valid DNR. A photocopy of a DNR is also a valid document.

There are two boxes to check on page one. The first is Full Cardiopulmonary Arrest (when both breathing and heartbeat stop), and the box to be checked is followed by the words, "Do not attempt cardiopulmonary resuscitation (CPR)." The second box is Pre-Arrest Emergency (when breathing is labored or stopped and the heart is still beating). Under this heading is the option to check that a person wants or does not want CPR in this situation.

Many people, lawyers included, have come to believe that signing a DNR in some manner is a substitute for having a valid health-care power of attorney or a living will. However, due to the narrowness of the scope of authority of a DNR, it is not a substitute. The entire scope of the DNR is listed in those items one and two. A DNR only covers full cardiopulmonary arrest or pre-arrest emergency. It has nothing to do with any other circumstance as far as dealing with life-prolonging treatment. If a client is in a coma or a vegetative state and wants to die with dignity, a DNR will be powerless to help.

A DNR is not a substitute for a valid health-care power of attorney or even a living will. It is a very specific declaration of "don't give me treatment if we're dealing with a medical condition called full cardiopulmonary arrest or medical condition called a pre-arrested emergency." It provides no guidance otherwise.

---

90. Cruzan v. Dir. of Mo. Dep't of Health, 497 U.S. 261 (1990).

The DNR may be invalidated if the immediate cause of a respiratory or cardiac arrest is related to trauma or mechanical airway obstruction. That means if someone has a DNR and is experiencing a respiratory or cardiac arrest, but it turns out that the person choked on a hotdog, when the EMT shows up and realizes that the person is choking and can't breathe, the EMT will remove that obstruction from the airway. The spouse can wave that DNR in front of the EMT and the EMT will pay no attention because the person is choking—from a traumatic cause, not a chronic condition.

CHOOSING AN AGENT

It is important for lawyers to remember that a client can appoint multiple agents. For example, lawyers may want to advise a client who is in the early stages of Alzheimer's to appoint one person to take care of finances (power of attorney for financial matters) and another to take care of personal and health-care decisions (power of attorney for health care).[91]

Family members typically act as the agent(s), but some clients may choose to ask a close friend to serve as their agent. Whomever clients pick as their agent, it is critical for the lawyer to advise them to pick someone that they really trust.

Practice Pointer:

In order to make certain that an individual chooses an agent carefully, it is imperative that the agent be on board with the decisions that the principal (the patient) is making regarding organ donations and life support.

Life support certainly is the crux of a durable power of attorney for health care. There are many examples of cases in which the appointed agent has refused to follow through on the direction provided by the principal. This often involves cases in which the principal does not want life support and the agent is incapable of removing life support. Frequently, this happens when a parent appoints a child to serve as agent.

Often, people are pressured to pick a family member, but that family member may not be the right choice for religious, moral, or other reasons. The family member is not willing to follow the wishes of an individual who wishes to be removed from life support. That is an example of choosing the wrong power of attorney agent.

---

91. HAMMOND ET AL., *supra* note 2, at 15.

Sometimes named agents may become unable, unavailable, or unwilling to fulfill their duties. Lawyers should offer to draft a client's power of attorney with alternate or even multiple agents. Of course, lawyers must check and make sure multiple agents are permitted in their state.

In the case of multiple agents, the documents may be drafted so that they are appointed severally and allowed to act independently. Or, the multiple agents may be appointed jointly so that they are required to act together and come to a consensus.[92]

Practice Pointer: Daughter Can't "Pull the Plug"

A lawyer and his staff met with their client to discuss her estate plan. Meeting together they spent close to two hours going over all of the client's wishes relative to her finances, her legacy, and, finally, her views regarding life-prolonging treatments that were incorporated into her health-care power of attorney. The client had been accompanied to this meeting by her daughter whom she had chosen to be her executor, her trustee, and her agent under her power of attorney for property and health care.

All seemed to be going well until reviewing the client's wishes relative to life-prolonging treatments and end-life decision making. At that point the daughter suddenly stated, "No mom, I could never direct a physician to withhold or remove life support." She was expressing her very strong religious beliefs as expressed by the Catholic Church regarding the sanctity of life and the Catholic definition of ordinary health care.

The client was stunned that her daughter would not fulfill her wishes regarding end-life decisions. After some time, certain adjustments needed to be made in the client's health-care decision-making process, and eventually she chose a different person to make the final life-prolonging decision.

It is important for clients to understand not only how their chosen agent may respond to their view on end-life treatment but also the position of the health-care provider. There are many charitable, religious hospitals and nursing homes that will not fulfill clients' desires relative to end-life decision making. In the event that a health-care provider is unwilling to comply with the legitimate end-life decision making elected by a client, the client and/or agent, under the health-care power of attorney, should request that the client be moved to a different facility that is willing to fulfill the client's wishes relative to end-life decisions.

---

92. *Id.* at 16.

POLST

Physician Orders for Life-Sustaining Treatment (POLST) programs were developed in response to a health-care system that is increasingly overlooking a patient's wishes in favor of other priorities. POLST programs provide a platform for end-of-life conversations between doctors and patients and a uniform way to document the wishes regarding those decisions so patients' desires are understood and properly prioritized.[93] POLSTs are designed to improve the quality of care that people receive at the end of their lives through effective communication of a patient's desires and comprehensive documentation of medical directives. Oregon was a leader in the development of POLST programs, beginning their programs in the middle of the 1990s.[94] Other states that have endorsed statewide POLST programs are Washington, California, Idaho, Montana, Utah, Colorado, Tennessee, North Carolina, Hawaii, West Virginia, Pennsylvania, and New York.[95] Twenty-three states are working toward developing programs, and some cities located in the 11 states that have neither endorsed nor are developing POLST programs are doing the same.[96]

---

93. *Physician Orders for Life-Sustaining Treatment (POLST)*, CAL. HEALTHCARE FOUND., (Feb. 2013) http://www.chcf.org/projects/2008/physician-orders-for-lifesustaining-treatment -polst.
94. TERRI SCHMIDT, OREGON POLST REGISTRY ANNUAL REPORT, OREGON POLST REGISTRY 3 (2011).
95. CTR. FOR ETHICS IN HEALTH CARE, *POLST State Programs*.
96. *Id.*

Appendix

HEALTH-CARE POWER OF ATTORNEY AND COMBINED ADVANCE DIRECTIVE LEGISLATION

SELECTED FEATURES COMPARED: DECEMBER 2009

Explanation: The descriptors in the chart are generalizations of statutory language and not quotations, so the statutes must be consulted for precise meaning. All states limit appointed agent's from acting over the objection of the principal, unless otherwise noted in the column under Limits on Agent's Powers.

Abbreviations:

LW = Living Will

DPA = Durable Power of Attorney

UHCDA = Uniform Health Care Decisions Act.

POLST = Physician Order for Life sustaining Treatment, or similar protocol

STATE	TYPE	PROVIDES FORM	LIMITS ON AGENT'S POWERS	PROHIBITED AGENTS
1. ALABAMA ALA. STAT. §§ 22-8A-2 to -14 (West 2007). Natural Death Act *See also* Durable Power of Attorney Act, § 26-1-2 *Separate LW Statute:* NO	Combined Advance Directive *[Modeled on UHCDA]*	YES Must be substantially followed	• Mental health facility admission and treatments • Psycho-surgery • Sterilization • Abortion • Pregnancy limitation • Nutrition & hydration—refusal permitted if expressly authorized	• Indiv. Provider* *Exception for relatives employed by the provider

FORMALITIES OF EXECUTION	PROHIBITED WITNESSES Note: "Provider" includes employees of provider	REGISTRY FOR ADVANCE DIRECTIVES	OUT-OF-STATE DIRECTIVES RECOGNIZED	POLST PROTOCOL STATEWIDE
• 2 or more witnesses age 19 or older	• Minor = 18 • Agent • Proxy signor • Relative/ Spouse • Heir/ Beneficiary • Person responsible for care costs		YES	

STATE	TYPE	PROVIDES FORM	LIMITS ON AGENT'S POWERS	PROHIBITED AGENTS
2. ALASKA Alaska Stat. §§ 13.52.010 to -.395 (West 2007). Health Care Decisions Act *Separate LW Statute:* NO	Combined Advance Directive *[Modeled on UHCDA]* plus incorporates mental health directive	YES Optional	• Psycho-surgery* • Sterilization* • Abortion* • Removal of bodily organs* • Temporary admission to mental health facility* • Electro-convulsive therapy* • Psychotropic mediation* • Life-sustaining procedures* • Pregnancy limitation *Consent/refusal permitted only if expressly authorized.	• Facility provider* *Exception for relatives
3. ARIZONA Ariz. Rev. Stat. Ann. §§ 36-3201 to -3262 (West 2007).	Combined Advance Directive	YES Optional	None specified	None specified

FORMALITIES OF EXECUTION	PROHIBITED WITNESSES Note: "Provider" includes employees of provider	REGISTRY FOR ADVANCE DIRECTIVES	OUT-OF-STATE DIRECTIVES RECOGNIZED	POLST PROTOCOL STATEWIDE
• 2 witness or notarized	• Agent • Facility provider *One* may not be: • Relative/ Spouse • Heir/ Beneficiary		YES	
• 1 witness or notarized	• Agent • Provider If only *one* witness, person may not be: • Relative/ Spouse • Heir/ Beneficiary		YES	

STATE	TYPE	PROVIDES FORM	LIMITS ON AGENT'S POWERS	PROHIBITED AGENTS
4. ARKANSAS ARK. CODE ANN. § 20-13-104 (2007). Durable Power of Attorney for Health Care Act *See also* ARK. CODE ANN. § 20-17-201 to -218 (proxy appointment in Living Will Declaration)	Special DPA	NO (But proxy appointment in Living Will Declaration does have optional form)	• Life-sustaining treatment— unless the DPA incorporates a proxy authorization from the Living Will Declaration statute, § 20-17-202 • Pregnancy limitation	None specified
5. CALIFORNIA CAL. PROB. CODE §§ 4600–4948 806 (West 2007). *Separate LW Statute: NO*	Combined Advance Directive	YES Optional	• Civil commitment • Electro-convulsive therapy • Psycho-surgery • Sterilization • Abortion	• Supervising Indiv. Provider* • Facility Provider* • Conservator— unless conditions are met. *Exception for relatives who are employees of.

FORMALITIES OF EXECUTION	PROHIBITED WITNESSES Note: "Provider" includes employees of provider	REGISTRY FOR ADVANCE DIRECTIVES	OUT-OF-STATE DIRECTIVES RECOGNIZED	POLST PROTOCOL STATEWIDE
• 2 witnesses	None specified		YES, if part of a (living will) declaration	
• 2 witnesses or notarized • Special institutional requirements	• Agent • Indiv. Provider • Facility Provider One may not be: • Relative/ Spouse • Heir/ Beneficiary	YES §§ 4800–4802	YES	YES Cal. Probate Code §§ 4780–4785 (8/4/08) "Physician Order for Life-Sustaining Treatment"

STATE	TYPE	PROVIDES FORM	LIMITS ON AGENT'S POWERS	PROHIBITED AGENTS
6. COLORADO Colo. Rev. Stat. §§ 15-14-503 to -509 (West 2007). Colorado Patient Autonomy Act *See also* §§ 15-14-501 to -502 and §§ 15-14-601 to -611 re DPA *Separate LW Statute*: Colo. Rev. Stat. §§15-18-101 to -113.	Special DPA	NO	None specified	None specified

FORMALITIES OF EXECUTION	PROHIBITED WITNESSES Note: "Provider" includes employees of provider	REGISTRY FOR ADVANCE DIRECTIVES	OUT-OF-STATE DIRECTIVES RECOGNIZED	POLST PROTOCOL STATEWIDE
None specified	N/A		YES	

STATE	TYPE	PROVIDES FORM	LIMITS ON AGENT'S POWERS	PROHIBITED AGENTS
7. **CONNECTICUT** Conn. Gen. Stat. §§ 19a-570 to -580d (West 2007). *See also §§ 1-43 et seq.* (2007) (statutory short form DPA) and § 1-56r (designation of person for decision making). *Separate LW Statute: NO*	Combined Advance Directive	YES Optional	None specified (but authority is described as authority to "convey" principal's wishes, rather than to make decisions for principal.) • Pregnancy limitation	• Facility Provider* • Attending physician • Administrator or employee of gov't agency financially responsible for care* *Exception for relatives
8. **DELAWARE** Del. Code Ann. tit. 16, §§ 2501–2518 (2007). *Separate LW Statute: NO*	Combined Advance Directive *[Modeled on UHCDA]*	YES Optional	• Pregnancy limitation	• Residential LTC Facility Provider* *Exception for relatives

FORMALITIES OF EXECUTION	PROHIBITED WITNESSES Note: "Provider" includes employees of provider	REGISTRY FOR ADVANCE DIRECTIVES	OUT-OF-STATE DIRECTIVES RECOGNIZED	POLST PROTOCOL STATEWIDE
• 2 witnesses • Special institutional requirements	• Agent		Not Addressed	
• 2 witnesses • Special institutional requirements	• Facility provider • Relative/ Spouse • Heir/ Beneficiary • Creditor • Person responsible for care costs		YES	

STATE	TYPE	PROVIDES FORM	LIMITS ON AGENT'S POWERS	PROHIBITED AGENTS
9. DISTRICT OF COLUMBIA D.C. CODE §§ 21-2201 to -2213 (2007). *Separate LW Statute:* D.C. CODE §§ 7-621 to -630 (2007).	Special DPA	YES Optional	• Decision to medicate defendant to render him/her competent to stand trial	• Indiv. Provider • Facility Provider
10. FLORIDA FLA. STAT. ANN. §§ 765.101 to -.404 (West 2007). *Separate LW Statute:* NO	Combined Advance Directive	YES Optional	• Mental health facility admission* • Electro-convulsive therapy* • Psycho-surgery* • Sterilization* • Abortion* • Experimental treatments not approved by IRB* • Life-sustaining procedures while pregnant* • Pregnancy limitation* *Consent/refusal permissible if expressly authorized	None specified

FORMALITIES OF EXECUTION	PROHIBITED WITNESSES Note: "Provider" includes employees of provider	REGISTRY FOR ADVANCE DIRECTIVES	OUT-OF-STATE DIRECTIVES RECOGNIZED	POLST PROTOCOL STATEWIDE
• 2 witnesses	• Principal • Individual Provider • Facility Provider *One* may not be • Relative/ Spouse or Heir/ Beneficiary		Not Addressed	
• 2 witnesses	• Agent *One* may not be • Relative/ Spouse		YES	

STATE	TYPE	PROVIDES FORM	LIMITS ON AGENT'S POWERS	PROHIBITED AGENTS
11. GEORGIA GA. CODE ANN. §§ 31-36-1 to -13 (West 2008). *Separate LW Statute: NO*	Combined Advance Directive	YES Optional	• Mental health facility admission or treatment (incl. mental retardation or addiction) • Psycho-surgery • Sterilization • Pregnancy limitation	• Indiv. Provider directly or indirectly involved
12. HAWAII HAW. REV. STAT. §§ 327E-1 to -16 (2007). *See also* HAW. REV. STAT. § 551D-2.5 re DPA for health care *Separate LW Statute: NO*	Combined Advance Directive *[Modeled on UHCDA]*	YES Optional	None specified	• Facility Provider* *Exception for relatives
13. IDAHO IDAHO CODE ANN. §§ 39-4501 to -4509 (West 2007), specifically § 39-4505. *Separate LW Statute: NO*	Combined Advance Directive	YES Optional	• Pregnancy limitation	• Indiv. Provider* • Community Care Facility Provider* *Exception for relatives who are employees of.

FORMALITIES OF EXECUTION	PROHIBITED WITNESSES Note: "Provider" includes employees of provider	REGISTRY FOR ADVANCE DIRECTIVES	OUT-OF-STATE DIRECTIVES RECOGNIZED	POLST PROTOCOL STATEWIDE
• 2 witnesses • Special institutional requirements	• Agent • Heir/ Beneficiary • Indiv. Provider *One* may not be • Institutional provider		YES	
• 2 witnesses *or* notarized	• Indiv. provider • Facility provider • Agent *One* may not be • Relative/ Spouse • Heir/ Beneficiary		YES	
• 2 witnesses *or* notarized	• Agent • Indiv. Provider • Community Care • Facility *One* may not be • Relative/ Spouse or Heir/ Beneficiary	YES § 39-4515	Not Addressed	YES

STATE	TYPE	PROVIDES FORM	LIMITS ON AGENT'S POWERS	PROHIBITED AGENTS
14. ILLINOIS 755 ILL. COMP. STAT. 45/4-1 to 4-12 (West 2007). *Separate LW Statute:* 755 ILL. COMP. STAT. 35/1 to 35/10.	Special DPA	YES Optional	None specified	• Indiv. Provider
15. INDIANA IND. CODE §§ 30-5-1-1 to 30-5-5-19 (2007), specifically §§ 30-5-5-16 and -17, and IND. CODE §§ 16-36-1-1 to -19, specifically §§ 16-36-1-6 and -7. *Separate LW Statute:* IND. CODE ANN. §§ 16-36-4-1 to -21 IND. CODE ANN. §§ 16-36-1-1 to -14 (West 2007).	General DPA with health powers. Health Care Consent Statute including appointment of health care representative	NO But mandatory language for authority re life-sustaining treatment (§ 30-5-5-17) NO But mandatory language above is incorporated by reference at § 16-36-1-14	None specified None specified	None specified None specified

FORMALITIES OF EXECUTION	PROHIBITED WITNESSES Note: "Provider" includes employees of provider	REGISTRY FOR ADVANCE DIRECTIVES	OUT-OF-STATE DIRECTIVES RECOGNIZED	POLST PROTOCOL STATEWIDE
None specified	None specified		YES	
• Notarized *or* one witness • 1 witness	• Agent • Agent		YES Not Addressed	

STATE	TYPE	PROVIDES FORM	LIMITS ON AGENT'S POWERS	PROHIBITED AGENTS
16. IOWA IOWA CODE ANN. §§ 144B.1 to .12 (West 2007). *Separate LW Statute:* IOWA CODE ANN. §§ 144A.1 to .12.	Special DPA	YES Optional	None specified	• Indiv. Provider* *Exception for relatives
17. KANSAS KAN. STAT. ANN. §§ 58-625 to -632 (2003). *Separate LW Statute:* KAN. STAT. ANN. §§ 65-28,101 to -28,109.	Special DPA	YES Must be substantially followed	• Cannot revoke previous living will	• Indiv. Provider* • Facility Provider* *Exception for relatives & religious community members
18. KENTUCKY KY. REV. STAT. §§ 311.621 to .643 (Baldwin 2007). *Separate LW Statute: NO*	Combined Advanced Directive (but called "Living Will Directive")	YES Must be substantially followed	• Nutrition & hydration* • Pregnancy limitation *Refusal permissible if specified conditions are met	• Facility provider* *Exception for relatives

FORMALITIES OF EXECUTION	PROHIBITED WITNESSES Note: "Provider" includes employees of provider	REGISTRY FOR ADVANCE DIRECTIVES	OUT-OF-STATE DIRECTIVES RECOGNIZED	POLST PROTOCOL STATEWIDE
• 2 witnesses *or* notarized	• Agent • Indiv. Provider *One* may not be • Relative/ Spouse		YES	
• 2 witnesses *or* notarized	• Agent • Relative/ Spouse • Heir/ Beneficiary • Person responsible for care costs		YES	
• 2 witnesses *or* notarized	• Relative/ Spouse • Facility Provider • Attg. physician • Heir/ Beneficiary • Person responsible for care costs		Not Addressed	

STATE	TYPE	PROVIDES FORM	LIMITS ON AGENT'S POWERS	PROHIBITED AGENTS
19. LOUISIANA LA. REV. STAT. ANN. §§ 40:1299.58.1 to .10 (2007). *See also* DPA (Procuration) statute, LA. CIV. CODE ANN. art 2985–3034 (2007), specifically art. 2997. *Separate LW Statute: NO*	Proxy contained in Living Will statute	YES Optional	• Powers implicitly limited to executing a living will declaration on behalf of principal. However, a DPA (a "procuration") may confer health decision powers generally on an agent (a "mandatory")	None specified
20. MAINE ME. REV. STAT. ANN. tit. 18A, §§ 5-801 to -817 (2007). *Separate LW Statute: NO*	Combined Advance Directive *[Modeled on UHCDA]*	YES Optional	• Mental health facility admission, consent permissible if expressly authorized	• LTC Facility provider* *Exception for relatives

FORMALITIES OF EXECUTION	PROHIBITED WITNESSES Note: "Provider" includes employees of provider	REGISTRY FOR ADVANCE DIRECTIVES	OUT-OF-STATE DIRECTIVES RECOGNIZED	POLST PROTOCOL STATEWIDE
• 2 witnesses	• Relative/ Spouse • Heir/ Beneficiary	YES § 1299.58.3D	YES	
• 2 witnesses	None specified		YES	

STATE	TYPE	PROVIDES FORM	LIMITS ON AGENT'S POWERS	PROHIBITED AGENTS
21. MARYLAND Md. Code Ann., Health-Gen. §§ 5-601 to -618 (2007). *Separate LW Statute: NO*	Combined Advance Directive	YES Optional	None specified	• Facility provider* *Exception for relatives
22. MASSACHUSETTS Mass. Gen. Laws Ann. ch. 201D (West 2007). *Separate LW Statute: NO*	Special DPA	NO	None specified	• Facility provider* *Exception for relatives

FORMALITIES OF EXECUTION	PROHIBITED WITNESSES Note: "Provider" includes employees of provider	REGISTRY FOR ADVANCE DIRECTIVES	OUT-OF-STATE DIRECTIVES RECOGNIZED	POLST PROTOCOL STATEWIDE
• 2 witnesses • Also recognizes oral directive to a physician with one witness	• Agent *One* must not be • Heir, or have any other financial interest in person's death	YES §§ 5-619 to -626	YES	YES* § 5-608.1 *Not technically POLST, but similar: "Instructions on Current Life-Sustaining Treatment Options"
• 2 witnesses	• Agent		YES	

STATE	TYPE	PROVIDES FORM	LIMITS ON AGENT'S POWERS	PROHIBITED AGENTS
23. **MICHIGAN** MICH. COMP. LAWS ANN. §§ 700.5506 to .5512 (West 2007). *Separate LW Statute: NO*	Special DPA	Only for agent's acceptance	• Pregnancy limitation • Life-sustaining procedures* *Refusal permissible if expressly authorized	None specified
24. **MINNESOTA** MINN. STAT. ANN. §§ 145C.01 to .16 (West 2007). *Separate LW Statute:* MINN. STAT. §§ 145B.01 to .17 (West 2007).	Combined Advance Directive	YES Optional	None specified	• Indiv. Provider* • Facility Provider* *Exception for relatives

FORMALITIES OF EXECUTION	PROHIBITED WITNESSES Note: "Provider" includes employees of provider	REGISTRY FOR ADVANCE DIRECTIVES	OUT-OF-STATE DIRECTIVES RECOGNIZED	POLST PROTOCOL STATEWIDE
• 2 witnesses Agent must accept in writing before acting as agent ("patient advocate")	• Agent • Relative/ Spouse • Heir/ Beneficiary • Indiv. Provider • Facility Provider • Employee of life/health insurance provider for patient		Not Addressed	
• 2 witnesses *or* notarized	• Agent • *One* may not be provider		YES	

STATE	TYPE	PROVIDES FORM	LIMITS ON AGENT'S POWERS	PROHIBITED AGENTS
25. MISSISSIPPI Miss. Code Ann. §§ 41-41-201 to -229 (West 2007). *Separate LW Statute: NO*	Combined Advance Directive *[Modeled on UHCDA]*	YES Optional	• Mental health facility admission, consent permissible if expressly authorized	• LTC Facility* *Exception for relatives
26. MISSOURI Mo. Ann. Stat. §§ 404.800 to .872 (West 2007) and cross-referenced parts of §§ 404.700 to .735 (DPA statute). *Separate LW Statute*: Mo. Ann. Stat. §§ 459.010 to .055 (West 2007).	Special DPA	NO	• Nutrition & hydration* *Refusal permissible if expressly authorized	• Attg. Physician* • Facility Provider* *Exception for relatives and members of same religious community

FORMALITIES OF EXECUTION	PROHIBITED WITNESSES Note: "Provider" includes employees of provider	REGISTRY FOR ADVANCE DIRECTIVES	OUT-OF-STATE DIRECTIVES RECOGNIZED	POLST PROTOCOL STATEWIDE
• 2 witnesses *or* notarized	• Agent • Indiv. Provider • Facility Provider *One* may not be • Relative/ Spouse or Heir/ Beneficiary		YES, but only if directive complies with this Act	
• Must contain language of durability and be acknowledged as conveyance of real estate (i.e., must be notarized)	None specified		YES	

STATE	TYPE	PROVIDES FORM	LIMITS ON AGENT'S POWERS	PROHIBITED AGENTS
27. MONTANA MONT. CODE ANN. §§ 50-9-101 to -206 (2007). Also incorporates by reference §§ 72-5-501 and -502 (DPA statute) *Separate LW Statute: NO*	Proxy contained in Living Will statute	YES Optional	• Pregnancy limitation	None specified
28. NEBRASKA NEB. REV. STAT. §§ 30-3401 to -3432 (2007). *Separate LW Statute:* NEB. REV. STAT. §§ 20-401 to -416 (2007).	Special DPA	YES Optional	• Life-sustaining procedures* • Nutrition & hydration* • Pregnancy limitation *Refusal permissible if expressly authorized	• Attg. Physician* • Facility* • Any agent serving 10 or more principals* *Exception for relatives who are employees of.

FORMALITIES OF EXECUTION	PROHIBITED WITNESSES Note: "Provider" includes employees of provider	REGISTRY FOR ADVANCE DIRECTIVES	OUT-OF-STATE DIRECTIVES RECOGNIZED	POLST PROTOCOL STATEWIDE
• 2 witnesses under LW statute • DPA statute: none, although customarily notarized	None specified	YES §§ 50-9-501 to -505	YES	
• 2 witnesses *or* notarized	• Agent • Relative/ Spouse • Heir/ Beneficiary • Attg. Physician • Insurer *One* may not be Facility provider		YES	

STATE	TYPE	PROVIDES FORM	LIMITS ON AGENT'S POWERS	PROHIBITED AGENTS
29. NEVADA Nev. Rev. Stat. §§ 449.800 to .860 (2007). *Separate LW Statute:* Nev. Rev. Stat. §§ 449.535 to .690 (2007) with proxy designation. NB. Living will statute recognizes an agent under a regular DPA with authority to withhold or withdraw life-sustaining treatment.	Special DPA	YES Form with disclosure statement must be substantially followed	• Mental health facility admission • Electro-convulsive therapy • Aversive intervention • Psycho-surgery • Sterilization • Abortion	• Indiv. Provider* • Facility Provider* *Exception for relatives
30. NEW HAMPSHIRE N.H. Rev. Stat. Ann. §§ 137-J:1 to -J:16 (2007). *LW Statute: Repealed*	Combined Advanced Directive	Form and disclosure statement must be substantially followed.	• Mental health facility admission • Sterilization • Pregnancy limitation • Nutrition & hydration* *Refusal permissible if expressly authorized	• Facility Provider* *Exception for relatives who are employees of

FORMALITIES OF EXECUTION	PROHIBITED WITNESSES Note: "Provider" includes employees of provider	REGISTRY FOR ADVANCE DIRECTIVES	OUT-OF-STATE DIRECTIVES RECOGNIZED	POLST PROTOCOL STATEWIDE
• 2 witnesses *or* notarized	• Agent • Indiv. Provider • Facility Provider *One* may not be • Relative/ Spouse or Heir/ Beneficiary	YES §§ 449.915 to -.965	Not Addressed	
• 2 witnesses or notarized • Principal must acknowledge receipt of mandatory notice	• Agent • Spouse • Heir/ Beneficiary • AH Physician • *One* may not be residential care provider		YES	

STATE	TYPE	PROVIDES FORM	LIMITS ON AGENT'S POWERS	PROHIBITED AGENTS
31. NEW JERSEY N.J. STAT. ANN. §§ 26:2H-53 to -81 (West 2007). *Separate Living Well Statute: NO*	Combined Advance Directive	NO	None specified	• Attg. Physician • Facility Provider* *Exception for relatives
32. NEW MEXICO N.M. STAT. ANN. §§ 24-7A-1 to -18 (West 2007). *Separate LW Statute: NO*	Combined Advance Directive *[Modeled on UHCDA]*	YES Optional	• Mental health facility admission	• LTC Facility Provider* *Exception for relatives
33. NEW YORK N.Y. PUB. HEALTH LAW §§ 2980–2994 (McKinney 2007). *Separate LW Statute: NO*	Special DPA	YES Optional	• Nutrition & hydration* *Principal must make his/her wishes "reasonably known"	• Attg. Physician* • Facility Provider* • Any agent serving 10 or more principals* *Exception for relatives who are employees of.

FORMALITIES OF EXECUTION	PROHIBITED WITNESSES Note: "Provider" includes employees of provider	REGISTRY FOR ADVANCE DIRECTIVES	OUT-OF-STATE DIRECTIVES RECOGNIZED	POLST PROTOCOL STATEWIDE
• 2 witnesses *or* notarized	• Agent		YES	
• 2 witnesses recommended, but not required	None specified		YES, but only if directive complies with this Act	
• 2 witnesses • Special institutional requirements	• Agent		YES	YES N.Y. Surr. Ct. Pro. § 1750-b "Medical Orders for Life-Sustaining Treatment"

STATE	TYPE	PROVIDES FORM	LIMITS ON AGENT'S POWERS	PROHIBITED AGENTS
34. NORTH CAROLINA N.C. Gen. Stat. §§ 32A-15 to -27 (2008). *Separate LW Statute*: N.C. Gen. Stat. §§ 90-320 to -323 (2008).	Special DPA	YES Optional	None specified	None specified
35. NORTH DAKOTA N.D. Cent. Code §§ 23-06.5-01 to -18 (2007).	Special DPA	YES Optional	• Mental health facility admission >45 days • Psycho-surgery • Abortion • Sterilization	• Indiv. Provider* • Facility Provider* *Exception for relatives who are employees of

FORMALITIES OF EXECUTION	PROHIBITED WITNESSES Note: "Provider" includes employees of provider	REGISTRY FOR ADVANCE DIRECTIVES	OUT-OF-STATE DIRECTIVES RECOGNIZED	POLST PROTOCOL STATEWIDE
• 2 witnesses *and* notarized	• Relative/ Spouse • Heir/ Beneficiary • Indiv. Provider • Facility Provider • Creditor	YES §§ 130A-465 to -471	YES	YES § 90-21.17 "Medical Orders for Scope of Treatment"
• 2 witnesses *or* notarized • Agent must accept in writing	• Agent * • Relative/ Spouse * • Heir/ Beneficiary * • Creditor * One may *not* be: • Indiv. Provider • Facility Provider *Also disqualifies notary	YES § 23-06.5-19	YES	

STATE	TYPE	PROVIDES FORM	LIMITS ON AGENT'S POWERS	PROHIBITED AGENTS
36. OHIO OHIO REV. CODE ANN. §§ 1337.11 to .17 (West 2007). *Separate LW Statute*: OHIO REV. CODE ANN. §§ 2133.01 to .15 (West 2007).	Special DPA	Only for mandatory disclosure statement	• Life-sustaining procedures* • Nutrition & hydration* • Pregnancy limitation *Refusal permissible if specified conditions are met	• Attg. Physician* • Nursing home administrator* *Exception for relatives who are employees of
37. OKLAHOMA OKLA. STAT. ANN. tit. 63, §§ 3101.1 to .16 (West 2007). *Separate LW Statute: NO*	Combined Advance Directive	YES Must be substantially followed	• Nutrition & hydration* • Pregnancy limitation *Refusal permissible if expressly authorized	None specified

FORMALITIES OF EXECUTION	PROHIBITED WITNESSES Note: "Provider" includes employees of provider	REGISTRY FOR ADVANCE DIRECTIVES	OUT-OF-STATE DIRECTIVES RECOGNIZED	POLST PROTOCOL STATEWIDE
• 2 witnesses or notarized	• Agent • Relative/ Spouse • Attg. Physician • Nursing home administrator		YES	
• 2 witnesses	• Heir/ Beneficiary	YES § 3102.1 to .3	YES	

STATE	TYPE	PROVIDES FORM	LIMITS ON AGENT'S POWERS	PROHIBITED AGENTS
38. OREGON OR. REV. STAT. §§ 127.505 to .660 & 127.995 (2007). *Separate LW Statute: NO*	Combined Advance Directive	YES Must be followed But recognizes that any other form "constitutes evidence of the patient's desires and interests"	• Mental health facility admission • Electro-convulsive therapy • Psycho-surgery • Sterilization • Abortion • Life-sustaining procedures* • Nutrition & hydration* *Refusal permissible if expressly authorized or if specified conditions are met	• Attending physician* • Facility provider* *Exception for relatives

FORMALITIES OF EXECUTION	PROHIBITED WITNESSES Note: "Provider" includes employees of provider	REGISTRY FOR ADVANCE DIRECTIVES	OUT-OF-STATE DIRECTIVES RECOGNIZED	POLST PROTOCOL STATEWIDE
• 2 witnesses • Agent must accept in writing • Special institutional requirements	• Agent • Attg. physician *One* may not be • Relative/ Spouse Heir/ Beneficiary, or facility provider	YES 2007 Or. Law Ch. 697 (S.B. 329) [not codified]	YES	YES No statute "Physician Order for Life-Sustaining Treatment"

STATE	TYPE	PROVIDES FORM	LIMITS ON AGENT'S POWERS	PROHIBITED AGENTS
39. **PENNSYLVANIA** 20 Pa. Stat. Ann. §§ 5401– 5416 (West 2007). *See also* 20 Pa. Cons. Stat. Ann. §§ 5601– 5611 (DPA).	Living Will Statute Statutory Form DPA includes health decisions powers	YES Optional	LW: Unclear whether agent is permitted to act *only* if principal is in a • terminal condition, or • state of permanent unconsciousness • Nutrition & hydration* • Pregnancy limitation *Refusal permissible if expressly authorized Statutory Form DPA defines powers specifically.	None specified
40. RHODE ISLAND R.I. Gen. Laws §§ 23-4.10-1 to -12 (2007). *Separate LW Statute*: R.I. Gen Laws §§ 23-4.11-1 to -15 (2007).	Special DPA	YES Not clear whether optional or mandatory	None specified	• Indiv. Provider* • Community Care Facility* *Exception for relatives who are employees of

FORMALITIES OF EXECUTION	PROHIBITED WITNESSES Note: "Provider" includes employees of provider	REGISTRY FOR ADVANCE DIRECTIVES	OUT-OF-STATE DIRECTIVES RECOGNIZED	POLST PROTOCOL STATEWIDE
• LW: 2 witnesses • Statutory Form DPA: None required	• LW: Person who signs declaration on declarant's behalf • Statutory Form DPA: None specified		• LW: Not Addressed • Statutory Form DPA: YES	
• 2 witnesses • Principal must be Rhode Island resident	• Agent • Indiv. Provider • Community Care Facility *One* may not be • Relative/ Spouse or Heir/ Beneficiary		YES	

STATE	TYPE	PROVIDES FORM	LIMITS ON AGENT'S POWERS	PROHIBITED AGENTS
41. SOUTH CAROLINA S.C. CODE ANN. §§ 62-5-501 to -505 (2007), particularly § 62-5-504. *Separate LW Statute*: S.C. CODE ANN. §§ 44-77-10 to -160 (also permits appointment of agent).	Special DPA (within general DPA statute)	YES Must be substantially followed (but conventional DPAs may also contain health powers)	• Nutrition & hydration necessary for comfort care or alleviation of pain* • Pregnancy limitation *Refusal permissible if expressly authorized	• Indiv. Provider* • Facility Provider* • Spouse of a Provider* *Exception for relatives
42. SOUTH DAKOTA S.D. CODIFIED LAWS §§ 59-7-1 to -9 (2007). *See also* §§ 34-12C-1 to -8 (health-care consent procedures). *Separate LW Statute*: S.D. CODIFIED LAWS §§ 34-12D-1 to -22 (2007).	General DPA that permits health decisions authority	NO	• Pregnancy limitation • Nutrition & hydration* *Refusal permissible if expressly authorized or other conditions are met	None specified

FORMALITIES OF EXECUTION	PROHIBITED WITNESSES Note: "Provider" includes employees of provider	REGISTRY FOR ADVANCE DIRECTIVES	OUT-OF-STATE DIRECTIVES RECOGNIZED	POLST PROTOCOL STATEWIDE
• 2 witnesses	• Agent • Relative/ Spouse • Heir/ Beneficiary • Attending physician • Creditor • Life insurance beneficiary • Person responsible for care costs • *One* may not be facility provider		YES	
None specified	None specified		YES	

STATE	TYPE	PROVIDES FORM	LIMITS ON AGENT'S POWERS	PROHIBITED AGENTS
43. TENNESSEE TENN. CODE ANN. §§ 68-11-1801 to -1815 (2007). *Separate LW Statute: NO*	Combined Advance Directive	NO	None specified	None specified
44. TEXAS TEX. HEALTH & SAFETY CODE ANN. §§ 166.001 to -.166 (Vernon 2007). *Separate LW Statute: NO*	(1) Special DPA (2) Proxy contained in LW	(1) Special DPA: (Medical PoA): YES. Must be substantially followed plus mandatory disclosure statement. (2) LW: YES Optional	• Mental health facility admission • Electro-convulsive therapy • Psycho-surgery • Abortion • Comfort care	• Indiv. Provider* • Facility Provider* *Exception for relatives who are employees of

FORMALITIES OF EXECUTION	PROHIBITED WITNESSES Note: "Provider" includes employees of provider	REGISTRY FOR ADVANCE DIRECTIVES	OUT-OF-STATE DIRECTIVES RECOGNIZED	POLST PROTOCOL STATEWIDE
• 2 witnesses *or* notarized	• Agent • Provider • Facility *One* may not be • Relative/ Spouse or Heir/ Beneficiary		YES	
• 2 witnesses	*One* may not be: • Agent • Attg. Physician • Relative/ Spouse • Facility • Heir/ Beneficiary • Creditor		YES	

STATE	TYPE	PROVIDES FORM	LIMITS ON AGENT'S POWERS	PROHIBITED AGENTS
45. UTAH Utah Code Ann. §§ 75-2A-101 to -125 (2008). New Law eff. Jan. 1, 2008. *Separate LW Statute: NO*	Combined Advance Directive	NO	• Pregnancy limitation • Long-term custodial placement in licensed facility other than for assessment, rehabilitative, or respite care.	• Indiv. Provider* • Facility Provider* *Exception for relatives who are employees of
46. VERMONT Vt. Stat. Ann. tit. 18, §§ 9700–9720 (2009).	Combined Advance Directive	NO	None Specified [May make certain decisions over the protest of the principal if certain conditions met]	• Indiv. Provider • Facility Provider* • Funeral/crematory/cemetery/organ procurement representative (when authorized to dispose of remains or donate organs)* *Exception for relatives who are employees of

FORMALITIES OF EXECUTION	PROHIBITED WITNESSES Note: "Provider" includes employees of provider	REGISTRY FOR ADVANCE DIRECTIVES	OUT-OF-STATE DIRECTIVES RECOGNIZED	POLST PROTOCOL STATEWIDE
• One witness	• Agent • Relative/ Spouse • Provider • Facility • Heir • Beneficiary under any instrument/ plan/account • Person responsible for care costs		YES	YES 75-2a-106 "Life with Dignity Order"
• 2 witnesses • Special institutional requirements	• Agent • Spouse or reciprocal beneficiary • Relative	YES §§ 9701, 9704, 9709, 9712, 9714, 9719	YES	YES 2009 Vt. Laws No. 25 (H. 435) § 97-1(6)

STATE	TYPE	PROVIDES FORM	LIMITS ON AGENT'S POWERS	PROHIBITED AGENTS
47. VIRGINIA VA. CODE ANN. §§ 54.1-2981 to -2993 (West 2007). *Separate LW Statute: NO*	Combined Advance Directive	YES Optional	• Mental health facility admission • Psycho-surgery • Sterilization • Abortion • Decisions about "visitation" unless expressly authorized [May make certain decisions over the protest of the principal if certain conditions met.]	None specified
48. WASHINGTON WASH. REV. CODE ANN. §§ 11.94.010 to .900 (West 2007). *Separate LW Statute*: WASH. REV. CODE ANN. §§ 70.122.0l0 to -.920 (West 2007).	General DPA	NO	Cross reference to guardianship law [RCWA 11.92.043(5)]: • Electro-convulsive therapy • Psycho-surgery • Other psychiatric • Amputation	• Indiv. Provider* • Facility Provider* *Exception for relatives

FORMALITIES OF EXECUTION	PROHIBITED WITNESSES Note: "Provider" includes employees of provider	REGISTRY FOR ADVANCE DIRECTIVES	OUT-OF-STATE DIRECTIVES RECOGNIZED	POLST PROTOCOL STATEWIDE
• 2 witnesses	• Relative/ Spouse	YES §§ 54.1-2983, -2985, and -2994 to -2996	YES	
None specified	N/A	YES § 70.122.130	YES	YES WASH. REV. CODE ANN. § 43.70.480 "Physician Order for Life-Sustaining Treatment"

STATE	TYPE	PROVIDES FORM	LIMITS ON AGENT'S POWERS	PROHIBITED AGENTS
49. WEST VIRGINIA W. VA. CODE ANN. § 16-30-1 to -25 (West 2007). *Separate LW Statute:* No	Combined Advance Directive (but maintains separate Living Will and Medical Power of Attorney documents)	YES Optional	• Limit on agent's authority to revoke a pre-need funeral contract	• Indiv. Provider* • Facility Provider* *Exception for relatives who are employees of

FORMALITIES OF EXECUTION	PROHIBITED WITNESSES Note: "Provider" includes employees of provider	REGISTRY FOR ADVANCE DIRECTIVES	OUT-OF-STATE DIRECTIVES RECOGNIZED	POLST PROTOCOL STATEWIDE
• 2 witnesses *and* notarized	• Agent • Attg. Physician • Principal's signatory • Relative/ Spouse • Heir/ Beneficiary • Person responsible for care costs		YES	YES § 16-30-25 and others "Physician Order for Scope of Treatment"

STATE	TYPE	PROVIDES FORM	LIMITS ON AGENT'S POWERS	PROHIBITED AGENTS
50. WISCONSIN WIS. STAT. ANN. §§ 155.01 to .80 (West 2007). *See* § 243.07(6m) (West 2007) (DPA cross-reference). *Separate LW Statute*: WISC. STAT. ANN. §§ 154.01 to -.15 (West 2007).	Special DPA	YES Optional, but disclosure statement is mandatory	• Admission to facility for mental health/retardation or other listed conditions • Electro-convulsive therapy • Mental health research • Drastic mental health treatment • Admission to nursing home or residential facility—very limited unless expressly authorized in the document • Nutrition & hydration* • Pregnancy limitation *Refusal permissible only if specified conditions are met	• Indiv. Provider* • Facility Provider* *Exception for relatives

FORMALITIES OF EXECUTION	PROHIBITED WITNESSES Note: "Provider" includes employees of provider	REGISTRY FOR ADVANCE DIRECTIVES	OUT-OF-STATE DIRECTIVES RECOGNIZED	POLST PROTOCOL STATEWIDE
• 2 witnesses	• Agent • Indiv. Provider • Facility provider* • Relative/ Spouse • Heir/ Beneficiary • Person responsible for care costs *Exception for chaplains & social workers		YES	

STATE	TYPE	PROVIDES FORM	LIMITS ON AGENT'S POWERS	PROHIBITED AGENTS
51. WYOMING Wyo. Stat. Ann. §§ 35-22-401 to -416 (2004). *Separate LW Statute*: Wyo. Stat. §§ 35-22-101 to -109 (2004).	Combined Advance Directive	YES Optional	None specified	• Residential or Community Care Provider* *Exception for relatives who are employees of
UNIFORM HEALTH-CARE DECISIONS ACT *Separate LW Statute: NO*	Combined Advance Directive	YES Optional	• Mental health facility admission, consent permissible if expressly authorized	• LTC Facility Provider

FORMALITIES OF EXECUTION	PROHIBITED WITNESSES Note: "Provider" includes employees of provider	REGISTRY FOR ADVANCE DIRECTIVES	OUT-OF-STATE DIRECTIVES RECOGNIZED	POLST PROTOCOL STATEWIDE
• 2 witnesses *or* notarized	• Agent • Indiv. Provider • Facility Provider		Not Addressed	
• 2 witnesses recommended, but not required	None		YES, but only if directive complies with this Act	

CAUTION: The descriptions and limitations listed in this chart are broad characterizations for comparison purposes and not as precise quotations from legislative language.
© 2009, American Bar Association, Commission on Law and Aging.

The American Bar Association acknowledges The West Group for providing access to online legal research.

 **EXPERT VIEW**

Surprising Truths Within Hospice Care

Carolyn Peterson is an RN who has worked as a nurse for 43 years. Seventeen years ago, she began to focus exclusively in the area of hospice care. She works for an organization that provides care for the dying and incurably ill.

Q: RNs have the capability of working in almost any area of medical care. What attracts you and keeps you working with hospice?

A: I think it's the humanity of the work. RNs enter a person's life at a time when the rest of the medical community seems to have abandoned them. When people get to the point in their illness where it can't be fixed, a lot of the medical community kind of give up on them. Many times when nurses first meet a patient or family, they might be the first one to have explained what's going on in terms of their disease and that, truthfully, there is no more treatment available except hospice. It takes quite a bit of finesse and compassion, and when a nurse has these conversations there are no do-overs.

Q: Would you explain to the lawyer readers of this book about the composition of a hospice team?

A: Medicare dictates who must be a part of the interdisciplinary hospice team. The top person is the medical director, who is an employee of the hospice and must be a doctor who is board certified in hospice and palliative care (relieving and preventing suffering). There must be a nurse case manager, a nondenominational chaplain, and a social worker.

Q: In a typical month, how many different patients or clients are cared for by a team?

A: Many hospice teams service 12 to 13 new families per month.

Q: What are the typical services that one could expect to find provided by a hospice on a per-day basis, and who pays for it?

A: Medicare Part A pays for hospice care at 100 percent. It does not require any supplemental insurance, because the Medicare hospice benefit covers it. Medicare provides for four different levels of hospice care. Some companies provide all four levels of care even though two of the levels can be financially risky (not profitable).

Medicare reimbursement is fixed at a maximum dollar amount, regardless of the level of care provided by a hospice.

Q: Could you clarify the four different levels of care?

A: The very basic level of care is called "routine level of care." That's the absolute minimum that Medicare expects a hospice to do. And that is where a patient can be seen anywhere from daily to every 14 days by the nurse, a certified nursing assistant, the chaplain, or a social worker. That's the very basic level of care.

The next level is called "respite care." Normally, seniors don't qualify for skilled nursing care unless they've been in an acute-care hospital for at least 72 hours. The exception to that is hospice, for a patient living at home when the person caring for them becomes injured or sick or perhaps when there's a fire in the house. The hospice will pay for that patient to be transferred to a nursing home and the hospice will pay for five nights at that facility while they sort out the situation. Or, let's say they're living at home with a daughter or son who needs a break. The hospice can bring the ill person to a nursing home, and that's one of the rare times that Medicare will pay for nursing home care without that initial acute-care hospitalization stay.

The third level of care is "continuous care" or "comfort care." This is the most financially risky area of care for the hospice agency. It enables putting a nurse at the bedside to manage pain symptoms and end-of-life care. There are very specific criteria—certain combinations of nursing home hours versus CNA [certified nurse assistant] hours. There are only so many hours per every 24-hour period that a patient receives care in order for the agency to be reimbursed. If they are off by even 15 minutes, the hospice may not get paid. But some hospices provide that level of care because it enables their patients to die at home. There are few agencies that do that.

The highest level of care is called "general inpatient care." That is done in a facility where there's a registered nurse on the premises at all times—a Medicare-accredited hospital setting or skilled nursing facility. It's the only time that Medicare allows the hospice to pay room and board in a skilled area. There are very specific criteria to qualify. An example would be somebody at home who is not doing well, but they would like to be around when their grandson comes home from college for a final goodbye. The decision might be made to take them to a hospital or nursing home to start an IV to get some hydration going and help make that wish come true.

Those are the four levels of care. All hospices do the routine level of care. Most will do respite care because there's no financial risk involved. There are very few hospital-based hospices that do all four levels. It is very important to interview different hospice options to ask them what levels of care they will provide.

Q: In your experience, what are the top three causes of death that are referred to a hospice?

A: Untreatable cancer would be right up there. End-stage dementia, where the patient has reached the point where the brain is no longer telling them that they're hungry or thirsty, or whether they're swallowing correctly, would be another. And lastly, with seniors, adult failure to thrive. Due to old age, a person's body is not utilizing the nutrition it's taking in and they're losing weight and just not thriving. And after that would be congestive heart failure and chronic obstructive pulmonary disease.

Q: How long does hospice care last?

A: Medicare is a six-month benefit, but as long as the person and hospice meet the criteria, that can be extended. And again, that's a financial risk that the hospice takes because there is a payment cap. A good hospice will keep you past six months if you still meet the criteria for whatever illness you've been admitted under.

Q: Who makes the decision about whether or not someone's still qualified?

A: Medicare insists on two doctors to certify that somebody has a prognosis of six months or less to live. Typically, those two doctors are the attending physician and the medical director of the hospice. It's called the certificate of terminal illness.

Q: Talk to me about end-stage dementia and a person's not being able to take hydration—death by dehydration.

A: When people get to the point where they're not eating or drinking on their own, it's usually because something is going on in their brain, whether it's advanced dementia, aggressive cancer, or a lack of oxygen because of congestive heart failure or a lung condition. You or I would feel hunger pangs and we would feel thirsty. People at that stage don't. As they become dehydrated, they get weak and sleepy. The kidneys are starting to shut down from lack of hydration. The individual goes into a coma, and from that coma they pass away. It's truly that simple. Hospice does not mean accelerating the death process.

 **EXPERT VIEW**

10 Tips for Caregivers

Jo Huey is nationally known as an author and trainer of those who provide care for people with Alzheimer's disease. One of her most memorable experiences was evacuating more than 30 New Orleans memory-care residents when Hurricane Katrina came to town. She and some of her staff spent the next two and a half months in temporary housing. All the residents had a diagnosis of Alzheimer's disease or some other type of dementia—individuals who typically would stay in an assisted-living facility until the end of their lives. Jo became affectionately known to her staff as "Hurricane Huey."

"We were required to do hurricane drills every year," she says, "but after the drill, you're actually able to go *back* to the residences that you evacuated. After Hurricane Katrina, we had nothing to go back to—and that leads to dealing with the difficult ambiguities of what to do next in the midst of a disaster." She has served as a nursing home administrator in Colorado and an assisted-living director in Louisiana.

Q: As you think of the years you've been dealing with persons with Alzheimer's, including your own mother, what would you love to have lawyers know about working with people with Alzheimer's and their families?

A: It's important to understand the complexity of what happens and to be able to look at the whole family situation. I think lawyers should know that when someone comes into your office complaining about certain problems within their family and saying that someone is trying to take away their money, you never know whether you're looking at a person who is unable to take care of their financial affairs, or whether there really is someone taking away their money.

People can present themselves so well—even a person with Alzheimer's. Often they are very angry at a family member, but many times that is the family member who is helping them the most. Once mom or dad is upset with the most caring family member, then other family members get involved and suddenly sibling rivalry is ignited, and any other historic family issues that have been simmering for a long time add fuel to the fire.

So the lawyer can easily get sucked into the middle of all of these family issues that are going on. . . . One of the most important things is making sure that the older person is able to make their own decisions, and that often gets overlooked. When families go to war with each other, the senior's wishes can be lost in the battles.

Q: Can you help us to sort out this issue of the person with dementia who is actually angry at the family member who is trying to help them the most? Because it really is quite common that people come in complaining about all the grievous and horrible things that some family member is doing to them, or taking their stuff. What's really going on there?

A: Very often it's just their fear of losing their things. They know something is really wrong with them, but if they let go of their things, then somebody will take advantage of them. That's one of the ways this disease presents itself. People are trying so hard just to hang on. And anyone that seems to disturb that, then that person becomes the most suspect. The targets of their anger, of course, are the ones that are present and helping them the most and are the ones who end up being accused of causing many of the bad things that are happening. The person with Alzheimer's no longer has the capacity to sort out complicated cause-and-effect.

For some reason, we just get angrier at the people who are closest to us. We get paranoid that somebody is hurting us when, in reality, they're doing everything they can to help.

Q: How do you think a lawyer could be alerted to the fact that it can be relatively common for an older person to falsely accuse a younger person of theft or manipulation?

A: I've seen some attorneys conduct family meetings in their office, and I believe that is the right strategy. You get everyone together and spend time just getting acquainted and then you can pick up on what's really happening by watching the body language of everyone in the room. Body language can be much more informative than just listening to their words. After the family meeting, have the people separate and then talk to each one about the same things. When interviewing the client, ask questions like, "Tell me what you need your money for. What are you going to do with it? What are your plans? Who do you want to have your money and things after you're gone? Why?" This type of interview will help the attorney sort out whether or not their client still has the ability to appreciate what they have and what is really happening around them.

I think the attorney needs to be very calm during these meetings. The attorney can provide great value to the client and family, because most families seldom get around to having those types of discussions.

If you look at the model of a geriatric care manager, one of the first things they do is go to the home and interview the individual who needs care as well as the family. They do this before they work on the care plan. If the attorney would consider the model of the geriatric care manager, they would get the family together and do an assessment before the attorney decides on the right course of action. Too often, I've seen situations where the attorney "charges the enemy" before really knowing who is hostile and who is a friend.

Q: Is it very common for people to go through the full Alzheimer's disease trajectory and then actually die of Alzheimer's?

A: Although Alzheimer's disease is an illness that ends in death, most often people die from other causes first, such as stroke or heart attack. The most common death for people with Alzheimer's or a related disorder is infections, especially pneumonia and sepsis (an infection that goes into the bloodstream).

The most common forms of sepsis for people with Alzheimer's tend to be from things the ordinary person wouldn't even think of, mainly urinary tract infection, also called UTI, or a bowel backup. The tough reality is that it's very difficult for a person with Alzheimer's to tell you what's going on internally and it tends to get overlooked by the care staff because the behaviors of somebody with a urinary tract infection often are not seen as an infection. They get very ill very quickly and it happens so fast.

Q: When I first met you, you shared with me some principles to improve communication with someone affected by Alzheimer's disease. What do we need to know?

A: The name of my book is *Alzheimer's Disease, Help and Hope: Ten Simple Solutions for Caregivers*. The 10 Absolutes are communication tools to allow caregivers (and perhaps lawyers) to know what to say and what not to say when working with people affected by Alzheimer's. My goal is to help people motivate those with Alzheimer's to do the right things, such as taking a bath. I also want to help people to avoid the nonstop battles and enjoy what time they have together. There are still lots of things that a person with Alzheimer's may be able to do, and they still need to have some meaning and purpose in their lives. Too often, everything is taken away from them and they feel like there is nothing left worth living for. The Ten Absolutes are

1. Never argue; instead, agree.
2. Never reason; instead, divert.
3. Never embarrass; instead, distract.
4. Never lecture; instead, reassure.
5. Never say, "Remember"; instead, reminisce.
6. Never say, "I told you"; instead, repeat/regroup.
7. Never say, "You can't"; instead, do what they can.
8. Never command/demand; instead, ask/model.
9. Never condescend; instead, encourage/praise.
10. Never force; instead, reinforce.

CHAPTER 4

SPECIAL-NEEDS TRUSTS AND POOLED TRUSTS

THIS CHAPTER WILL PROVIDE a basic introduction to the use of special-needs trusts (SNT) planning for a client with Alzheimer's disease. The goal is to retain any government benefits, preserve the client's dignity and independence, and pay for specific needs not covered by government benefits. After introducing the different types of special-needs trusts, this chapter will cover the following areas:

1. Help make non-elder-law lawyers aware of the value of an SNT in the inter-spousal and pooled trust context.
2. Illustrate common estate-planner errors and pitfalls that foil many attempts to create inter-spousal SNTs.
3. Make lawyer audience aware of the value of an SNT from the view of an aged person with Alzheimer's or other age-related disability to protect their adult child with a disability by a transfer to an SNT.

Case Study
A Tale of Three Widows: Shirley, Mary, and Zoe

Shirley, Mary, and Zoe were three aged widows who eventually developed dementia. They were all in their 80s at the time of receiving a diagnosis of Alzheimer's-type dementia. Like the majority of seniors, they were women of moderate middle-class means. In other words, they essentially had middle-class income and corresponding net worth. None of them had sufficient income or assets to provide private-pay, luxury nursing home care for the full period of time that they had dementia. Most seniors in the United States do not have sufficient resources to pay for even one full year of private pay at either an assisted-living facility or a skilled-care nursing home.

Since dementia is a progressively debilitating condition, many of those affected will need multiple years of ever-more-expensive care. Once one's personal resources have been exhausted, each state has a nursing home Medicaid benefit program, which may become the sole resource to pay for skilled nursing home care for those affected by Alzheimer's disease. Although nursing home Medicaid benefit eligibility varies from state to state, an institutionalized person occupying a Medicaid-funded bed is essentially asset-less and income-less.

Let's explore the impact upon dignity and quality-of-care life differences that can be achieved when an appropriate special-needs trust is used to supplement the very limited nursing home Medicaid resources available to a person with Alzheimer's.

Shirley:

At one time, Shirley and her husband, Curly, had enjoyed a life of health and prosperity. Like most men, Curly's health began to deteriorate several years before Shirley had any significant aging-related health issues. And as is quite common, Shirley provided most of the care for her husband for many years. During the time of his decline in health they spent a substantial amount of their marital assets on Curly's ever-increasing health-care needs. Eventually, Curly had to be moved out of the home and had to be institutionalized in a skilled nursing home setting. By the time he died, Shirley was substantially impoverished—so she was unable to continue to afford their marital home or to remain in the neighborhood that they had enjoyed for many years. She was forced to move to a small apartment where she lived frugally on one Social Security check of $1,200 per month. Her assets were $120,000 in total, which represented the proceeds from the sale of their home. A few years later Shirley developed dementia of the Alzheimer's type. After she became unsafe in a normal environment, she needed to live in a skilled nursing care setting. In her state of residence, one does not qualify for nursing home Medicaid until all assets above $2,000 have been "spent down" on health care. In addition, once a person has qualified for nursing home Medicaid benefits, all of the income is assigned to the care facility in which they reside. The only exception is that the institutionalized person may keep $1 per day, which is referred to as the "personal needs allowance."

Near the end of Shirley's life, she was out of money and out of options. With only $30 per month for her personal-needs allowance and less than $2,000 in assets, she was bereft of any resources beyond the state nursing home Medicaid benefits. If she needed dental care, new dentures, hearing aids, modified mobility devices, specialized therapies, foot care, or other such services, the likelihood of the state meeting her needs was remote.

Shirley powerlessly lived out her final days warehoused in a nursing home Medicaid bed.

Mary:

Mary's life history during her younger years was very similar to Shirley's. She and her husband, Larry, enjoyed health, happiness, and modest success for many decades. After reaching retirement age, Larry began to notice that Mary's memory was slipping. Within a few years, Larry had changed from being Mary's husband and best friend to being her full-time caregiver. Larry vowed that Mary would never go to a nursing home.

It would be wonderful if such sentiments could always be fulfilled. Unfortunately, the realities of life and long-term care often thwart such commitments. And so it was to be for Larry and Mary.

Then one day, Larry, who had been a lifelong smoker, was diagnosed with inoperable cancer. He was told to go home and get his affairs in order. Larry remained stoic about his own condition, but he was distraught about what was going to happen to Mary. He worried about how to provide the best care for her after he was gone. A friend whom he had come to know through an Alzheimer's support group encouraged him to see an elder-law estate planner. This attorney understood estate planning, long-term care options, and nursing home and Medicaid law. Under the direction of the lawyer, Larry modified his estate plan to create a new will, which included a testamentary SNT for the sole benefit of Mary during the balance of her life. In addition, the testamentary SNT provided that any assets remaining in the trust after Mary's death were to be distributed to their children and certain selected charities.

The lawyer explained that the testamentary SNT for the benefit of Mary did not need to include a provision for Medicaid payback to the state.

According to federal law, a testamentary SNT for a spouse is treated as if it was a third-party, non-payback SNT. Larry died, and Mary did qualify for nursing home Medicaid—which provided for her room, board, and basic health care in a nursing home. However, Mary's life during her final years was much better than Shirley's. Mary could look to her SNT trustee, who had access to ample funds from the sale of the couple's home and other assets. Having money available for hearing aids, mobility devices, specialized therapies, trips, personal attendance, room enhancements, special events, and more is a marvelous way to increase the dignity of a person's life while still qualifying them for nursing home Medicaid benefits.

Zoe:

In the early years, Zoe and her husband Moe's story was much like that of Shirley and Curly, and Mary and Larry. The distinctive difference in its final scene is how Zoe achieved a nursing home Medicaid qualifications and a dignity-preserving SNT.

Zoe was fortunate to live in a state that allowed her personal representative, guardian, or power of attorney to fund a pooled trust from Moe's assets. This is allowable in certain states even though the person may be over 65. (This provision was provided for in the 1993 Omnibus Reconciliation Act legislation.) This is referred to as a d4C Pooled Trust. The virtue of the d4C is that it can be funded with a senior's assets so as to provide and pay for special needs that would not be covered by the state's nursing home Medicaid program. But regardless of the amount of money in the pooled trust, Zoe can still be eligible for nursing home Medicaid. There was a state Medicaid payback requirement from any funds remaining in the pooled trust after Zoe's death.

For Zoe, she was able to use her assets to fund the pooled trust and qualify for institutionalized care paid for by the state's Medicaid program. Because of the funding of her pooled trust, she enjoyed a much higher level of services in her time of greatest need. Her trustee used her pooled trust funds to pay for things such as

- out-of-pocket medical and dental costs,
- personal care attendance,
- nursing home advocate,
- rehabilitation services,
- legal fees,
- clothing and eyeglasses, and
- many other needs, as long as they were solely for the benefit of Zoe.

Even though Moe had never considered creating a testamentary SNT for Zoe, she still was able to enjoy the benefits of an SNT—but it was created via a different route.

TRUSTS BACKGROUND

When a lawyer is presented with a situation wherein one member of a family has a diagnosis of Alzheimer's disease, quite frequently there is a healthy spouse. The concern of dealing with a person with Alzheimer's is being able to provide long-term health care, even when the healthy spouse predeceases the person with the diagnosis. The circumstances that cause an event such as a healthy spouse predeceasing a person diagnosed with Alzheimer's is statistically significant. And when doing planning for a husband and wife when one of the two of them has been diagnosed with a long-term illness, it is extremely important to not make the assumption that the person with the long-term disease trajectory is going to die before the healthy spouse.

Without proper planning, lawyers could have one of two results: the client didn't do the proper estate planning and now the spouse has inherited all of the assets, or the client bypassed the spouse with the hopes that the children would simply "do the right thing" and take care of the spouse, and they didn't.

The savior is the testamentary SNT. This tool will not interrupt public benefits, but will provide for the special needs until the beneficiary's death.

Special-Needs Trusts

One of the best ways to protect the individual with Alzheimer's disease is to set up a special-needs trust or, in some states, to transfer monies to what has been referred to as a "pooled trust." The type of special needs trust or other trust to be selected depends upon the goals and circumstances of both the donor, who is often referred to as the grantor, and the person with the diagnosis or beneficiary. There is much more to this decision making than merely deciding to put money and property into a trust.

There are two synonymous ways to refer to a special-needs trust—simply a "special-needs trust" or a "supplemental needs trust." In both, the language of the trust must specifically state that the assets in the trust are not available to be used for anything that would be covered by governmental benefits but, instead, are used to complement—to supplement but not supplant—whatever care would be provided for by governmental benefits.

That's a key concept, and that's what makes this type of a trust—what is referred to as a "dignity for client trust," (d4C)—because what is being provided is more care than what would be available through the overburdened governmental Medicaid system.

A properly drafted supplemental-needs trust that is funded appropriately is going to wind up in one of two categories: it may be a pay-back trust, meaning at the end of a person's life any funds in the trust will need to be repaid to the state for a Medicaid lien, or it may be a non-payback trust. Non-payback trusts most often are the special-needs trusts created by a third party where the third-party was never legally obligated to pay for the person's health care.[1]

In too many circumstances, lawyers try to use special-needs trusts that do not fit the circumstances of an aged individual needing long-term care. The most common uses of special-needs trusts are to assist either younger individuals who receive monies from a personal injury award due to an accident, or a child with special needs who has been left money in the estate of a parent. These are the types of special-needs trusts that most practitioners are familiar with, but they are not appropriate for elderly clients with Alzheimer's disease.

When trying to determine the proper use of a special-needs trust when dealing with a mature couple, lawyers are trying to assist their clients in making sure that dignity is preserved for the ill spouse in the unlikely, but still extremely possible, event that the healthy spouse pre-deceases the ill spouse.

One of the real challenges of trying to create a special-needs trust when one spouse is the grantor and the other spouse is to be the special-needs trust beneficiary is that typical state and federal laws view spouses as having a duty of paying for the health care of their spouses. This concept goes back to the middle ages under common law; it was deemed

---

1. *POMS SI 01120.203*, Soc. Sec. Admin., https://secure.ssa.gov/apps10/poms.nsf /lnx/0501120203 (last visited Nov. 12, 2012).

that spouses have a duty to pay for the necessaries of their spouse and nothing could be more necessary than health care.

However, with the proper planning and administration, the funds in such a trust may be devoted to enhancing the quality of life of a person with disabilities, while at the same time allowing the person to still qualify for as many governmental benefits as possible.

Practice Pointer: Special-Needs Trust for the Spouse Must Be Drafted Carefully

When someone tries to create a special-needs trust for a spouse, it typically is not going to be allowable in its ordinary style, because a spouse has a legal duty to pay for medical care.

In addition, typically the assets between spouses are attributed to each other because it is deemed that spouses are responsible for each other's "necessaries." Necessaries include food, clothing, shelter, and health care.

Therefore, when a spouse tries to set up a special-needs trust for another spouse, in most cases, the Medicaid rules for long-term care and Medicaid do not allow those funds to be treated as being segregated and unavailable to the individual. (Medicaid is discussed in chapter 6.) They treat those assets as being available. Therefore, they require them to be spent down on care before the person becomes impoverished enough to receive Medicaid.

The goal of using a special-needs trust is to get around these issues by drafting properly and carefully and using the right strategy so that if a healthy community spouse predeceases the institutionalized ill spouse, they can create a special-needs trust that provides supplemental care for things that the governmental benefits will not pay for, while allowing the spouse to be able to have food, clothing, shelter, and the basics of health care paid for by the long-term-care benefits of nursing home and Medicaid.

OBRA 93

The Omnibus Budget Reconciliation Act of 1993 (OBRA 93) sets forth the federal requirements for special-needs trusts.[2] The act applies to trusts established on or after August 11, 1993.[3]

The federal statute that creates these trusts deals with trusts established by the individual (that is, that are self-settled) and how the transfer

---

2. 42 U.S.C. § 1396p (2009).
3. *Id.*

of assets to and existence of the trust affects the individual's eligibility for benefits under a Medicaid State Plan.[4]

42 U.S.C. § 1396p(d) lays out the general rules that govern special-needs trusts and the transferring of assets. The statute tells us that assets of a revocable trust will be considered to be available to the individual. On the other hand, the transfer of assets to an irrevocable trust is subject to the Medicaid transfer-of-assets period-of-ineligibility rules. These rules are explained in 42 U.S.C. § 1396p(c). When lawyers are dealing with an irrevocable trust, the assets are available to the individual "if there are any circumstances under which payment from the trust could be made to or for the benefit of the individual."[5]

However, in drafting the legislation that would become OBRA 93, the drafters created exemptions that would turn into important tools for elder-law lawyers. These exemptions from the trust transfer rules are the "d4A," "d4B," and "d4C" trusts.[6] These trusts are discussed in more detail in the following sections.

The Social Security operations manual, called the Program Operations Manual Systems (POMS), defines "Medicaid trusts" as any type of trust established by an individual on or after August 11, 1993, made up in whole or in part of assets (resources and/or income) of the individual and that are created by a means other than by will.[7]

The POMS establish the requirements for self-settled and third-party trusts. Practitioners should be aware that the POMS are not the law, but they do illustrate the Social Security Administration's (SSA) views and practices. They demonstrate how the SSA determines eligibility for Social Security income, and thus Medicaid for individuals in states where Medicaid eligibility depends on being eligible for Social Security income.

The POMS address regional and local issues such as the interpretation of a specific state law or issue related to a particular SSA region or locale.[8] This makes the POMS a very useful tool for lawyers who may not be as familiar with their state laws in this field.

---

4. *Id.*
5. Interview with Timothy L. Takacs; 42 U.S.C. § 1396p(d)(3)(A)–(B).
6. Interview with Takacs, *supra* note 5.
7. *POMS SI 01730.048 Medicaid Trusts*, Soc. Sec. Admin., at B.2, https://secure.ssa.gov /apps10/poms.nsf/lnx/0501730048 (last visited Nov. 12, 2012).
8. Interview with Takacs, *supra* note 5.

A trust is deemed to be established by an individual if it is established by the individual; the individual's spouse; or a person, including a court, or administrative body with legal authority to act for the individual or spouse or who acts at the direction or request of the individual or spouse.[9] A Medicaid trust will either be a revocable or irrevocable trust.[10]

REVOCABLE TRUSTS

The principal of a revocable trust is considered to be a resource to the individual, and payments from the trust to or for the benefit of the individual are considered income to the individual. Any other payments are considered assets disposed of by the individual.[11]

IRREVOCABLE TRUSTS

If there are any circumstances under which payment from an irrevocable trust could be made to or for the benefit of the individual, the portion of the principal (or income on that principal) from which payment to the individual could be made is considered resources.[12] Payments from the trust or income on the trust for the benefit of the individual are considered income, while payments for any other purpose are determined to be a transfer of assets by the individual.[13]

Any portion of the trust or income on the trust from which no payment could be made under any circumstances to the individual is considered to be transferred assets on the date the trust was/is established. If, however, the access by the individual was "blocked" later, the date of the transferred assets will be the date that access was "blocked" (foreclosed).[14]

---

9. *Id.*
10. *Id.*
11. *POMS SI 01730.048.B.2, supra* note 7, at C.2.
12. *Id.*
13. *Id.*
14. *Id.*

D4A: SELF-SETTLED MEDICAID PAYBACK TRUST

A d4A trust is one that contains the assets of a person with disabilities under the age of 65. This type of trust is established for the benefit of such individual by a parent, grandparent, legal guardian, or court.[15] The state receives all the assets that remain in the trust when the beneficiary dies, up to the amount of the total medical assistance paid by the state to the beneficiary.[16] This is the type of trust that is the most common special-needs trust and thus is the one of which most practitioners are aware.

Unfortunately, it is of extremely limited value in dealing with people with Alzheimer's or other long-term-care conditions.

D4B: MILLER TRUST

D4B trusts, or Miller trusts as they are commonly known, are composed entirely of pension, Social Security, and other income to the individual (and accumulated income in the trust). Much like with the d4A trust, the state will receive all of the assets remaining in the trust upon the death of such individual up to an amount equal to the total medical assistance paid on behalf of that individual. But with this type of trust, the state does not make payments for nursing facilities; those payments would come from the trust.[17]

The main benefit of the Miller trust is that it is a useful tool for an individual who is applying for Medicaid but has too much income and wants to qualify for Medicaid in a hurry. The excess income can be transferred into a Miller trust, and the individual will be eligible for Medicaid benefits. However, Miller trusts are not much help in any other situation and are significant only in those states that impose an income cap on Medicaid long-term-care eligibility.

D4C: CHARITABLE POOLED TRUST

Zoe, the wife in the third introductory example, was fortunate enough to have a d4C trust. As mentioned in Zoe's story, the virtue of the d4C

---

15. 42 U.S.C.A. § 1396p (2009).
16. *Id.*
17. *Id.*

is that it can be funded with a senior's assets so as to provide and pay for special needs that would not be covered by the state's nursing home Medicaid program. But regardless of the amount of money in the pooled trust, Zoe can still be eligible for nursing home Medicaid.

A d4C trust is funded directly by an inter vivos transfer of assets of the person with disabilities or with assets from a living spouse.

If lawyers create a special-needs trust with the client's own assets or create one for the spouse while he or she is alive, this trust is referred to as "self-settled," and at the death of the person with disabilities, the remaining assets are subject to claims by the state up to the amount expended on the person through public benefits. This trust is also commonly referred to as a "pooled trust" and can be used when a person with disabilities who is on public benefits receives an inheritance or a lump-sum settlement.

The d4C trust must be established and managed by a nonprofit association. A separate account is maintained for each beneficiary of the trust, but, for purposes of investment and management of funds, the trust pools these accounts.

A spouse could create such a trust for the spouse with disabilities with a certain amount of funds during the healthy spouse's lifetime in order to protect that amount of money for the special needs of the spouse with disabilities.[18]

Administration Expenses

It is less expensive to administer a d4C trust than a d4A counterpart, and it is possible for individuals to find charitable institutions that are willing to manage a d4C that are not managing d4A trusts.

Around the country, there are more charitable organizations that were organized to handle pooled trusts because of the efficiencies of scale than there are typically those that handle d4As. Most d4A trusts are handled by bank trust departments and Merrill Lynch Trust Departments or other large financial institution trust departments, and for the most part those institutions want anywhere from the minimum of $250,000 to $500,000 and up to manage the trust, whereas many charitable organizations will handle deposits for pooled trusts of even less than $100,000. That is another one of the virtues of the d4C.

---

18. *Id.* § 1396p(d)(4)(C).

In 2012, Illinois passed a Medicaid reform law that eliminated the use of a d4C pooled trust for individuals 65 or older. The d4C, which is a self-settled pooled trust, had been the number one planning tool used by Illinois elder-law practitioners to provide the preservation-of-dignity resources for their clients while qualifying for nursing home Medicaid benefits. One of the most common uses was the circumstance in which aged individuals had been living in their home and had depleted all of their liquid assets on their living expenses and care. Upon selling their home, they needed to be relocated to a skilled-care nursing facility. Proceeds from the sale of the home would be transferred to a charitable organization that administers a pooled trust, and institutionalized individuals' assets would be reduced to no more than $2,000. The nursing home would be paid by Medicaid, and individuals would have supplemental-care needs funded from their own funds held in the charitable pooled trust. At the end of their lives, any funds remaining in the pooled trust were subject to distribution to the charitable entity and reimbursement to the state for Medicaid expenses incurred.

Although the statutory underpinnings for the d4C trust are expressed in federal law, the pooled trust is under attack in numerous states.

In the spring of 2012, d4C trusts were significantly damaged by two cases coming out of the Dakotas that are now known as the "Badland Decisions."[19] The Badland Decisions are *In re Pooled Advocate Trust*[20] and *Center for Special Needs Trust Administration, Inc. v. Olson*,[21] and both decisions involve senior citizens who contributed to a pooled trust and then applied for Medicaid at some later date.[22]

In *Center*, the senior citizen involved was a 78-year-old man who applied for Medicaid. When he applied, he submitted records disclosing that funds had been put into a d4C trust. Upon his death, the Medicaid agency made a claim to have all of the funds returned and even accused the Center for Special Needs Trust Administration of making a fraudulent conveyance.[23] The Medicaid agency was forced to drop the charges of fraudulent conveyance during discovery.[24]

---

19. William J. Browning, *Pooled Trusts Under Attack from CMS*, Oct.–Nov. 2012, NAELA NEWS, at 24.
20. 813 N.W.2d 130 (S.D. 2012).
21. 676 F.3d 688 (8th Cir. 2012).
22. Browning, *supra* note 19.
23. *Id.*
24. *Id.*

The Eighth Circuit Court ruled that the residual amounts that remained in a pooled trust after the beneficiary's death do not have to be paid back to the state and could remain in the trust so that the nonprofit could use the funds for other members of the trust.[25] However, the court went further and through its interpretation of 42 U.S.C. § 1396p(c)(2)(B)(iv) held that for individuals that are 65 and older, transfers to a pooled trust are improper transfers and create a penalty period.[26]

The South Dakota Supreme Court also dealt a blow to d4C trusts in its decision in *Pooled Advocate Trust*, just weeks later, when it held that the transfer penalty period for Medicaid eligibility will be triggered by transfers of assets into pooled trusts for less than fair market value.[27]

There is some hope for d4C trusts, though, as the Third Circuit Court of Appeals ruled that the states have a binding obligation to hold that the assets-counting rules do not apply to pooled trusts under the Medicaid Act.[28] The court also noted that nonprofits were entitled by federal law to keep the residual amounts left in the pooled trust after the death of the beneficiary.[29]

However, the Third Circuit noted that under the Medicaid Act, individuals 65 and older would create a period of ineligibility for Medicaid if they transferred assets to a pooled trust.[30] The court admitted that this was an "error" in the act, but stated that it did not have the judicial power to correct the error.[31]

There will certainly be more challenges in this arena, and practitioners need to be aware that creating pooled trusts for their clients who are 65 and older is no longer a safe option.

Unfortunately, at least to this date, there are no current legal challenges pending in Illinois against the most recent state ban against the pooled trust.[32] The loss of the availability of a pooled trust has already begun to force thousands of Illinois citizens to face their final months or years limited to a meager $1 a day personal-needs allowance and an ever-decreasing level of care as provided by nursing home Medicaid.

---

25. *Id.*
26. *Id.*
27. *Id.*
28. *Id.* (citing Lewis v. Alexander, 685 F.3d 325 (3d Cir. 2012)).
29. *Id.*
30. *Id.*
31. *Id.*
32. As of December 1, 2012.

HOW TO TAKE CARE OF THE SPOUSE

One of the main goals in creating a special-needs trust when dealing with Alzheimer's is to make sure the spouse is taken care of.

A great way to protect the spouse is to draft a testamentary SNT. Mary, in our introductory case study, benefitted from having a testamentary SNT in place.

Testamentary Trusts

A trust established by a will or a "testamentary trust" is established under the terms of a will and is only effective upon the individual's death. A trust to which property is transferred during the life of the individual who created the will is not a trust established by a will, even if the will transfers additional property to that trust.[33]

According to federal law, a testamentary SNT for a spouse is treated as a third-party non-payback SNT.[34]

A testamentary special-needs trust is created under a will and allows a community spouse (i.e., the noninstitutionalized spouse) to leave assets for the benefit of the institutionalized spouse in order to cover supplemental needs not covered by Medicaid. Money stays in the trust until the institutionalized spouse needs such goods or services as differentials in the cost between private and shared rooms, dental procedures, hearing aids, dentures, special wheelchairs/mobility devices, and other quality-of-care needs not provided for by governmental benefits.

The advantage of the testamentary special-needs trust is that while there may be substantial assets in trust for the institutionalized spouse, these assets may not be counted against the spouse for Medicaid eligibility purposes. Therefore, Medicaid coverage continues and there is a source of money available for additional or supplemental needs.

If a trust is properly drafted and the proper strategy is used, and if a community spouse leaves the assets to the institutionalized spouse through a testamentary means, then potentially unlimited amounts of assets can be left for the beneficiary.

This is because the person who is institutionalized is not treated as having those assets available to pay for care; the reason for that is

---

33. *POMS SI 01120.201*, SOC. SEC. ADMIN., at B.6, https://secure.ssa.gov/apps10/poms.nsf /lnx/0501120201 (last visited Nov. 12, 2012).
34. 42 U.S.C.A. § 1396p(d)(2)(A) (2009).

because a properly drafted special-needs trust that is also properly funded in allowable manners has funds in it that are not treated as having come from the individuals themselves. Therefore, the amount of money in the trust is irrelevant because it didn't come from someone who has a duty of care.

Interestingly enough, the definition of "trust" under OBRA 93 specifically excludes testamentary trusts and trusts established by a person other than the beneficiary or beneficiary's spouse, as long as the person is not acting with legal authority or under the direction of the beneficiary or spouse. A third-party special-needs trust, therefore, is not subject to OBRA 93 rules.[35]

When the institutional spouse dies, the balance of the trust goes to the person's heirs. Many states subject the remaining fund balance in a special-needs trust to a state recovery.

Practice Pointer: Logic Behind Testamentary Special-Needs Trust

The reason that a testamentary special-needs trust seems to be allowable is that it was apparent to the federal government that nobody is going to be transferring assets to a spouse to avoid Medicaid by choosing to die to get those assets transferred to the spouse. Therefore, it is an allowable route to use a testamentary manner, typically a will, to create a special-needs trust. Some of the community spouse's assets may be channeled into a special-needs trust for the benefit of the spouse and it will be an allowable transfer. That may be the reason that the testamentary language is in the law.

Practitioners need to keep in mind that one of the most difficult problems in dealing with a testamentary trust is that they do not begin to function until the death of the testator. There are many circumstances in which a special-needs trust may be needed prior to the death of the individual who may wish to fund a trust for a person with Alzheimer's. Trusts written within a will are sometimes deemed to be "trapped inside the will." This means that they are absolutely ineffective unless and until the grantor dies.

Therefore, practitioners need to understand that the trust will be trapped inside the will when considering drafting a testamentary trust for a client. While these trusts can be a powerful tool, they are not the best tool for every situation.

---

35. *Id.* § 1396p(d)(2)(A)(ii).

> **Practice Pointer: Drafting Requirements for Trusts for Spouses**
>
> When drafting a trust for a spouse, it is actually a requirement that a special-needs trust for a spouse be testamentary in order to protect the assets from Medicaid spend-down.
>
> In the case of anyone other than a spouse, there is no need for the trust to be testamentary. Any third party that is not legally responsible for the health care of an ill person may create a Medicaid no-payback special-needs trust for an ill person. They may use either an inter vivos trust or a testamentary trust to accomplish that goal.

The federal guidelines do not provide clear guidance on the issue of whether a spouse must renounce a will and take a statutory share instead. At best, it appears that the federal guidelines would require a determination on a case-by-case basis. Practitioners should check the laws of their respective states on this issue.

> **Practice Pointer: Bypass Estate Planning**
>
> There are many times elder law lawyers work with a family and create a hybrid of special-needs trust planning and disinheritance, or what is referred to as "bypass estate planning."
>
> In bypass estate planning, there is a couple wherein either the husband or the wife has been diagnosed with Alzheimer's or other long-term condition. The healthy spouse wants to do everything possible to be able to provide additional care and additional dignity care for the ill spouse. But in the event that the healthier spouse was to predecease the ill spouse, the ill spouse may well have become qualified for Medicaid. If the ill spouse has been qualified for Medicaid and the healthy spouse dies, then under the most common will distribution language used by married couples, all assets are left to the surviving spouse (a "sweetheart will"). The inheritance may make the ill spouse ineligible for Medicaid due to the receipt of assets. In addition, the state will have a claim for Medicaid health-care costs expended on behalf of the surviving ill spouse.
>
> If the healthy spouse wants to provide dignity care for the ill spouse and currently qualify for Medicaid, what lawyers often have them do is "carve out"

a portion of the estate and create a testamentary special-needs trust, which is funded with a portion of the estate. The balance of the estate bypasses or disinherits the ill spouse who is already on Medicaid and then will pass directly to the children, grandchildren, or other designated beneficiaries.

A properly drafted special-needs trust can only pay for supplemental care that governmental benefits do not cover.

Another powerful tool is the third-party trust created for a public benefits recipient. Because this type of special-needs trust is more commonly used to protect a child with disabilities, it is covered in more detail in part 3.

Common Mistakes When Creating a Spousal Special-Needs Trust

The number one mistake lawyers make in creating a spousal special-needs trust for a client is assuming that the creation of that trust is patterned upon either asset-protection-trust concepts or language applicable to the creation of a special-needs trust by a parent for a child with special needs. Neither of these two concepts will succeed in the creation of a special-needs trust between spouses. In the intraspousal special-needs trust arena, there is a hidden adversary that can pierce the shield of the purported special-needs trust erroneously founded on the traditional concepts noted above.

This hidden and powerful adversary is the state's Medicaid department. The Medicaid department has the power to deem any assets funded into an unallowable special-needs trust "available" to be used for an individual's care in the event that the individual applies for nursing home Medicaid benefits. Failure to consider the destructive power of this adversary can leave many practitioners subject to malpractice claims.

Practice Pointer:

It is almost impossible to successfully use an inter vivos trust to transfer assets to a special-needs trust for the benefit of a spouse and also protect those assets from being deemed available by a state's Medicaid authorities.

Many estate-planning lawyers think that they can use the same for-mat for a special-needs trust no matter what the circumstances. This is the kind of logic that can get lawyers into a lot of trouble.

As mentioned earlier in the chapter, special-needs trusts are most commonly used to protect younger individuals who receive monies from a personal injury award, or a child with special needs who has been left money in the estate of their parent. These are the types of special-needs trusts that most practitioners are comfortable drafting, but they are not the right type of document for elderly clients with Alzheimer's disease.

Practice Pointer: Cookie-Cutter Planning Will Not Work

Lawyers need to be aware that simply going about special-needs trust planning for elderly clients as they would in their normal special-needs planning is inappropriate.

Specialized planning is necessary when dealing with Alzheimer's disease, and if lawyers are not aware of the nursing home Medicaid rules within a state, then they need to seek the advice of an elder-law lawyer.

The authors have included in the appendix an example of a special-needs trust that is flawed. (See appendix A.)

This is an actual trust that was an attempt at a spousal SNT. The trust was presented to one of the authors when the daughter, who was a beneficiary of her mother, wanted to help her mother apply for long-term-care medical benefits under Medicaid. The daughter told the author that the lawyer who drafted the trust knew that her father, the trustmaker, was terminally ill and that her mother was mentally ill and confined to a mental health long-term-care facility. The goal of the trust had been to make the father's assets not countable for Medicaid purposes. The trust became irrevocable upon the death of the father.

Unfortunately, the author had to recommend that the daughter con-sider a malpractice suit against the drafting lawyer. The goal of creating a spousal SNT had not been met and now the trust was irrevocable.

This trust is fatally flawed. OBRA 93 reformed the law regarding which trusts would be considered to not be treated as available. Only a testamentary trust was excluded from the OBRA reform. The flawed trust fails in that it is not a testamentary trust created by will. Even if it was not flawed on those grounds, it also has conflicting language that the Medicaid department would interpret to require a trustee to pay for health care. The trust explicitly states that the trustee is to consider the health needs of the survivor spouse. Most jurisdictions find a duty to pay for care, even when the trustmaker adds "do not pay when government benefits are available."

The drafting lawyer should have created a testamentary SNT and then would have been operating outside of OBRA 93. This was a very significant error considering that the drafting lawyer knew the father was terminally ill.

Second, on the fourth page of the flawed trust, under "Third: Section 1," the drafting lawyer inserted qualifying language in an attempt to keep the assets as not countable. However, the qualifying language does not negate spouse-to-spouse distributions because husbands and wives are generally legally responsible for each other's medical expenses.

A trust created by a spouse for the benefit of another spouse is a trust that is treated, for Medicaid purposes, as a self-settled trust. There are only two distinct types of self-settled SNTs recognized and allowed by Medicaid, and they both require a payback to the state for any Medicaid-related expenditures made on behalf of the trust beneficiary.[36]

There is an example of a properly drafted spousal SNT that shows how to couple a trust distribution for an inter-spousal special-needs trust "pourback to will" to create and fund trust via probate in the appendix. (See appendix B.)

HOW TO PROVIDE FOR AN ADULT CHILD WITH DISABILITIES

Another situation that can arise is the elderly parent with Alzheimer's who has an adult child with disabilities and who wants to be able to provide for the child.

It has often been said that the death of child is a parent's worst nightmare. However, for some parents, the fear is that they will predecease the child with disabilities. These parents are faced with the additional questions or fears of "Who will care for my child when I am gone?," "No one loves him/her like I do," and "He/she has never known any home but this one."

---

36. *Id.* § 1396p(d)(4)(A), (C).

So what happens when people get a diagnosis of Alzheimer's and they realize that they may not die suddenly and leave their assets to that wonderful special-needs trust (trapped inside the will or trust) for the child as they had planned? They now know that with Alzheimer's they will slowly need more care than the child does. All of the assets will be used up to pay for that care. They will not be able to care for the child in the manner they had imagined.

Under current law, a transfer of assets to a special-needs trust for a child with disabilities is an allowable transfer under the Medicaid rules. Practitioners who have elderly clients with adult children with disabilities need to advise their clients to have any inheritance going to the child with disabilities going into a special-needs trust.

In planning for an elderly parent of a child with disabilities, lawyers must consider the possibility that the parent and the child may both need long-term care. The parent can create a "stand alone" special-needs trust for the child with disabilities, and lawyers should make sure that the agent under the durable power of attorney has instructions to fund that trust even in the event the client does not have capacity. This will ensure that if the parent gets a diagnosis of Alzheimer's, the agent can immediately fund that special-needs trust for the child with no negative consequences for the parent, who then applies for nursing home Medicaid benefits.

Another advantage of a stand-alone special-needs trust is that others can leave assets to that trust either in life or at death. So if Sister Sally wants to leave $10,000 to Eddy in her will, she only has to point to the already existing special-needs trust. If Aunt Alice never married and never had any children and always had a special place in her heart for Eddy, she doesn't have to reinvent the wheel in her documents. She can simply leave something or everything to "The Eddy Smith Special-Needs Trust dated November 14, 2012."

Practice Pointer:

Don't trap the special-needs trust for a client's estate planning documents (will or trust) for a child or grandchild with disabilities. Prepare a stand-alone special-needs trust that can be funded during life.

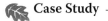 **Case Study** ——————————————————————————————

When Clark went to his lawyer's office, he was 72, and his adult son, Tommy, had had mental disabilities since birth. Although Tommy was high functioning, he still needed a lot of help.

Clark's wife Cynthia had passed away two years earlier and Clark had begun to wonder what would happen to Tommy when Clark died. Clark told the lawyer, "I guess we always thought that with Tommy's disabilities, he would not have a normal life expectancy. Some doctors had even suggested that he would not live past 30."

Now Clark had come face-to-face with a harsh reality. If Clark's health was in trouble, Tommy was in trouble. And there was trouble. Clark had been having trouble remembering where he put things: his keys, his wallet, his watch. Things just kept getting lost. He noticed that at church he would see people he had known for quite some time, but he couldn't remember their names. The final incident that sent him to the doctor was when he took Tommy to visit Tommy's brother and he got lost and very confused coming home.

The doctors did several tests and determined that Clark had Alzheimer's disease. Clark was concerned about his own health, but, as most parents, he was most concerned about Tommy.

Clark wanted to make sure that Tommy would be taken care of and get to do the things he loved and that he would not become a burden to his siblings. He wanted to be sure that Tommy would be cared for—maybe not just like he and Cynthia had cared for him, but the best care possible. Clark wanted to make sure that his own health-care needs would not exhaust all of his assets and leave nothing for Tommy.

Fortunately, a well-drafted special-needs trust was able to provide Clark with peace of mind and Tommy with a secure future.

Practice Pointer:

The special-needs trust will not supplant public benefits for the child (or grandchild). Transfers to that trust during a parent's (or grandparent's) lifetime will not prevent the child from receiving public benefits for care when the time comes.

Lawyers should learn the rules of their state and help clients provide for their children or grandchildren with disabilities.

Non-Spouse Third-Party Trustor

A less common, but additional, possibility that exists when dealing with individuals with dementia is the possibility of a special-needs trust created by a non-spouse third party. This non-spouse third party could be a well-to-do child, a sibling, or a significant other who loves but is not married to the ill individual. Third-party discretionary special-needs or supplemental-needs trusts are used to protect the governmental benefits eligibility of individuals with disabilities who are to receive assets through inheritance or gifting from third parties. These special-needs trusts allow trust assets to be reserved for expenses not covered by governmental benefits. Property held in properly drafted special-needs trusts will not affect the eligibility of the person with disabilities for such benefits.[37]

One of the great virtues of having a non-spousal third party create a discretionary special-needs or supplemental-needs trust is that a non-spouse is not treated as if assets belonged to the ill person.

Third-party special-needs trusts generally fall under two categories.

Third-Party Trust Created for a Public Benefits Recipient

A special-needs trust may be created by a grantor to set aside or bequeath assets to another individual without jeopardizing the individual's eligibility for public benefits.[38] This trust is most often used where a parent seeks to establish a trust for the benefit of a child with disabilities.

However, the third-party trust created for a public-benefits recipient may also be useful when the spouse of a Medicaid recipient, or potential Medicaid recipient, wishes to leave the couple's estate, or a portion of it, in trust for the benefit of the spouse.[39] Therefore, this can be an important tool for clients with Alzheimer's.

Third-Party Trust Created for Another Where the Grantor Seeks Public Benefits

A grantor may create a special-needs trust to set aside assets in a trust for a child with disabilities or individual under age 65 with disabilities where at least a portion of the grantor's motive is to attain Medicaid

---

37. *POMS SI 01120.201*, Soc. Sec. Admin., https://secure.ssa.gov/apps10/poms.nsf /lnx/0501120201 (last visited Nov. 12, 2012).
38. Interview with Takacs, *supra* note 5.
39. *Id.*

eligibility. These types of transfers to a trust would not disqualify the grantor from Medicaid eligibility under the exceptions provisions in 42 U.S.C. § 1396p(c)(2)(B)(iii) and (iv).

When a grantor-parent transfers recurring monthly income into an inter vivos, third-party special-needs trust created for a child with disabilities, the transfer is counted toward the grantor-parent's net available monthly income when determining the amount of the Medicaid benefits to which the grantor-parent will be entitled to after being determined to be eligible for Medicaid benefits.[40]

Practice Pointer: Agencies Attacking the Trust Will Look for a Duty Owed

Lawyers need to be aware that when government agencies look at money in a special-needs trust coming from a third party, they look to see if the third party had any sort of duty to provide care for the individual for a special-needs trust was created.

If there is no duty and the person creating the trust happens to be especially generous, the trustmaker can put a large amount of assets in the trust, and any of those assets that are available at the end of the person's life will be distributed to the residuary beneficiaries that the trustmaker puts into the trust.

A third-party trust is a trust established with the assets of someone other than the beneficiary. If the beneficiary of the trust is a child or any person with disabilities other than the spouse, it is a third-party special-needs trust. For example, the trustmaker creates a trust for another person (not a spouse) and funds that trust with money that did not belong to the person with disabilities.[41]

Practitioners need to be alert for situations in which a trust is allegedly established with the assets of a third party, but in reality is created with the beneficiary's property. In such cases, the trust is not a third-party trust, but rather a grantor trust.[42]

In a properly created third-party trust, the assets in the trust can be used for the beneficiary's special needs to supplement and not supplant public benefits.

---

40. *Id.* (referencing *In re* Jennings v. Commissioner of N.Y.S. Dep't of Soc. Servs., 893 N.Y.S.2d 103 (2010)).
41. *POMS SI 01120.200*, Soc. Sec. Admin., at B.17, http:/policy.ssa.gov/poms.nsf /links/0501120200 (last visited Nov. 12, 2012).
42. *Id.*

An advantage of the third-party special-needs trust is that the trust-maker can choose what happens to any remaining trust assets when the person with disabilities passes away. If the trust is created as a stand-alone trust, trustmakers can fund the trust during their lifetime, and other relatives (e.g., siblings of the person with special needs) can direct assets for the trust or designate assets to pass to this trust. Since the trust is already in existence, another person, such as a brother, may reference this trust in the estate plan.

The most common sources of that funding are grandparents, siblings, other loved ones, aunts, uncles, and, of course, parents. But of course, when the diagnosis is Alzheimer's, most often there are no parents still left alive. However, in some cases there are clients who have what's called "young onset Alzheimer's," and in one instance a client with young onset Alzheimer's was diagnosed at the age of 39.

Appendix A

DECLARATION OF TRUST (Excerpt)

THIRD:

SECTION 1: Upon my death the trustee shall administer the trust estate, including any amounts added thereto from my probate estate, for the benefit of my wife, _____, upon the following terms:

> The trustee may pay to her such sums from income and principal as the trustee deems necessary or advisable from time to time for her health, maintenance in reasonable comfort, and best interest, considering her income from all sources known to the trustee. However, the trustee shall withhold payment for the costs of services from governmental and private sources, and the trustee shall be prohibited from using trust assets for services provided by and funded by governmental bodies.

> The express purpose of this trust is to provide for _____'s extra and supplemental needs, over and above the benefits _____ otherwise received as a result of her handicap or disability from any local, state, or federal government or from private agencies, any of which provide services or benefits to disabled persons. Anything to the contrary herein notwithstanding, no trust income or principal shall be paid to or expended for the benefit of _____ so long as there are sufficient monies available to her for her care, comfort, and welfare from federal, state, and local government agencies and departments. The trustee shall consider such governmental funds in determining whether there are funds available to the beneficiary from sources other than the trust estate and shall use trust assets only to supplement and never to substitute for such funds. In no event may trust income or principal be paid to or for the benefit of a governmental agency or department, and the trust estate shall at all times be free of the claims of such governmental bodies.

Appendix B

Will of John Pourback

I, JOHN POURBACK, a resident of Kane County, Illinois, revoke any prior wills and codicils made by me and declare this to be my Will.

Article One
Family Information

I am married to my beloved spouse, JANE POURBACK. We were married on February 1, 1965.

I have two children. Their names and dates of birth are:

JIMMY JOHN POURBACK, born on March 1, 1970;

BILLY BOB POURBACK, born on April 1, 1975; and

All references in my will to "my children" are references to these children.

Article Two
Distribution of My Property

SECTION 2.01 DISPOSITION OF TANGIBLE PERSONAL PROPERTY

I direct that my Executor shall distribute my tangible personal possessions according to a separate "Personal Property Memorandum" or other similar writing, which shall be signed by me and kept with my personal records. It is my intent that such writing qualifies to distribute my tangible personal possessions under applicable state law. If such writing is not found at the time of my death, or ruled an improper disposition, this bequest shall lapse and my tangible personal possessions shall become part of my living trust. If any items of tangible personal property I happen to own are not mentioned in such list, such items shall become part of my living trust. If any such gift shall lapse, then such items shall become part of my living trust.

SECTION 2.02 POUR-OVER TO MY LIVING TRUST

Except to the extent my Executor establishes and funds a testamentary trust as provided in Section 2.03, all of my probate estate, excluding any property over which I might have a power of appointment, and after payment of expenses and taxes which are paid pursuant to this will, I give to the then acting Trustee of the JOHN POURBACK LIVING TRUST dated JANUARY 01, 2007 and executed prior to this will, to be added to the property of that trust. I direct that the Trustee administer the property as provided in the trust agreement and any amendments prior to my death.

SECTION 2.03 ESTABLISH AND FUND TESTAMENTARY TRUSTS

I authorize my Executor to establish, with the assets of my probate estate, if any, or with any property distributed to my personal representative from my Trustee, testamentary trusts for the benefit of my beneficiaries under the same terms and conditions of my revocable living trust as it exists at the date of my death. I appoint the Trustee and successor Trustees named in my revocable living trust as the Trustee and successor Trustee of my testamentary trusts. The Trustee of my testamentary trusts shall have all the administrative and investment powers given to my Trustee in my revocable living trust and any other powers granted by law.

My Trustee is under no obligation to distribute property directly to my Executor, but rather may distribute such property directly to the Trustee of the testamentary trusts. Any property distributed to my testamentary trusts by the Trustee of my revocable living trust shall be distributed by the Trustee of my testamentary trusts in accordance with the terms and conditions of my revocable living trust as it exists on the date of my death.

In the event that my wife JANE POURBACK survives me, the Trustee of my revocable living trust has been authorized to create via probate, a supplemental needs trust, the JOHN POURBACK TESTAMENTARY TRUST, for the lifetime benefit of my wife with any residual interests passing to my children.

The JOHN POURBACK TESTAMENTARY TRUST shall be administered as follows:

1. *Until the termination of the Trust, the Trustee shall distribute for the benefit of my beloved spouse, JANE, so much or all of the net income and principal thereof as the Trustee, in its sole and absolute discretion,*

determines from time to time to be desirable to meet the supplemental needs of my beloved spouse over and above the support and benefits she either receives through retirement income or becomes eligible to receive as a public and/or governmental benefit.

2. *It is my intent in the establishment of this Trust that it be used first (1st) to meet the supplemental needs of my beloved spouse, as the primary beneficiary hereof, and then secondarily (2nd) for the benefit of the remainder beneficiaries (i.e., any children). As to the primary beneficiary, my beloved spouse, it is my further intent that this Trust be used only to meet my beloved spouse's supplemental needs over and above her care, support and maintenance and that it not be used to provide the basic necessities of her care, support and maintenance. In the even my spouse is unable to support, maintain, and care for herself, it is contemplated that public and/or governmental benefits be procured to provide the basic needs of my spouse's support, care and maintenance and that the Trustee, in its sole and absolute discretion, apply part or all of the net income (and, if the Trustee deems it desirable, part or all of the principal) to meet her supplemental needs not otherwise provided by public and/or governmental benefits. By "supplemental needs" I mean those needs or desires which my spouse is unable to provide for herself and which are not provided by public and/or governmental benefits and which go beyond the basic necessities of care, support and maintenance. In its determination of what, if anything, constitutes my spouse's supplemental needs, the Trustee shall include in the consideration of expenditures such provisions, services and experiences as will contribute to and help make my spouse's life as pleasant, comfortable and happy as possible. When speaking of support and benefits provided "by public and/or governmental benefits," I mean any and all benefits, support, maintenance, care, financial assistance or resources available to or received by my spouse at any time from any local, county, state, federal or other public government, agency, or department or combination thereof, in cash or in kind, regardless of whether or not such benefits or resources are currently publicly available. It is expressly my intent that this Trust not jeopardize or in any way reduce, restrict or prevent such benefits, support, maintenance, care, financial assistance or resources that are or may become available to my spouse by public and/or governmental benefits, and in all matters relating to the administration and management*

of this Trust, it shall be interpreted consistent with my express intent that this Trust be limited to the application of both income and principal to provide supplemental benefits to those provided by public and/or governmental benefits. Within the limits of the use of the Trust monies, as aforesaid, it is my intent that sums spent for contribution, medicine, surgical and dental care, clothing, recreation, entertainment and the like be deemed proper expenditures from the income and principal of this Trust, provided that the furnishing of such sums, goods or services shall not be paid by the Trustee if in its judgment such payment will jeopardize or permanently reduce the benefits, support, maintenance, care, financial assistance, or resources that are or may become available to my spouse by public and/or governmental benefits.

3. *In keeping with the foregoing, I expressly state that the Trustee, in its sole and absolute discretion, may accumulate income of the Trust and that any income so accumulated shall be distributed or expended in accordance with the provisions of the Trust and my express intention in the establishment hereof, provided, however, that the Trustee shall not be required to distribute any income or principal during the administration and management of the Trust.*

4. *The Trustee may apply to any and all appropriate local, county, state and federal governments, agencies and departments for the payment of such benefits, support, maintenance, care, financial assistance, resources, or entitlements as my spouse is or may be entitled to by reason of her age or handicapping condition as aforesaid.*

5. *In addition to the provisions of Section 7.10 of this document, it is expressly stated that because this Trust is to be conserved and maintained for the supplemental needs of my spouse, no interest of my spouse's under this Trust shall be subject to the claims of voluntary or involuntary creditors for the provision of care and services, including residential and/or institutional care, by any public entity, office, department or agency of the State of Illinois, or any other state, or the United States, or any other governmental agency, or be lienable for any debt to any public government, agency or department or subject to the process of seizure of any court.*

6. *This Trust shall terminate when my spouse dies, if not previously terminated pursuant to Section 2.03, Paragraph (7), or upon my death if my spouse does not survive me; whereupon the Trustee shall*

distribute the principal and accrued or undistributed net income of the Trust to my residuary beneficiaries under the terms of Article Eight of my revocable living trust.

7. In the event that any creditor of my spouse's by whatever description whatsoever, including any public entity or agency or department thereof, shall be held to be entitled to share in the Trust or in the event that in the Trustee's opinion the purpose for which the Trust was established, as aforesaid, will not be accomplished, then the Trust shall immediately terminate and the principal and accrued or undistributed net income thereof shall be distributed pursuant to Section 2.03, Paragraph (6). For purposes of the previous sentence, my spouse shall be deemed to have predeceased me.

8. At the time of its formation, the Trust will include 110 assets contributed by or belonging to my spouse, and the trustee may not accept future contributions of assets by or belonging to my spouse. No public and/or governmental assistance benefits for my spouse may be added to this Trust. My spouse shall have no access to the income or principal of the Trust and shall have no power to direct the trustee to make distributions of income or principal from the Trust.

9. Subject to the foregoing limitations of Section 2.03, Paragraph (8), the trustee, in its sole discretion, may accept and receive property from anyone other than my spouse during the lifetime of the Trust.

10. The Trustee shall, on an annual or more frequent basis, consult with an attorney with appropriate expertise in the area of public benefits and trust law to review state and federal legislation, regulations, and other requirements so that the public benefits eligibility of the beneficiary is not jeopardized by inappropriate actions or distributions by the Trustee. The cost of such attorney consultations shall be paid by the Trustee from Trust assets. In addition to the foregoing, if the assistance of an attorney or other professional is desirable in connection with any proceeding to obtain, retain or increase public or governmental benefits for my spouse, the trustee is empowered to hire or retain such professional and pay the professional's fees from the income or principal of the Trust.

11. As often as the Trustee deems such action to be advantageous to the Trust or any beneficiary, it may, by written instrument, resign and appoint as substitute trustee any bank or trust company, wherever

situated. The substitute trustee shall have all of the powers and discretions of the Trustee, but shall exercise the same under the supervision of the Trustee. The Trustee may remove the substitute trustee at any time and re-appoint itself as Trustee. The Trustee's power and discretion to appoint a substitute trustee shall extend to appointing a co-trustee or to contracting with a professional trustee for investment services. If the assistance of professional trustee or investment services is desirable in connection with the administration of this Trust, the trustee is empowered to hire or retain such professional and pay the professional's fees from the income or principal of the Trust.

Section 2.04 Alternate Disposition

If the trust referred to in Section 2.02 is not in effect at my death or if for any other reason the pour-over cannot be accomplished, I specifically and completely incorporate the terms of the trust into this will by reference. In such a situation, I direct my Executor to establish a trust in accordance with the provisions of such trust and give the remainder of my estate, excluding any property over which I might have a power of appointment, to the Trustee of said trust to be administered as provided in the trust agreement.

Article Three
Designation and Succession of Fiduciaries

Section 3.01 Executor

I nominate JIMMY JOHN POURBACK as my Executor. If JIMMY JOHN POURBACK fails or ceases to act as my Executor, I nominate BILLY BOB POURBACK as my successor Executor.

 **EXPERT VIEW**

The Marriage of Technology and Alzheimer's Caregiving: Staying Safely at Home Longer

The Oaks, a United Methodist Continuous Care Retirement Community, is located in Orangeburg, which is inland from Charleston, South Carolina. What attracted us was the exciting work being done there to give people diagnosed with dementia the ability to live at home with dignity while providing peace of mind for family members and caregivers. The Oaks provides traditional senior services and care combined with a look to the future, recognizing that there is extraordinary pressure to move long-term care from the institutional facility back into the community.

The visionary leader of the Oaks is the Rev. James McGee, CEO. When we met with him and Stacie Pierce, the director of the technology/caregiving solution program called Live at Home Technologies, they had recently returned from meeting with IT wizards in Israel. The purpose of the trip was to further their research, development, and implementation of innovative technologies to provide remote in-home care for people affected by dementia. Some of the activities monitored include motion of an individual or lack of motion, bed and chair activities, medication access, patterns of movement through the home, daily body weight, daily blood pressure and blood glucose, time spent in the bathroom, the opening and closing of interior and exterior doors, and appliance usage. Stacie answered a few questions we had.

Q: Tell me about how technology is helping seniors to live at home longer.

A: This is something I'm passionate about. I'm a caregiver first and foremost. We take care of people, and we use technology to enhance that care so that when they're not safe anymore, they understand what their other choices are.

There are more than 70 million baby boomers about to hit the market. We need to have choices available. When you talk about Alzheimer's, it's an epidemic, and people are living longer and the disease is being diagnosed earlier. Technology gives people more living options.

We help people live at home with the support of honest and reliable family members who live nearby. One family lives 90 minutes from our facility. The daughter-in-law and son-in-law live about 500 yards away from the two disabled family members. The father has Alzheimer's and his daughter, who lives with him, is 62, and she's developmentally delayed and has an IQ equivalent to a three- or four-year-old. The wife recently died of a massive heart attack, most likely due to caregiver fatigue. This woman was taking care of her husband with Alzheimer's and her disabled 62-year-old daughter. So now you have a family who is asking, what can we do? The man was born in this house and the daughter was raised there. They have been a part of each other's lives for 62 years, and they have their patterns. If we separate them, she'll go to an institution and he'll go to assisted living or a nursing home, and they'll both probably die much sooner.

We examined their living patterns. We worked with the family to figure out what the rules will be. He still likes to go out and get the mail. They live on a busy road, so we put a door sensor on the door. Then I started thinking, If he leaves the door open, how am I going to know if he came back in? So I put a floor mat down on the inside. So if he opens the door and there's no pressure on the floor sensor within 20 minutes, then I know he didn't come back in. We've had that system in place for three years now. Anytime an alert is sent out, it goes to one of the other family members who live nearby.

The daughter had a history of falling in the bathtub. So we established a rule that if there's pressure on a mat in the bathroom for more than 30 minutes, then an alert is sent to one of the family members. We can set it up so that an alert goes to one of the family members, on their cell phone or their computer, and then they can connect to the house, turn on the camera inside, and actually view to see if someone is on the floor. We here at the Oaks do not have access to the cameras—only family members do.

You can't have technology without some sort of caregivers, as well. Nonetheless, the technology can make the caregiver's life more livable. Otherwise there's a much higher likelihood that the caregiver will die before the person being cared for.

I met with a man yesterday who's in his mid-80s and still an active businessman. His wife has Alzheimer's and he needs help with care. He says, "I still enjoy my work. I have to go out of town to do business. I can't take care of my wife 24/7." He wants to have a solution so his wife can continue to live at home and to provide the family with some sanity at the same time. We can put in a system that will allow him to go out and play poker and still keep his wife safe by providing alerts to him or other caregivers.

Most people don't even know that these types of solutions are available. I have been certified as an assistive technology practitioner and an aging-in-place specialist. This type of training allows us to work with homebuilders and remodelers to design appropriate systems within residences.

Q: Let me introduce you to Scott Ewing, chief operating officer at the Oaks. The Oaks is providing caregiver monitoring for his 87-year-old mother who still lives at home 600 miles from Orangeburg. Without the technology in her home, she would need to live at an assisted-living facility. Scott, how does this technology help your mother?

A: I'm a nursing home administrator so I understand costs very well. I had to have a discussion with my family about the risks versus reward of keeping Mom at home. My fear is not that she falls, because I know she's going to fall—she's elderly—but if she falls and something happens and she's undiscovered, that would be terrible. But with this technology, we can know that if she falls we'll get an alert. My mother is a retired schoolteacher and not particularly affluent. The cost of a nursing home where she lives in Maryland is $7,000-plus a month. Assisted living would be $5,000-plus a month.

When you put in the technology, you have up-front costs for the system—but that is less than one month of assisted living. With what we have put in, my mother can continue to live in her home of 53 years, and all her neighbors are around to help and support her. If I get an alert, I call a next-door neighbor and they'll check on her. She's had some of the same neighbors all her life. It's been tremendous and very liberating for her to have the technology so she can stay at home.

(While we were doing this interview, Scott got an alert that his mother had been in the bathroom more than one hour. He excused himself and went to make a call. He returned and told us that she had responded somewhat sheepishly, "I'm sorry, son, I must have fallen asleep.")

CHAPTER 5

GOVERNMENT
BENEFITS

Winning the Diagnosis Lottery

When it comes down to it, the health-care system isn't a whole lot different from a lottery system. If someone gets a diagnosis that there is a Medicare reimbursement code for, then Medicare cares about that person's care and will cover it. If someone gets a diagnosis that's not covered by Medicare, Medicare does not care about that person's care and that person will have to spend down until that person qualifies for Medicaid.

There's a story of two sisters of the same relative age, sharing the same genes and even living on the same street. One sister had heart issues and was able to rely on Medicare. The other sister was not so "lucky" and had Alzheimer's disease and was unable to use Medicare. In essence, the first sister won the diagnosis lottery.

Medicare cares about helping seniors to not die of heart attacks or strokes. For the sister that had a heart problem, there was a Medicare reimbursement code to take care of almost everything that she needed: medication, health services, rehab services, hospital services, doctor services. She was provided an enormous amount of care—probably half a million dollars or more because there was a Medicare reimbursement code for the diagnosis that she had.

Medicare didn't completely abandon the sister with Alzheimer's. When she got a urinary tract infection and had to go to a hospital as an inpatient, Medicare paid for her acute care. Part B paid for doctor services. Part D helped pay for medications, such as Aricept and Risperdal.

But look at what's not covered. Someone who has memory issues and starts to need assistance will not be able to access Medicare benefits for care. As the sister with Alzheimer's started to have memory issues, she was living at home. One day she decided to turn on the water in the bathtub upstairs and she didn't turn it off. She didn't turn it off for a couple of days. At this point it became obvious that the sister was no longer safe in a normal environment and somebody needed to be overseeing her activities of daily living. She needed in-home care.

Medicare does not care about in-home care, assisted-living care, or nursing home care. There are no Medicare reimbursement codes for that kind of care. So the sister diagnosed with Alzheimer's starts to have memory issues that cause her to be unsafe in her own environment and she even needs to have someone coming in to be with he or she needs to go somewhere where she is supervised and the environment is controlled, but Medicare does not care about providing that kind of care.

That means the sister with Alzheimer's will have to pay for her care out of her pocket, out of her savings account. If she had a long-term-care policy—she didn't, and most people don't—it may have helped pay for care. With a long-term care policy, Medicare continues to pay for all the things that it paid for before: acute care.

So, the sister with Alzheimer's has had to pay for care at home. When she finally gets down to $2,000 or less of assets (because she's a single individual), she can qualify for Medicaid nursing home benefits and she can move to a nursing home.

Up the street, the other sister has had over $500,000 of health care provided by Medicare and hasn't had to spend down all of her assets.

Today, it's common that people don't like the fact that someone is helping people to get qualified for Medicaid, because Medicaid is taking money from the government. However, think of it this way: The first sister didn't do anything wrong and she got a heart attack and the government happily paid for her benefits. But the second sister worked all of her life, saved her money, and also did everything right. Why should she be denied care?

In 1965, a political decision was made that Medicare would cover acute care because the "Big Killers" of the time were all acute problems such as stroke, heart attack, and cancer. Now a couple of generations have passed, and the problems of the elderly are no longer just acute-care issues. Today's big aging issues are long-term illnesses: Alzheimer's disease, other dementia, and Parkinson's disease.

Many seniors believe that Medicare will pay for their nursing home costs. After all, the language states that Medicare will pay for "skilled care," and we refer to facilities as independent, assisted, and skilled. Many clients are shocked to discover that the benefits they paid into will not pay for their "skilled care" in the nursing home.

Both sisters paid into the Medicare system through contributions from employment income. However, the hard truth is that one will be able to access those benefits and one will not.

MEDICARE VERSUS MEDICAID

Medicare is the federal medical insurance plan for senior citizens and individuals with disabilities, but the program does not cover the kind of long-term care that those inflicted with Alzheimer's disease require.

Medicare provides care for individuals who are blind, have disabilities, or are over the age of 65 and need acute medical care. "Acute medical care" means an individual has been diagnosed with an illness or other medical issue where there is a high probability that the individual can recover and return to a normal life.[1]

When Medicare was born in 1965, the average male died before ever reaching 65 years of age and the average female lived to be about 70. So when Medicare was first designed, it was created in a society where most people would never qualify for it or, if they did qualify, they would qualify for a relatively short amount of time.

Looking to the other side of the equation, many people believe that Medicaid is just about paying for care for poor people. Medicaid was designed to be the part of the social safety net that provided health care for people who were too poor to be able to have their own health care. It was limited in what it was going to do because it was means tested,

---

1. WILLIAM G. HAMMOND, RICK L. LAW, KAREN HAYS WEBER & MARY HELEN GAUTREAUX, THE ALZHEIMER'S LEGAL SURVIVAL GUIDE: ACTION GUIDE 51 (2009).

meaning that it was only available if someone qualified for certain poverty limitations.

Practice Pointer: Medicare Versus Medicaid

Lawyers will need to be familiar with the differences between Medicare and Medicaid and what type of coverage they provide. Lawyers may have to give clients the bad news that what they think about Medicare coverage is incorrect.

In 1965, there was no such thing as assisted-living facilities. Assisted living is for a person who has gotten to the point in life to have chronic-care conditions—chronic meaning the person is never going to get well. That is an important difference between Medicare and Medicaid.

Medicare does not cover chronic medical care services for most individuals who are suffering from a long-term illness or medical problem where there is a high probability that they will not recover and will not return to a normal life.[2]

Many people believe that Medicare will provide them with long-term-care benefits if they need to be in an assisted-living facility or a nursing home, but they are mistaken.

MEDICARE

Medicare is primarily designed to provide care for people over the age of 65 who can get well. Medicare is supposed to pay for acute care assuming the person needing the care is placed as an inpatient.

"Inpatient" is a key term and has become a controversial issue. Hospitals are starting to have people who are there to undergo tests, but these people are determined to be "under observation," which means they are on their own when it comes to paying their medical bills. Medicare helps pay for inpatient care in the hospital or skilled nursing facilities following a hospital stay. And it's not just any hospital stay; basically, a person has to have three midnights in the hospital before qualifying for skilled nursing care in a rehab center or home health care. A person could actually be in the hospital multiple days, having multiple tests, and seeing multiple doctors, and if that person has not been "admitted" but is merely "under observation," they need to be prepared to pay multiple bills.

---

2. *Id.*

Medicare is concerned about care only as long as a person can get well. There are a few exceptions to that, due to political lobbies that were strong enough to make changes. For instance, Medicare cares for people who have amyotrophic lateral sclerosis, or Lou Gehrig's disease, and about people with chronic renal failure. Why? Because these diseases or conditions had a big enough lobby to get the Medicare law changed. Medicare does not care about Alzheimer's disease and was never designed for long-term care.

Although Medicare can sometimes cover up to 100 days in a skilled-nursing facility, it is intended for patients who need recovery or rehabilitation from surgery or illness. For Medicare to pay for a stay in a nursing home, patients must continue to recover during their stay.

Individuals in the middle to late stages of Alzheimer's require custodial care instead of rehabilitative care.[3] "Custodial care" means assistance with preparing meals, bathing, grooming, toileting, and other activities of normal daily life. It may appear that this is skilled care, and even involves measures to keep individuals from harming themselves or others, but Medicare is not going to pay for this custodial care.

There are four parts of Medicare coverage: hospital insurance, medical insurance, Medicare advantage plans, and Medicare prescription drug plans, all with their own eligibility requirements.

Hospital Insurance (Part A)

Most people age 65 or older who are citizens or permanent residents of the United States are eligible for free Medicare hospital insurance (Part A). You are eligible at age 65 if:

- You receive or are eligible to receive Social Security benefits; or
- You receive or are eligible to receive railroad retirement benefits; or
- Your have a spouse who is eligible; or
- You or your spouse (living or deceased, including divorced spouses) worked long enough in a government job where Medicare taxes were paid; or
- You are the dependent parent of a fully insured deceased child.[4]

---

3. *Id.*
4. Soc. Sec. Admin., Pub. No. 05-10043, Medicare 5–6 (June 2011), *available at* http://www.socialsecurity.gov/pubs/10043.html#a0=2.

Individuals who do not meet these requirements may be eligible for Medicare hospital insurance for a monthly premium. Usually, this hospital insurance is only available during certain enrollment periods.

Before age 65, you are eligible for free Medicare hospital insurance if:

- You have been entitled to Social Security disability benefits for 24 months; or
- You receive a disability pension from the railroad retirement board and meet certain conditions; or
- [You] receive Social Security disability benefits because [you] have Lou Gehrig's disease (amyotrophic lateral sclerosis); or
- You worked long enough in a government job where Medicare taxes were paid and you meet the requirements of the Social Security disability program; or
- You are the child or widow(er) age 50 or older, including a divorced widow(er), of someone who has worked long enough in a government job where Medicare taxes were paid and meet the requirements of the Social Security disability program; or
- You have permanent kidney failure and receive maintenance dialysis or a kidney transplant and:
  - You are eligible for or receive monthly benefits under Social Security or the railroad retirement system; or
  - You have worked long enough in a Medicare-covered government job; or
  - You are the child or spouse (including a divorced spouse) of a worker (living or deceased) who has worked long enough under Social Security or in a Medicare-covered government job.[5]

Benefits

Part A helps pay for inpatient care in a hospital or skilled-nursing facility (following a hospital stay), some home health care, and hospice care.[6]

Medicare covers 100 percent of medically necessary home health-care services, but the individual pays 20 percent of the cost for medical equipment.[7]

Medicare covers hospice care once a doctor certifies an individual as terminally ill with six months or less to live. Coverage here includes

---

5. *Id.*
6. *Id.*
7. Ctrs. for Medicare & Medicaid Servs., Medicare & You 33 (2012).

drugs and medical costs, including equipment and services. Medicare usually does not cover things like spiritual and grief counseling.[8] An individual pays nothing for hospice care, but does pay up to $5 per prescription for outpatient drugs and 5 percent of the costs for inpatient respite care.[9]

The individual pays a deductible of $1,156 and no copayment for the first 60 days each benefit period, $289 for days 61 to 90 each benefit period, and $578 per "lifetime reserve day" after day 90 each benefit period (up to 60 days over a lifetime). Individuals pay all costs for each day after the lifetime reserve days. Inpatient mental health care in a psychiatric hospital is limited to 190 days in a lifetime.[10]

Medical Insurance (Part B)

Anyone who is eligible for free Medicare hospital insurance (Part A) can enroll in Medicare medical insurance (Part B) by paying a monthly premium. An individual who is not eligible for free hospital insurance can buy medical insurance, without having to buy hospital insurance, if that person is age 65 or older and is

- a U.S. citizen or
- a lawfully admitted noncitizen who has lived in the United States for at least five years.

Benefits

Part B helps pay for doctor services and many other medical services and supplies that are not covered by hospital insurance.

Under Original Medicare, if the Part B deductible applies, a person must pay all costs until that person meets the yearly Part B deductible ($140 in 2012) before Medicare begins to pay its share. Then, after the deductible is met, the person typically pays 20 percent of the Medicare-approved amount of the service, if the doctor or other health-care provider accepts assignment. There is no yearly limit for what a person pays out-of-pocket.[11]

---

8. *Id.* at 33.
9. *Id.* at 34.
10. *Id.* at 34.
11. *Id.* at 36.

Medicare Advantage Plans (Part C)

Individuals who have Medicare Parts A and B can join a Medicare Advantage plan. Medicare Advantage plans are offered by private companies and approved by Medicare. Medicare Advantage plans generally cover many of the same benefits that a Medigap policy (discussed below) would cover, such as extra days in the hospital after having used the number of days that Medicare covers.

Benefits

Part C plans are available in many areas. People with Medicare Parts A and B can choose to receive all of their health-care services through one of these provider organizations under Part C.[12]

Medicare Prescription Drug Plans (Part D)

Anyone who has Medicare hospital insurance (Part A), medical insurance (Part B) or a Medicare Advantage plan (Part C) is eligible for prescription drug coverage (Part D). Joining a Medicare prescription drug plan is voluntary and requires an additional monthly premium for the coverage. Some beneficiaries with higher incomes will pay a higher monthly Part D premium.

Benefits

Part D helps pay for medications that doctors prescribe for treatment.[13]

Practice Pointer: Medicare Part D

One problem lawyers may run into is that most clients have not signed up for Medicare Part D at its inception. Many clients state that the cost of the insurance was more than they were paying for drugs at the time. There was a specific enrollment period and many people simply did not enroll. Lawyers must inform their clients that a nursing home resident who is applying for Medicaid must have a Medicare Part D plan in order to have their pharmacy costs covered. There is open enrollment to a nursing home resident, but the family must work with a social worker or go to the Medicare website and enroll the resident. Copayments, deductibles, and the infamous "donut hole" (this is where Medicare has paid $2,500 of the drugs' costs and will not stop

---

12. *Apply for Medicare, supra* note 6.
13. *Id.*

paying until the costs reach $5,000) are waived when the individual is dual eligible—enrolled in both Medicare and Medicaid.

So do clients who have not yet enrolled in a Medicare Part D plan need to do so if they are applying to receive Medicaid benefits for nursing home costs? Not so fast.

If clients did not enroll in Medicare Part D because they have insurance coverage as part of their pension plan and drug coverage is part of their supplemental coverage through that plan, this can cause a very interesting dilemma. If they applied for a Medicare Part D plan, the insurance company would discontinue all coverage under the pension plan. In several instances, the nursing home resident was the husband, and if he enrolled in a Medicare Part D Plan, the company was not only dropping him from coverage, his wife would lose her insurance coverage as well. This can happen under very good insurance plans from reputable companies.

So what are the options? Don't enroll in Medicare Part D and just continue to use the pension plan and pay copays and deductibles? Drop the insurance and buy Medicare supplement plans along with the drug plans for both husband and wife? Neither seems very appealing. However, if clients chose option one, they could deduct any amount they paid for the drugs from whatever they were contributing from the income portion. Problem solved? Maybe, but what if they didn't have any income contribution? Each client situation is different and it is important to be able to discuss options with each client.

Medigap Policies

Medicare supplement insurance fills the "gaps" between Medicare benefits and what a person must pay out-of-pocket for deductibles, coinsurance, and copayments. Medigap policies are sold by private insurance companies that are typically licensed and regulated by their state Department of Insurance. These policies only pay for services that Medicare deems as medically necessary, and payments are generally based on the Medicare-approved charge. Some plans offer benefits that Medicare does not, such as emergency care while in a foreign country.[14]

---

14. *Medicare Supplement Insurance*, ILL. DEP'T OF INS. (Jan. 2011), http://insurance.illinois .gov/healthinsurance/MedSupplement.asp.

Practice Pointer: Know the State's Medigap Policies

Each state has different "Medigap policies" in place, so lawyers need to be familiar with their state's policies and requirements. For example, in Illinois, all policies sold after June 1, 2010, must offer hospice coverage; while preventive services and in-home recovery benefits are no longer sold.

Illinois requires Medigap companies to sell a person a policy—even if that person has health problems—provided that the person is at least 65 and applies within six months after enrolling in Medicare Part B, or is turning 65 and have been on Medicare due to disability previously. During this open enrollment period, a company must allow a person to buy any of the Medigap plans it offers. A person can use the open enrollment rights more than once during this six-month period. Lawyers should investigate which policies are offered within their jurisdiction.

For example, people may change their minds about a policy they bought, cancel it, and buy any other Medigap policy within six months of enrolling in Medicare Part B. Although a company must sell a policy during the open enrollment period, it may require a waiting period of up to six months before covering any preexisting conditions unless a person has had other health coverage ("creditable coverage") for at least six months on the day of applying. Preexisting conditions are conditions for which a person received treatment or medical advice from a physician within the previous six months.

An individual's right to open enrollment is absolute beginning with enrollment for Medicare Part B, even if a person waits for several years after becoming 65 to enroll in Medicare Part B because of continued employment or other reasons.

Illinois residents under age 65 who receive Medicare because of disabilities have the same open enrollment rights as seniors. A person under 65 who qualifies for Medicare because of disabilities and who applies for a Medigap policy within six months after enrolling in Medicare Part B has a six-month open enrollment period beginning the day of enrollment in Medicare Part B.

Individuals can return their Illinois Medigap policy within 30 days after receiving it and get a full refund with no questions asked.

California, Florida, and New York have supplemental policies very similar to that of Illinois.

MEDICAID

Medicaid is a hybrid program between both the federal government and the individual states. Therefore, its implementation in each state is remarkably different because the actual rules for Medicaid are created within the state and reviewed by the federal government to ensure that the states don't violate the federal rules. This leads to a wide variety of application implementations.

It is absolutely critical for a lawyer doing estate planning—or any lawyer for that matter—to know and have a good relationship with an eldercare lawyer who is experienced in assisting clients with filing for Medicaid and long-term Medicaid benefits in the state.

Case Study
The Danger of Not Being Familiar with Medicaid

One of the authors notes, "I would never want to disparage another lawyer, but sometimes I am amazed at what I hear from a client who received really bad advice from their family lawyer."

The author actually had one such client whose father was in the late stages of Parkinson's disease. The client had a very capable estate-planning lawyer work with her parents to create their estate plan. When the estate-planning documents had been prepared and signed (and the plan was simply "sweetheart" planning: "If I die, you take everything, Sweetheart. Same goes for me, Sweetheart."), one of the four daughters turned to their family lawyer and said, "What if my dad needs to go to a nursing home?" To which the lawyer replied, "You don't want to put your dad in a nursing home."

Most people don't want to put a loved one in a nursing home, but many times it cannot be avoided. Needless to say, this daughter was pretty upset when she found out that there was other planning (and better planning) that could be done. When the family lawyer called the author's firm wondering why his clients were so upset and the author mentioned the nursing home Medicaid program and the possible need for that program, the family lawyer said, "I don't know anything about nursing home Medicaid." The author replied, "That's what you should have told your clients in the first place."

The author points out that he has never received a call from an estate planner who said, "I'm doing an estate plan and I would like to make sure that I'm not doing anything to violate the Medicaid rules." However, he has seen the aftermath of mistakes made and the problems those mistakes created for people who later need these benefits. These are mistakes that would have been avoided had the lawyers known their state's Medicaid rules or sought advice from a lawyer who does.

Practice Pointer:

Lawyers should familiarize themselves with their state's Medicaid rules. If lawyers don't know them, they should refer the client to someone who does.

Most people believe that Medicaid is only for the really poor members of society and that they will never use Medicaid. There is a stigma attached to Medicaid in many people's minds because of this nearly universal belief. However, in the fight against Alzheimer's disease, Medicaid is a very important program, and lawyers must be cognizant of how it works.

The Mythology of Medicaid:

A former Illinois senator who had been a very successful accountant and had dealt with senior issues for years told one of the authors, "I don't quite understand what Medicaid has to do with senior citizens."

The author said, "In the state of Illinois, the average senior citizen does not have enough personal resources, savings, IRA, etc. to pay privately for even one year of long-term care services out-of-pocket. Therefore, almost every Illinois senior citizen's family who winds up with a loved one requiring long-term care will need to deal with Illinois's Medicaid nursing home benefit qualification rules. That's what Medicaid has to do with senior citizens."

This politician was a very capable politician who had been voting on senior issues for over 20 years. But in his position as a local layperson relative to Medicare and Medicaid, even as a politician, he had no idea that the words senior citizen and Medicaid applied to each other at any point.

The former senator is not alone in his thinking. This is an example of how little people understand Medicaid and, unfortunately, the federal government is not working very hard to break this myth. People assume that Medicare will provide care from age 65 to the grave, and that is simply not true.

Medicaid is a means-tested entitlement program that provides medical benefits to eligible individuals. The federal government gives grants to the states, covering about 50 to 80 percent of the program costs, with the state paying the balance. Each state adopts its own rules, within the federal guidelines, for administering the program.

Medicaid pays for nursing home costs for qualified individuals. It can also cover home- and community-based services such as assistance with bathing, light housekeeping, cooking, and laundry while an eligible patient with Alzheimer's remains at home if a state offers these community programs.

People sometimes forget that Alzheimer's disease will alter the life of the spouse in dramatic ways, and there are consequences that can continue long after the spouse with Alzheimer's is gone.

Practice Pointer: Burden on the Caregiving Spouse

An often overlooked aspect of Alzheimer's disease is the burden placed on caregiving spouses, who often need care themselves later.

One of the book's authors had a client whose husband had Alzheimer's disease and eventually needed long-term care beyond what his wife could provide. Despite the husband's macho declaration that he would put a gun to his head before ever going to a nursing home, the sad truth is that his wife would be the one to bear the burden caused by his long-term-care needs and her own aging challenges.

The husband and wife in this example are frugal people who worked hard all their lives. They live on two Social Security checks, his modest pension, and minimal investments. They are able to pay their bills and enjoy simple luxuries—until the out-of-pocket expenses of long-term care begin to drain what they worked a lifetime to save.

The wife selflessly provides in-home care for her beloved husband, but eventually the day will come when her strength is not enough to pick him up or keep him from wandering away from home. On that day, it might be a doctor, a discharge planner, or a police officer who looks into her eyes and speaks the harsh truth: "I'm sorry, ma'am. You can't take care of him by yourself anymore."

This poor woman will then face a nightmare as she walks the eldercare journey with a frail and declining husband. First, she will learn that neither Medicare nor their health insurance provides any payment for home health-care costs. Later, when her husband must be relocated to a long-term care facility, she will discover that neither Medicare nor Medicaid supplemental insurance will pay the facility's $3,000 to $8,000 monthly cost.

Quickly, she also will discover that Medicaid is not available because she has "too much money." Her husband's care will be offset by Medicaid only if she and her husband meet stringent income and asset limitations. If they have assets over $109,560, they will be forced to "spend down" their life savings, which Medicaid defines as "excess assets." When all excess assets have been spent on her husband's medical care, then Medicaid will also control her monthly income. In Illinois, she will be restricted to $2,739 per month from the couple's joint income. If she has more income than this of her own not counting her husband's income, the state (again, Illinois) will seek a support amount from her to contribute to the payment of his care.

Later, when her husband dies, she will receive more bad news. She may lose all or half of his pension, and as the "survivor spouse" she loses one of the two Social Security checks. She has spent nearly all of their assets to provide for her husband's care, and now she can't even afford to live in her own home. The nightmare of long-term care will leave her impoverished and will steal her independence after she has spent many years providing for his care.

She will not have the luxury of a spouse who will serve her as she served him. No one will be there to dutifully care for her at home and to delay the day that she must move to a long-term-care facility. She will not have the financial resources that he had, because Medicaid called them "excess nonexempt assets" and she spent those assets paying for her husband's care. As a single person, she will not be provided with assistance by the Medicaid system until she has become impoverished to the point of a paltry $2,000 or less in total assets. The indignity committed against her does not stop there, for now she must sign over all her income to the nursing home as well, except for a miserly personal-needs allowance of $30 per month, which is not enough to get her hair done much less to pay for personal items and replace clothing that is worn or that does not come back from the laundry at the nursing home.

The loving wife who faithfully cared for her husband is now out of money and out of options. She is alone—and living the nightmare of long-term care in America.

Practice Pointer:

Lawyers should be aware of the burden imposed on the caregiving spouse and the physical and financial dangers she faces. Someone needs to look out for her as she is busy looking out for her husband's care.

Eligibility

Eligibility is based on the applicant's medical condition and assets and income. For example, an individual must either live in a nursing home or have a medical need, such as Alzheimer's, that requires nursing home care to apply for Medicaid to cover residential long-term-care costs.

A medical assessment is necessary to establish medical eligibility in order to identify the long-term health-care needs.

It is also necessary to be a U.S. citizen or be lawfully admitted for permanent residence in the United States. Individuals are required to live in the state where they apply for Medicaid and must intend to make that state their home.

Medicaid strictly limits the assets people may own while accepting benefits. While each state has its own limits and its own exempt assets, the following are generally exempt assets that do not count against the beneficiary:

- the principal place of residence in certain situations
- household and personal belongings
- one car
- burial plot/prepaid funeral plan
- cash value of permanent life insurance policies up to $1,500
- a small amount of cash (this varies from state to state, but typically a single Medicaid applicant may keep $2,000 while married couples who both require Medicaid may keep about $3,000)

All other assets are "countable assets" and count toward the state-determined maximum. Countable assets are bank accounts, CDs, money market accounts, stocks, mutual funds, bonds, retirement accounts, pensions, second cars, second or vacation homes, and any other item that can be valued and turned into cash.

Principal Place of Residence

When there is a community spouse (the spouse still living at home), the home is considered an exempt asset. In most states, the community spouse could continue to keep a home of any value. With the passing of the Deficit Reduction Act of 2005,[15] there is now in many states a limit on the equity value that a person can have in a home. In other words, the community spouse does not have to sell the home to qualify the spouse for Medicaid.

Lawyers need to be informed of the rules in the state regarding liens placed against the home. In some states, although the home is "exempt," the state stands ready to file a lien for the amount paid toward the institutionalized spouse at the time the community spouse passes away.

When lawyers are dealing with a single individual and that individual moves out of the house to go to a nursing home, the rules change. In this scenario, the individual in the nursing home is not allowed to keep a home in most states. In some states, if the person does keep the home, the state will file a lien against that home. In Illinois, the state files a lien, but if the person moves home, a lawyer can have the lien removed.

Most states have certain limitations, ranging from $750,000 to $5 million of equity, on the maximum amount of equity that a person can have in a home or be forced to sell it. In many states, including Illinois, if a person is a single individual and goes into a nursing home, it is presumed that the person is not going home. Therefore, the state will require that the home be listed for sale if the person has not returned to the home after 120 days. That person can claim what is called an "intent to return" and not have to sell the home, but the state of Illinois will place a lien against the house, and the lien is based on whatever is the eventual total amount of Medicaid that is expended on that person's behalf, so that when that house is sold, the state has a claim against the proceeds.

The federal government allows the states to choose levels of exempt assets within a range of what's allowable under the federal standards.

---

15. Pub. L. No. 109-171 (2006).

These exempt assets, called the community spouse resource allowance (CSRA), will be the amount of money available to a community spouse as a resource allowance when an institutionalized spouse applies for benefits under the Medicaid program. Most states require full disclosure of all assets owned jointly or individually by either spouse. Illinois and many other states are not interested if this is a second marriage or if there is a prenuptial agreement.

Practice Pointer: Prenuptial/Antenuptial Agreements

When drafting clients' prenuptial or antenuptial agreements, lawyers should advise clients that if one of them has to go to a nursing home, both of them are responsible to pay for the car. Thus, the agreement may not be worth the paper on which it is written.

Additionally, in instances where one spouse needs nursing home services to be paid for by the state through the Medicaid program, there also is a limit to the income for the community spouse.

If community spouses have income of their own, lawyers need to be aware of their state's minimum monthly marital needs allowance (MMMNA).

For example, the MMMNA in Illinois is $2,739 per month. The best way to describe this MMMNA is that the state of Illinois does two levels of testing to determine whether or not there would be some sort of diversion of the institutionalized spouse's income to the healthy community spouse. Following are two examples to illustrate this point.

MMMNA Example No. 1—Alone and Making Adjustments:

The husband has a Social Security check of $1,200 per month and a pension from Ford Motor Company for another $1,200 a month. The wife has a Social Security check of $600 a month.

So, the husband is getting $2,400 a month. The only income that's coming to the wife in her name is the $600 social security check. Now, the husband needs to apply for Medicaid nursing home benefits, because he has Alzheimer's. In Illinois, the only amount of money he can keep to spend on himself is $30 per month, as a personal-needs allowance. The only other deduction from income for the husband is what he pays for supplemental insurance.

Let us assume that the husband pays $220 for his Medicare supplement (the wife's cost of insurance is not a part of the income calculation). From that $2,400, there is $2,150 left. In Illinois, the MMMNA is $2,739. What does that mean? Up to $2,139 can be diverted to the wife from what is remaining of her husband's income. So the balance of $19 must be paid to the nursing home each month. From that income, the wife now must continue paying the electric, gas bill, and grocery bill; auto gas, insurance, and maintenance; house maintenance, insurance, and taxes (hopefully not a mortgage payment); her own health insurance supplement, doctor, and pharmacy bills; and her own personal everyday needs.

When the husband dies, she will lose her $600 and probably all or half of his pension. She will go from receiving $2,739 a month down to $1,200 or $1,800 a month.

Now, by changing a few numbers, we can illustrate how harsh the MMMNA can be for individuals that are used to a slightly different lifestyle.

MMMNA Example No. 2—Drastic Lifestyle Alteration:

In this example, the community spouse still has her $600 Social Security check from working at a bank for a few years, but she became a teacher later in life and is now a retired teacher. She has a small income, but she actually wound up having a very large teacher's pension and is getting $2,100 a month for her pension. Her husband is also a retired teacher and he was a principal and has $4,000 a month for his teacher pension.

The income in his name is $4,000. The income in the wife's name is now $2,700. He gets to keep $30 for the personal-needs allowance. His teacher pension provides his insurance, so there's no deduction for a Medicare supplement. In Illinois, $39 per month is all that is going to be diverted to the community spouse, the wife, because that brings her up to the $2,739 maximum.

What happens to the rest of his money? Now, $3,961 must be paid to the nursing home and the state of Illinois only pays the difference—which truthfully won't be much due to the fact that the state does not pay the private-pay rate but pays a much smaller daily rate in most cases.

Here we have a wife who was used to living on $6,700 a month for two people, and now she's down to $2,739. That's quite a change.

These examples illustrate why people (including lawyers) who think that Medicaid is only for poor people need to rethink that idea.

Spending Down

Individuals with more assets than allowed by Medicaid must "pay down" or "spend down" their assets before they can qualify to be eligible for Medicaid benefits. If someone applies for Medicaid before "spending down" to the allowable assets, some states will deny the application and others will place the applicant in a "spend down" and require that all assets over the allowable amount be spent on care before eligibility is triggered. Although that might seem harmless, it is not!

 Case Study ───────────────────────────

Why Seeing an Elder Law Lawyer Early Is Crucial

This is an actual email that the author received from a client:

"I don't know if you can help me. My mom doesn't have a lot of assets. She owns a home and she has about $42,000 of assets. She went into the hospital but she wasn't there long enough before she was transferred to a skilled nursing facility, the nursing home rehab."

Typically that person is going either to long-term care or skilled rehab. The basic rule is that the person has to have three midnights as an inpatient in a hospital to trigger Medicare paying for a skilled-nursing facility post-hospital stay. What's happening now is that the centers for Medicare or Medicaid services have hired recovery audit contractors, who are independent contractors who get paid a lot of money to deny care, in order to save money for Medicare. Right now the recovery audit contractors are disallowing about 90 percent of one- to two-day stays in the hospital. In order to get to a skilled-nursing care facility, a person has to have a stay of three nights, or three midnights, to trigger the skilled-nursing care facility coverage that follows up.

So the client is saying her mother was on her own dime in the hospital. Now she's on her own dime in a skilled-nursing facility. They don't know what's going to happen next and don't know what they should do.

The nursing home may have even volunteered to work with the family to submit the Medicaid application. If they provide the asset information and she is approved for a spend down, the remaining $42,000 plus any sale proceeds from the home (in states where the home will not remain exempt) MUST be spent on care.

What if she needed a lawyer for powers of attorney or estate planning? What if she has not yet paid for her funeral? What if she has some credit card debt? What about the ongoing expenses related to the home? What if the real estate taxes come due next month? See, not as harmless as one might think.

Under the Deficit Reduction Act, if she made any "non-allowable transfers" in the past five years, the transfers would be totaled and a penalty assessed, and that penalty will not start to run until she is "otherwise eligible," which means not until she has completed her spend down—then the penalty period will begin, and she won't get benefits until it ends. In Illinois, no partial returns will cure a penalty after decision.

Could something have been done to start the penalty or cure it so she does not end up destitute and with Medicaid refusing to pay until the penalty is over? Yes.

Could she have used some of the $42,000 to hire a lawyer to do her estate plan and review her five years of records? Yes.

Could she have used some of the $42,000 to prepay her funeral expenses? Yes.

Could she have paid off her credit card debt and her real estate taxes? Yes.

Can she do it now after she has applied and been put in a spend down? No. All of the $42,000 must be paid to the nursing home, and all the proceeds from the sale of the home as well.

It is very important that individuals in this situation consult an experienced elder law lawyer because there are some planning steps one can take to preserve portions of current assets, pay off existing debt, purchase needed items, and still allow them to qualify for Medicaid benefits. There may be some "non-allowable" transfers (gifts) that must be cured before Medicaid benefits will be approved.

Practice Pointer:

Lawyers need to advise clients that attorney fees will be part of the allowable spend down and could provide them with a financial benefit and peace of mind. Directing the spend down before going to Medicaid will help clients pay for things they need or want (or need to pay) before the money is all designated for care.

Fortunately, lawyers' legal fees are considered a fair market expenditure for purposes of spending down. So, frankly, lawyers dealing with Medicare and Medicaid issues should be saying to their clients, "You know what, you only have X amount of money left, which you're going to spend down on care anyway, and the money you're going to pay to me as a lawyer is going to be spent down anyway, so you might as well buy my services to make life better and maybe get a better result than you would get otherwise. You might as well use the money you're going to spend anyway on hiring a lawyer to represent you and your family member who needs Medicaid to deal with these issues they have."

What about a couple? What happens when they are above the asset or "resource" allowance?

When one spouse has a disease such as Alzheimer's and needs Medicaid assistance, but the other spouse is still healthy, the couple is faced with dividing their assets. (Another less conventional approach—divorce—is discussed in chapter 6.)

Division of assets is the common term for the spousal impoverishment provision of the Medicare Catastrophic Coverage Act (MCCA) of 1988. The law was written with the intent to not impoverish both spouses when only one needs Medicaid, but it can still have harsh implications for the community spouse—the spouse not needing Medicaid.

Most states require some sort of allocation of assets between the community spouse and the institutionalized spouse. Exempt assets do not count toward the state's maximum figure. Any amount of assets over the state's maximum must be spent down prior to qualifying for Medicaid.

A couple's countable assets are calculated as of the date that the institutionalized spouse is placed in a Medicaid-certified bed. Typically this date, or the "snapshot date," is the date that the spouse enters a hospital or nursing home for a continuous stay of at least 30 days.

Thus, a couple would add up all of their countable assets as they stand on their snapshot date and divide by two. The community spouse is entitled to keep half, up to the federal maximum. For example, the federal maximum CSRA for 2012 was $113,640.[16]

16. *New York State Medicaid Update—December 2011 Volume 27—Number 16*, N.Y. DEP'T OF HEALTH, http://www.health.ny.gov/health_care/medicaid/program/update/2011/2011-12.htm (last updated Mar. 2012).

It is very important to know how the state calculates what the community spouse can keep. Although it could be as much as $113,640, it could be much less. Furthermore, the institutionalized spouse can have as much as $2,000 in countable assets in some jurisdictions, or it may be much less. Lawyers should verify asset allowances for healthy and ill spouses in their jurisdiction.

CSRA asset example and spend down:

First, a look at the "exempt assets." A couple has a house that is valued at approximately $300,000 and two vehicles. In Illinois, the community spouse can have one vehicle of any value and the institutionalized spouse can have a vehicle as long as the value is not more than $4,500 (unless it is a special vehicle for transportation due to medical needs—i.e., a wheelchair van). So, for this example, their house and cars are exempt.

In addition to the house and the cars, they have an annuity of $100,000 that is non-qualified and held jointly, they have a couple of CDs of $20,000 each, a brokerage account of $50,000, and a checking and savings account of about $15,000 total.

In Illinois, the community spouse can protect under the CSRA $109,560 and the institutionalized spouse can have a maximum amount of assets of $2,000. Anything over the $111,560, regardless of the type of asset (even IRAs), must be spent down prior to qualifying for Medicaid for the institutionalized spouse.

Lawyers can apply the same spend-down strategies to the couple as to the single individual so they can pay down any debt. They have an equity line on the house that they used to put on a new roof and siding last year. They owe $30,000, so the lawyers advise them to pay that off. They have credit card debt of $10,000. They pay off that $10,000. Two prepaid funerals of $15,000 each can be part of the spend down.

The clients just spent $70,000 to benefit themselves. They are now about $24,500 away from the allowable assets. They could upgrade the main exempt vehicle. They might need a new furnace or a new mattress or landscaping. Also, they need to pay the lawyer for helping them with this difficult and dangerous process of long-term-care planning. Now they are eligible for Medicaid and the community spouse is better protected for the future.

The department caseworker and the social worker at the nursing home will not be telling the applicant about possible spend-down strategies—this is the job of the lawyer. Clients must not go to Medicaid until they are ready. Lawyers should guide them to the spend down that best benefits them.

If a couple has substantially more assets, a good tool to keep in mind is irrevocable trust (which is discussed more in detail in chapter 4). This tool isn't for everyone, because assets cannot be returned to the person who put the money in the trust, but it is a great tool for setting aside gifts. Of course, it must survive the five-year look-back period for Medicaid purposes.

Improperly Spending Down Assets

If a spouse has Alzheimer's and needs to qualify for Medicaid, but the assets are too high, that person cannot simply give away assets until reaching the maximum figure. Spending down has to be done within the Medicaid regulations.

Lawyers need to keep in mind that there is a five-year look-back period when it comes to assets and qualifying for Medicaid. That means if the client has Alzheimer's and needs to qualify for Medicaid, any gifts the client made in the last five years can, and probably will, be scrutinized.

When a person needs to qualify for Medicaid, it is very difficult to prove that gifts made in the last five years were not made to qualify for Medicaid. In fact, it can seem like proving the client is eligible for Medicaid is tougher than defending a client charged with a serious criminal offense.

In order to put someone in prison, the government generally has a burden of proof of proving beyond a reasonable doubt that a person intended to do a bad thing. But when it comes to getting the government to write a check, for nursing home Medicaid, the burden is on the person. The general rule is that money being transferred between generations will be presumed to have been given to qualify for nursing home Medicaid. Lawyers must rebut the presumption that if the person gave away money within five years of needing nursing home Medicaid, that it was done in order to qualify for nursing home Medicaid. If lawyers do not rebut the presumption, the person will earn a penalty period of ineligibility.

This can be a substantial burden to overcome, but lawyers can help clients prevail by having them document everything.

Document Gifts to Family Members

Lawyers need to help clients create contemporaneous affidavits of transfers of money. Creating an affidavit provides some evidence to help rebut the presumption that money was given away to qualify for Medicaid. The affidavit should say, "Here are the facts and circumstances that surround my gift of $20,000 to my beloved daughter Marilyn. Marilyn needed $20,000 for emergency surgery due to a car injury" (attach a copy of the hospital bills).

The better a non-allowable transfer is documented, the better chance lawyers will have to give credible evidence that their clients were not trying to transfer money to qualify for Medicaid benefits.

Gift Tax Issues

Clients can give away up to $13,000 per recipient without filing a gift tax return. Most people hear that but do not really understand it. Lawyers know that gifting rules change almost annually. They also know that clients can give away more than $13,000 per recipient and still not pay taxes.

One of the most common myths of gifting is that the recipient of the gift pays taxes. It is counterintuitive that the person making a gift may be responsible for gift taxes on the amount gifted. Clients can give away money, and if they don't go beyond the lifetime limit, they are likely to have no gift tax issues, but they will certainly have Medicaid problems if they need nursing home care within five years of the date of the gift.

Practice Pointer: Potential Issues with Gift Tax

The fact that people don't have gift tax issues does not mean they are home free. Medicaid and the IRS don't agree on the issue of gifting.

With five years of records under scrutiny and all transfers being aggregated and brought forward to the date that the applicant is otherwise eligible, penalty periods will be imposed and the client will have no way to pay for care. The total amount of the non-allowable transfers will be divided by either the state-specific divisor or (in Illinois) by the client's semiprivate room rate in the facility.

Thus, if a client has transferred $60,000 over a five-year period, these transfers are deemed non-allowable (not for fair market value) transfers, and the client has a divisor of $6,000, the penalty period, or period of ineligibility, is 10 months. The 10-month period will not start until the client is down to the asset limit and receiving an institutionalized level of care. So, who will pay? The client is out of money. Will the community spouse have to spend down from the CSRA? Will the nursing home issue a 30-day notice that the resident must vacate the facility?

There's a chance that more and more seniors will be dumped in the emergency room due to improper spending down disqualifying people from Medicaid. These people won't be eligible for Medicaid, but they won't be able to afford private care. Unfortunately, there's no long-term-care facility that's going to take them.

Caregiver Contracts

As one generation ages, the children often take on caregiver roles. It usually starts out with things like picking up groceries for mom and dad, driving them to their appointments, and maybe giving them $100 here and there. Pretty soon the caregiver children are preparing meals, cleaning, doing the laundry, and stopping by at least once a day to check on them. At some point, a child may decide to quit a job because taking care of mom or dad has become a full-time job itself.

And what are mom and dad are doing? They are writing checks to the caregiver child for gas, for food, and for time spent cleaning and doing laundry. We're not illustrating elder abuse here. The adult child is taking care of mom and dad, but money gets commingled. The child is buying her groceries and their groceries and they're paying some and she is paying some.

In some cases, a child will move in with the parents to better care for them. Maybe the child is the power of attorney for property or at least the power of attorney for health care. Maybe the parents add that child to their bank accounts so that the child can pay bills for them, including reimbursements to the child.

Illinois actually passed a new, anti-elder-abuse power of attorney law that went into effect July 1, 2012, and there is a flat-out presumption that if agents are writing checks to themselves, that is per se abuse of the principal.

The scenario may be that a dutiful daughter, who is also the power of attorney, is taking care of her parents' accounts and is writing herself checks to cover her expenses and also to cover the fact that she has left her gainful employment in order to care for her parents. According to Illinois law, she may be considered to be committing elder abuse. She may certainly be violating the power of attorney statute. When the time comes that the parents require a higher level of care than she can provide and one or both of them go to a nursing home and they apply for Medicaid, all those checks written by the daughter will be scrutinized by the state. The caregiver may be accused of abuse, and the seniors may have a penalty period of ineligibility for nursing home Medicaid benefits.

If there was no contract in place between the parents and the daughter outlining the care to be provided and the compensation to be paid, the state will consider the transfers as non-allowable.

The current Illinois Administrative Rules state that care provided to a senior by a friend or family member is presumed to be "gratuitous."[17] The rules further state that "transfers for love and affection are not considered transfers for fair market value and thus are non-allowable and subject to penalty periods."[18] It does not stop there. The rules go on to state that if care was given in the past for free, the person giving the care (friend or family member) cannot charge for care at any time in the future. In other words, if children started caring for their parents and didn't enter into a contract and charge them for that care, they should not plan on doing it—ever. If they moved their parents in with them and the parents lived there for free, they cannot decide later to charge them rent either.

Practice Pointer:

Lawyers should prepare a care contract immediately for clients who are receiving care from friends or family members—or face the consequences later. Make sure clients understand that any care they pay for must be backed up with a contract. Lawyers must explain to the children that payments made to them for assisting their parents with care or other services will be scrutinized and can create eligibility problems down the line.

---

17. 89 ILL. CODE R. 120.388(f)(3) (LexisNexis 2012)
18. *Id.*

This is why it is so important for clients to document these situations. Here is a dutiful child trying to help out her parents, and she has unknowingly created the perfect storm by serving as a caregiver without a contract, starting out doing things for free and then taking payments and perhaps even writing the checks. She is facing potential elder-abuse accusations, and the parents, who may have dementia at this point, may not be eligible for Medicaid benefits when they need them.

This horrible situation can be avoided through a well-drafted caregiver contract.

Powerful Caretaker Contract

First, hire a geriatric care manager to go to the house and create a personalized care plan for the individual. Then draft a caregiver contract that's tied in to the care that the care manager says needs to be done. The care manager highlights what can be done by a non-licensed individual. This approach provides a very personal plan rather than drafting a generic contract once and using it for multiple situations.

Sometimes there will be a caregiver that actually is a nurse or an occupational therapist and can do some things that a typical layperson couldn't do. Often, though, it is a family member who is either out of a job or willing to leave a job to help take care of the parents, and this person needs to get paid. In addition, the lawyer should work with the family to get them set up with a bookkeeping service. That way they can accurately keep track of their time. It's also a good idea to have them come back in to go through their first month of logs to make sure they really know what they're doing and that they're doing it the right way. Sooner or later, lawyers will be dealing with those logs, and if they didn't take care of them, they are not going to pass the evidentiary test.

This type of contract allows lawyers to know that they are setting this whole family up to make sure that money passing from the senior to the junior will pass the caregiver contract test. Depending on the mental condition of the principal, someone might need to evaluate the principal's capacity to make these kinds of statements.

Lawyers also need to modify the statutory power of attorney to specifically state that agents have authority to hire themselves on behalf of the principal, as a caregiver.

A lot more goes into drafting a good caregiver contract than one would originally think.

Some lawyers might think this level of drafting is unnecessary, but if the contract is not drafted correctly, a client runs the risk of being accused of being an elder abuser. On top of that, lawyers may have senior clients who wind up with penalty periods of ineligibility for Medicaid benefits that they need to pay for care.

Employment Taxes

Under a caregiver agreement, family caregivers do not owe self-employment tax on the payment for a family member unless they are in the business of providing care to others.[19]

According to the Internal Revenue Service, special rules apply to workers (caregivers) who perform in-home services for the elderly or individuals with disabilities. Caregivers are typically employees of the individual for whom they provide services because they work in the homes of the elderly or individuals with disabilities and these individuals have the right to tell the caregivers what needs to be done. These services may or may not be provided by a family member. If the caregiver employee is a family member, the employer may not owe employment taxes even though the employer needs to report the caregivers' compensation on a W-2. (See Publication 926 Household Employers Tax Guide for more information.) However, in some cases, the caregivers are not employees. In such cases, the caregiver must still report the compensation as income on Form 1040 and may be required to pay self-employment tax depending on the facts and circumstances.[20]

State Examples of Medicaid

Below are the Medicaid statutory requirements for Illinois, Florida, California, and New York. While the requirements may be generally similar from state to state, individual states may have nuances that require knowledge of the state's statutes.

Illinois

The Illinois Department of Human Services website states that, for medical assistance, a person has to be either blind, disabled, or aged

---

19. *See* IRS Form 1040; *see also Family Caregivers and Self-Employment Tax*, INTERNAL REVENUE SERV., http://www.irs.gov/Businesses/Small-Businesses-&-Self-Employed/Family-Caregivers-and-Self-Employment-Tax (last updated May 3, 2013).
20. *Id.*

(65 or older); have children under the age of 19; or be pregnant.[21] The person must also meet financial eligibility criteria, meet residency requirements, and in most cases be citizens (except for children).[22]

The eligibility requirements for Medicaid or medical assistance in Illinois are set out in detail in several statutory provisions. Illinois Compiled Statutes chapter 305, act 5, section 5-2 addresses the general eligibility requirements. It contains 16 "classes of persons" who are eligible.[23]

Recipients of basic maintenance grants are defined by sections 3-1 and 4-0.5. Section 3-1 provides Medicaid coverage to people who are 65 or older, are blind, or have disabilities.[24] There is an additional requirement under section 3-1 that in order to be eligible, the person must be receiving Supplemental Security Income (SSI) or have been found ineligible for SSI on the basis of income.[25]

Section 3-1 states, "'Aged person' means a person who has attained age 65, as demonstrated by such evidence of age as the Illinois Department may by rule prescribe."[26]

The same section defines "disabled person" as

a person age 18 or over who has a physical or mental impairment, disease, or loss which is of a permanent nature and which substantially impairs his ability to perform labor or services or to engage in useful occupations for which he is qualified, as determined by rule and regulation of the Illinois Department. For purposes of this Act, an Illinois Disabled Person Identification Card issued pursuant to The Illinois Identification Card Act, indicating that the person thereon named has a Type 1 or 2, Class 2 disability shall be evidence that such person is a disabled person under this Section; however, such a card shall not qualify such person for aid as a disabled person under this Act, and eligibility for aid as a disabled person shall be determined as provided in this Act. If federal law or regulation permit or require the inclusion of blind or disabled persons whose blindness or disability is not of the degree specified in the foregoing definitions, or permit or require the inclusion of disabled persons under age 18 or aged persons under age 65, the Illinois Department, upon written approval of the

---

21. *See Medical Assistance Programs*, ILL. DEP'T OF HUMAN SERVS., http://www.dhs.state.il.us /page.aspx?item=30359 (last visited May 24, 2012).
22. *Id.*
23. *See* 305 ILL. COMP. STAT. 5/5-2 (2011).
24. *See id.* 5/3-1.
25. *See id.*
26. *See id.*

Governor, may provide by rule that all aged, blind or disabled persons toward whose aid federal funds are available be eligible for assistance under this Article as is given to those who meet the foregoing definitions of blind person and disabled person or aged person.[27]

The statutes also provide that people who would qualify as 65 or older, blind, or with disabilities but would *not* qualify under that section on a need basis may still be eligible if they meet certain financial-need requirements.[28] Those requirements are as follows:

(i) their income, as determined by the Illinois Department in accordance with any federal requirements, is equal to or less than 70% in fiscal year 2001, equal to or less than 85% in fiscal year 2002 and until a date to be determined by the Department by rule, and equal to or less than 100% beginning on the date determined by the Department by rule, of the nonfarm income official poverty line, as defined by the federal Office of Management and Budget and revised annually in accordance with Section 673(2) of the Omnibus Budget Reconciliation Act of 1981, applicable to families of the same size; or

(ii) their income, after the deduction of costs incurred for medical care and for other types of remedial care, is equal to or less than 70% in fiscal year 2001, equal to or less than 85% in fiscal year 2002 and until a date to be determined by the Department by rule, and equal to or less than 100% beginning on the date determined by the Department by rule, of the nonfarm income official poverty line, as defined in item (i) of this subparagraph (a).[29]

People who would "otherwise qualify for Aid to the Medically Indigent under Article VII" are also eligible.[30] It should be noted that it is not clear whether this class is still relevant since the statutory section it references has been repealed.

Additionally, people otherwise ineligible who "fall sick, are injured, or die" and could not afford "necessary medical care or funeral and burial expenses" qualify.[31]

---

27. *See id.*
28. *See id.* 5/5-2 (2)(a)(i)–(ii).
29. *Id.*
30. *See id.* 5/5-2(3).
31. *See id.* 5/5-2(4).

People who were previously eligible but have become ineligible due to employment earnings, when they satisfy certain additional requirements, are eligible.[32]

Those people who are employed and disabled and also meet certain federal Medicaid requirements under the Social Security Act qualify for Illinois Medicaid as well.[33]

There are additional qualifying classes of people in Illinois, but those classes do not pertain directly to this book.

Florida

Florida's eligibility requirements are quite distinct from those in Illinois. In Florida the Department of Children and Family Services make eligibility determinations.[34]

Eligible classes of people to receive *mandatory* payments for medical assistance and related services are set out in the Florida Statutes, title XXX, section 409.903.[35]

Although there are several groups or classifications that qualify for Medicaid in Florida, we will focus on those that apply to Alzheimer's disease.

One eligible group is people who receive benefits from or who did receive and lost benefits from the SSI program. "This category includes a low-income person age 65 or over and a low-income person under age 65 considered to be permanently and totally disabled."[36]

Another eligible group classification is a "person who is age 65 or over or is determined by the agency to be disabled, whose income is at or below 100 percent of the most current federal poverty level and whose assets do not exceed limitations established by the agency."[37]

There is an additional group of people who *may* receive assistance with their medical costs, subject to availabilities of moneys. Those groups are defined under Florida Statues section 409.904.[38]

The first group of optional Medicaid recipients is for, "[s]ubject to federal waiver approval, a person who is age 65 or older or is determined

---

32. *See id.* 5/5-2(8).
33. *See id.* 5/5-2(11).
34. *See* FLA. STAT. ANN. § 409.902 (West 2012).
35. *See id.* § 409.903.
36. *See id.* § 409.903(2).
37. *See id.* § 409.903(8).
38. *See id.* § 409.904.

to be disabled, whose income is at or below 88 percent of the federal poverty level, whose assets do not exceed established limitations, and who is not eligible for Medicare or, if eligible for Medicare, is also eligible for and receiving Medicaid-covered institutional care services, hospice services, or home and community-based services. The agency shall seek federal authorization through a waiver to provide this coverage."[39]

The second group of optional aid recipients is for "[a] family, a pregnant woman, a child under age 21, a person age 65 or over, or a blind or disabled person, who would be eligible under any group listed in s. 409.903(1), (2), or (3), except that the income or assets of such family or person exceed established limitations."[40]

The third group of optional aid recipients is for "[a] person who is in need of the services of a licensed nursing facility, a licensed intermediate care facility for the developmentally disabled, or a state mental hospital, whose income does not exceed 300 percent of the SSI income standard, and who meets the assets standards established under federal and state law."[41] This section also includes several steps to be taken in determining the person's income.[42]

The fourth group is for people who meet all the Medicaid requirements but are not citizens and who need emergency medical services.[43]

California

California's Department of Health Care Services website provides a fairly clear breakdown of those who are eligible for Medi-Cal (California's Medicaid program).[44]

The department's website indicates that enrollment in several state or federal programs may create eligibility for Med-Cal. Those programs include "SSI/SSP, CalWorks (AFDC), Refugee Assistance, Foster Care or Adoption Assistance Program, and In-Home Supportive Services (IHSS)."[45] The website also indicates other ways one can qualify for Medi-Cal, if the person is

---

39. *See id.* § 409.904(1).
40. *See id.* § 409.904(2).
41. *See id.* § 409.904(3).
42. Id.
43. *See id.* § 409.904(4).
44. *See Do I Qualify for Medi-Cal Benefits?*, Dep't of Health Care Servs., http://www.dhcs
     .ca.gov/services/medi-cal/Pages/DoYouQualifyForMedi-Cal.aspx (last visited May 10,
     2013).
45. *Id.*

65 or older, blind, disabled, under 21, pregnant, in a skilled nursing or intermediate care home, on refugee status for a limited time, depending how long you have been in the United States, a parent or caretaker relative or a child under 21 if: the child's parent is deceased or does not live with the child, or the child's parent is incapacitated, or the child's parent is under employed or unemployed, or have been screened for breast and/or cervical cancer.[46]

California's statutory scheme, which creates these groups and benefits, is very complex, with each group being granted an entitlement through a separate statutory section, to be distinguished from Illinois and Florida where the classes of benefited people were all contained within a single statute.[47]

Section 14005.40, for example, qualifies people 65 or older and people with disabilities for Medi-Cal, assuming that those individuals satisfy certain financial-need requirements as set out in that section.[48]

Section 14005.30 (eligibility for Medi-Cal benefits) is a somewhat broader-reaching provision, which qualifies people for Medi-Cal who satisfy the requirements of section 1396u-1 of title 42 of the United States Code.[49] Thus, by satisfying the federal requirements a person is qualified to receive Medi-Cal in California.[50]

Section 14005.42 (individuals receiving aid under Kinship Guardian Assistance Payment Programs; full-scope benefits) grants eligibility to all people "on behalf of whom kinship guardians are receiving aid under any of the Kinship Guardian Assistance Payment Programs pursuant to Article 4.5 (commencing with Section 11360) of Chapter 2."[51]

Section 14006.01 (continuing care retirement community that collects an entrance fee; resident; eligibility for Medi-Cal benefits) qualifies any person for Medi-Cal benefits who is living in a continuing care retirement community that requires an entrance fee.[52]

There are many additional sections that cover Medi-Cal qualifications that are not pertinent to this book.

---

46. Id.
47. *See* CAL. WELF. & INST. CODE § 14005.40 (West 2009).
48. *See id.*
49. *See id.* § 14005.30; 42 U.S.C.A. § 1396u-1 (West 1999).
50. *See* CAL. WELF. & INST. CODE § 14005.30.
51. *See id.* § 14005.42.
52. *See id.* § 14006.01.

New York

New York's Department of Health website contains a lot of useful information for determining eligibility for Medicaid.[53] Of particular interest is a chart on the website that indicates how much income people can receive monthly or annually and still qualify for Medicaid. It also indicates the quantity of resources that people retain and still qualify for Medicaid.[54]

Also available on New York's Department of Health website is a Medicaid Reference Guide, available for download as a PDF.[55] This guide, whose introduction indicates it should be used as an almanac, reference, or dictionary, covers the eligibility requirements for receiving Medicaid.[56] The reference guide indicates that an applicant may be eligible for Medicaid in any one of the following categories:

- receiving Supplemental Security Income (SSI);
- eligible under Low Income Families (LIF); or
- SSI-related (Aged, certified blind/disabled); under age 21.[57]

The statute that regulates the qualifications for Medicaid in New York is Social Services Law section 366.[58] This statute makes several different groups of people eligible for Medicaid, including, but not limited to,

- a person that is eligible for the safety net program, a public assistance program for the needy;[59]
- a person that is eligible for federal SSI, assuming there are not duplicative payments to the people who are blind, are 65 or older, or have disabilities, from both the federal and state Medicaid programs;[60]
- a person that meets certain financial need requirements and "is (i) sixty-five years of age or older, or certified blind or certified dis-

---

53. *Medicaid in New York State*, N.Y. Dep't of Health, http://www.health.ny.gov/health
_care/medicaid/ (last visited May 25, 2012).

54. *Id.*

55. N.Y. Dep't of Health, Medicaid Reference Guide (2012), *available at* http://www
.health.ny.gov/health_care/medicaid/reference/mrg/mrg.pdf.

56. *Id.*

57. *Id.* at 3.

58. *See* N.Y. Soc. Serv. Law § 366 (McKinney 2011).

59. *See id.* § 366(1)(a).

60. *See id.* § 366(2).

abled or (ii) for reasons other than income or resources, is eligible for federal supplemental security income benefits and/or additional state payments"; or [61]

- a person that is "a resident of a home for adults operated by a social services district or a residential care center for adults or community residence operated or certified by the office of mental health" and is unable, due to insufficient income or resources, to meet all the costs of required medical care and services.[62]

VETERANS AFFAIRS BENEFITS

There are substantial benefits that may be available to wartime veterans who are now senior citizens and are facing the burden of long-term care due to a host of diseases, including Alzheimer's disease. It is important for lawyers to be aware of these benefits because the Department of Veterans Affairs (VA) estimates that millions of wartime veterans and their spouses may be eligible for special monthly pension benefits and are not even aware of the benefits.[63]

There are many types of benefits available to veterans through the VA for things such as education, life insurance, health care, home loans, and burial benefits. The two major categories of benefits are compensation and pension.[64]

Compensation is a benefit that veterans receive when the veteran has a disability caused by, or exacerbated by, military services and is not applicable for this book. However, the non-service-connected pension is very applicable.

Non-Service-Connected Disability Pension

A pension is a benefit for veterans or their surviving spouses with low incomes who are permanently and totally disabled when that disability is *not* related to military service. This is often referred to as a "special monthly pension" (or sometimes an "improved pension"). Veterans are considered to have a permanent and total disability if they are:

---

61. *See id.* § 366(5).
62. *See id.* § 366(6).
63. LAW ELDERLAW, THE NUTS AND BOLTS GUIDE TO VETERANS BENEFITS (rev. ed. Dec. 30, 2010).
64. *See* U.S. DEP'T OF VETERANS AFFAIRS, VA FORM 21-0501, VETERANS BENEFITS TIMETABLE (2009), *available at* http://www.vba.va.gov/pubs/forms/VBA-21-0501-ARE.pdf.

- patients in a nursing home for long-term care because of disability;
- receiving Social Security disability benefits;
- unemployable as a result of a disability that is reasonably certain to continue throughout their life; or
- suffering from any disease or disorder determined by the Secretary of the Department of Veterans Affairs to be a permanent or total disability.[65]

In 2011, the maximum disability pension rate for a veteran with no dependents was $11,830, which worked out to $995 per month. The rate for a veteran with one dependent or for two veterans married to each other was $15,493, or $1,291 per month. Each additional dependent child added $2,020, or $168 per month, to the pension.[66]

The amount of the special monthly pension increases if the veteran with permanent disabilities is also housebound. People are considered housebound if they have a permanent and total disability and either have an additional disability, or disabilities, ratable at 60 percent or more or are substantially confined to their residence or the immediate premises due to a disability that is reasonably certain to remain throughout their lifetime.[67]

In 2011, the maximum pension for a housebound veteran with no dependents was $14,457, or $1,204 per month. If the housebound veteran had one dependent, the maximum pension was $18,120, or $1,510 per month. If a surviving spouse was housebound, the maximum pension was $9,696, or $808 per month. With a dependent child, the maximum pension was $12,144, or $1,012 per month. Again, each additional dependent increased the pension $2,020, or $168 per month.[68]

If the veteran is in need of regular aid and attendance, the maximum special monthly pension is increased further to $19,736, or $1,644 per month (using 2011 figures) if the veteran has no dependents. With one dependent, the maximum pension in 2011 was $23,396, or $1,949 per month. To be in need of regular aid and attendance, the veteran or spouse must have a permanent or total disability and be (1) a patient in a nursing home; (2) blind, or nearly blind; or (3) needing the regular

---

65. N.Y. Soc. Serv. Law § 366(6).
66. Id.
67. Id.
68. Id.

aid and attendance of another person to perform basic activities of daily living, such as dressing, bathing, and attending to the wants of nature.[69]

Low-income, wartime veterans who attain the age of 65 are also entitled to a pension, known as a service pension, whether or not they have a disability. The amount of the maximum pension is the same as the special monthly pension.

Income/Net Worth Requirements

In order to be eligible to receive any of the above non-service-connected pensions, the veteran must meet income and net worth requirements.

First, the annual maximum pension amount is decreased, dollar for dollar, by the veteran's countable income. Income that is countable is generally all of the veteran's income, including that of a spouse or any dependents, *minus* unreimbursed medical expenses. Unreimbursed medical expenses include doctor fees, dentist fees, Medicare premiums and copayments, insurance premiums, transportation to physician offices, and the costs of assisted-living facilities or in-home aides.[70]

> **Example**
>
> If a veteran has $20,000 in income and $10,000 in unreimbursed medical expenses, the countable income is $10,000. The $10,000 in countable income is deducted from the maximum annual special monthly pension of $11,830 for a benefit of $985. As another example, suppose the veteran is in a nursing home (and so qualifies for the additional pension for aid and attendance) and has an income of $50,000. If the unreimbursed medical expenses for the nursing home are $5,000 per month, or $60,000, the veteran's countable income is negative $10,000. Any negative income is counted as an income of $0, and the veteran will be eligible for the maximum annual special monthly pension for aid and attendance of $19,736.

In addition to low income, the veteran must also have a limited net worth. The VA has not specifically defined "limited net worth"; however, a general guide is that the veteran must have a net worth lower than $50,000 if single or $80,000 if married.

---

69. *Id.*
70. *Id.*

> **2011 Income Figures for Eligibility**
>
> This is a needs-based program with income and asset tests.
>
> - Income limitation
>   - Gross income minus certain expenses
>   - Unreimbursed medical expenses of veteran and his/her household
>   - Certain educational expenses
>   - After reducing gross income by the above expenses, net income must be lower than $11,181 to $22,113, depending on a person's circumstances
> - Net worth limitation
>   - In addition to house, car, life insurance, burial policies, and annuities in payout status, a person can generally have between $50,000 and $80,000 in assets, including CDs, stocks, bonds, etc.

Possible Medicaid Trap

It is important for lawyers to be aware of the Medicaid qualifications and rules when considering whether one meets the VA asset limitation test. Lawyers should advise their clients that giving away cash or other things of value can create terrible problems for senior citizens if or when they later need to apply for Medicaid to assist them with skilled-nursing care. Giving away assets can create a long penalty period of ineligibility for Medicaid benefits.

DIC Benefits

Under Dependency and Indemnity Compensation (DIC), the unmarried spouses, dependent children, and parents of veterans can all potentially be eligible for the wide variety of benefits the VA offers.[71]

Spouses and children of service members may also qualify for certain group life insurance programs.[72]

---

71. See *Dependency and Indemnity Compensation (DIC)*, U.S. Dep't of Veterans Affairs, http://www.benefits.va.gov/BENEFITS/factsheets/survivors/dic.pdf (last visited June 26, 2012).
72. See U.S. Dep't of Veterans Affairs, Family Servicemembers' Group Life Insurance, http://www.benefits.va.gov/BENEFITS/factsheets/insurance/SGLI.pdf (last visited June 26, 2012).

Parents who are dependent on a veteran may qualify for financial support benefits. This benefit is based on need.[73] There are also benefits for the "dependents of a deceased wartime veteran."[74]

A surviving spouse is eligible for DIC benefits if the spouse:

- validly married the veteran before January 1, 1957;
- was married to a service member who died on active duty;
- married the veteran within 15 years of discharge from the period of military service in which the disease or injury that caused the veteran's death began or was aggravated;
- was married to the veteran for at least one year, *or*
- had a child with the veteran, *and*
- cohabited with the veteran continuously until the veteran's death or, if separated, was not at fault for the separation, *and*
- is not currently remarried.[75]

A child qualifies for DIC benefits if the child is

- not included on the surviving spouse's DIC;
- unmarried; and
- under the age 18, or is between the ages of 18 and 23 and attending school.[76]

In situations where a veteran died on or after January 1, 1993, the spouse gets a basic monthly rate of $1,195.[77] There are additional allowances for when the veteran was eligible for service-related disability at the time of death and if the spouse is eligible for aid and attendance or housebound benefits pursuant to 38 U.S.C. 1311(c) and (d).[78]

However, a spouse who remarries cannot generally receive benefits. There is an exception for a spouse who remarries on or after December 16, 2003, and on or after turning 57, to continue receiving DIC benefits.[79]

73. *See Veteran's Dependent Parent Benefit*, U.S. Dep't of Veterans Affairs, http://www .benefits.va.gov/BENEFITS/factsheets/misc/DependentParent.pdf (last visited June 26, 2012).
74. *See Survivors Pension Benefits*, U.S. Dep't of Veterans Affairs, http://www.benefits .va.gov/BENEFITS/factsheets/survivors/Survivorspension.pdf (last visited May 10, 2013).
75. U.S. Dep't of Veterans Affairs, Dependency and Indemnity Compensation (DIC) (2008) http://www.benefits.va.gov/BENEFITS/factsheets/survivors/dic.pdf.
76. *Id.*
77. 38 U.S.C. § 1311(a)(1) (2012).
78. *Id.* § 1311(c)–(d).
79. *Veteran's Dependent Parent Benefit, supra* note 73.

In cases where the spouse is entitled to DIC benefits, each additional child over the age of 18 may receive $251 a month if in school and $505 if determined to be "helpless."[80]

The amount of benefits for parents varies on income and whether there are one or two surviving parents and whether they are living with the spouse.[81]

As always, lawyers should familiarize themselves with all of the benefits available for veterans and their dependents and to consider the interplay between these benefits and other benefits, such as Medicaid, prior to advising clients.

California Medigap

http://www.medicare.gov/Publications/Pubs/pdf/02110.pdf

Florida Medigap

http://www.myfloridacfo.com/consumers/Guides/Health/docs
/Med%20Supp%20Insurance%20Overview.pdf

New York Medigap

http://www.dfs.ny.gov/insurance/medplan/Medsup_coverage.pdf

---

80. *Compensation*, U.S. DEP'T OF VETERANS AFFAIRS, http://www.benefits.va.gov /COMPENSATION/index.asp?expandable=0 (last visited May 10, 2013).

81. *Id.*

 **Expert View**

The Red Flag of Alzheimer's: A Change of Character

Dr. William Thies is currently the senior scientist in residence at the Alzheimer's Association, having served previously as the chief medical and scientific officer. Before joining the Alzheimer's Association, Dr. Thies worked at the American Heart Association. Prior to that, he held faculty positions at Indiana University in Bloomington and the University of Pittsburgh.

Q: Dr. Thies, lawyers are laypeople when it comes to Alzheimer's disease. From your point of view, what are some of the most important things that lawyers need to understand?

A: The worst part of Alzheimer's disease is the later stages of the disease, and if we actually found ways to keep people from getting into those late stages, we would save an immense amount of human suffering, because people's quality of life goes to zero, plus the fact that their family is devastated by it and it can rob them of all of their resources at the same time.

    This disease is one of the major cost drivers in a health-care system that is becoming a major cost driver for our whole economy—and we've got to find ways to lighten the load or it's going to wreck the whole economy.

Q: What factors are observable to lawyers and other people to be able to say, "I think Chris or Mary may be suffering from Alzheimer's disease"?

A: Changes in behavior—that is the biggest thing to look for. For example, losing interest in hobbies—the guy who always got the newspaper first thing in the morning so he could do the crossword, and now he doesn't do it anymore. Look for changes in sleeping patterns. The person who was always up early and worked all day in one way or the other, and now all of a sudden he or she is sleeping a lot during the day. Drinking—certainly whether that's a cause or an effect, I think is open to debate—but somebody who never drank and all of a sudden is drinking a significant amount. Those sorts of changes are markers of something different going on.

    If they have a spouse, they're going to be driving that spouse crazy because they have become totally undependable. They're driving them crazy asking them about 150 times from about 3:30 to 5:30, "What's for dinner?" That's really significant.

Think about what nine out of 10 people would say about your father. For example, was he funny or was he serious? Was he very punctual? Good with money? Interested in certain things? And if any of that starts to deteriorate, you should start thinking, "Gosh, this is serious."

One of the things that's very clear is that a fairly large portion of our population is living at home in early stages of Alzheimer's disease, early stages of dementia—and unless the community gathers around and tries to help them, they are in great danger. A lot of people live alone—more people are living as singles who have lost their spouse, and their children have grown up and moved away, and now they are by themselves. Nobody sees their decline in cognitive function. They fall off the radar at their doctor's office, and even if they have an attorney, they fall off the radar there as well. No one calls and says, "How are you doing?" I think that's a significant worry for a substantial portion of our population. It's a societal problem.

There was the notorious case of a car dealer that sold a gentleman eight new cars in nine months because the man couldn't remember that he had recently bought a car. He would purchase the car, park it someplace, and not remember where he parked it. He had a distant memory that he needed a car and where to buy a car, but not where he parked the new car. When this problem was discovered, the car dealer was unapologetic. He said, "I sell cars, what do I know? The guy kept coming back and saying he wanted a new car, and I'm just trying to meet my customers' needs."

A man puts on a new roof after only three years—not that he has forgotten what a new roof is for, but rather he doesn't remember that he already did it.

Q: What else should lawyers keep in mind?

A: Subtle cognitive decline may come to the attention of a lawyer much earlier than an actual diagnosis of dementia. In helping lawyers to make assessments of individuals, we don't want to turn lawyers into doctors—you don't want the lawyers doing diagnoses in their office—but they are potentially an early warning group because a frequent early characteristic of Alzheimer's disease is that a person becomes less effective at something he or she was very good at, and it's clearly a change. The same thing can apply to financial decisions. It's one thing to be looking at all kinds of legal or insurance documents and not be able to understand them, but when you add a relatively modest amount of decline in cognitive function, those sorts of things get harder and harder.

The client is not showing up for appointments when they schedule them; they're making three appointments for the same thing.

There's going to be cognitive impairment—which is distinguished from dementia because it comes sooner and it's much more subtle—for example, the person who was always considered a careful dresser, but now you see her mismatched and slightly disheveled, or the person who was always scrupulously on time, and all of a sudden that begins to deteriorate. Those are the habits of a lifetime, and when those start to disappear, you're looking at somebody who is having some substantial cognitive difficulties.

Q: Is there anything else you would like to add?

A: Another thing that happens in families that causes havoc is that people don't see these changes as a manifestation of disease. They see it as the emergence of some sort of character flaw in their loved one. Dementia tends to aggravate a lot of the dysfunction within a family, and I think one of the key things that a lawyer can do in that setting is to try and get those people some education about the disease. There's real science behind the idea that people cope better with Alzheimer's if they understand that it is a disease and if they understand the sequence and can anticipate what's coming next, and if they understand that other people have gone through this and survived. It's great to get education to people, and that's one of the reasons for the support program of the Alzheimer's Association.

CHAPTER 6

GUARDIANSHIPS AND CONSERVATORSHIPS

"Circling Schemers," by Shay Jacobson, RN, MA, NMG, President Life Care Innovations, Inc.

Mrs. Weiss was in the throes of a "casual care" relationship when referred as a possible guardianship candidate. "Casual care" refers to the complex web of neighbors, acquaintances, service providers, and others who occupy the periphery of a client's life and then gradually (or suddenly) find a pivotal role for themselves in the care and oversight of a vulnerable person. They appear to be well-meaning, sincere, and good-hearted, but are not.

Mrs. Weiss and her husband were financially successful, had assets that hovered in the area of $35 million, and had established a solid estate plan. However, when Mr. Weiss died, Mrs. Weiss's world spun in an unexpected orbit.

Mr. Weiss had always taken care of all of their finances. Tackling this unknown and unsavory job at the age of 84 was not an appealing proposition for Mrs. Weiss.

Compounding her lack of interest in managing her finances was Mrs. Weiss's situational depression following her husband's unexpected death, and the mild dementia she was hoping no one had noticed over the past couple of years. That dementia was an obstacle to the development of new skills. Even if she had an interest in juggling the details of her $35 million estate, her dementia would have precluded the acquisition of these new skills.

Fortunately, Mrs. Weiss had a number of financial professionals charged with managing her estate.

Sadly, it was one of these financial representatives who let her down first. His fees for managing her IRAs had, on average, run about $7,000 annually before Mr. Weiss died. In the first year after Mr. Weiss's death, those fees spiked to a shocking $200,000. While it's entirely possible there was a bit of extra management needed in those post-mortem months, an increase of this magnitude is strongly suggestive of opportunism. Mrs. Weiss's ability to recognize the irregularity of a staggering fee hike was clouded by her depression and blossoming dementia.

The next person to see the glow of illicit opportunity in Mrs. Weiss's situation was the relative of a neighbor. She was in the area just enough, and had heard just enough, to understand that a lonely, grieving, and slightly demented woman with a great deal of money might appreciate some company. She might even appreciate it so much she would pay for it. Maybe she would even add her to the will!

The neighbor's relative started popping by quite often to see Mrs. Weiss. Now, she was playing the role of a close and dear friend whose every moment was consumed with the comfort and well-being of Mrs. Weiss.

The new friend, who we'll call Bonnie, ingratiated herself initially by offering to help out around the house and shop for groceries. There were probably a lot of lingering conversations over coffee as groceries were dropped off and the garden was tended, and Mrs. Weiss quickly warmed to the idea of having someone fussing over her with great regularity.

Bonnie's next offer involved all that pesky money and property management. She put her name on a $400,000 bank account as co-owner with Mrs. Weiss. She became power of attorney. Long-standing relationships with financial professionals and institutions were systematically terminated, which was, in the end, Bonnie's undoing.

The trust officers who had dutifully and honorably served Mrs. Weiss for 20 years would not merely stand by and allow this new best friend to unravel Mrs. Weiss's estate plan. They decided to stop Bonnie by pursuing guardianship.

The longtime trust officers brought the matter to the guardianship court for assessment of Mrs. Weiss's competencies and protection of her person and assets. Mrs. Weiss went through a battery of tests and was diagnosed with moderate dementia and depression. It was determined that she was not able to manage her finances but should participate in her personal life choices. A third-party guardian was appointed to sort out the web of intrigue that surrounded this gentle woman.

The guardian sifted through the rubble of Bonnie's activities. The $400,000 bank account that she put her name on as co-owner was returned to its prior sole owner, Mrs. Weiss. The new will Bonnie had orchestrated, and the relocation of the trusts to new financial institutions, was determined by the court to have been done after Mrs. Weiss's testamentary capacity had waned. The original plan was thus honored. Mrs. Weiss was provided professional caregivers that came from a licensed, bonded, and insured agency.

Mrs. Weiss now lives in her home with a 24-hour caregiver. She travels weekly to the university where she once worked to attend lectures and remain a part of the professional community that was her family. The guardian serves as insulation from professional opportunists that recognize her vulnerability. Without the protection of a guardian, her world would predictably remain in a helter-skelter pattern, and her financial investments would fill the pockets of the circling schemers who prey on the vulnerable.

Guardianship is designed to protect those who are overwhelmed due to age-related frailties, disabilities, or injuries. The goal is to maximize independence but also to protect and proactively prevent exploitation. Mrs. Weiss is living in the community, using her resources to enhance her person-centered care plan as she ages in safety.

Now that the era of casual care has ended, Mrs. Weiss is thriving in a structured setting, and her plan, as designed by her and her husband, is back on track.

GUARDIANSHIP TO THE RESCUE

A guardianship is a legal relationship that is established and monitored by state courts under state laws. It is a mechanism for empowering someone (the guardian) to act on behalf of an incapacitated individual (the ward).

In the case of estate planning for a client with Alzheimer's, guardianships are usually a last resort. Unfortunately, if lawyers are approached by a client with a loved one suffering from Alzheimer's and proper planning was not undertaken prior to them becoming a client—that last resort will become a necessity, unless a geriatric psychiatrist or other appropriate health-care professional finds that the client retains sufficient testamentary capacity. (See chapter 2.)

Each state has its own statutes, rules, and procedures for initiating guardianships and for managing the personal and financial affairs of adults who have disabilities or are incapacitated for whom a guardian is appointed. The terminology associated with these legal relationships varies a bit by state. Some states use the terms "guardians" and "conservator" interchangeably while some states use the term "guardian" to refer to a guardian of the person, and "conservator" to apply to a guardian of the estate.

Whatever term a state uses, the purpose of the guardianship or conservatorship is to ensure the financial and personal well-being of adults who are incapacitated or have disabilities.

Most states tend to impose the least restrictive guardianship or conservatorship as is necessary to maintain the well-being of the incapacitated person so as to preserve as many rights of the incapacitated person as possible.

Practice Pointer: Guardianship versus Powers of Attorney

An agent under a power of attorney trumps a guardian with respect to the exercise of any powers covered by the power of attorney. This is because courts defer to the person who was nominated by the person with alleged disabilities at a time when the person was not under a disability.

GUARDIAN DEFINED

A guardian is someone appointed by the court to serve as a representative of the person with a legal disability—for purposes of this book, Alzheimer's disease or other dementia.

A court-appointed guardian has the authority to make decisions for the person with Alzheimer's without judicial involvement, provided the decisions are consistent with the procedures and requirements of the governing statutes or regulations of that state. Guardians typically are required to provide periodic accounting to the court.

Disability must be assessed according to statutory definitions and "cannot be inferred merely from old age."[1]

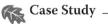 **Case Study**

Age, by Itself, Is Not a Disability

Some people are the subject of guardianship proceedings because their conduct is somewhat contrary to our natural norms of society.

A 96-year-old man wanted to go to Las Vegas and marry his caregiver. Some of his family members questioned whether he was competent and started a guardianship proceeding to try to stop him. The judge did find that although he, too, thought it was a stupid decision to marry the caregiver, this man was competent to make those stupid decisions. The man did not need a guardian and was free to make bad personal decisions.

One of the authors, Kerry Peck, notes that, "Competent people are able to make stupid decisions, and we hear judges say that on a pretty regular basis."

Practice Pointer: Ask "Orientation Questions"

It is a good idea for lawyers to ask "orientation questions" when dealing with potential clients who may come in for an estate plan or ask for a lawyer to defend them against a guardianship action, and always when they ask a lawyer to act in the role of guardian ad litem. Orientation questions are simply questions to see if clients can understand the time and the place they are in, who they are, and what's going on currently in the world.

Basic orientation questions would involve asking individuals their address, how many children they have, their age, their name, and, if they are old enough, about their grandchildren.

Of course, lawyers are going to need some family collaboration on whether these answers are correct. It is also good to ask about current events. Is there a presidential election coming up? Who are the candidates? Is there some major world event, such as a hurricane, that has occurred? Where did it occur?

Check a client's accuracy in sequencing various events in their own lives.

---

1. *In re* Estate of Neprozatis, 378 N.E.2d 1345, 1349 (Ill. App. Ct. 1978) (citing White v. White, 169 N.E.2d 839, 844 (Ill. App. Ct. 1960)).

The answers to the orientation questions will give lawyers a good jumping-off point, but they will need a medical expert to examine the individual to be absolutely sure when it comes to issues of dementia.

Practice Pointer:

One of the key things lawyers should do is bring in clinical professionals when their "gut" tells them something is not quite right with a client. Many lawyers think they understand dementia, but lawyers really need a clinical assessment.

It is not unusual for clients with dementia to fool a lawyer into thinking they have capacity because they can be socially appropriate. They can work their way through a situation and look totally normal, but if a lawyer asks the right questions and they don't have the mental flexibility to answer them perfectly, then a bona fide doubt exists.

A lot of court cases drag on longer than they should because the lawyers truly don't understand the person's mental capacity. The best lawyers utilize all available resources to totally understand their client and the type of problem that may be affecting their client.

There is no downside to getting a clinical assessment even if the subject ends up being totally normal. It adds to the case and it gives the case more bite. For example, if somebody has changed a will and has already had a clinical assessment, it stops a lot of arguments and saves the client and the families a lot of aggravation.

Practice Pointer: Disability Definition

When stating the reasons a guardian is needed for a person with disabilities, the petitioner needs to be sure that the allegations as stated on the petition conform to the statutory definition of a "disabled person" (i.e., mental deterioration, physical incapacity, mental illness, or development disability that renders a person incapable of making personal or financial decisions).

There are several definitions of "disability" and lawyers need to know how their state defines the term.

For example, a severe loss in memory—brought on by Alzheimer's—can support a finding that an individual is disabled and unable to manage personal affairs in many states.

In Illinois, "disability" is defined as a person's inability to manage one's person or estate due to "mental deterioration or physical incapacity."[2]

In most states, an individual may be adjudged to have a disability by a court after a competency hearing. If the individual is determined to be disabled in Illinois, the court will appoint a guardian to promote the well-being of the disabled individual, to protect the individual, and to "encourage development of his maximum self-reliance and independence."[3]

CURRENT ESTATE PLAN

As soon as lawyers learn that a client has Alzheimer's, they need to examine the current estate plan. If the individual has a well-drafted power of attorney or living will, the client (and the lawyer) is in good shape. (See chapter 3 for a description of powers of attorney and living wills.)

However, lawyers will often find that people are not well prepared for the unexpected and many people do not have a power of attorney or living will. In these situations, lawyers may need to turn to a guardianship.

MENTAL CAPACITY

As mentioned in chapter 3, capacity is not an all-or-nothing concept. Capacity runs along a continuum and may vary according to several factors, such as the time of day, the task presented, and life stressors.

Practice Pointer:

Document conversations with a memo to the file. In cases in which there is likely to be a question about the capacity of an individual, lawyers should write a memorandum to the file as soon as possible to document the conversations with the individual, generally focusing on surrounding events, current events, and things of that nature.

---

2. 755 ILL. COMP. STAT. 5/11a-2(a) (2008).
3. *Id.* 5/11a-3(b).

Practitioners must keep in mind that even when their clients have Alzheimer's, they may still have valid preferences when they apparently cannot think clearly about complicated matters.

If a client is determined to be incompetent, another hearing will be held and the court will appoint a conservator to handle the client's financial affairs and/or a guardian will be appointed to tend to the client's personal and health-care needs.

Practice Pointer:

It is important to keep in mind that even though a client has Alzheimer's, that client's abilities and wishes should be honored as long as possible. Just because the client is diagnosed with dementia does not mean that the client loses all rights at the point of diagnosis.

The client's competency may need to be determined, but a diagnosis of Alzheimer's does not instantly signal that a person is totally incapacitated. Dementia, like some other mental disorders, is progressive and degenerative. Professional evaluation is necessary to determine a person's competencies as they change over the trajectory of the disease.

Practitioners need to be aware that when clients with Alzheimer's do lose the ability to make decisions for themselves, it will be absolutely necessary to have a guardian to legally make the decisions for the client if the proper planning was not put in place earlier.

SUBSTITUTED JUDGMENT STANDARD

When a guardian makes decisions on behalf of a ward, they should be made by conforming as closely as possible to what the ward, when competent, would have done or intended under the circumstances. The guardian must take into account evidence that includes, but is not limited to, the ward's personal, philosophical, religious, and moral beliefs, and ethical values relative to the decision to be made by the guardian. Whenever possible, the guardian should determine how the ward would have made a decision based on the ward's previously expressed preferences, and make decisions in accordance with the preferences of the ward.[4]

---

4. *Id.* 5/11a-17(e).

It is important to note that the "substituted judgment" statutory language refers to the preferences of the ward that were "previously expressed" (i.e., before the ward became incompetent). The ward's *current* desire, even if clearly and consistently expressed over the course of the proceedings, does not automatically trump all other considerations.[5]

Practice Pointer: Estate Planning Problems

If a person with Alzheimer's is incapable of executing powers of attorney or other estate-planning documents, it will become necessary to create a guardianship to transfer the assets of the individual with Alzheimer's. However, this leads to some problems:

- A guardianship adds time, expense, and uncertainty to any proposed transfers of assets from the ward to the spouse and/or child with a disability.
- Guardians may not be authorized to make gifts in the same manner as would be possible through powers of attorney signed while a person is still mentally capable.

CONFLICT

Issues of representation can be murky in Alzheimer's cases. It is almost inevitable that the medical interests of the individual with disabilities and the financial interests of the heirs will conflict because the more money spent on caretaking, the less there will be to inherit.

An objective third party can always be appointed guardian to avoid family conflict.

Practice Pointer: Consider Hiring Professional Care Managers

Care managers, such as nurses, social workers, and licensed clinical counselors, are licensed clinical professionals, usually with advanced degrees, with extensive knowledge of health care, aging, and different issues that affect people with disabilities. They understand the health-care system and they know the right people to contact for specialized services.

When families are fighting, lawyers need to take a step back and make an independent judgment of the decision rather than relying on

---

5. *In re* Estate of K.E.J., 887 N.E.2d 704 (Ill. App. Ct. 2008).

what they are told by a client. Many times, family members can be very convincing in telling lawyers how much they care about the relative in question, but they are really interested in the money. Therefore, lawyers should take the time to examine the situation and see who really is the "caring child" and who is just after the money. Some of the issues that are the most difficult arise when there are multiple marriages and multiple sets of children. There is often a preexisting conflict in those sets of children, and lawyers need to have great caution in counseling and representing them.

> **Practice Pointer: Dealing with Large Families**
>
> When there are multiple adult children with multiple views about what a parent needs, the children need to pick a spokesperson. The children need to have all their arguments with themselves, and the spokesperson is the only person that may speak with the lawyer. This strategy forces the family into a situation where they have to come to a consensus, and it can reduce fees, which diminish the estate of the ward.

Types of Guardianships

This section will walk the reader through the different types of guardianships available in Illinois and provide similar information for California, Florida, and New York. Most states treat guardianships similarly, but often have variations, so it is important that lawyers become familiar with a state's laws or contact a lawyer who is.

In Illinois, if the court adjudges a person to have a disability, the court may appoint (1) a guardian of person, if it has been demonstrated by clear and convincing evidence that because of the disability the person lacks sufficient understanding or capacity to make or communicate responsible decisions concerning the care of person; (2) a guardian of the estate, if it has been demonstrated by clear and convincing evidence that because of the disability the person is unable to manage his estate or financial affairs; or (3) a guardian of person and the estate.[6]

Guardianships are only to be utilized as is necessary to promote the well-being of the person with disabilities; to protect the person from neglect, exploitation, or abuse; and to encourage development of maxi-

---

6. 755 Ill. Comp. Stat. 5/11a-3(a).

mum self-reliance and independence. A guardianship will be ordered only to the extent necessitated by the individual's actual mental, physical, and adaptive limitations.[7]

Practice Pointer: Determining Whether a Client Has Disabilities

The following determinations should be made by a qualified medical professional:

- the actual determination of whether an individual has a disability
- the extent of their disability's practical impact on their ability to make decisions
- the assessment of the least restrictive options for care and treatment

Disability must be assessed and cannot be inferred merely because someone is elderly.

The three main types of guardianships are the plenary guardianship, the limited guardianship, and the temporary guardianship.

The two main subsets of plenary guardianships are guardians of the person and guardians of the estate.

Guardian of Person

The guardian of the person may

- make medical decisions;
- oversee the residential placement of their ward (with court approval);
- ensure that the ward receives proper professional services; and
- release medical records and information.

The guardian will assist the ward in the development of maximum self-reliance and independence.

The guardian of the person may petition the court for an order directing the guardian of the estate to pay an amount periodically for the provision of the services specified by the court order. If the ward's estate is insufficient to provide for education and the guardian of the ward's person fails to provide education, the court may award the custody of the ward to some other person for the purpose of providing education. If a person makes a settlement upon or provision for the support

---

7. *Id.* 5/11a-3(b).

or education of a ward, the court may make an order for the visitation of the ward by the person making the settlement or provision as the court deems proper.[8]

A guardian of the person may not admit a ward to a mental health facility except at the ward's request as provided in article IV of the Mental Health and Developmental Disabilities Code and unless the ward has the capacity to consent to such admission as provided in article IV of the Mental Health and Developmental Disabilities Code.[9]

Surrogate Decision Maker

Another reason that it is important to create a guardian of the person is to avoid having a surrogate decision maker assigned. While the courts will try to assign someone with the individual's best interests at heart, it does not always work out that way.

In some cases, for example, where an incapacitated patient is in the hospital and does not have a living will or a power of attorney, the attending physician may appoint a surrogate decision maker who would then be authorized to make health-care decisions for the patient. These decisions include whether to forgo life-sustaining treatment. The order of priority for being appointed a surrogate decision maker varies from state to state but is generally similar to the example below from Illinois:

1. the patient's guardian of the person;
2. the patient's spouse;
3. any adult son or daughter of the patient;
4. either parent of the patient;
5. any adult brother or sister of the patient;
6. any adult grandchild of the patient;
7. a close friend of the patient;
8. the patient's guardian of the estate.[10]

Guardian of the Estate

The guardian of the estate may do the following for the ward:

- make financial decisions
- enter into contracts

---

8. *Id.* 5/11a-17(a).
9. *Id.* 5/11a-17(a).
10. *See* 755 Ill. Comp. Stat. 40/25 (2012).

- estate planning
- file lawsuits
- sell real estate
- apply for government benefits

The guardian has a fiduciary duty to investigate and pursue eligibility for government benefits to conserve estate assets.

In cases involving substantial assets, the court may require (or the family or the parties may request) a corporate guardian of the estate. All of the major banks and many of the mid-tier banks have trust departments that act as guardian of the estate. However, it should be noted that a bank will not act as guardian of the person.

To the extent specified in the order establishing the guardianship, the guardian of the estate will be responsible for the care, management, and investment of the estate. In some states, a guardian of the estate is referred to as a conservatorship.

The guardian of the estate must manage the estate frugally and apply the income and principal of the estate so far as necessary for the comfort and suitable support and education of the ward, his minor and adult dependent children, and persons related by blood or marriage who are dependent upon or entitled to support from the ward, or for any other purpose that the court deems to be for the best interests of the ward. The guardian may make disbursement of the ward's funds and estate directly to the ward or other distributee or in such other manner and in such amounts as the court directs.[11]

Short-Term Guardian

A guardian of a person with disabilities may appoint in writing, without court approval, a short-term guardian to take over the guardian's duties each time the guardian is unavailable or unable to carry out those duties.[12]

The guardian must consult with the ward to determine a preference concerning the person to be appointed as short-term guardian, and the guardian is required to give due consideration to that preference in choosing a short-term guardian. The written instrument appointing a short-term guardian must be dated and must identify the appointing

---

11.   755 Ill. Comp. Stat. 5/11a-18(a).
12.   *Id.* 5/11a-3.2(a).

guardian, the ward, the person appointed to be the short-term guardian, and the termination date of the appointment. The written instrument has to be signed by, or at the direction of, the appointing guardian in the presence of at least two credible witnesses at least 18 years of age, neither of whom is the person appointed as the short-term guardian. The person appointed as the short-term guardian is also required to sign the written instrument, but not at the same time as the appointing guardian.[13]

Temporary Guardian

There are certain circumstances, including a guardian's death, incapacity, or resignation, in which the court may appoint a temporary guardian.[14] For a temporary guardian to be appointed, it must be deemed necessary for the immediate welfare and protection of the person or the estate on such notice and subject to such conditions as the court may prescribe. In determining the necessity for temporary guardianship, the immediate welfare and protection of the person and estate must be of paramount concern, and the interests of the petitioner, any care provider, or any other party will not outweigh the interests of the ward. The temporary guardian will have all of the powers and duties of a guardian of the person or of the estate that are specifically enumerated by court order. The court order has to state the actual harm identified by the court that necessitates temporary guardianship or any extension thereof.[15]

 Case Study ─────────────────────────────

Temporary Guardianship Cases Are Emergency Situations

A lawyer was appointed guardian ad litem in a temporary guardianship case in which the children couldn't agree whether their mother should have neurosurgery. The court directed that the hearing occur the same day as it was filed. The guardian ad litem was directed to go out and talk to the doctors, examine the records, and come back and make a report to the court that was made in ad litem.

This is an extreme example, but time is of the essence in temporary guardianship situations.

---

13. *Id.*
14. *Id.* 5/11a-4(a).
15. *Id.* 5/11a-4(a).

In almost every scenario, by the time a family files for guardianship of someone with Alzheimer's disease, they want a full plenary guardian. However, they may also have a need to file a temporary guardianship, typically in instances of financial exploitation. (Financial exploitation is examined in detail in chapter 7.)

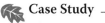

Case Study
The Neglectful Agent

A charitable group contacted a professional care manager about an elderly immigrant with Alzheimer's disease who needed help because the woman's agents under her powers of attorney were not acting on her behalf.

The woman did not have adequate food and was literally starving. She was giving all of her money away to her neighbors. She had a caregiver, but the caregiver was an alcoholic who kept taking the woman to the emergency room to get Tylenol with codeine and taking it all herself.

The woman had congestive heart failure that was not being treated. She had pain that was not being treated. She had oxygen tanks, but they were all empty. The powers of attorney would not help her. They were located two states away and would not provide any service for her because they thought she was fine.

The care managers were able to be named temporary guardians and were able to provide caregivers. Fortunately, the care managers were able to inform the woman's family. The family finally realized that if they did not step up to the plate and do the job, somebody else would and they would lose control.

One of the family members actually moved in with the woman and became her caregiver. The elderly woman was able to stay in her own home with care, and the care managers turned the guardianship over to the family with court supervision.

This is an example of excellent work by a lawyer who knows the system, and who knows the preference of the court to have family manage things. But if the family is not doing a good job, then they start getting supervised by the court because the courts are going to protect the person with disabilities.

That's the role of a good guardianship lawyer. Lawyers have to be prepared to do whatever it takes to protect the ward. Once the guardianship process is in place, the least restricted environment principle needs to apply, but sometimes it takes an iron fist to ensure the family does a good job.

Practice Pointer: Guardianship for an Interim Period

A temporary guardianship is available to authorize limited substitute decision making, where necessary for the immediate protection of the "alleged disabled individual" between the time that the petition for appointment of a guardian is filed and the date of the hearing for the petition.

The guardian ad litem is often referred to as the eyes and ears of the court. Before the temporary guardianship hearing is held, the court appoints a guardian ad litem to visit the person, make a determination, and report back to the court as to whether emergency relief is necessary and reasonable under the circumstances.

Practice Pointer: Temporary Guardianships

Because temporary guardianship petitions are granted in emergency situations, it is important to clearly identify the cause of the emergency and to detail how the current situation jeopardizes the person's financial or personal well-being.

In most courts, the petition for appointment of a temporary guardian is required to be filed contemporaneously with a plenary or limited guardianship petition. However, in some courts, a temporary guardian petition may be filed, and relief granted, with no further action required of the petitioner.

Although orders may be entered ex parte, or without notice to the person with alleged disabilities, many courts insist on the appointment of a guardian ad litem in temporary guardianship situations.

The steps to petition for a temporary guardianship are as follows:

Step 1: Obtain a physician's report and file an appropriate court form.

- The report must be completed by a physician (M.D. or D.O.).
- The judge cannot approve a temporary guardian without an accompanying doctor's evaluation.

Physician's Report should include

- a diagnosis that the respondent suffers from one of the following that renders the person partially or totally incapable of making personal or financial decisions:

- mental deterioration
- physical incapacity
- mental illness
- developmental disability
- a description of the nature and type of person's disability
- how the disability affects the patient's functioning and decision making
- an analysis of the results of evaluations of the person's mental and physical condition
- information on educational condition, adaptive behavior, and social skills
- whether the person is in need of a guardian and the type and scope of the guardianship needed
- a recommendation of the most suitable living arrangement for the person

Step 2: File the petition for plenary and temporary guardianship simultaneously.

- The temporary guardianship petition must state why a temporary guardian is necessary.
- Focus on "the immediate welfare and protection of the alleged disabled person and/or his estate."

Step 3: After filing the temporary guardianship petition, a guardian ad litem must be appointed.

Practice Pointer: Temporary Guardianship Powers

Because a temporary guardian is authorized to have all the powers and duties available to a plenary guardian as listed in the appointing order, it is imperative to carefully detail any and all powers sought in the temporary petition.

 Case Study
Guardian Ad Litem

A lawyer was appointed guardian ad litem in a case in which the son of the person with alleged disabilities filed a case seeking to remove life support. The lawyer was told that the patient was in a deep coma and was dying from lung cancer. The court directed the lawyer to go out on a very expedient basis and then return for a hearing. After spending hours with the doctors and medical team, the lawyer then went in and attempted to communicate with the person. The lawyer got down and spoke very loudly into the patient's ear (the patient was wearing an oxygen mask) and told the patient the reason for his visit. The patient promptly sprung up out of bed, used a variety of profanities relative to his son and indicated that he was sure his son had come to town to get his money because he hadn't seen him in about 10 years.

The fact that the third-party guardian ad litem was able to go and advise this man of the situation, the existence of this case against him to remove life support, and the fact that it worked because he obviously opposed the removal of life support is demonstrative of the due process system that's in place to protect people's rights. This man was on the verge of being taken advantage of, and in essence losing his life.

Limited Guardianship

A limited guardian is appointed by taking away certain rights of an individual and giving certain rights. For example, the person with disabilities may lose the right to contract but may retain the right to receive $500 a month of personal discretionary spending money.

Practice Pointer: Limited Guardianships May Cause Trouble Down the Line

The parties may attempt to settle a guardianship dispute before trial by agreeing to the appointment of a limited guardian of the respondent's person, estate, or both. Practically speaking, however, the appointment of a limited guardian can pose problems in the future. For example, for a respondent with a diagnosis of progressive dementia, the duties and powers of the guardian and the legal disabilities that must be included in the limited guardian order will change over time based on the very nature of the respondent's disability.

In addition, the duties and powers of the limited guardian must be specifically laid out in the order to distinguish between the authority of the limited guardian and the powers retained by the respondent. As a result, the practitioner may be forced to go into court on multiple occasions to modify the terms of the limited guardianship as the respondent's disability progresses.

California

Individuals with dementia, as defined in the last published edition of the *Diagnostic and Statistical Manual of Mental Disorders*, should have a conservatorship to serve their unique and special needs.[16]

A conservatorship of the person, the estate, or both may be established for adults who are unable to care for their person or estate.[17]

A conservatorship is established for people who are so incapacitated as to be unable to provide properly for their personal needs or to "manage [their] own financial resources or resist fraud or undue influence."[18]

The guardian, conservator, or limited conservator, to the extent specifically and expressly provided in the appointing court's order, has the management and control of the estate and, in managing and controlling the estate, must use ordinary care and diligence. What constitutes use of ordinary care and diligence is determined by all the circumstances of the particular estate.[19]

The guardian or conservator is authorized to exercise a power to the extent that ordinary care and diligence requires that the power be exercised.[20]

Generally, the guardian or conservator must apply the income from the estate, as necessary, to the comfortable and suitable support, maintenance, and education of the ward (including care, treatment, and support of a ward who is a patient in a state hospital under the jurisdiction of the state Department of Mental Health or the state Department of Developmental Services). This also applies to those individuals legally entitled to support, maintenance, or education from the ward, taking into account the value of the estate and the condition of life of the person required to be furnished such support, maintenance, or education.[21]

All conservators of the estate have general powers specified in the Probate Code and may have additional powers as the court may designate. These additional powers must be specifically set forth in writing.[22]

16. CAL. PROB. CODE § 2356.5(b) (West 2005).
17. *Id.* § 1800.3.
18. *Id.* § 1801(a)–(b).
19. *Id.* § 2401(a).
20. *Id.* § 2401(b).
21. *Id.* § 2420(a).
22. CAL. WELF. & INST. CODE § 5357 (West 1994).

Limited conservatorship of person: Unless specifically requested in the petition for appointment of a limited conservator and granted by the court, a limited conservator does *not* have any of the following powers or controls over the limited conservatee to (1) fix the residence or specific dwelling; (2) access the confidential records and papers; (3) consent or withhold consent to the marriage of, or the entrance into, a registered domestic partnership; (4) contract; (5) give or withhold medical consent; (6) control one's own social and sexual contacts and relationships; or (7) make decisions concerning the education.[23]

Temporary conservatorship: A temporary conservatorship may be established by the court for up to 30 days. The court may appoint a temporary conservator on the basis of the comprehensive report of the officer providing conservatorship investigation, or on the basis of an affidavit of the professional person who recommended conservatorship stating the reasons for the recommendation.[24]

Florida

In Florida, "guardian" means a person who has been appointed by the court to act on behalf of a ward's person or property, or both. "Limited guardian" means a guardian who has been appointed by the court to exercise the legal rights and powers specifically designated by court order entered after the court has found that the ward lacks the capacity to do some, but not all, of the tasks necessary to care for one's person or property, or after the person has voluntarily petitioned for appointment of a limited guardian. "Plenary guardian" means a person who has been appointed by the court to exercise all delegable legal rights and powers of the ward after the court has found that the ward lacks the capacity to perform all of the tasks necessary to care for one's person or property.[25]

Emergency temporary guardian: A court, prior to appointment of a guardian but after a petition for determination of incapacity has been filed, may appoint an emergency temporary guardian for the person or property, or both, of an alleged incapacitated person. The court must specifically find the appearance of imminent danger that the physical or mental health or safety of the person will be seriously impaired or

---

23. CAL. PROB. CODE § 2351.5(b).
24. CAL. WELF. & INST. CODE § 5352.1(a) (West 1971).
25. FLA. STAT. ANN. § 744.102(9) (West 2006).

that the person's property is in danger of being wasted, misappropriated, or lost unless immediate action is taken. The powers and duties of the emergency temporary guardian must be specifically enumerated by court order. The court will appoint counsel to represent the alleged incapacitated person during any such summary proceedings, and such appointed counsel may request that the proceeding be recorded and transcribed. The court may appoint an emergency temporary guardian on its own motion if no petition for appointment of guardian has been filed at the time of entry of an order determining incapacity.[26]

New York

The court may appoint a guardian for a person if the court determines it is necessary to provide for the personal needs of that person, including food, clothing, shelter, health care, or safety and/or to manage the property and financial affairs of that person. Second, the ward must either agree to the appointment or be incapacitated (as defined in section 81.02(b) of New York's Mental Hygiene Law). In deciding whether the appointment is necessary, the court must consider the report of the court evaluator and the sufficiency and reliability of available resources to provide for personal needs or property management without the appointment of a guardian. A court-appointed guardian will be granted only those powers that are necessary to provide for personal needs and/or property management of the incapacitated person in such a manner as appropriate to the individual and that will constitute the least restrictive form of intervention.[27]

New York defines "guardian" as a person who is 18 years old or older, a corporation, or a public agency, including a local department of social services, appointed in accordance with the statutory terms by the supreme court, the surrogate's court, or the county court to act on behalf of an incapacitated person in providing for personal needs and/or for property management.[28]

Appointing a guardian: If the person alleged to be incapacitated is found to have agreed to the appointment of a guardian and the court determines that the appointment of a guardian is necessary, the order of the court will be designed to accomplish the least restrictive form of intervention by appointing a guardian with powers limited to those that the court

---

26. *Id.* § 744.3031(1)–(2).
27. N.Y. MENTAL HYG. LAW § 81.02(a) (McKinney 1992).
28. *Id.* § 81.03.

has found necessary to assist the person in providing for personal needs and/or property management. If the person alleged to be incapacitated is found to be incapacitated and the court determines that the appointment of a guardian is necessary, the order of the court must be designed to accomplish the least restrictive form of intervention by appointing a guardian with powers limited to those the court has found necessary to assist the incapacitated person in providing for personal needs and/or property management. The order of appointment is required to identify all people entitled to notice of all further proceedings.[29]

Procedure: Although creating a guardianship is often considered a last resort, it is still important to carefully pick the guardian. The guardian may be a family member, friend, or an agency that competently provides guardianship services.

Petition: The petition is broken down into the content, the nomination, and where to file.

Content: The petition for adjudication of disability and for the appointment of a guardian of the estate, the person, or both of an alleged disabled person must state, if known or reasonably ascertainable,

    a.   the relationship and interest of the petitioner to the respondent;
    b.   the name, date of birth, and place of residence of the respondent;
    c.   the reasons for the guardianship;
    d.   the name and post office address of the respondent's guardian, if any, or of the respondent's agent or agents appointed under the Illinois Power of Attorney Act, if any;
    e.   the name and post office addresses of the nearest relatives of the respondent in the following order: (1) the spouse and adult children, parents and adult brothers and sisters, if any; if none, (2) nearest adult kindred known to the petitioner;
    f.   the name and address of the person with whom or the facility in which the respondent is residing;
    g.   the approximate value of the personal and real estate;
    h.   the amount of the anticipated annual gross income and other receipts; and
    i.   the name, post office address and in case of an individual, the age, relationship to the respondent and occupation of the proposed guardian.

---

29. *Id.* § 81.16(c).

In addition, if the petition seeks the appointment of a previously appointed standby guardian as guardian of the person, the petition must also state:

a. the facts concerning the standby guardian's previous appointment and

b. the date of death of the person's guardian or the facts concerning the consent of the person's guardian to the appointment of the standby guardian as guardian, or the willingness and ability of the person's guardian to make and carry out day-to-day care decisions concerning the person with disabilities.[30]

A petition for adjudication of disability and the appointment of a guardian of the estate, the person, or both of an alleged disabled person may not be dismissed or withdrawn without leave of the court.[31]

Nomination: The petition for adjudication of disability and for the appointment of a guardian of the estate, the person, or both of an alleged disabled person must state, among other information, the name, post office address, and, in case of an individual, the age, relationship to the respondent, and occupation of the proposed guardian.[32]

A person, if still of sound mind and memory, may designate in writing a person, corporation, or public agency qualified to act under Section 11a-5, to be appointed as guardian or as successor guardian of the person, the estate, or both, in the event a person is adjudged to have a disability. The designation may be proved by any competent evidence, but if it is executed and attested in the same manner as a will, it will have prima facie validity. If the court finds that the appointment of the one designated will serve the best interests and welfare of the ward, it will make the appointment in accordance with the designation. The selection of the guardian will be in the discretion of the court whether or not a designation is made.[33]

Where to file: If the alleged ward is a resident of Illinois, the proceeding must be instituted in the court of the county in which that person resides. If the alleged ward is not an Illinois resident, the proceedings

---

30. 755 ILL. COMP. STAT. 5/11a-8 (West 1998).
31. *Id.*
32. *Id.* 5/11a-8(i) (West 1998).
33. 755 ILL. COMP. STAT. 5/11a-6 (West 1979).

are required to be instituted in the court of a county in which the real or personal estate is located.[34]

Practice Pointer: Changing the Ward's Residence or Domicile

Generally, only duly appointed public guardians and the Office of State Guardian have the power to place a ward in a residential facility. Other appointed guardians usually may only do so if specified by court order.

The guardianship order may specify the conditions on which the guardian may admit the ward to a residential facility without further court order. In making residential placement decisions, the guardian must make decisions in conformity with the preferences of the ward unless the guardian is reasonably certain that the decisions will result in substantial harm to the ward or to the ward's estate.

When the preferences of the ward cannot be ascertained or where they will result in substantial harm to the ward or to the ward's estate, the guardian must make decisions with respect to the ward's placement that are in the best interests of the ward.

The guardian may not remove the ward from the ward's home or separate the ward from family and friends unless such removal is necessary to prevent substantial harm to the ward or to the ward's estate. The guardian has a duty to investigate the availability of reasonable residential alternatives. The guardian must monitor the placement of the ward on an ongoing basis to ensure its continued appropriateness, and is tasked with pursuing appropriate alternatives as needed.

Contested

Many judges will not appoint a guardian ad litem when the underlying petition seeks only the appointment of a guardian of the person (not estate) and when the respondent plans to appear in court. This is frequently done as a practical matter to avoid the generation of fees of a guardian ad litem.

Most state courts require the appointment of a guardian ad litem in all cases except temporary guardianships.

---

34. *Id.* 5/11a-7.

Practice Pointer: Separate the Legal from the Emotional Issues

The dynamic issues facing practitioners in contested guardianship litigation are factually and legally complex and often bring forward sensitive and personal issues. It is the lawyer's responsibility to separate the legal issues from the often complex emotional matters while zealously advocating for the client and still maintaining the integrity of the person with alleged disabilities and the parties involved.

Practice Pointer: Get Court Authority for Legal Action

The guardian should always seek court authority to commence, prosecute, or defend any suit on behalf of the ward. After appointment, all suits and proceedings on behalf of the ward should be brought by the guardian in the capacity as guardian, rather than in the name of the person with disabilities. The guardian of the estate may settle any lawsuit involving the ward, but the probate court must first approve settlement as in the best interests of the ward.

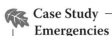 **Case Study**
Emergencies

A care manager was notified of an elderly woman who was living alone. She was suffering from a lot of physical deficits and allegedly had two bad sons. A capable lawyer presented the case as an emergency because one of the sons was a convicted felon who was getting out of jail in three days and was going to move back in with his mother. In the past, the son prevented her from getting any care because he would threaten caregivers with knives and various other forms of violence.

The woman had slight Alzheimer's and a fierce loyalty to her son and insisted that her son was fine and wasn't causing problems. However, the caregivers would all leave, which then put her in a dire situation. So the lawyer's job was to go into court, get a temporary guardianship in place, and protect the woman by stopping the convicted felon son from moving back into her house.

The experienced lawyer on the case was able to present the urgency of moving forward and getting orders of protection through the guardianship court (which not all lawyers realize can be done) to protect this woman from the convicted felon. Checking past police reports, the lawyer found reports of 46 police visits to the home for violent episodes. These reports included domestic violence, violence against the neighbors, brandishing a butcher knife, and chasing caregivers around the apartment.

The woman had forgotten about these incidents due to her Alzheimer's. The lawyer was able to get an emergency guardianship in place within 24 hours. Professional caregivers were appointed to manage the care environment and care providers.

With the ex-con son out of the picture, the care managers discovered that the other son wasn't really a bad guy. It turned out that he was petrified of his brother and wouldn't go and help in the house when his brother was present because he feared for his safety. They were able to work with the other son, and the mother actually moved in with her "better son." A 24-hour caregiver was put in place to monitor the situation.

After a short period of time, it was prudent to pull out the 24-hour caregiver. The good son has been able to take care of his mother for the last two years. The other son is not disrupting the care anymore, and it's actually a very successful and economical outcome.

Many lawyers in the guardianship court do not realize that protective orders can be issued from the guardianship court. The purpose of guardianship is to guard and protect, and lawyers need to be aware of all of the available tools to guard and protect wards and their assets.

Notice: Illinois requires that the respondent be personally served with a copy of the petition and a summons at least 14 days before the hearing. The summons must be printed in large, bold type and include the statutory language for notice.[35]

Practice Pointer:

Often laypeople don't realize that the basis of a guardianship is a finding of incompetency to manage one's own affairs and results in taking away one's civil liberties. So it's a serious issue, because when appointing a person to be someone's plenary guardian, it is taking away the right to marry, right to vote, and right to drive. Essentially, it's saying that the person is totally incapable and forfeits any rights as a citizen.

This strips individuals of very substantial civil rights and civil liberties.

35. 755 Ill. Comp. Stat. 5/11a-10(c) (West 2012).

That's why the Illinois Probate Act provides that individuals who are the subjects of a guardianship case can have a court-appointed attorney, a court-appointed doctor evaluate them, and a jury trial if they seek such. Generally, the court system will bend over backward to make sure that a person with disabilities is not taken advantage of. Due process is required by the Constitution of the United States whenever one's civil liberties are jeopardized by judicial action.

Notice of the time and place of the hearing must be given by the petitioner by mail or in person to those people, including the proposed guardian, whose names and addresses appear in the petition and who do not waive notice not less than 14 days before the hearing.[36]

Practice Pointer: Notice via Certified Mail

If a contested hearing over who should act as guardian is anticipated, sending notice via certified mail is a good way to thwart future allegations of improper service as a basis for overturning the appointment of a guardian for the person with disabilities.

Hearing

The hearing may be held at such convenient place as the court directs, including at a facility in which the respondent resides.[37]

In the Illinois guardianship hearing,

- the person with alleged disabilities has the right to be present;
- the person with alleged disabilities must be given at least 14 days advance notice of the hearing;
- the rules of civil procedure apply;
- witnesses generally include doctors, social workers, caregivers, and family members;
- courts accord equal weight to medical and lay testimony;
- the guardian ad litem will frequently be appointed to serve as defense council;
- the person with alleged disabilities must be adjudged disabled by clear and convincing evidence before a guardian will be appointed;

---

36. *Id.* 5/11a-10(f).
37. *Id.* 5/11a-10(d).

- if there is an existing power of attorney for the ward, it can be used as a defense against the appointment of a guardian;
- upon the death of the respondent, pending litigation regarding the appointment of a guardian terminates.

The respondent is entitled to be represented by counsel, to demand a jury of six people, to present evidence, and to confront and cross-examine all witnesses. The hearing may be closed to the public on request of the respondent, the guardian ad litem, or appointed or other counsel for the respondent. Unless excused by the court upon a showing that the respondent refuses to be present or will suffer harm if required to attend, the respondent will be present at the hearing.[38]

In deciding whether to include a request for the appointment of a guardian of the estate or merely a request for the appointment of a guardian of the person, it is important to note that the court probably will allow a petitioner to drop a request for appointment of a guardian of the estate at the hearing date, but may not later allow the petitioner to simply amend the petition to include such a request due to a lack of jurisdiction as a result of improper notice to both the respondent and those people entitled to receive notice under 755 Illinois Compiled Statutes act 5, section 11a-8.

Upon oral or written motion by the respondent or the guardian ad litem or on the court's own motion, the court must appoint one or more independent experts to examine the respondent.

At the hearing the court must inquire regarding

1. the nature and extent of respondent's general intellectual and physical functioning;
2. the extent of the impairment of the respondent's adaptive behavior if he or she is a person with a developmental disability, or the nature and severity of the mental illness if he or she is a person with mental illness;
3. the understanding and capacity of the respondent to make and communicate responsible decisions concerning the respondent's person;
4. the capacity of the respondent to manage his or her estate and financial affairs;

---

38.   755 Ill. Comp. Stat. 5/11a-11(a) (West 1995).

5. the appropriateness of proposed and alternate living arrangements;

6. the impact of the disability upon the respondent's functioning in the basic activities of daily living and the important decisions faced by the respondent or normally faced by adult members of the respondent's community; and

7. any other area of inquiry deemed appropriate by the court.[39]

Practice Pointer: Physician Testimony

The physician should provide testimony as to the exact diagnosis of the respondent including the effect that such a diagnosis has on the respondent's cognitive functioning. At trial, the petitioner's counsel should elicit testimony from the physician as to the respondent's prognosis or the permanency that the diagnosis has on the respondent's cognitive functioning. This can be very important in early stages of Alzheimer's disease when the disease may not be so easy to spot to the layperson.

Practitioner should speak to the physician regarding this issue prior to trial and should already know the answer that the physician will provide.

If the physician concludes that the respondent is only partially incapable of making personal and financial decisions, the physician also must provide testimony as to which types of decisions the respondent can or cannot make. Lay witness testimony can substantiate the physician's opinion.

Before stating an opinion as to the respondent's level of incompetency at trial, physicians should clearly establish and testify as to the date(s) they evaluated the respondent, the length of time spent during the evaluation(s), whether they reviewed any medical records prior to the evaluation(s), whether they relied on the opinions of other medical professionals before formulating their opinion, and the types of questions that were asked of the respondent at the evaluation.

Practitioners should also have the proposed guardian testify as to the proposed care plan for the person with alleged disabilities, the appropriateness of which can then be supported by additional expert testimony of a social worker, care manager, or physician.

---

39. *Id.* 5/11a-11(e).

The medical report of the person must be prepared by the physician within the state-mandated time period after the date of the filing of a petition.

> **Practice Pointer:**
>
> It might seem obvious, but medical reports need to be legible. Often, the judge will say, "What does this say?" and the lawyer might have to reply, "I have no idea."
>
> Some lawyers will actually prepare a transcript and type out what the physician's report says because doctors have terrible handwriting. It is a good idea to type out the report for the judge.

Another good idea is to review the medical report before filing the case so there's actually a basis to file the case. If a lawyer files the case and tells the court to appoint a guardian ad litem and the medical report comes back and it turns out that the person who was supposedly incapacitated is actually fine, the lawyer may be embarrassed and even sanctioned by the court.

> **Practice Pointer: Physician's Report**
>
> It is important for all practitioners to avoid inadvertently making the report a part of the public record through the use of the report as an exhibit in subsequent pleadings.

REPORTING REQUIREMENTS

The Illinois requirements will provide a general idea of how the process works, followed by a brief synopsis of the requirements for California, Florida, and New York. Although most states have similar requirements, there are bound to be some differences, so practitioners need to be familiar with the requirements of their state.

Guardian of Person

If directed by the court, the guardian of the person must file with the court at intervals indicated by the court, a report that must state briefly

1. the current mental, physical, and social condition of the ward and the ward's minor and adult dependent children;
2. the present living arrangement, and a description and the address of every residence where the guardian lived during the reporting period and the length of stay at each place;
3. a summary of the medical, educational, vocational, and other professional services given to the guardian;
4. a résumé of the guardian's visits with and activities on behalf of the ward and the ward's minor and adult dependent children;
5. a recommendation as to the need for continued guardianship;
6. any other information requested by the court or useful in the opinion of the guardian.[40]

The Office of the State Guardian will assist the guardian in filing the report when requested by the guardian. The court is authorized to take such action as it deems appropriate pursuant to the report.[41]

Guardian of Estate

The probate court, upon petition of a guardian for an adult with disabilities, and after notice to all other people interested as the court directs, may authorize the guardian to exercise any or all powers over the estate and business affairs of the ward that the ward would be able to exercise if present and able.[42]

The court has the power to authorize actions or the application of funds to meet the ward's wishes so far as they can be ascertained. The court must consider the permanence of the ward's disabling condition and the natural objects of the ward's bounty in making these decisions.[43]

In ascertaining and carrying out the ward's wishes, the court may consider minimization of State or federal income, estate, or inheritance taxes; and providing gifts to charities, relatives, and friends that would be likely recipients of donations from the ward. The ward's wishes must be carried out as best they can be ascertained, whether or not tax savings are involved.[44]

---

40. 755 Ill. Comp. Stat. 5/11a-17(b) (West 2010).
41. *Id.* 5/11a-17(b).
42. 755 Ill. Comp. Stat. 5/11a-18(a-5) (West 2007).
43. *Id.*
44. *Id.*

> **Practice Pointer: Who Should Be the Guardian?**
>
> It is crucial to examine the potential guardians' abilities and skill set when choosing a person to serve as guardian. The correct choice may be a spouse, adult child, or friend. However, if there is no one in the person's life with the correct abilities and skill set, lawyers need to consider other options.
>
> Two such options: Some states and/or counties have officials who serve as public guardians. Private professional guardians are certified by the National Guardianship Association, Inc. (www.guardianship.org).

Family members and friends will often disagree about who should act as the person's guardian, and lawyers may have to actually prove in court who is the right guardian. The task at trial simply may be presenting evidence to distinguish between the proposed guardians and convincing the trier of fact of one's superiority to meet the respondent's needs, whether personal, fiscal, or both.

Frequently, the parties will indicate that they're fighting for the parent's medical care and control when they're really fighting for control of the money, how much is going to be spent on the parent in his or her lifetime, and if that's affecting their inheritance.

However it is best to try to avoid a full-blown contested hearing to choose a guardian, so many parties attempt to settle matters by agreeing to the appointment of financial institutions, geriatric care managers, county public guardians, or any other neutral party as guardian when family members and friends are contesting the choice of guardian.

Often not-for-profit guardianship agencies act as guardian of the person, and some of them act as both guardian of the estate and guardian of the person.

TERMINATION/REMOVAL OF THE GUARDIAN

Getting a guardian removed for improper conduct is not an easy thing to do unless it's clearly a case of theft. It can happen when the lawyer finds out that the person who is the guardian is inappropriate or making bad decisions, but it is a difficult evidentiary task.

Petition to terminate guardianship of person and/or of estate: The court may determine that it is in the best interest of the ward to terminate or limit the authority of a standby or short-term guardian. This is done through a petition by any interested person (including the standby or short-term guardian) with notice to all interested people. The petition for termination or limitation of the authority of a standby or short-term guardian may, but need not, be combined with a petition to have another guardian appointed for the person.[45]

Temporary guardianships: A temporary guardianship expires within 60 days after the appointment or whenever a guardian is regularly appointed, whichever occurs first. Extensions are normally not granted.

In the case where there has been an adjudication of disability, an extension may be granted (a) pending the disposition on appeal of an adjudication of disability; (b) pending the completion of a citation proceeding brought pursuant to section 23-3; (c) pending the appointment of a successor guardian in a case where the former guardian has resigned, has become incapacitated, or is deceased; or (d) where the guardian's powers have been suspended pursuant to a court order. The ward has the right to petition the court to revoke the appointment of the temporary guardian anytime after the appointment is made.[46]

California

A conservatorship may be reviewed by the court at the expiration of six months after the initial appointment of the conservator. The court investigator will visit the conservatee (ward) and conduct an investigation into the appropriateness of the conservatorship and whether the conservator is acting in the best interests of the conservatee regarding the conservatee's placement, quality of care (including physical and mental treatment), and finances. In response to the investigator's report, the court may take appropriate action, including

- ordering a review of the conservatorship or
- ordering the conservator to submit an accounting.[47]

The court may also review conservatorships one year after their appointment and annually thereafter. However, at the review that occurs one year after the appointment of the conservator, and every subsequent review, the court may set the next review in two years if the

---

45. 755 Ill. Comp. Stat. 5/11a-17(f); 755 Ill. Comp. Stat. 5/11a-18(f) (West 2010).
46. 755 Ill. Comp. Stat. 5/11a-4(b) (West 2012).
47. Cal. Prob. Code § 1850(1) (West 2012).

court determines that the conservator is acting in the best interests of the conservatee.[48]

In these cases, the investigator must conduct an investigation one year before the next review and file a status report in the conservatee's court file regarding whether the conservatorship still appears to be warranted and whether the conservator is acting in the best interests of the conservatee. If the investigator determines that the conservatorship still appears to be warranted and that the conservator is acting in the best interests of the conservatee, no hearing or court action in response to the investigator's report is needed.[49]

Florida

The guardian is required to file an initial guardianship report and must also file a guardianship report annually.[50]

Unless the court requires filing on a calendar-year basis, each guardian of the person has to file the annual guardianship plan within 90 days after the last day of the anniversary month the letters of guardianship were signed.[51] The plan must cover the coming fiscal year, ending on the last day in such anniversary month. If the court requires calendar-year filing, the guardianship plan must be filed on or before April 1 of each year.[52]

The purpose of the annual guardianship plan is to provide updated information about the condition of the ward. The annual plan must specify the current needs of the ward and how those needs are proposed to be met in the coming year. Each plan for an adult ward must, if applicable, include

    a.   Information concerning the residence of the ward, including
        1.   the ward's address at the time of filing the plan;
        2.   the name and address of each place where the ward was maintained during the preceding year;
        3.   the length of stay of the ward at each place;
        4.   a statement of whether the current residential setting is best suited for the current needs of the ward; and

48. *Id.* § 1850(2).
49. *Id.*
50. Fla. Stat. Ann. § 744.361(2)–(3) (West 2007).
51. Fla. Stat. Ann. § 744.367(1) (West 2006).
52. *Id.*

    5. plans for ensuring during the coming year that the ward is in the best residential setting to meet the ward's needs.

  b. information concerning the medical and mental health conditions and treatment and rehabilitation needs of the ward, including

    1. a résumé of any professional medical treatment given to the ward during the preceding year.

    2. the report of a physician who examined the ward no more than 90 days before the beginning of the applicable reporting period (the report must contain an evaluation of the ward's condition and a statement of the current level of capacity of the ward); and

    3. the plan for providing medical, mental health, and rehabilitative services in the coming year.

  c. information concerning the social condition of the ward, including

    1. the social and personal services currently used by the ward;

    2. the social skills of the ward, including a statement of how well the ward communicates and maintains interpersonal relationships; and

    3. the social needs of the ward.[53]

Each guardian of the property must file an annual accounting on or before April 1 of each year with the court, unless the court requires or authorizes filing on a fiscal-year basis. The annual accounting must cover the preceding calendar year. If the court authorizes or directs filing on a fiscal-year basis, the annual accounting must be filed on or before the first day of the fourth month after the end of the fiscal year.[54]

The annual guardianship report of a guardian of the property has to consist of an annual accounting, and the annual report of a guardian of the person must consist of an annual guardianship plan. The annual report is required to be served on the ward, unless the ward is a minor or is totally incapacitated, and on the lawyer for the ward, if one is in place. The guardian must also provide a copy to any other person that the court directs.[55]

---

53. *Id.* § 744.3675.
54. *Id.* § 744.367(2).
55. *Id.* § 744.367(3).

The annual accounting is to include

- a full and correct account of the receipts and disbursements of all of the ward's property over which the guardian has control and a statement of the ward's property on hand at the end of the accounting period; however, this does not apply to any property or any trust of which the ward is a beneficiary but which is not under the control or administration of the guardian; and
- a copy of the annual or year-end statement of all of the ward's cash accounts from each of the institutions where the cash is deposited.[56]

The guardian is required to obtain a receipt, canceled check, or other proof of payment for all expenditures and disbursements made on behalf of the ward. The guardian must preserve all evidence of payment, along with other substantiating papers, for a period of three years after the discharge. The guardian does not need to file the receipts, proofs of payment, and substantiating papers with the court, but the documents must be made available for inspection and review if the court orders an inspection and review.[57]

Emergency temporary guardians: An emergency temporary guardian has to file a final report no later than 30 days after the expiration of the emergency temporary guardianship.

In cases where the emergency temporary guardian is a guardian for the property, the final report must consist of a verified inventory of the property as of the date the letters of emergency temporary guardianship were issued, a final accounting that gives a full and correct account of the receipts and disbursements of all the property of the ward over which the guardian had control, and a statement of the property of the ward on hand at the end of the emergency temporary guardianship. If the emergency temporary guardian becomes the successor guardian of the property, the final report must satisfy the requirements of the initial guardianship report for the guardian of the property.[58]

If the emergency temporary guardian is a guardian of the person, the final report must summarize the activities of the temporary guardian with regard to residential placement, medical condition, mental

56. FLA. STAT. ANN. § 744.3678(2) (West 2008).
57. *Id.* § 744.3678(3).
58. FLA. STAT. ANN. § 744.3031(8) (West 2006).

health and rehabilitative services, and the social condition of the ward to the extent of the authority granted to the temporary guardian in the letters of guardianship. If the emergency temporary guardian becomes the successor guardian of the person, the report must satisfy the requirements of the initial report for a guardian of the person.[59]

Judicial review of guardianships: The court retains jurisdiction over all guardianships. The court will review the appropriateness and extent of a guardianship annually and

1.   if an objection to the terms of the guardianship report has been filed;
2.   if interim review has been requested;
3.   if a person, including the ward, has filed a suggestion of increased capacity; or
4.   if the guardianship report has not been received and the guardian has failed to respond to a show cause order.[60]

New York

Guardians have to file with the court that appointed them a report stating the steps taken to fulfill their responsibilities within 90 days of the issuance of the commission to the guardians. Guardians are also required to file proof of completion of the guardian education requirements with the initial report.[61]

To the extent that the guardian has been granted powers with respect to property management, the initial report must contain a verified and complete inventory of the property and financial resources over which the guardian has control; the location of any will executed by the incapacitated person; the guardian's plan, consistent with the court's order of appointment, for the management of such property and financial resources; and any need for any change in the powers authorized by the court.[62]

The initial report must also document the guardian's personal visits with the incapacitated person, in cases where the guardian has been granted powers regarding personal needs, and the steps the guardian has taken, consistent with the court's order, to provide for the personal needs

---

59.   *Id.*
60.   Fla. Stat. Ann. § 744.372 (West 1990).
61.   N.Y. Mental Hyg. Law § 81.30(a) (McKinney 2004).
62.   *Id.* § 81.30(b).

of that person; the guardian's plan, consistent with the court's order of appointment, for providing for the personal needs of the incapacitated person; a copy of any directives, any living will, and any other advance directive; and any necessary change in the powers authorized by the court.[63]

The plan for providing for the personal needs of the incapacitated person will include the following information: (1) the medical, dental, mental health, or related services that are to be provided for the welfare of the incapacitated person; (2) the social and personal services that are to be provided for the welfare of the incapacitated person; (3) any physical, dental, and mental health examinations necessary to determine the medical, dental, and mental health treatment needs; and (4) the application of health and accident insurance and any other private or government benefits to which the incapacitated person may be entitled to meet any part of the costs of medical, dental, mental health, or related services provided to the incapacitated person.[64]

Annual report: Every guardian must file an annual report in May, or at any other time upon motion or order of the court. The report has to include the following information:

1. the present address and telephone number of the guardian;
2. the present address and telephone number of the incapacitated person; if the place of residence of the incapacitated person is not a personal home, the name, address, and telephone number of the facility or place at which the person resides and the name of the chief executive officer of the facility or person otherwise responsible for the person's care;
3. any major changes in the physical or mental condition of the incapacitated person and any substantial change in medication;
4. the date that the incapacitated person was last examined or otherwise seen by a physician and the purpose of that visit;
5. a statement by a physician, psychologist, nurse clinician, social worker, or other person that has evaluated or examined the incapacitated person within the three months prior to the filing of the report regarding an evaluation of the incapacitated per-

---

63. *Id.* § 81.30(c).
64. *Id.*

son's condition and the current functional level of the incapacitated person;

6. to the extent the guardian is charged with providing for the
   personal needs of the incapacitated person,
   a. a statement of whether the current residential setting
       is best suited to the current needs of the incapacitated
       person;
   b. a résumé of any professional medical treatment given to
       the ward in the preceding year;
   c. the plan for medical, dental, and mental health treatment,
       and related services in the coming year;
   d. information concerning the social condition of the
       incapacitated person, including the social and personal
       services currently utilized by the incapacitated person,
       the social skills of the incapacitated person, and the social
       needs of the incapacitated person;

7. to the extent the guardian is charged with property
   management, information required by the provisions of the
   surrogate's court procedure act prescribing the form of papers
   to be filed upon the annual accounting of a general guardian of
   a ward's property;

8. where the guardian has used or employed the services of the
   incapacitated person or where moneys have been earned by or
   received on behalf of such incapacitated person, an accounting
   of any moneys earned or derived from such services;

9. a résumé of any other activities performed by the guardian on
   behalf of the incapacitated person;

10. facts indicating the need to terminate the appointment of the
    guardian, or for any alteration in the powers of the guardian
    and what specific authority is requested or what specific
    authority of the guardian will be affected;

11. any other information the guardian may be required to file by
    the order of appointment.[65]

---

65. *Id.* § 81.31(b).

Practice Pointer: Getting Paid

If a respondent hires a lawyer for representation in a guardianship matter and the lawyer's assessment is that the client is less than fully competent, it is advisable that the lawyer seek to become the "court-appointed attorney." If the respondent is eventually adjudicated as having disabilities, the estate may be unwilling to pay the lawyer, arguing that the respondent did not have the requisite capacity to contract for or supervise services. If the lawyer becomes "court-appointed," however, then obtaining full payment for services becomes much more likely.

ADULT GUARDIANSHIP AND PROTECTIVE PROCEEDINGS JURISDICTION ACT

While state laws almost exclusively govern guardianships and conservatorships,[66] the Uniform Law Commission completed the Adult Guardianship and Protective Proceedings Jurisdiction Act in 2007.[67] The act has been enacted in the following states: Alabama,[68] Alaska,[69] Arizona,[70] Arkansas,[71] Colorado,[72] Connecticut,[73] Delaware,[74] District of Columbia,[75] Hawaii,[76] Idaho,[77] Illinois,[78] Indiana,[79] Iowa,[80] Kentucky,[81]

---

66. Federal laws, especially Medicaid laws, have a significant effect on guardianships and conservatorships.
67. Fact Sheet, *Adult Guardianship and Protective Proceedings Jurisdiction Act*, UNIFORM LAW COMM'N, http://www.uniformlaws.org/LegislativeFactSheet.aspx?title=Adult%20 Guardianship%20and%20Protective%20Proceedings%20Jurisdiction%20Act (last visited May 3, 2013).
68. ALA. CODE § 26-2B-101 (2012).
69. ALASKA STAT. ANN. § 13.27.010 (West 2008).
70. ARIZ. REV. STAT. ANN. § 14-12101 (2010).
71. ARK. CODE ANN. § 28-74-101 (West 2008).
72. COLO. REV. STAT. ANN. § 15-14.5-101 (West 2008).
73. Conn. Gen. Stat. 45a-644-45a-663 (2012).
74. DEL. CODE. ANN. tit. 12, § 39A-101 (West 2011).
75. D.C. CODE § 21-2401.01 (2008).
76. HAW. REV. STAT. § 551G-1 (West 2012).
77. IDAHO CODE ANN. § 15-13-101 (West 2011).
78. 755 ILL. COMP. STAT. 8/102 (West 2010).
79. IND. CODE ANN. § 29-3.5-1-1 (West 2011).
80. IOWA CODE ANN. § 633.700 (West 2010).
81. KY. REV. STAT. ANN. § 387.810 (West 2011).

Maine,[82] Maryland,[83] Minnesota,[84] Missouri,[85] Montana,[86] Nebraska,[87] Nevada,[88] New Jersey,[89] New Mexico,[90] North Dakota,[91] Oklahoma,[92] Oregon,[93] Pennsylvania,[94] South Carolina,[95] South Dakota,[96] Tennessee,[97] Utah,[98] Vermont,[99] Virginia,[100] Washington,[101] and West Virginia.[102]

Massachusetts, Mississippi, New York, and Ohio all introduced legislation to adopt the act in 2012.

The legislation establishes a uniform set of rules for determining jurisdiction. The act is intended to simplify the process for determining jurisdiction between multiple states in adult guardianship cases, as well as making it easier for state court judges in different states to work together in such cases.

One of the issues that the act is designed to eliminate is multistate jurisdictional issues in "granny snatching" cases. Typically, the fact pattern arises when an older adult resident visits a child in another state (Washington) for vacation, or a child comes to the older adult's state of residence (Illinois) and kidnaps and takes the person to the home (Washington) of the visiting children in a state other than her home state.

Frequently, the misconduct is designed to financially exploit the parent and deprive the court of jurisdiction in the parent's home state.

---

82. ME. REV. STAT. ANN. tit. 18-A, § 5-511 (2011).
83. MD. CODE ANN., EST. & TRUSTS § 13.5-101 (West 2010).
84. MINN. STAT. ANN. § 524.5-602 (West 2010).
85. MO. ANN. STAT. § 475.501 (West 2011).
86. MONT. CODE ANN. § 72-5-602 (West 2009).
87. NEB. REV. STAT. ANN. § 30-3902 (West 2012).
88. NEV. REV. STAT. ANN. § 159.1991 (West 2009).
89. N.J. STAT. ANN. § 3B:12B-1 (West 2012).
90. N.M. STAT. ANN. § 45-5A-102 (West 2012).
91. N.D. CENT. CODE ANN. § 28-35-01 (West 2009).
92. OKLA. STAT. ANN. tit. 30, § 3-302 (West 2010).
93. OR. REV. STAT. ANN. § 125-800 (West 2010).
94. 20 PA. CONST. STAT. ANN. § 5901 (West 2012).
95. S.C. CODE ANN. § 62-5-700 (West 2011).
96. S.D. CODIFIED LAWS § 29A-5A-101 (2011).
97. TENN. CODE ANN. § 34-8-101 (West 2011).
98. UTAH CODE ANN. §75-5b-101 (West 2009).
99. VT. STAT. ANN. tit. 14, § 3151 (West 2011).
100. VA. CODE ANN. § 64.2-2100 (West 2012).
101. WASH. REV. CODE ANN. § 11.90.010 (West 2010).
102. W. VA. CODE ANN. § 44C-1-1 (West 2009).

Such conduct is also intended to take the parent out of the reach of a guardianship in the parent's home state. However, if both states have adopted the act, there is a framework for determining jurisdiction and protecting the older adult.

DIVORCE AND GUARDIANSHIP ISSUES FOR INDIVIDUALS WITH ALZHEIMER'S DISEASE

Several states have enacted statutes giving guardians/conservators general authority to act on behalf of wards and conservatees. It is well accepted that these general grants of power usually include the authority to make personal decisions about the ward's health care, end-of-life treatment, place of residence, and visitors. However, one area that many jurisdictions still find too personal to allow a guardian or conservator to act on behalf of the ward is divorce.

The majority rule is that guardians and conservators cannot bring a divorce action on behalf of a ward unless a statute expressly grants such authority. However, an increasing minority of states are beginning to hold that a guardian or conservator can bring a divorce action on behalf of a ward even without express statutory authorization.

Illinois and the "Best Interests" Hearing

In 2012, the Illinois Supreme Court overturned its long-standing decision in *In re Marriage of Drews* and now allows guardians to initiate divorce actions on behalf of their wards pursuant to a "best interests" hearing.[103]

In *Drews*, the court had adopted the majority rule that, "absent statutory authorization, a guardian cannot maintain an action, on behalf of a ward, for the dissolution of the ward's marriage."[104] Illinois's Probate Act authorizes a guardian to act on behalf of a ward in all legal proceedings.[105] However, the court in *Drews* interpreted this authority as applying to legal proceedings that are financial, but not personal, in nature. Furthermore, the court did not find any "explicit authorization"

---

103. Karbin v. Karbin, No. 112815, 2012 Ill. LEXIS 1011, at *28, *30 (Oct. 4, 2012).
104. *In re* Marriage of Drews, 503 N.E.2d 339, 340 (Ill. 1986).
105. 755 ILL. COMP. STAT. 5/11a-18(c) (2012).

for a guardian to initiate a divorce action in sections 5/11a-17(a)[106] and 5/11a-18[107] of the Probate Act.[108]

In *Karbin*, the court had to decide the issue of whether a guardian has the authority to proceed with a counter-petition for divorce on behalf of the ward, after the competent spouse voluntarily dismissed his petition for divorce, making the counter-petition filed on behalf of the ward the sole petition.

The Illinois Supreme Court ultimately decided that, under Illinois law, guardians do have the authority to initiate a divorce action on behalf of a ward for several reasons.

First, the court explained how its decisions in cases it decided subsequent to *Drews* had been inconsistent with the principles set out in *Drews*.[109] After *Drews*, Illinois courts granted guardians the authority to make very personal decisions on behalf of wards without express statutory language granting guardians the authority to make these types of decisions.[110] In these cases the courts found that guardians are broadly empowered "to perform an act which is within the implied authority granted by the Probate Act."[111]

Second, the court noted that the divorce petition in *Drews* was filed prior to the enactment of Illinois's no-fault divorce statute.[112] The court found it "difficult . . . to accept the view that the decision to divorce is qualitatively different from any other deeply personal decision, such as the decision to refuse life-support treatment or the decision to undergo

---

106. Provides that the duties of a guardian of the person include providing for the ward's "support, care, comfort, health, education and maintenance, and professional services as are appropriate."
107. Provides that the duties of the guardian of the estate include "the care, management and investment of the estate."
108. *In re Drews*, 503 N.E.2d at 341.
109. *Karbin*, 2012 Ill. LEXIS 1011, at *11.
110. *In re* Marriage of Burgess, 725 N.E.2d 1266 (Ill. 2000) (construing sections 11a-17 and 11a-18 broadly and allowing guardian to continue divorce action previously begun by ward prior to adjudication of disability) (holding later codified at 755 Ill. Comp. Stat. 5/11a-17(a-5); *In re* Estate of Greenspan, 558 N.E.2d 1194 (Ill. 1990) (rejecting arguments that Probate Act did not provide guardian with the authority to consent to removal of life support); *In re* Estate of Longeway, 549 N.E.2d 292 (Ill. 1989) (reading section 11a-17 broadly to authorize plenary guardian to make decision on behalf of ward regarding use of life-sustaining treatment); *In re* Estate of K.E.J., 887 N.E.2d 704 (Ill. App. Ct. 2008) (authorizing guardian to seek to have ward undergo involuntary sterilization under section 11a-17(a)).
111. *Karbin*, 2012 Ill. LEXIS 1011, at *12 (quoting *In re Greenspan*, 558 N.E.2d at 1199; *In re Longeway*, 549 N.E.2d at 298).
112. *Karbin*, 2012 Ill. LEXIS 1011, at *20.

involuntary sterilization" without an injury being required for divorce.[113] The court stated that the majority rule in *Drews* is inconsistent with Illinois's policy of no-fault divorce and the policy of the Probate Act.[114]

The Illinois court further explained under the Probate Act that a person with disabilities is entitled to "vigilant protection" under the law.[115] However, the court noted that a spouse with disabilities is left at a disadvantage when only the competent spouse may file for divorce. In this situation, the competent spouse essentially has complete control over the marriage, leaving the spouse "trapped in an unwanted, potentially abusive, marriage."[116]

Ultimately, the Illinois Supreme Court remanded the case directing the circuit court to hold a "best interests" hearing pursuant to section 5/11a-17(e) of the Probate Act, which sets forth the factors[117] to be considered in determining the best interests of the ward.[118] The court also held that a guardian needs to meet a clear and convincing standard to prove that the divorce is in the best interest of the ward.[119]

Prior to the *Karbin* decision, Senate Bill 2547 was introduced in the Illinois Senate in 2012. The proposed bill would authorize a guardian to initiate a divorce action on behalf of a ward only when there is a court order granting the guardian such authority. As a threshold inquiry, the court has to determine whether the ward has the capacity to consent to a divorce. Ultimately, if the court determines that the ward does not have the capacity to consent and is not expressing a clear desire for the divorce, the court has to find the following factors by clear and convincing evidence: the ward lacks decisional capacity, the benefits of the divorce outweigh the harm to the ward, the court has considered less intrusive alternatives, and the divorce is in the best interest of the ward.

113. *Id.* at *21.
114. *Id.* at *22.
115. *Id.* at *23.
116. *Id.* at *22–23 (quoting Mark Schwarz, *The Marriage Trap: How Guardianship Divorce Bans Abet Spousal Abuse*, 13 J.L. & Fam. Stud. 187, 191 (2011)).
117. "In determining the ward's best interests, the guardian shall weigh the reason for and nature of the proposed action, the benefit or necessity of the action, the possible risks and other consequences of the proposed action, and any available alternatives and their risks, consequences and benefits, and shall take into account any other information, including the views of family and friends, that the guardian believes the ward would have considered if able to act for herself or himself."
118. *Karbin*, 2012 Ill. LEXIS 1011, at *29–30.
119. *Id.* at *31.

If this bill were ever to be passed, it would go a long way in codifying the Illinois Supreme Court's decision in *Karbin*.

Divorce is frequently an economic issue, but it may also be a scenario in which the husband and wife have clearly drifted apart. Maybe one is living in a nursing home or long-term-care facility and the other is living in the community, and it's in the best interests of both of them to be able to get out of the marriage and move on.

Another thing to keep in mind is that, for Medicaid planning, sometimes it's important to consider a legal separation as opposed to a divorce. Sometimes people are opposed to a divorce for religious reasons, but they want to have a legal separation in order to get a court order on who retains what assets. (Medicaid planning is discussed in chapter 5.)

Florida

Florida guardians are now authorized to initiate a divorce action on behalf of a ward against a competent spouse if the guardian is given permission to do so by a guardianship court.[120] A guardianship court may authorize such an action as long it holds a noticed evidentiary hearing to determine whether it can be shown by clear and convincing evidence that the divorce is in the ward's best interest and whether the ward's spouse has consented to the divorce.[121] Prior to *Vaughn v. Guardianship of Vaughn*, Florida adhered to the majority rule that a guardian does not have the power to initiate a divorce action on behalf of a ward absent specific statutory authorization for such power.[122] In *Vaughn*, the court ruled that "the question of who will bring the [divorce] action is merely

---

120. FLA. STAT. § 744.3215(4)(c) (2012); Vaughn v. Guardianship of Vaughn, 648 So. 2d 193, 195–96 (Fla. Dist. Ct. App. 1994) (despite guardianship court's authority to permit guardian to initiate divorce action on behalf of ward, court decided that guardianship court erred in granting guardian such authority because it did not hold evidentiary hearing that allowed competent spouse to present evidence that divorce was not in ward's best interest).

121. Other evidentiary hearing requirements are: appoint independent lawyer to act on ward's behalf; obtain independent medical, psychological, and social evaluations about ward; personally meet with ward to afford ward opportunity to express any personal views on divorce issue before court; and find by clear and convincing evidence that wards lacks capacity to make decision about divorce issue before court. FLA. STAT. § 744.3725; *Vaughn*, 648 So. 2d at 195–96.

122. Scott v. Scott, 45 So. 2d 878 (Fla. 1950); Cohen v. Cohen, 346 So. 2d 1047 (Fla. Dist. Ct. App. 1977); Wood v. Beard, 107 So. 2d 198, 199 (Fla. Dist. Ct. App. 1958).

procedural."[123] The court went on to state that a guardian's authority to initiate a divorce is really derived from section 61.052 of Florida's no-fault divorce statute,[124] which was enacted several years after the Florida Supreme Court's adoption of the majority rule.

Section 61.052(b) provides that one of the grounds for divorce is the mental incompetence of a spouse so long as the spouse has been adjudged incompetent for at least three years. This section also states that the competent spouse must file for divorce and serve the guardian or nearest blood relative of the incompetent spouse who is entitled to appear and be heard on the issues. The guardian must defend and protect the interests of the ward. If the guardian is the spouse of the ward, then the court must appoint a guardian ad litem to represent the ward in the divorce action in order to avoid a conflict of interest between the spouses.

New York

The New York courts are undecided on the issue of guardian-initiated divorces. In *McRae v. McRae*, the court opined that the state's divorce statute did not expressly prohibit an incompetent individual from bringing a divorce action through the guardian. In this case, the incompetent spouse/husband had been residing in a mental institution for several years when he brought a divorce action upon the ground of his wife's adultery. He asked the court to appoint a guardian ad litem to represent him in the divorce action. The wife contended that a divorce is personal and cannot be maintained by anyone other than one of the spouses. The court rejected the wife's argument and authorized the appointment of a guardian ad litem for the husband.[125]

However, in *Mainzer v. Avril*,[126] a New York court held that no one could bring a divorce action on behalf of an incompetent spouse due to a lack of express statutory authority allowing someone besides the parties to bring such an action. Also, in *Mohrmann v. Kob*, the court came to a similar conclusion. A wife brought an action against her husband who had a disability to enforce the terms of a separation agreement. The husband's guardian counterclaimed for a divorce on the ground of the wife's

---

123. *Vaughn*, 648 So. 2d at 195.
124. Fla. Stat. § 61.052.
125. McRae v. McRae, 250 N.Y.S.2d 778, 780–81 (N.Y. App. Div. 1964).
126. 177 N.Y.S. 596 (N.Y. Sup. Ct. 1919).

adultery, but the court held that a statutory grant of general power to a guardian to maintain any action on behalf of an incompetent individual is not sufficient to authorize a guardian to specifically bring a divorce action on behalf of an incompetent person.[127]

California

In California, a guardian or conservator has the power to initiate a divorce action on behalf of an incompetent individual. Section 372(a) of the California Code of Civil Procedure states that "when . . . an incompetent person, or a person for whom a conservator has been appointed is a party, that person will appear either by a guardian or conservator of the estate or by guardian ad litem appointed by the court in which the action or proceeding is pending." Also, in *In re Marriage of Higgason*,[128] the California Supreme Court held that a guardian may bring a divorce action on behalf of an incompetent spouse "provided it is established that the spouse is capable of exercising judgment, and expressing a wish, that the marriage be dissolved on account of irreconcilable differences and has done so."[129] In *Higgason*, the incompetent wife was able to satisfy these requirements by signing and verifying her divorce petition and testifying in a deposition that she wanted a divorce.[130]

Vermont

The Vermont Supreme Court has issued an opinion following the majority rule.[131] In *Samis v. Samis*, the wife suffered from dementia, and her guardian filed for divorce on her behalf. The husband filed a motion to dismiss the divorce petition on the basis that Vermont's guardianship statute[132] does not authorize a guardian to initiate a divorce action on behalf of a ward. The family court denied the motion and allowed the divorce action to proceed.

The family court acknowledged that there is no specific authorization for a guardian to file a divorce complaint in the guardianship statute. The court instead based its decision on Vermont Rule for Family

127. Mohrmann v. Kob, 51 N.E.2d 921, 924 (N.Y. 1943).
128. 516 P.2d 289, 294 (Cal. 1973), *overruled on other grounds by In re* Marriage of Dawley, 551 P.2d 323 (Cal. 1976).
129. *In re Higgason*, 516 P.2d at 294.
130. *Id.*
131. Samis v. Samis, 22 A.3d 444 (Vt. 2011).
132. Vt. Stat. Ann. tit. 14, § 3069 (2012).

Proceedings 4(b)(1)(A), which it interpreted as authorizing a guardian to sign a divorce complaint on behalf of a ward.[133]

The Vermont Supreme Court declined to affirm the family court's decision on these grounds, stating that a guardian's authority to initiate a divorce on behalf of a ward cannot come from a procedural rule promulgated by the supreme court. Rather, the guardian's authority has to come from a statute created by the legislature.

The court went on to examine section 3069(c)(6) of the guardianship statute that gives a guardian general authority to obtain legal advice and initiate court actions on behalf of the ward. The court ultimately concluded that the legislature did not intend for this general grant of authority to a guardian to include the power to initiate a divorce action on behalf of a ward and reversed the decision of the family court.

Connecticut

In *Luster v. Luster*,[134] a Connecticut appellate court held that a conservator may bring a divorce action on behalf of a conserved person. The non-disabled spouse filed a divorce action against her husband, who suffered from senile dementia and was found by the probate court to be incapable of caring for himself. The husband's two daughters were appointed as his permanent conservators of his person and estate. The daughters filed a counter-petition for divorce on behalf of their father. The court concluded that the daughters, as conservators of the person and estate of their father, could not bring a counter-petition on his behalf.

The appellate court reversed the lower court's dismissal of the counter-petition for divorce basing its decision in part on section 45a-650(k) of Connecticut's General Statutes, which states that a "conserved person shall retain all rights and authority not expressly assigned to the conservator." Under Connecticut's General Statutes, a conservator is not given express authority to initiate a divorce action on behalf of a conserved person. The court also based its decision on the common-law rule that, generally, a conserved person can only bring a civil action through the conservator. Taking the statute and common law into consideration, the court concluded that "given that . . . an action for dissolution of marriage is a civil action . . . a conservator may bring a civil

---

133. *Samis*, 22 A.3d 444.
134. 17 A.3d 1068 (Conn. App. Ct. 2011).

action for dissolution of marriage on behalf of a conserved person."[135] The Connecticut Supreme Court granted an appeal of this case in July 2011. As of April 16, 2012, the status of this appeal was disposed by nisi disposition.

Overall, these recent decisions in the various state courts demonstrate that there is still a split in the jurisdictions over whether a guardian has the authority to initiate a divorce action on behalf of a ward. Although these courts reached different decisions, it is apparent that this issue is not going away and will ultimately be up to the state legislature to decide the issue and enact a statute accordingly.

135. *Luster*, 17 A.3d at 1080.

 **Expert View**

Even Experienced Lawyers Make These Mistakes

Dr. Sanford Finkel is *both* a clinical professor of psychiatry at the University of Chicago Medical School and an active clinician. He has been retained as an expert consultant who has reviewed and testified in a wide variety of court cases involving contested wills, testamentary capacity, and undue influence.

Q: What mistakes do attorneys make when trying to determine capacity?

A: First of all, lawyers must realize that, with Alzheimer's disease, a person who loses his cognitive capacity and functional abilities doesn't always lose his social abilities. In a superficial conversation, the person can respond and, on the surface, connect. But if you ask him detailed questions, he may say, "My daughter will answer that." He will defer or deflect the question. Or he may answer your question with a question. In other words, he will give you something with a little piece of your question—two words maybe—or he will answer a question you haven't asked.

People may stay alert and remain pleasant until very late in their illness. Some lawyers (as well as others) may be very ready to believe anyone who is socially pleasant. Lawyers like people who are alert and not difficult. People stay alert until very late in the illness.

Lawyers often ask yes or no questions. When dealing with a controversial will, the defense may arrange for videos in an attempt to prove that a person has capacity. I remember one situation where the testatrix was leaving her assets to charity. The lawyer brought her husband to the nursing home to film the signing. She asked the testatrix, "You do want to leave your money to this person, right?" The testatrix replied, "Yes." The next question from the attorney was, "You don't want to leave your money to these people here, do you?" The testatrix answered, "No." The lawyer asked, "It is July 8, 2007, isn't it?" The testatrix answered, "Yes."

The problem is that this woman had been seen by a psychiatrist at the nursing home, and every time he had examined her he found her completely disoriented. The day before the signing, she thought the year was 1923, and she did not know the date or the season. So, in contrast to what the lawyer intended, the video showed that by the use of biased yes or no questions the lawyer was trying to unduly influence the testatrix.

In another case, the attorney was on the boards of many charities. The testator had only one relative, a cousin with whom he had been close. While the testator was in a nursing home, he made a new will, leaving his entire $2 million estate to the charities of which the attorney was a board member. The cousin was bequeathed nothing. The lawyer next asked, "You *do* want to leave all of this to the charities, *don't you?*" The man nodded and didn't even say yes. The next question was, "You *don't* want to leave anything to your nephew? Right?" The testator smiled and nodded affirmatively.

So the testator was able to smile and nod just like a young child, but he was unable to sign his name. The lawyer and his witnesses said that the testator, a high school graduate, signed with an X on the designated page. There was no X on any of the other pages.

To overcome the problem of assuming that socially pleasant people are cognitively competent, one must *ask open-ended questions.* If someone is changing his will, you need to ask him, "Why are you doing this? Why did you decide to change the percentages between your daughter and your son? What do you think is going to happen upon your death, if you change your will this way? How do you think your next of kin will react?" Sometimes it's possible to have the person who is creating a controversial will re-think his decisions. Perhaps reconciliation with an out-of-favor family member is possible. This course of action may avoid will contest litigation.

My advice to a lawyer with a client with a controversial will is to ask the client to see a mental health specialist for an evaluation. A videotape, an audiotape, or a written report should suffice.

A person could have Alzheimer's and still might have testamentary capacity. It depends on the complexity of the task, the context, and the degree of cognitive impairment. For example, once I was asked to give an opinion on the testamentary capacity of an 89-year-old man who was in the moderate stage of Alzheimer's disease. He had insisted on making a will and said, "I have a wife I've been married to for 65 years. I have two daughters who fight all the time. I want my wife to get everything."

I asked him, "What are your assets?" He answered, "I have a bank account." "What do you have in it?" He responded, "I don't know, maybe half a million. I'd have to look at my statement." He took out a folder, and he had accurately approximated his existing cash assets (I verified there were no other cash or cash-equivalent accounts).

I then asked, "What other assets do you have?" He answered, "I have the condo."

I asked, "How much was the condo worth?" He responded, "I would have to ask my real estate agent or my secretary. I think it's about $300,000." So, I concluded that he did have the elements of testamentary capacity.

But the story does not end here. Two months later, his wife died, and he incurred a fall and hip fracture and was rehabilitating in a nursing home. His two daughters were fighting with each other, and one daughter was able to get him to sign an amendment, leaving everything to her. In a week's time he had been taken out of his home where he had lived for decades. His situation had vastly changed in two months. He was disoriented to time and place. He scored a 12/20 on the Mini-Mental State Examination. He had no idea what his assets were at that point in time. In a new environment without the calm structure his wife had provided, and in the middle of family conflict, he no longer had testamentary capacity.

Q: What other advice would you like to share with lawyers?

A: It is also important to obtain previous estate-planning documents. If you are going to amend an estate-planning document involving a substantial shift in bequests, one must know what documents already exist. If there is a major change, then the testator needs to explain his rationale. At this critical juncture, it might be possible for the attorney to take action (e.g., by referring to a mental health expert) to avoid expensive and painful litigation after the testator dies. In many cases, the attorney has never seen the prior documents. Often they are surprised to learn about their client's prior long-standing estate plans.

One of the common challenges I face in these cases is: "Dr. Finkel, you never met the individual or you only spoke to them one time, but the general practitioner saw this person 112 times. The general practitioner disagrees with you, and the treating doctor must be right, if he says that the testator has (or doesn't have) testamentary capacity!"

However, in my opinion, the general practitioner is rarely in a better position than the expert to determine mental capacity, even if the expert has never seen the testator. Often I have reviewed thousands or even tens of thousands of pages of medical records and other documents, those of the primary care physicians, but also other physicians and health care providers, hospital and nursing home records, and home health care information. It's the rare primary care physician who has done that. A primary care physician has a few notes; maybe over 15 years she has accumulated 100–300 pages of notes. But after my review of many thousands of health care and medical records, I generally have a much broader understanding of the cognitive capacity of the individual than the primary care doctor. In addition, evaluating cognitive capacity and mental illness of older people is my specialty as a geriatric psychiatrist—this is my expertise. The primary care physician or the non-psychiatrist specialist has other expertise and responsibilities.

For example, a cardiologist or pulmonologist is trying to save a man's life in the hospital. These specialists may never do a complete mental status evaluation. I have been in situations when such a specialist may testify, "Well, I knew he knew what he was doing." If asked, "How did you know?" The specialist might respond, "I always asked him, 'How are you doing? How is your family?' And he would answer, 'Great,' so I knew that he was mentally OK."

Q: You've been hired by attorneys to provide expert advice in many prominent cases. Do you ever have to tell the attorney who has hired you that there is a problem with the case?

A: If my opinion is contrary to her client's position, I try to help the attorney understand the clinical shortcomings in her case and what clinical or factual avenues to explore to enhance her understanding of the case. I'm an advocate for my opinions, not an advocate for the case. I don't proceed with cases if I do not support the retaining attorney's client's position. When I first started expert work, I thought that if I came up with the "wrong" opinions, the lawyers were going to be mad at me, but so be it. In fact, they are almost never angry, because lawyers do not want to spend a few years investing their time gathering and then, at the end, find out that they have a clinically (and legally) weak case.

CHAPTER 7

FINANCIAL EXPLOITATION

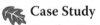 **Case Study** ───────────────────────
   Sex for Signatures

On a warm Friday afternoon in Chicago, a boomer son and daughter of a physically healthy 86-year-old man named Eugene sat across the desk from a respected and experienced elder law litigator. They had come to see the lawyer for advice regarding concerns they had about their father and his new friend Olga. This is the story they shared.

"Dad married his high school sweetheart—that was our mom, Doris. They were married for over 60 years. Mom and Dad were always devoted to each other. For many years Mom suffered from debilitating diabetes, and then cancer. Mom loved Dad with all her heart. For the last 10 years, Dad has been Mom's full-time caregiver.

"Mom and Dad had always been very religiously conservative—but for the last fifteen years or so, Mom wasn't even able to attend church. After Mom's death, there was a funeral at the church. It seemed like everyone in the community turned out, because Mom and Dad were so respected. A woman named Olga attended the funeral whom none of us had ever met before. She warmly addressed all of the family members and expressed her condolences for our loss. She appeared to be about 65 years of age and fit as a fiddle.

"After the funeral, Olga began attending church and all of the older adult activities. She publicly declared her faith and volunteered to help out wherever she was needed. After a while, people told us that everywhere that Dad went, Olga was sitting right beside him. I think our dad was quite flattered to have the attention of a younger woman, after all those years of caring for Mom. The relationship seems to have become romantic within a matter of months after Mom's funeral.

"We children had noticed that Dad was becoming 'a little forgetful,' but we considered that just a normal part of old age. Dad has always been close with all of us kids, and he told us about Olga. We were very happy for him to have a companion and to be getting out of the house. Everything seemed to start out okay—but during the last few months Dad has become more withdrawn from family activities. He doesn't call or return calls like he used to. He stopped sending birthday cards to the grandkids (which always had a $50 bill in them). Some of us kids attempted a trip home to see Dad for Thanksgiving—but we were told quite bluntly, 'No, please don't come. I'm going to have Thanksgiving with Olga and her family.'

"Right after Thanksgiving we got a call from a lifelong family friend who is Dad's accountant. He urged us to visit Dad, because he had been visited by Dad and Olga. He indicated that substantial changes in ownership of assets were being discussed. He recommended that we contact you, Mr. Attorney."

After listening to this story, the wise yet cynical lawyer stated, "From my experience, this is probably a case of *professional* financial exploitation—especially due to the fact that your father may suffer from a bit of dementia. I think it's very probable that there is sexual activity going on between Olga and Eugene. I refer to this as the 'sex for signatures' scam."

Immediately the son and daughter stood up, outraged. "Sir—you have no business insulting our family and our father. Our dad has always been an upstanding man of the faith! I resent your comments and your lack of empathy!" After saying that, they promptly left the office.

On the following Monday morning, the first call into the lawyer's office was from the son and daughter, who had spent the weekend at the dad's house. As soon as the phone was answered, they blurted out to the lawyer, "We can't believe it! You were right. During the weekend we heard the unmistakable sounds of intimacy coming from our father's room. And that's not the worst of it! There was a brand-new Lexus sitting in the driveway, for which Dad had taken out the loan. But the car title is in Olga's name."

> **The Most Fleeting Human Emotion**
>
> "I have observed over 200 contested guardianships with an elder abuse component. In my opinion, guilt is the most fleeting human emotion. From what I have seen, if the abuser had any guilt at the beginning when first reaching over and taking something from a frail, vulnerable senior, it didn't last long. Interestingly, it doesn't stop there. Over time, the thief rationalizes that they are actually owed the money by the parent or grandparent or elderly neighbor from whom they are stealing. Amazingly, it goes even further—to the point that, eventually, the bad guy sees himself as the victim!"—Shay Jacobson, RN, MA, NMG (National Master Guardian), President of Lifecare Innovations, Inc.

FINANCIAL EXPLOITATION

Instances of financial exploitation are on the rise and senior citizens are frequent targets.

What is even more disturbing is that about 90 percent of the financial exploitation of seniors is committed by family members or people that they should be able to trust, such as caregivers.

Seniors, and especially seniors with dementia, are the perfect victims because they generally won't report the abuse. They won't report the exploitations for a variety of reasons, ranging from being embarrassed to fear that if they turn in their relative or caregiver they will be put in a nursing home because there will be nobody left to care for them in their home.

Amy Flynn, an elder abuse supervisor at Senior Services, states that a significant amount of the financial exploitation cases that she sees involve an abuse of a power of attorney.

Flynn notes that the majority of the cases combine financial exploitation and emotional abuse. "They go hand in hand together because an abuser will manipulate mom or dad's emotions in order to exploit money from them. More often than not, those cases do involve some form of abuse of a power of attorney."

 Case Study
Financial Exploitation and Emotional Abuse

In a recent elder abuse case, the daughter constantly told her elderly mother, "You were never there for me as a child. You were a horrible mother. You never bought me the things that I wanted." The mother was suffering from dementia and the daughter convinced her to sign paperwork giving the daughter power of attorney for financial matters.

Soon after the documents were signed, the daughter used her mother's funds to buy herself a vacation home in Florida. Likely, the daughter felt entitled to the vacation home.

Another example of financial exploitation and emotional abuse is when adult children who have drug or alcohol problems move into their parent's home. The children often end up living off of the parent and then they become verbally abusive to obtain money for the purchase of drugs or alcohol. In some cases, they will get their parent to sign documents giving them power of attorney, thus providing easy access to money for drugs and alcohol.

Charles Golbert, deputy public Guardian and supervisor of the Adult Guardian Subdivision with the Cook County (Illinois) Public Guardian's Office, agrees that powers of attorney documents can be problematic.

"They're just too easy to fill in and forge or have somebody who doesn't have capacity to sign," he says. "People are entitled to rely on the documents as long as there is nothing facially problematic about them. They're very dangerous for that reason as well. In fact, I tell people powers of attorney are kind of the scariest documents that I know. I'd say they're the single most abused document we see in our financial exploitation practice."

Practice Pointer: Client Capacity Before Creating a Power of Attorney

It is very important to have a doctor examine a client if there might be any issue with capacity. (See chapter 2 and Rule 1.14.) Always err on the side of being overly cautious.

Amy Flynn has asked many lawyers, "Why did you go ahead and do this power of attorney paperwork when we have documentation that shows that the individual had dementia?" The lawyer will always respond, "Well, they appeared to be absolutely fine when I sat down and met with them."

One of the challenges with some forms of dementia is that it is very hard for a layperson to determine capacity, and even giving a *Mini Mental Status Exam* (MMSE) can still lead to a false conclusion that people have capacity but, in reality, don't understand the consequences of their acts.

An awful lot of lawyers treat powers of attorney as if they are an unimportant throwaway document, but in a senior's life (particularly one with dementia) it is not a throwaway document. It is empowering somebody to have an absolute license to steal.

It is worth revisiting author Kerry Peck's thoughts on the dangers of the misuse of a power of attorney from chapter 3: "Unfortunately, when a durable power of attorney for property is used inappropriately, it can be used on a regular basis to exploit individuals. People no longer use guns to rob banks; today they use a durable power of attorney. A durable power of attorney, when presented to an unsuspecting teller of a bank, will be used to withdraw massive sums of money."

 Case Study

The Crooked Attorney and a Broad Power of Attorney

Susie never married or had children and ended up outliving all of her relatives. As various family members passed away, Susie inherited their estates. Susie's last living relative, her brother, died when she was 66. After inheriting her brother's estate, Susie had about $350,000 in investment accounts and owned her longtime home outright.

Susie had no other sources of income and needed this money to last for the rest of her life. After her brother died, Susie had no family to look after her. When she reached her early 70s, Susie developed Alzheimer's disease and was soon unable to protect her interests. She began to rely more and more on the family's longtime, trusted lawyer to help her with finances. Susie was incapacitated, but the lawyer had her sign a very broad power of attorney agreement granting the lawyer virtually unfettered access to all of her moneys. Shortly after Susie signed the instrument, the lawyer started to plunder her funds.

Over an eight-year period, the lawyer stole $176,000 from Susie's accounts. He also squandered away large portions of Susie's pension and social security. When the lawyer had worked his way through Susie's savings and investment accounts, he sold her longtime home to his friend and client for far less than its market value. He then helped himself to much of the remaining sale proceeds.

After selling Susie's home, the lawyer moved her into a very small apartment on the other side of town, away from the neighborhood where she had lived her entire life. At this point, her old neighbors became suspicious and called the police, who referred the case to the Public Guardians Program. The Public Guardians Program subsequently became Susie's guardian and sued the lawyer for recovery of Susie's home and the moneys he stole. They also reported him to the lawyer registration and disciplinary commission. The case eventually settled, and Susie's house and her savings were returned to her. She was able to move back into her longtime home, where she lived out the remaining years of her life. The lawyer was disbarred.

Financial fraud may be experiencing an uptick in activity, but it is interesting to note that many scams that are prevalent now are not really new or unique.

"While the Internet has made financial fraud more pervasive, law enforcement said most online scams are not much different than those employed by snake oil salesmen in the 19th century and Florida swampland salesmen in the 1960s. Unsuspecting consumers are deceived over and over again with the same schemes, failing to realize that scammers are infinitely creative in making them believe they're offering something new and lucrative."[1]

One type of financial scam that seems to have been around since the dawn of time is the sudden appearance of the wolf in sheep's clothing.

"Cloaked in a new disguise, con men appeal to the individual's weak spot: a desperate shortage of money before payday, a need to earn more than the yield on their certificate of deposit, a need to pay medical bills."[2]

These scams are most popular in times of financial uncertainty and are likely to target vulnerable seniors who are worried about their retirement and having to financially support their adult children.

"Economic hardship means more people have less money to risk with shady deals. But economic hardship also makes people more vulnerable—and scammers more desperate and creative—authorities said. Alabama's [Joe] Borg [head of Alabama's Securities Commission] said the financial market collapse in 2008 created new potential targets, whether young working professionals distrustful of traditional stock

---

1. Kimberly Blanton, TRS. OF BOS. COLL., CTR. FOR RET. RESEARCH, THE RISE OF FINANCIAL FRAUD: SCAMS NEVER CHANGE BUT DISGUISES DO (2012).
2. *Id.*

and bond markets, baby boomers panicking about insufficient retirement savings, the unemployed living on the edge, or retirees dissatisfied with the historically low rates they are earning on their assets."[3]

Most senior citizens are probably very trusting of police officers, especially their neighborhood beat cop. Unfortunately, this trust is not always warranted.

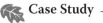 **Case Study**

The Bad Cop

Jerry was a lifelong bachelor. He worked for the city for 30 years and was able to retire with a modest pension. He had lived a frugal life and had paid off his house and accumulated modest savings, which he kept in certificates of deposit.

Jerry turned 80 and became afflicted with dementia. He started becoming confused and disoriented. One day, Jerry mistakenly entered a neighbor's home believing it was his home, and refused to leave. Not knowing what to do, the neighbor called the police. A beat officer responded to the call and took Jerry home.

Shortly after, the police officer began taking advantage of Jerry's dementia to enrich himself. The officer had Jerry sign documents designating the officer as the primary beneficiary of Jerry's retirement death benefit. He also had Jerry name him as the beneficiary of Jerry's certificates of deposit. Next, the officer had Jerry execute trust documents naming the officer as beneficiary, under which he would receive Jerry's entire trust estate, both real and personal. He even had Jerry execute a pour-over will, leaving all of his real and personal property to the trust.

Jerry's nephew came to town to visit his uncle and some friends and take in a baseball game. When the nephew visited Jerry, the police officer was in the home, which made the nephew suspicious. The nephew began to investigate and learned what had happened to his uncle's estate. The nephew contacted the Public Guardians Program. After an investigation, the Public Guardians Program petitioned the probate court to become Jerry's guardian. The petition was granted, and the Public Guardians Program sued the police officer to invalidate the above transactions.

After a long and testy trial, the judge invalidated all of the transactions. The judge also awarded Jerry $50,000 in punitive damages.

The cases of Susie and Jerry illustrate a common theme in many financial exploitation cases: the exploiter is often someone in a position

---

3. *Id.*

of trust and authority who abuses this power for financial gain. While some cases involve strangers who exploit the vulnerable, the majority of cases involve people who are uniquely positioned to take advantage of the disabled person, such as fiduciaries, family members, and trusted members of society.

Golbert notes that another growing area of concern in financial exploitation cases is sloppy lawyering. In many of the cases where a power of attorney or other document was created after the person signing over the power or changing a will was clearly incapacitated due to dementia; it's not a case of the lawyer being a crook. It is more likely that the lawyer was sloppy. For example, somebody says: "My grandmother wants a will, and she wants to make me agent of power of attorney. Can you prepare the documents?" Amazingly, the lawyer just prepares the documents, having never seen or met the grandmother who is actually the client under the law. Most of the time, the lawyer charges the typical fee, not a kick back from what was stolen using the power of attorney. The lawyer wasn't involved in the finance exploitation, but it is sloppy lawyering. Lawyers must be vigilant to avoid becoming unwitting coconspirators to elder abuse.

Practice Pointer: Keep in Mind Who the Client Is

Lawyers have to be sure they know who the client is and that they talk with their clients in private.

When a person brings an elderly relative to a lawyer's office and wants paperwork drawn up so that the person can have power of attorney over the elderly relative, the lawyer has a duty to talk to the elderly adult—who is the actual client—and should do so in private.

If there are concerns about the mental capacity of the client, then a doctor should be brought in to make an independent judgment on capacity.

Golbert says lawyers need to have a healthy suspicion, and should always be on the lookout and have their antennas up. They should be suspicious of anything that doesn't quite smell right or sit right, and should follow up on it.

Another big issue in financial exploitation is the monitoring of guardians. If the guardian is financially exploiting the ward, who is looking out for the ward? Ideally, the court system is overseeing the monitoring of the guardianship process, but the reality is that frequently that is not the case.

The courts in some states and counties do a great job monitoring guardians, but many do not. The courts that are doing a better job have mechanisms in place so that when a guardian does not file accounting paperwork, it sets off a red flag and a citation is sent to the guardian.

In many counties, specialized probate judges actually review all the annual accountings. In those counties, the judges are able to intelligently review accountings and catch red flags because of their training. There are other jurisdictions where there isn't any mechanism to track when an accounting has not been filed for years.

In some counties, the same judges that hear traffic cases, divorce cases, and contract disputes also hear probate and guardianship matter. Those judges might not have much familiarity with what to look for when they review accountings. They might not pick up on something that might be a red flag to a judge that specializes in this area.

FORENSIC ACCOUNTING

At the Elder Justice Center in Tampa, Florida, the probate judges have larger-than-average caseloads, but they have something called a guardian monitor that is part of the center. The guardian monitors are hired and trained and supervised by the center, but they serve the courts. They may not qualify as actual forensic accountants, but they have training in reviewing accountings and are trained to recognize the red flags.

Every accounting gets scrutinized not by the judge, but by one of these guardian monitors. The guardian monitor reports any suspicion or concern to the judge, and the judge will call the parties in to follow up on it and appoint a guardian ad litem if necessary and appropriate.

A system does not necessarily have to use licensed certified public accountants with specialized certification in forensics to monitor the guardians in order to be successful. It could be modeled on Tampa, where the guardians ad litem get training in forensic accounting. As long as the people reviewing the accountings know what they're doing and know what they're looking for, the system can work.

If the county isn't as well prepared to monitor guardians as the system in Tampa, it is a good idea to have a general idea of what to look for when a lawyer suspects an elderly client who is suffering from dementia is being financially abused by the guardian.

Practice Pointer: Clues to Financial Exploitation

If lawyers suspect that a client is the victim of embezzlement, one of the first things to look for when examining the client's financial records is anything that ends in all zeros. Because real, typical checks that people write are for amounts like $517.33. So lawyers should look for everything that's $2,500, $500, $1,500. Those kinds of numbers are where to actually start looking to see if somebody is taking money.

Another thing to look for is the use of ATMs. Most elderly people do not use ATMs. They typically will be more likely to go into the bank and deal with someone face-to-face. If there are a lot of ATM withdrawals, that should be a red flag. This is especially true if lawyers see they've never used an ATM for the 30 years they've had a bank account, and then, right when somebody new enters their life, there are a significant number of ATM transactions.

Another red flag is that they are purchasing things that elderly people with dementia don't normally buy. An 80-year-old person who doesn't drive anymore is not going to buy a BMW. Lawyers need to look at the person's finances and ask themselves if these types of expenditures make sense for the elderly client's specific situation.

STRANGER DANGER

When it comes to the other 10 percent of financial exploitation, lawyers are dealing with stranger danger.

Just as seniors are easy prey for family and caregivers, they are prime targets for criminals. Criminals see seniors as easy marks for financial scams for many of the same reasons as family and caregivers, but also because seniors are easy to reach.

They can get seniors by the phone. Many seniors are lonely, so they'll talk. Cherie Aschenbrenner, an elder-service officer with the Elgin (Illinois) Police Department, works with the elderly in her community to help them be more aware of financial exploitation. Aschenbrenner notes that the elderly will almost always answer the phone, even if the caller ID says Kingston, Jamaica. In fact, when people are not on alert when the caller tells them they have won a foreign lottery, they have self-identified themselves as an easy victim.

Criminals can get seniors by the mail, too, because seniors tend to read every piece of mail front and back. They look forward to the mailman bringing them their mail. Studies have shown that seniors place unusually high validity in direct-mail solicitations. Additionally, seniors are usually home a lot and tend to answer the door. This means seniors are susceptible to financial exploitation scams over the phone, through the mail, and face-to-face.

Aschenbrenner also points out that many criminals and scam artists can spot a senior's home just by looking at it. Houses that have an American flag flying, a Buick in the driveway, and well-tended flowers often are owned by senior citizens. Bad guys from all over the world can target seniors using online maps and street views because of these distinctive features on homes owned by seniors.

Now add the fact that the senior is suffering from dementia and there's a lot of opportunity for criminals to financially exploit this group.

One of the most common tools being used by scammers today is the green dot MoneyPak. The green dot MoneyPak is at most big-box stores, and the card itself is perfectly legitimate. It is simply a card to put money on for use as a debit card of sorts. This card plays a large role in the grandma scam and lottery scams.

GRANDMA SCAM

Another common scam is for the scammer to call an elderly woman up and say, "Hi grandma, this is your granddaughter." The senior responds, "Oh, is this Kim?" Now the scammer has the senior on the hook and can reel her in.

The scammer proceeds to tell the senior, "I am going to a wedding in Niagara Falls and I got into this car accident and I need money." Or "Grandma, I'm in jail and they got me for drug charges. But I know it doesn't sound like me because I got a cold, the guy next to me on the plane had a cold so I got it. So I took Nyquil and that's why I have drugs in my system. I need you to send money, Grandma."

The scammer then instructs the senior to get a green dot MoneyPak and put money on the card and to await the call back.

If the senior pays the court costs, the scammers will probably make up another reason that they need more money and will continue to take the senior's money until the senior runs out of money or figures out it's a scam.

Fortunately, education does help. Aschenbrenner was happy to get a call from one of the seniors who heard Aschenbrenner's seminar on avoiding financial exploitation and was able to use that knowledge to defeat a scammer. The senior was the intended victim of the grandma scam, but instead of running to Wal-Mart to put money on a green dot MoneyPak, she called her son and asked if her granddaughter was in Niagara Falls. When the scammer called back, she was able to say, "I know this is a scam because my granddaughter is home."

Sadly, Aschenbrenner estimates that this scam probably works 50 percent of the time.

Lottery Scam

The typical lottery scam works as follows: Seniors receive a call from outside the country and are told they won a foreign lottery. However, they have to prepay the taxes before the winnings can be released to them. The caller will tell them to go to Wal-Mart and pick up a green dot MoneyPak, place $500 on the card, and go back home to await the next phone call in an hour.

The scammer is attempting two things here. First, by sending the senior to a big-box store, it is less likely that the senior will know the cashier and talk about the lottery winnings. Second, by saying he will call back in an hour, the caller is not giving the senior time to think clearly or talk to family about the phone call.

When the scammer calls back, he will have the senior read the 14-number code on the back of the MoneyPak. Once the scammer has the code, he has access to the money on the card and can steal it from the senior.

A variation of the lottery scam involves sending checks to seniors. The senior then tries to cash the check and the check bounces. The bounced check is returned to the scammer with the senior's bank account information on the check and the senior is hit with a fee for the bounced check.

Spoofing

Another phone-related scam is called spoofing. Spoofing is when a person can change the caller ID. Sophisticated criminals can make the caller ID appear to be that of a bank's. They then call up seniors and tell them that there is a problem with their account and ask them to verify their account number, etc. And soon enough, they have the senior's account information.

RUSE ENTRY

A ruse entry involves scammers faking their way into a senior's home for the purposes of robbing them. It works best if they can catch seniors out in the yard. They may tell them that they are new neighbors and ask if they could come into the backyard just a couple of seconds and see the garden. What they're really doing is distracting the senior while someone else comes in the front door and going straight to the bedroom to steal whatever they can.

Another scam is to claim they are from the city's water department and that they were digging in the yards and hit a line. They just need to come in for one minute and check out the basement. They get the senior downstairs, run water, make noise, etc. Meanwhile, the second guy is in the bedroom robbing the senior.

DRIVE-BY CONTRACTORS

Another scam to be on the lookout for is the door-to-door contractor scheme. For example, some men show up and claim to have just finished reroofing a garage down the street. They claim to have extra materials and offer the homeowner a "great deal." If the homeowner accepts, they will try to get paid up front and then will either do shoddy work or start the job and then disappear.

Practice Pointer: Never Respond to People Soliciting for Business

Lawyers should advise their clients to never respond to people who are soliciting them for business.

Never use people who go door to door to work on the house. People who have good business reputations for house repair don't go door to door. They have enough business as it is. Stockbrokers who are making cold calls probably are not very good stockbrokers, even if they are honest. Never, ever respond to solicitations by e-mail, in person, or on the phone.

Aschenbrenner states that a big reason these scams work on seniors so often is because they are so trusting. Because they trust people, they don't want to say, "I don't know who you are. Where's your car? I don't see your vehicle. Let me see your identification." They'll think they'll offend them, so they won't ask them. They'll just let them in their home.

There is also a fear of retaliation with elderly victims. There could be a fear of going to court and being unfamiliar with where to go and what to do. However, the main reason most seniors don't want to contact the police is because they are embarrassed.

Some financial exploitation doesn't start out as a scam. Elderly individuals suffering from dementia who forget to pay their bills or taxes can also become victims of financial exploitation.

Unfortunately for many seniors who have lost their ability to handle their bills, legislators have put into place real estate tax and judgment creditor collection laws based on the assumption that the debtor has the legal capacity of a fully functional 30-year-old adult. Professional real estate tax and debt collection scavengers have developed profitable systems to acquire homes from the vulnerable.

 Case Study ———————————————————————
Legally Protected Exploiters

Maxine was in the early stages of dementia. She owned a house with her husband and had lived in that house for 20 years. They owned the house outright. Maxine's husband always paid the bills and took care of the financial matters. Maxine's husband died and her dementia worsened. At one point, the police found her wandering naked in the streets on a freezing January night.

Maxine was then put in a hospital instead of returning to her home.

While she was hospitalized, Maxine's property taxes were sold to a tax scavenger for nonpayment. The scavenger forced a tax deed sale of Maxine's home for the nonpayment of the taxes. The property taxes at issue amounted to less than $350. The notices of the tax deed sale were sent to Maxine's home, but she was residing at a state mental health hospital. The mailman was aware of her hospitalization and returned the tax sale notices to the sender with the notation "Person is hospitalized" written on the envelopes.

No one ever contacted the mailman or anyone else at the post office about the returned envelopes. Even though the scavenger knew that the notices of the tax deed sale of Maxine's longtime home had been returned unserved, and even though important clues as to Maxine's whereabouts were written on the faces of the returned envelopes, the scavenger proceeded with the forced tax lien sale and obtained a tax deed to Maxine's home.

The trial judge involved in the forced tax sale would later testify in an affidavit that if this information had been disclosed to him, he would not have approved the forced sale.

Shortly after the tax sale, the Office of Public Guardian was appointed guardian on behalf of Maxine. Her guardian immediately moved to vacate the tax deed and argued that Maxine had never received the returned notices that she was about to lose her home due to unpaid taxes. The guardian also presented uncontroverted expert medical evidence that, even if Maxine had received the notices, she would not have been able to understand their import or act to protect herself, due to her mental illness.

The guardian further argued that the scavenger was obligated to follow up on the notations on the returned envelopes and that the notations on the returned notices, along with the fact that a valuable house with no mortgage, liens, or encumbrances was being lost over a mere $347 in unpaid taxes, put the scavenger on notice that something was amiss.

After a lengthy trial, the court denied the motion to vacate the tax deed. The court agreed that Maxine did not receive the notices. The court also agreed with the expert witness psychiatrist that, even if she had received the notices, Maxine would not have been able to understand their meaning or to act. However, the court held that, although the scavenger was on notice that Maxine was hospitalized, he was not on notice that she was hospitalized due to a mental disability.

In addition, the court opined that the scavenger was under no legal obligation to follow up on the information on the returned notices. The state appellate court and state supreme court both affirmed the trial court's decision.

The U.S. Supreme Court granted certiorari, vacated the decision of the state supreme court, and remanded the case for reconsideration in the state supreme court. However, after supplemental briefing and argument, the state supreme court again affirmed the trial and appellate courts.

VULNERABILITY

A 2012 University of California–Los Angeles study conducted by Shelley E. Taylor, a distinguished professor of psychology, found that older people are more likely to fall for scams because they have a greater tendency to fail to interpret an untrustworthy face as potentially dishonest.[4] Apparently, this is because a region of the brain called the anterior insula, which is linked to distrust and is important for discerning untrustworthy faces, is less active in older adults.[5]

"Older adults are more vulnerable. It looks like their skills for making good financial decisions may be deteriorating as early as their early-to-mid-50s," said Taylor, founder of the field of health psychology who was honored in 2010 with the American Psychological Association's Lifetime Achievement Award.[6]

Not only is this fascinating, but this really drives home the very important point that seniors are vulnerable to financial exploitation before the point where they are legally incapacitated.

When drafting estate-planning documents, lawyers always have to be thinking about what has to happen for a person to be determined to be incapacitated. Lawyers should plan for the fact that their clients have a high probability of becoming unable to handle their financial affairs long before they are legally incapacitated. Most often it will be apparent to a spouse and other family members before it ever comes to the notice of either medical or legal professionals.

When drafting estate-planning documents such as a revocable living trust, lawyers should consider offering clients different options for the determination of sufficient incapacity to trigger the removal of the trustee. The traditional options have been to suggest to clients that when two or more attending physicians agree that the individual lacks legal capacity, then the trustee is to be removed and the successor trustee is then empowered. That traditional view has a glaring weakness due to the fact that most physicians do not want to ever have to go to court. In addition, most attending physicians do not want to give a diagnosis of dementia or incapacity, because they do not want to deliver that bad news.

The drafting lawyer should consider discussing with the client the idea of creating a disability panel. Most clients and their spouses

---

4. Press Release, UCLA Office of Media Relations, Why Older Adults Become Fraud Victims More Often (Dec. 3, 2012), *available at* http://newsroom.ucla.edu/portal/ucla/why-older-adults-become-fraud-241076.aspx.

5. *Id.*

6. *Id.*

embrace the idea of a disability panel for the determination of sufficient incapacity so as to remove a *financially vulnerable* trustee.

This concept works well for both married couples and single individuals, in that clients may identify certain trusted friends or family who they believe would make a proper decision when and if the clients become sufficiently incapacitated to handle their own affairs. Many clients choose to include family members and one attending physician. They often empower a majority to rule in the decision making. In other cases, clients may be more comfortable with a unanimous decision.

The concept of a disability panel is very important because physicians are reluctant to take the liability of determining that a person is incapacitated. Because of this reluctance, it's becoming harder and harder to have the traditional language in a trust that actually works to provide the protections people want. People want the trust to be able to relieve an incapacitated trustee of authority and replace him or her with a successor to take over. If a client has chosen one or two physicians, lawyers may have difficulty getting one or both of them to say the client is incapacitated.

One of the authors actually heard a physician say, "I would not determine a person to be incapacitated unless I was convinced that if there was a fire in their home, they would not know enough to leave."

This is troubling because people become vulnerable from a financial standpoint long before they would know to leave if the room was on fire. Many people become vulnerable to financial exploitation and financial error long before they're incapacitated. They are vulnerable.

The author then asked the doctor, "What, if anything, could you do if a person was losing their ability but it hadn't reached the level of incapacity?"

The doctor replied: "Well, there's no Medicare reimbursement code for the determination of vulnerability. There's no protocol for vulnerability. I could not do anything."

Linda Voirin, a licensed social worker at the Kane County (Illinois) State's Attorney Office, is a victim advocate specifically for seniors and people with disabilities. She believes that about 75 percent of the elderly victims she sees are suffering from some sort of vulnerability because of aging. Many times that vulnerability does not render the victim legally incapacitated.

Often the vulnerability is mental, but sometimes it is physical. Voirin explains that physical vulnerability doesn't just mean a physical disability that can be seen, but can also mean that people are not able to get out and go to the bank themselves to do some things that they might have done. Maybe there is vision loss and they have to have someone else sign a check. That vision loss opens up a door for someone else to take advantage of them without them ever knowing it.

It isn't easy for lawyers to always notice the declining mental abilities of their senior clients, because it is such a gray area. Voirin notes that the legal and medical communities need to develop better tools to figure this out. Without better tools, too many vulnerable seniors are left with no legal protection when vulnerability leaves them defenseless.

Voirin says: "The reality is there has been changes in the brain and some of those changes are important changes having to do with decision making, which I would think any private attorney needs to verify that it has not been affected. Because with changes in the brain, in the frontal cortex, they can sit and have tea and coffee and talk about the sports, Fox News, and everything else, but yet, when it comes to their checkbook, they may not be able to understand as well as they have in the past. They will not tell you they are forgetful and confused, but someone living with them will be able to identify it and begin to take advantage of it." [7] (See chapter 2 for an in-depth explanation of Rule 1.14 and dealing with capacity.)

These changes to the senior's brain help explain why people that no one ever would have expected are giving money away to the Canadian lottery or all these other scams. Ten years earlier, they would have said, "Are you kidding me? What are you thinking? Of course it's a scam." But now, all of a sudden, many things are believable to them, because of changes in the brain.

If an unscrupulous caregiver is taking care of a person with Alzheimer's and says to this person, "You owe me $6,000 for this week because I did just a few extra loads of laundry," that person isn't going to hesitate before paying someone far more than what should be paid. It is even easier just to fill out a check for $6,000 and put it in front of seniors to sign—they often will.

Shay Jacobson, a registered nurse and president of Lifecare Innovations, Inc., points out that practitioners need to be looking for red flags in their elderly clients' behavior. One such red flag is that people that

---

7. Linda Voirin's professional opinion and observation based on experience. Phone interview with Linda Voirin, 2012.

have early-stage Alzheimer's may have difficulty with sequencing. They cannot remember which child was born first, second, or third. They can't remember what year they were married.

People in the early stages of Alzheimer's also usually have more difficulty with short-term memory deficits than long-term. So they'll make appointments and then they'll call the office five times to verify the appointment. Each time they call, they will have no recollection of already having called.

Officer Aschenbrenner laments the fact that there is very little that the police can do to protect the vulnerable elderly until they are actually incapacitated. In cases where an elderly person is being financially exploited by a child, about all that can be done is to give the person a Mini Mental Status Exam (MMSE) and try to prove the need for a guardianship. Then hopefully somebody honest in the family would take over.

The law is not going to protect someone with capacity from making bad mistakes. If people have the legal capacity, they are free to make bad mistakes.

WOLF IN SHEEP'S CLOTHING

Vulnerable seniors are very susceptible to the wolf in sheep's clothing. Seniors are trusting and want to believe people.

 Case Study ———————————————————————————

The War Hero from Church

Take, for example, somebody who is supposedly a sophisticated developer/investor who takes an 85-year-old man and his wife to a fancy dinner. They trust him because he is a member of their church and, like the 85-year-old man, is a veteran. In addition, he is supposedly a war hero.

He invites them over and drives them around his big apartment complex. He points out where he provides a free apartment for one of the church's ministers. He's taking care of the minister for the church and basically tells them that they will get a better-than-market return if they invest with him and God's Kingdom. Oh, and by the way, he suggests that they get a reverse mortgage on their house because that's free money and he will help them invest that money to get a big "above market rate" return.

The couple invests $220,000, but the promissory notes are nonrecourse notes signed by the developer on behalf of illusory entities. Not surprisingly, the provider of the investment product, the promissory note, is a non-registered entity. The lawyer for the couple filed suit using a consumer fraud statute.

 Case Study
The Wayward Priest

A local priest was going through the neighborhood surrounding his parish and offering Holy Communion to the homebound members of his church. On the surface, this seems like a normal activity that one might expect a priest to do for his congregation. However, this priest had a lawyer accompanying him. The pair would come into the homes of the sick or the old or those that just couldn't make it into the church for whatever reason, and the priest would perform a mass and offer them Holy Communion right in their living room.

After the priest was done, the lawyer would then offer his estate-planning services to the homeowner. The homeowners, people too old and frail or too sick to attend church, trusted the lawyer, because he was accompanied by their priest.

It turned out that the beneficiary of the estate-planning documents was none other than the priest. The priest owned properties in Florida and was hiding money in multiple locations. (So much for his vow of poverty.) And, naturally, the lawyer was receiving healthy kickbacks from the priest for his part of the exploitation.

Golbert tells us that, unfortunately, it is becoming more and more common to see cases involving trusted lawyers who are either the exploited (and guilty of sloppy lawyering) or who are involved in the exploitation by drafting documents. He says that the Attorney Registration & Disciplinary Commission says the fastest-growing area of lawyers to discipline is the group exploiting elderly clients and taking advantage of their age and their condition.

 Case Study
The Longtime Partner

Two friends fresh out of law school started a firm together 30 years ago. For 30 years they worked side by side and were the best of friends out of the office. Everything seemed great until one of them was diagnosed with Alzheimer's disease.

Inexplicably, the other partner turned on his best friend and started stealing all of his money shortly after the diagnosis.

These cases of the wolf in sheep's clothing serve to remind lawyers of the importance of speaking with their senior clients alone at various times. Lawyers need to ask these clients questions that will help give them a feeling for how much influence a person that clients want to give more and more power and control to has over the client.

Linda Voirin says that lawyers are doing a disservice to seniors by not speaking with them privately, because they certainly aren't going to get an honest answer with the caregiver—or son, daughter, granddaughter, etc.—sitting right in front of them.

This is especially important when someone new shows up in the client's life and seems to be influencing the client.

DEFENSES AGAINST FINANCIAL EXPLOITATION

The increasing frequency of financial exploitation of seniors paints a grim picture. The seniors' reluctance to report the instances and the murkiness of vulnerability versus incapacity makes the lawyer's job even more difficult.

The following are a few tips that Golbert and forward-thinking practitioners are using to combat the financial exploiters.

Probate/Citations

Citations to discover and recover assets are important tools to be aware of when lawyers need to recover money and property of a client who is the victim of financial exploitation because they allow for discovery without having to file a lawsuit.[8]

Citations can be found in the probate codes of many jurisdictions.

Citations to Discover Assets

Guardians and representatives of the estates of elderly clients with dementia are at a considerable disadvantage compared with lawyers representing adult clients without disabilities when it comes to investigating financial exploitation. Clients with dementia will have a much more difficult time identifying the exploiter and explaining how they were financially exploited. Because of this disadvantage, many jurisdictions' probate codes allow for a citation to discover assets. A citation to discover

---

8. CHARLES P. GOLBERT & DAWN LAWKOWSKI-KELLER, ADVOCATING FOR THE MOST VULNERABLE: PURSUING RECOVERY OF ASSETS STOLEN FROM OUR WARDS 9 (2012).

assets "is a broad, pre-complaint discovery tool designed to 'level the playing field' for guardians and representatives of persons who may not understand or be able to articulate what happened to their assets."[9]

Article XVI of the Illinois Probate Act permits a disabled person's guardian, representative, or "any other person interested in the estate" to file a petition for the issuance of a citation to discover assets against any person who the petitioner believes

> (1) to have concealed, converted or embezzled or to have in his possession or control any personal property, books of account, papers or evidences of debt or title to lands which belonged to a person whose estate is being administered in that court or which belongs to his estate or to his representative or (2) to have information or knowledge withheld by the respondent from the representative and needed by the representative for the recovery of any property by suit or otherwise. The petition shall contain a request for the relief sought.[10]

Citations to discover assets are useful because they allow lawyers to obtain discovery without having to file suit and without having to plead facts requisite to survive a motion to dismiss.[11] That makes them a great discovery tool in financial exploitation cases involving clients with dementia.

The petition for the issuance of a citation to discover assets should lay out the facts as to why the respondent would have information regarding the disabled person's assets.

Citations to discover assets are meant to create a quick and comprehensive means of discovery of assets and their value.[12] They are generally not subject to dispositive motions for failure to state a claim such as a motion to dismiss or for summary judgment as one only is required to allege that the respondent has knowledge of estate assets and/or their value.[13]

The court may question the respondent under oath regardless of whether the petitioner has proved the matters alleged in the petition.[14] Article XVI empowers the court to hear evidence offered by any party and allows the court to determine all questions of title, claims of adverse

---

9.   *Id.* at 10.
10. 755 Ill. Comp. Stat. 5/16-1(a) (1995).
11. Golbert & Lawkowski-Keller, *supra* note 8, at 10.
12. *Id.* at 11.
13. *Id.*
14. 755 Ill. Comp. Stat. 5/16-1(d).

title, and the right of property, and enter such orders and judgment as the case requires.[15]

The court may compel the appearance of the respondents, compel discovery, and enforce its orders through its contempt powers.[16]

Citations to Recover Assets

On the other hand, citations to recover assets are subject to dispositive motions.[17]

Filing a petition for the issuance of a citation to recover assets is basically saying, "This money has been stolen and we have a citation against you." It means the people served have to appear in court and prove that they didn't steal the money. If it's proven that they stole money, then the lawyer can issue a rule to show cause against them if they do not put the money back. And if they do not comply, they're in contempt of court, which means they can go to jail.[18] This power is typically found in a state's Probate Act and the Code of Simple Procedures as well.

Lawyers do not have to prove the theft first. They just have to have permission to file the citation. So, lawyers go in on a petition and ask for the citation to be granted.[19]

Practice Pointer: Discover, Recover, or Both?[20]

Charles Golbert warns that lawyers must clearly designate whether they are seeking discovery of assets, recovery of assets, or both. If the initial petition only requests discovery, the court may not enter any orders for the recovery of property until lawyers file an additional petition to recover assets.

Another thing to keep in mind is that the petition to recover assets is subject to dispositive motions for failure to state a claim.

Although a citation to recover assets is a procedural mechanism, it does not typically create any substantive legal rights.[21] So when using a citation to recover assets, lawyers must plead cognizable legal theories

---

15. *Id.*
16. *Id.*
17. Golbert & Lawkowski-Keller, *supra* note 8, at 11.
18. 755 Ill. Comp. Stat. 5/16-1(d) (1995).
19. *Id.*
20. Charles P. Golbert, *Using the Probate Act to Recover Assets Stolen from Persons with Disabilities*, 88 Ill. B.J. 510, 511 (2000).
21. Golbert & Lawkowski-Keller, *supra* note 8, at 11.

such as incapacity or undue influence, coercion, and duress.[22] Undue influence, coercion, and duress are very often pleaded in the alternative.

To win on the theory of incapacity, lawyers have to show that at the time of execution of whatever was executed, clients lacked the requisite mental capacity to understand what they were signing. That usually involves a combination of expert testimony. Lawyers need to get all the medical records going back as far as possible, and talk to all the treating doctors if the clients were going to a doctor. Lawyers need to have a doctor, such as a forensic psychiatrist, review the records and try to make a determination as to when capacity would have kicked in and at what level.

Lawyers need to combine that with whatever environmental evidence there is. For example, neighbors might say this person loved the rose garden and was meticulous about it, but around a certain period of time, the neighbors noticed that they never saw the person leave the house, and the garden became weed infested and the lawn overgrown.

Family members can often provide environmental evidence. Piecing together the medical evidence with the environmental evidence helps to create the story of backdating the disability to whenever the document in question was signed.

However, even if the client was not incapacitated, other legal theories would include undue influence, coercion, duress, or conversion. If someone just plunders somebody's bank account and didn't have permission and there is no consideration, that's simply conversion. People don't need to be incapacitated to be a victim of conversion.

Another legal theory that is very common in these cases is fraud. When an exploiter promises the clients that they would get this great rate of return and that was not true, that is fraudulent misrepresentation under the common law.

Many states have great consumer fraud statutes that are very consumer friendly and in some cases allow for attorney fees.

When lawyers sue under the theory of fraud, the client can be awarded punitive damages, which is a great incentive when it comes time to talk about settlement talks. When it's time to sit down to talk settlement, lawyers can state that all they really want is the money that was stolen and the assets that were stolen. They can tell the other side

---

22. *Id.* at 12.

that they are not really looking for a windfall and will go away if they just give back what was taken. However, if this goes to trial, they have intentional counts pending, including fraud, and they're going to ask for punitive damages as well as giving it back. So that's a very helpful bargaining chip in settlement talks.

If the victim of financial exploitation was adjudicated disabled and/or had a guardian appointed at the time the document was executed, the document is void ab initio as a matter of law (in most jurisdictions).[23]

However, if documents were signed before the date of adjudication, there will need to be a hearing to demonstrate incapacity at the time of the signing. In order to show incapacity, lawyers will usually need expert medical testimony.[24]

Fortunately, there is another option if lawyers cannot demonstrate that a client was incapacitated at the time of the financial exploitation.

Lawyers need to look at changing what they perceive to be a relatively equal relationship into fiduciary obligations on the part of the exploiter.

FIDUCIARY RELATIONSHIP

Fiduciary relationships exist as a matter of law in certain relationships, such as lawyer-client. According to Charles Golbert, a fiduciary relationship can also be found as a matter of fact. Courts consider such factors as

- the degree of kinship between the parties;
- disparity in age;
- disparity in health;
- disparity in mental conditions;
- disparity in education and/or business sophistication;
- the degree of trust placed in the dominant party; and
- the degree of dependence or reliance placed in the dominant party.

The idea that someone can create a fiduciary responsibility by disparity of knowledge and a whole host of other things, even though the person may not be in what would be considered the traditional law of fiduciary, is very important. If lawyers can show, based on the facts and

---

23. *Id.*
24. *Id.*

circumstances, that a fiduciary duty existed, the burden shifts to the other side—to the fiduciary.

So now, from an evidentiary standpoint and from a trial strategy standpoint, lawyers do not have as big a problem as they thought they had; they now have to spend substantial amounts of time convincing the court of differences between individuals that should create a fiduciary obligation, even though it's not a traditional fiduciary obligation like lawyer-client accounts or client trust officer accounts.

Golbert has proved fiduciary obligations, not just in the difference between sophistication and education, but even in caregiver situations. Golbert has successfully argued that this person bathes this person every day. This person has access to all of the stuff in the house. This person had a fiduciary obligation because of the high level of trust and care between the two and the vulnerability of the individual who was cared for.

Once lawyers have a fiduciary duty by fact patterns, they can argue undue influence. For example, if the client is not incapacitated but is vulnerable and is taken in by a con man and tricked into signing away the house, that could be undue influence. The courts look at the disparity in needs, health, and education and business sophistication, the degree of trust placed on the dominant party and dependents or reliance, etc.

Going back to the case study earlier in this chapter involving the war hero from church who tricked an elderly couple out of $220,000 by using nonrecourse promissory notes, apply a fiduciary duty by fact pattern and suddenly the defense of the elderly couple may be more promising.

Lawyers might have thought that if the couple duped out of their life savings are found to have been competent at the time they signed the notes, there is no recourse.

However, Golbert suggests that a fiduciary relationship can be found in this case based on a disparity in education and/or business sophistication.

There is often a fiduciary relationship between home-care workers and the person they take care of because of the degree of dominance and reliance and trust for somebody who is bathing a person, taking the person to the bathroom, and feeding the person. So lawyers can establish a fiduciary relationship for home-care workers.

Once a fiduciary relationship is established, either by law or by fact, the defendant now bears the burden of proving that the transaction was objectively fair and reasonable and of benefit to the ward. Now, the transaction will be presumed invalid.

Creating a nontraditional fiduciary relationship is a great way to protect the client and to aggressively go after the perpetrator of the financial scam. It can be a lifesaver when the elderly victim is in the early stages of dementia and is vulnerable, but not yet incapacitated. However, getting the victim to report the exploitation or go along with the prosecution of the exploiter is often a battle itself.

SENIORS TOLERATE LESSER OF TWO EVILS

Seniors with dementia are more likely to put up with financial exploitation rather than report it. They know that they are vulnerable, but they don't want to turn in their abuser. They don't want their child or grandchild arrested, so they'll just put up with it. Sometimes, the relative exploiting them is the only person that can help them continue to stay in their own home. Maybe they don't drive anymore and they depend on that son or daughter to take them everywhere.

The worst part is that their children usually know this and take advantage of it. They think, Well, it's going to be my money anyway; I'll just use it now. They don't think the parents will live another 10 or 20 years. They don't care about that. A lot of times, in this economy, maybe the abuser is not even working. They move into the parents' house and live off social security. Sometimes they will threaten the parents with putting them in a nursing home (although they'd never do that since they are living off of their social security checks).

Oftentimes other family members will call the police and say, "I think my brother is taking advantage of my mom and I don't like it one bit." More often than not, though, according to Officer Aschenbrenner, when the police talk to the mom, she says, "No, I want him to live here. I'm fine." Sometimes she will simply say, "I don't want to make things worse than what they are." At that point, there is nothing the police can do.

Linda Voirin adds that older people will tolerate abuse because it is the lesser of two evils. "That is probably the number one reason why the abuse is never reported, because the need of the senior to live at home is so great."[25]

---

25. Linda Voirin's professional opinion and observation based on experience.

Seniors are so afraid that if someone takes their son, grandson, whatever person away, now they will have to go to a nursing home. Given those two scenarios, they'll put up with the abuse so that they can stay in their home.

Seniors who have been scammed by strangers don't want to tell their family because they are embarrassed, but they are afraid if they do tell their adult child, the adult child would say, "Dad, you can no longer care for yourself. We need to take you to look at other living options." Seniors know that is a euphemism for the nursing home.

The fear of going to a nursing home is legitimate. Voirin states, "We are probably fast-tracking someone's demise when we take them out of what they've known and where they want to be and where they need to be in their home. If that is the trade off, then we have to look at that pretty carefully."[26]

Voirin adds that "there is empirical evidence that when a senior has been a victim of crime, that it has hastened their death. Being a victim, because it is so disrupting in their life at a vulnerable time in their life when trust is so important, hastens their demise." Then add the guilt of their grandson, or whoever was exploiting them, being put in jail and the stress of them moving to a nursing home—that's a lot of stressors.[27]

GOING FORWARD

As more people are made aware of the widespread financial exploitation against seniors, more states will address these serious crimes.

For instance, Illinois recently amended its criminal code by making the "financial exploitation of an elderly person or a person with a disability" a felony.[28] The section reads in part:

> A person commits financial exploitation of an elderly person or a person with a disability when he or she stands in a position of trust or confidence with the elderly person or a person with a disability and he or she knowingly and by deception or intimidation obtains control over the property of an elderly person or a person with a disability or

26. Id.
27. Id.
28. 720 ILL. COMP. STAT. 5/17-56 (2013).

illegally uses the assets or resources of an elderly person or a person with a disability.[29]

A person is in a position of trust when

he (i) is a parent, spouse, adult child or other relative by blood or marriage of the elderly person or a person with a disability, (ii) is a joint tenant or tenant in common with the elderly person or a person with a disability, (iii) has a legal or fiduciary relationship with the elderly person or a person with a disability (iv) is a financial planning or investment professional, or (v) is a paid or unpaid caregiver for the elderly person or a person with a disability.[30]

Subsection (v) above was just added effective January 1, 2012.

From looking at the Illinois Criminal Code and the definition of a person in trust, it gives hope that the task of protecting seniors, especially seniors suffering from dementia, from financial exploitation may get easier.

---

29. *Id.* 5/17-56(a).
30. *Id.* 5/17-56(c).

 **Expert View**

When the Indispensable Caregiver Is the Abuser

Linda Voirin, LSW, is the victims' advocate for the Seniors and Persons with Disabilities Unit, Office of Joseph H. McMahon, Kane County (Illinois) state's attorney. The key point of this interview is the difficulty in prosecuting senior financial exploitation and elder-abuse cases.

Q: Linda, you're not an attorney, but you've been a victims' advocate for over 10 years in the state's attorney's office and you deal specifically with seniors and persons with disabilities. Describe your role as it relates to the whole team.

A: We have some attorneys who have been specifically trained in dealing with the issues of abuse and the needs of the elderly, as well as attorneys who are trained specifically for the crimes that are committed against the elderly, such as financial exploitation. In addition, there is the concept of aggravated theft or aggravated assault. So as a victims' advocate, we are helping the elderly victim to understand, first of all, what's happening in the court system, being in communication with them as to court dates, and what's happening in meetings with the attorney.

  Often, if they have been victimized, it's a sign that there are other areas in their life that need looking at. Maybe they were particularly sought out as a victim because of a weakness that they had. Maybe they need extra care. So we try to assess their situation and then get them tied into services. We don't actually provide those services; rather, we make referrals.

Q: How often would you say that the person is victimized because, even though they're not technically incapacitated, they become vulnerable due to aging?

A: At least two-thirds of the time. It's usually some vulnerability that's been identified by the abuser. Sometimes it's mental; sometimes it's physical. It can be as simple as the person no longer being able to do their banking by themselves and so they're asking others to do it. Maybe there is a vision loss and they are asking others to sign checks. These disabilities open the door for someone to be able to take advantage of them.

  One of the biggest problems is that the abuser often is the person providing care to the older person. And the older person needs that help so much that they often tolerate the abuse. That is the number one reason why most abuse is never reported—because the senior's need is so great. For example, if you take away their son, grandson, or whoever away from them who is assisting them in being able to stay at home, now they are in great fear that they are going to have to go to a nursing home—and often that's the truth. So when the senior reviews the two scenarios—stay at home and put up with the abuse, or don't put up with the abuse and go to the nursing home—they decide to put up with the abuse. It's the lesser of two evils.

An additional issue is the embarrassment and the shame. We see this on the witness stand. They admit that they didn't want to tell anybody that they have a disability, because if they tell their family members, they'll say, "Dad, you can no longer take care of yourself. We're going to need to look into other options" (go to a nursing home).

So that's an important piece to address before you can be serious about taking an abuser out of a home. When you go in and take the adult-child caregiver from a home and disrupt the senior's life, we have to know what kind of an impact that has. If the senior has to move to an assisted-living facility, the lack of familiarity can be difficult to manage. It may be necessary; however, the elderly person might feel a sense of loss of independence.

Q: So it's a tradeoff that the abused person might not be eager to make, in spite of the abuse.

A: We have seen some difficult situations involving financial abuse. We recently had a person whose grandson was living in the basement. The elderly person never went downstairs because she physically could not handle the stairs. And the grandson was downstairs dealing drugs and doing drugs. But yet, he was the caregiver. Now that's a very dangerous situation on many levels for this elderly person. However, when we got involved, she was adamant, telling us that he was the only one able to keep her in her home. She was visually limited as well as physically limited. And we had to get a lot of care people to come in and come together to be able to begin a transition from that home. But if we had gone in and just ripped that guy out of the house and said, "That's the end of this!" prior to putting anything in place to assist with transitions, that would have been just devastating to her. It was devastating anyway, but it certainly would have been worse and could have hastened her death.

As you can imagine, after going through the traumatic experience of some form of abuse, the victim often feels lonely and depressed. If takes a lot of emotional and physical effort for the aged person to leave the comforts of their home and familiar surroundings and adapt to a new place. He or she will find the new environment strange and will miss the familiar. It may very well cause a decline, both physically and emotionally.

In addition, there is empirical evidence that when a senior has been a victim of a crime, it hastens their death. Just being a victim in and of itself is so disrupting at this vulnerable time in their life when trust is so important.

The older person can't handle the stress, and on top of that, how are you going to get them to handle the guilt of putting a person who is close to them in jail? A huge amount of guilt is put on the abused senior, especially if it's a family member. The same is true when it's not a family member but, rather, a caregiver who has been a person of trust for any length of time. The fact that that person is now no longer trustworthy and has turned on them and taken advantage of them in one way or another, this is a tremendous stressor. Often, we find caregivers who are stealing some of the medication and then there's that break in trust. It's a very difficult thing for someone to get over, and sometimes they don't get over it. And then they begin to question everyone, and now they say, "I don't know who I can trust, now I don't know if I can trust any caregiver or if I can begin to trust someone in a long-term-care facility."

So it makes it extremely difficult to get people to testify against the ones who have betrayed their trust and financially abused them. And that's one of the reasons that so few elderly abuse cases are reported—and even the ones that are reported can be difficult to prove.

CHAPTER 8

PERSONAL-CARE AGREEMENTS AND NURSING HOME CONTRACTS

"Colicky Dementia" by Shay Jacobson

"Dementia" is a term that brings to mind a pleasantly confused, grandmotherly figure—sweet, gentle, and very compliant. But what happens when an already misfiring mind responds chaotically to the world around it, veering drastically from the peaceful path?

Dementia presents itself differently in different people. Untreated mental illness, undetected substance abuse, and personality disorders can all result in dementia presenting itself in a frenzied manner.

There is a very common condition among healthy babies called colic. Wikipedia defines colic as "a condition in a healthy baby in which it shows periods of intense, unexplained fussing/crying lasting more than three hours a day, more than three days a week, for more than three weeks."[1] Let us consider a person suffering from dementia that manifests itself in a colic-like condition. For explanatory purposes, I have coined the phrase "Colicky Dementia."

---

1. Shay Jacobson, President, CEO Life Care Innovations.

Colicky Dementia is unpredictable, inconsolable, and results in dispropor-tionate behavior reactions to the reality of the individual's environment, inner health, and caretaking. The individual exhibits a chronic state of anxi-ety, panic, and circular thinking that lasts for periods exceeding three hours a day, more than three days a week, for more than three weeks.

This condition ensnarls the individual in a continuous fight-or-flight response with their caregivers and environment. Individuals react with fear and panic when they feel unsafe, uneasy, or not in control. Since they can-not communicate normally with those who care for them, they react with escalating and circular panic. They resort to undesirable behaviors such as shouting, biting, crying, and hitting.

This is more than a nuisance to the caregiver, as it leads to serious caretaker stress. Caregivers dealing with individuals suffering from this condition are faced with an unrelenting assault upon their own mental health. The result-ing impact on caregivers includes depression, exhaustion, anger, major ill-ness, isolation, and chronic health problems.

Someone calls a lawyer and asks for a "simple contract" because an adult child is going to be compensated for providing in-home care for a frail parent. Most of the time, neither the caller nor the lawyer can imagine the powerful, invisible forces arrayed against this agreement—cultural and religious tradition, judicial bias, elder abuse statutes, and the state Medicaid department.

The lawyer's role in serving clients and their families is most often determined by the care needs of the family member affected by Alzheimer's disease (the "affected loved one"). One of the key challenges of serving as the lawyer is the difficulty in understanding who the client is and how best to serve that client. It is important for the lawyer to carefully define whether the client is the affected loved one or one of the healthier members of the family. Nonetheless, the lawyer will be faced with carefully representing the client within the context of a disease that is impacting an entire family unit.

Millions of people are currently providing in-home caregiving ser-vices for a loved one. Providing those services is done at great personal cost and sacrifice.

People on the Alzheimer's care journey often progress through a trajectory as follows (covered in more detail in chapter 1):

- memory loss ignored
- memory loss masked/denied
- unsafe alone
- aid needed, but fights back
- assisted living required
- nursing home required
- hospice care required/death

As the affected loved one's care needs increase, the lawyer needs to understand how best to draft personal-care agreements and how to review assisted-living facility and nursing home contracts (referred to hereinafter as "nursing home contracts"). This chapter will focus on revealing the invisible obstacles that confront lawyers and their clients when drafting a personal-care agreement among family members and the hidden traps within many standard nursing home contracts.

The first stage of this journey, "memory loss ignored," does not mean that loved ones are ignoring the senior's memory loss. The person affected, as well as the loved ones, may be dismissing the memory loss as part of the aging process. An individual in the early stages of Alzheimer's is often in good physical health, which makes it much easier to dismiss the occasional lapses in memory. The person feels good, looks good, and makes perfect sense most of the time.

 Case Study ——————————————————————————
Affected Loved Ones Are Often on a Similar Journey

A woman received a phone call from her grandmother asking her how to make spaghetti. The grandmother had been making spaghetti for more than 50 years, but now her memory was failing her in simple daily tasks. The woman visited her grandmother and was shocked to see the messy condition of the home and her grandmother's personal appearance.

Even more surprising was her grandfather's state of confusion. Clearly, both of them were in need of assistance, but neither one was willing to ask for help.

When memory loss is first detected, one of the authors refers to this as "smoke in the kitchen." In many cases, there literally is smoke in the kitchen because one of the most common dangers of memory loss is that the senior forgets and leaves a burner on or does not turn off the oven, and eventually starts a fire in the kitchen.

Often seniors will either ignore their memory loss or will attempt to hide the behavior. In many cases, they are aware of their worsening condition but are afraid of being put in a nursing home.

Once the memory loss has been detected by family or friends, the next stage is coming to the decision that the senior is "unsafe alone" and needs aid. It is not unusual for the senior to resist and fight to avoid assisted-living situations. While men seem to be more likely to fight back since control can be a bigger issue for a man facing Alzheimer's, it is not out of the norm for women to plant their feet and say, "I am not leaving my home."

On the Alzheimer's journey, the goal for many seniors and their families is to keep the seniors in their home (or in the home of an adult child) for as long as possible. This will necessitate the need for in-home care.

There are several hiring options when it comes to in-home care. The important thing to remember is that anyone hired directly usually creates an employer-employee relationship. It is critically important to examine the relationship in light of both federal and state labor and tax laws. Most often, if an individual is being hired who will perform services and be under the direction and control of another, an employer-employee relationship is created. Many individuals ignore this concern at their peril because they prefer to either pay cash to the caregiver or report the compensation paid on a Form 1099. While it is the preference of private individuals to avoid and even evade tax rules, lawyers are obligated to inform families of the employer-employee obligations inherent in this type of arrangement.

There are many companies that specialize in in-home care, but even among such companies there are different protocols. Many companies are the employer of the caregivers that they provide. Lawyers should check to be sure that their caregivers are insured and bonded. The client pays the company and the company pays the caregiver. From a legal standpoint, this is the simplest arrangement, since the client does not have to do any bookkeeping, employment law, and/or tax reporting.

Some companies that may appear to be employers of caregivers are actually in the business of merely placing freelance caregivers with families. These companies are being compensated by a finder's fee and sometimes by taking an override from the caregivers' compensation. The contract provided by this type of quasi-employment agency and in-home health-care provider clearly stipulates that the company is not the employer of the caregiver. The lawyer will need to make the legal determination as to whether or not the client has become the employer.

The majority of clients and their families do not have formal employer-employee contracts with their caregivers. Instead, most families prefer to handle these arrangements "below the radar." This means that by the time the lawyer gets a call, there are substantial issues of unpaid employment-related taxes, workers' compensation, and grossly inadequate bookkeeping.

Whenever the client employs a family member, neighbor, friend, or freelance caregiver, there needs to be an employment contract in place. This contract will need to be reviewed so that the client and the client's family understand all the provisions. (Caregiver contracts are discussed briefly in chapter 5 in the context of Medicaid qualifications.)

Practice Pointer:

Read the in-home care contract carefully. When hiring in-home care, people need to understand the finer points of the contract. One family was surprised to discover that the in-home care provider whom they thought they were paying $18 an hour got paid time and a half on Saturday, double time on Sunday, and double time on holidays.

They were shocked when they got a bill of $72 an hour for eight hours of care on Sunday, the Fourth of July—four times the rate that they thought they had agreed upon!

ADULT CHILDREN PROVIDING CARE

Situations in which adult children provide care for their elderly parents often start out as very casual arrangements. Many times, the first stage involves the adult children picking up some groceries for the parents while doing their own shopping or driving the parents to an appointment. Maybe they start giving their parents some money, or maybe they are coming over and cooking and cleaning and checking in on their elderly parents.

Then, all of a sudden, a parent is diagnosed with Alzheimer's and the adult child has to quit his or her job or cut back hours because taking care of the parent has become a full-time job.

Most adult children don't think that they need to have a lawyer draft a personal care contract, but that is exactly what needs to happen if they are providing care for their parents.

The elderly parent may well be writing checks to the caregiver child for gas, food, and time spent cleaning and doing laundry. However, in all likelihood, everything is getting commingled and no one is keeping records. The child is buying the parent's groceries and his or her own groceries and both are paying some.

If clients are not keeping adequate records, they run the risk of the caregiver client being accused of elder abuse and the senior receiving the care being ineligible for Medicaid benefits.

Sometimes the child will move in with the parents to better care for them, and sometimes it is easier to have the parents move into the child's home. Often in these situations the child is appointed the power of attorney for property or at least the power of attorney for health care for the parent. In many cases the parents add that child to their bank accounts so the child can pay bills for them, including reimbursements to the child.

Many states have passed legislation that has greatly expanded the definition of elder abuse. Family members who take on the role of caregiver may find themselves within the definition of people who have heightened duties relative to their loved one. Neglect of those duties can lead to both civil and criminal liability. Illinois passed an anti-elder-abuse power of attorney law that went into effect July 1, 2012, which creates a presumption that if people who are agents are writing checks to themselves, that is per se abuse of the principal, the parent. This presumption can be rebutted with the existence of a written agreement that stipulates clear terms and conditions that justify payments from the principal to the agent.

A properly drafted personal-care agreement is required as the foundational document to rebut accusations of elder abuse within the familial-care arrangement. Proper and timely bookkeeping is also required—and unfortunately is the Achilles' heel of many of these contracts. Eventually the parents may need a higher level of care than their child can provide. When one or both of them go to a nursing home and then apply for Medicaid, all those checks written by the child on the parents' account will be scrutinized and audited by the state. If there was no personal-care contract in place between the parents and the child clearly describing the care to be provided and the compensation to be paid, many states will consider the transfers as non-allowable. A non-allowable transfer will create a penalty period of ineligibility for nursing home Medicaid benefits for the affected loved one. The lawyer needs to have provided appropriate written advice and counsel to the client so as to avoid being liable for creating a personal-care agreement relationship that led to a denial of nursing home Medicaid benefits.

For example, the current Code of Illinois Rules state that care provided to a senior by a friend or family member is presumed to be "gratuitous." The rules further state that "transfers for love and affection are not considered transfers for fair market value and thus are non-allowable and subject to penalty periods."[2] This can make it difficult in cases where a family member has been caring for a senior and not charging for the care or not keeping adequate records.

Perfect World Versus Real World

In a perfect world, clients will approach their lawyers before providing any care for their elderly parent who is suffering from Alzheimer's disease and give lawyers the opportunity to create a personal-care contract for them. Unfortunately, it is much more likely that clients will wait and tell their lawyers that they have been caring for their mother for the last several months free of charge, and now their mother's Alzheimer's is getting worse and they need to spend more time caring for her. Perhaps they need to cut back their hours at work. Whatever their situation, they have now realized that they need to have their mother pay them for the care.

While it is much easier to draft the personal-care agreement prior to the start of the care, lawyers can still draft the agreement after care has started. The key is to demonstrate an increase or escalation in the care needs of the senior. However, the personal-care agreement can only be for services to be given commencing from the date of that agreement. It could be considered fraud by the state Medicaid department to create a personal-care agreement for services that had originally been rendered gratuitously. Lawyers cannot predate a personal-care agreement.

---

2.   89 Ill. Code R. 120.388(F)(3) (2012).

Case Study
Escalation of Care Required

A client walks into a lawyer's office and says, "I have been going over and taking care of my elderly mother for the past few months for a few hours a day. Now she's been diagnosed with Alzheimer's, and this is going to take up a lot more of my time and energy. I may need for her to move in with me and my husband, and I am going to need to start charging her. I want to set up a personal-care agreement for her."

In this situation it is not too late to create a valid personal-care agreement even though care has already been provided for free, because at this point the client is saying that the care needs have intensified and it's time for them to start being paid.

The key for Medicaid eligibility is that someone can never be compensated for care that was being provided gratuitously. In the Medicaid context, care provided without a properly drafted and medically justified personal-care agreement is presumptively gratuitous. For example, the parents lived with their son for two years and he did many things for them gratuitously, and then suddenly he says he wants to receive payment. He says that not only does he want to receive payment going forward, he wants to be compensated for all that previous care. That will be a big issue for Medicaid eligibility for the affected loved one, because a retroactive payment will be viewed as a gift and could create a substantial period of ineligibility for the person needing Medicaid.

The reality is that a lot of times people incrementally get into these situations. So if clients go to lawyers early in that process, lawyers would probably want to have them set up a low-level personal-care agreement. As the care increases, lawyers would increase the amount that clients are being paid proportionally to the amount of hours they're working over time. Lawyers need to have ancillary documentation in place to validate the changes of care level needed.

It can be very difficult for the caregivers if they first performed services for free and later request payment. In these situations a written agreement is almost certainly required.[3]

3. Sheena J. Knox, *Eldercare for the Baby-Boom Generation: Are Caregiver Agreements Valid?* 45 Suffolk U.L. Rev. 1271, 1288 (2012) (citing Ctrs. For Medicare and Medicaid Servs., U.S. Dep't of Health and Hum. Sers., State Medicaid Manual § 3258.1(A)(1) (2001) [hereinafter State Medicaid Manual] (explaining care provided without contemporaneous payment presumed gratuitous, unless tangible evidence rebutting presumption exists)); Gauthier v. Dir. of Office of Medicaid, 956 N.E.2d 1236, 1242–43 (Mass. App. Ct. 2011) (determining exchange not for fair market value because of "lump-sum up-front payment"). *But see* Weitzel v. Dehner, No. 08-0627-D (Mass.

HOW TO DRAFT A POWERFUL PERSONAL-CARE AGREEMENT

From time to time, one of the authors has received calls from other lawyers requesting a copy of his personal care employment agreement. The requesting lawyer has made an erroneous assumption that drafting an interfamilial care agreement is a one-size-fits-all, cookie-cutter task. Unfortunately, simply pulling out a standard, generic employment agreement and changing the names will not do in this situation.

After meeting with the client and family, the next step in the process involves obtaining a personal-care plan. A personal care plan can be initiated by a telephone conference involving the client, the family, and the affected loved one's personal physician. A personal-care plan is the foundation upon which the personal-care agreement is built. In addition, it provides written evidence of the health condition that necessitates and justifies in-home personal care. This is vitally important when defending payments being made between family members.

For people with Alzheimer's, the care plan recommendation will state that the caregiver is needed for health care, hygiene, welfare monitoring, nutritional management, and assistance with various activities of daily life. The recommendation will typically end with the statement that "without this care, the patient would require care in a nursing facility." Most family members are not licensed health-care professionals. A licensed health-care professional, such as a medical doctor, physician's assistant, or other qualified individual, needs to be in charge of the case management and serve in an oversight capacity.

An alternative method of creating a care plan is to hire a licensed geriatric care manager to go to the person's house and do an assessment of the person's needs. The geriatric care manager is trained to do a survey of the physical environment within the home and an inventory of all resources available to the individual. After completing the assessment of the individual, the environment, and the resources, a personalized care plan is created. With the assessment in hand, the lawyer will be able to draft a customized personal-care agreement. The agreement is tailored around what the care manager has identified as necessary care and other circumstances.

Super. Ct. Dec. 30, 2008) (allowing agreement in which daughter provided care without compensation and only later began receiving payments).

Practice Pointer: Personalizing the Care Contracts

Lawyers need to customize the personal-care agreement as much as possible to make it a powerful document that will stand up to potential legal challenges. A generic contract that simply states that the elder is being provided care is not going to stand up to the scrutiny of either the state's Medicaid department or the Department of Veterans Affairs. The affected loved one may need to qualify for public benefits; therefore, compliance with the often unfathomable regulations of the Medicaid department and Veterans Affairs must be taken into consideration.

Lawyers need to include specific items to clearly demonstrate what activities of daily living are being provided. Personal-care agreements should incorporate the elder's answers to questions like, "What do you like to eat? What do you hate to eat? Would you like to rise early or sleep in? How often do you wish to have your hair done?" This level of personalizing the care contract can give a much more persuasive argument if the contract is later challenged.

Lawyers need to include sample daily log sheets so that the caregiver can record activities on a daily basis. Refer the family to a bookkeeping and payroll service to handle the appropriate and timely employment and tax-return filings.

On occasion the affected loved one has an adult child who is a nurse, occupational therapist, or other licensed health-care professional who is legally qualified to do more health care than a typical layperson. In those situations, it is important to draft those health-care details into the agreement so as to provide a legal and contractual basis for a higher level of compensation than could be paid to a nonprofessional. The typical nonprofessional caregiver will be compensated based on the normal regional private-pay rate for a non-skilled in-home care provider. A professional may be compensated at a professional rate for performing a care service within that person's scope of expertise. It will always be necessary to keep proper records noting the hours worked, as well as the type of care given during those hours.

Practice Pointer: Demonstrate Fair Market Value Wages

It is important to demonstrate that the caretaker is being paid fair market value, particularly if the caregiver is a relative or friend. Documentation will help fight the presumption that the arrangement is a scheme to cheat Medicaid by passing the senior's assets to a relative or friend.

If adult-child caregivers have moved the affected loved one into their home and need to make some accommodations within the home, then these changes must be documented as medically necessary if funds for the remodeling will be taken from the elder's accounts. Caregivers should be advised by the lawyer regarding the extent of authority provided to them for the expenditure of funds. Family members serving as caregivers and agents under powers of attorney consistently rationalize an expansion of their authority to dip into the resources of the principal. Lawyers should provide clear and simple written letters of instruction to the parties involved in a personal-care agreement.

Practice Pointer: Use a Bookkeeping Service

Set the caregiver up with a bookkeeping service so that the caregiver is able to accurately record time and expenses. It is a good idea to have the caregiver come in after a month to review the logs and ensure that that the caregiver is keeping proper records.

If the agreement is later challenged in court, the caregiver's logs will need to be reasonably precise, accurate, and timely.

At some point after a personal-care contract has been created, people receiving care will continue to decline as they move through the Alzheimer's care journey. Unfortunately, the majority of those individuals will exhaust their personal resources and be compelled to apply for nursing home Medicaid benefits. The Medicaid application process will include the state agency questioning the payments that were made to the caregiver.

If the personal-care agreement is not drafted correctly, or proper records were not kept, clients could end up with costly penalty periods of ineligibility for Medicaid benefits during which they need to pay for care. Without appropriate evidence, which usually is provided by contemporaneous logs of daily caregiving services, a caregiver could be accused of being an elder abuser.

Practice Pointer:

Draft the care contract with the state Medicaid department in mind. Lawyers' legal expertise cannot be limited to the review of a care contract as if it were equivalent to a lawn care services agreement. Lawyers need to draft the care contract so that it meets all the standards required by state Medicaid regulations. The Medicaid department is not a lawyer's friend, and it is not the client's friend. Even though criminals are provided with a presumption of innocence, a Medicaid applicant is burdened with a presumption that any transfer of money or other asset not for value is deemed to have been motivated to qualify for state nursing home Medicaid benefits.

The authors provide a binder along with the personal care contract. The binder includes the following items:

1. The service contract (drafted pursuant to the personal-care plan provided by the licensed health-care professional and the Medicaid rules) that outlines the activities of daily living and other assistance being provided to the elder(s) by caregiver(s) and the compensation being paid for said services.
2. Forms to be completed by the physician and a "needs assessment" to be filled out by a professional geriatric care manager regarding of the needs of the elder(s). It also contains a "Personalizing Your Care Agreement" that should be completed by the elder(s) and caregiver(s) in order to provide appropriate and satisfactory care and to have a record of the likes and dislikes of the elder(s) for said caregiver(s) or any subsequent person providing care in the absence of the caregiver(s).
3. Informational material regarding selecting a caregiver if one needs to be retained in the absence of the caregiver(s) and a home safety checklist for the safety and protection of elder(s). Additionally, it includes a nursing home checklist in the event nursing home care becomes necessary in the future.
4. Instructions for the caregiver(s) regarding keeping track of activities, time spent, and any out-of-pocket expenses, including, but not limited to, mileage incurred on behalf of elder(s). Also, forms for recording the dates, description of activity, expenses, mileage, and time, along with a sample form. Also, invoice forms to use for billing the elder(s).
5. A household Employer's Tax Guide (IRS Publication 926) covering the rules regarding payment of federal employment tax (Social Security, Medicare tax, etc.) on a household employee as well as whether one needs to pay state unemployment tax for the household employee. Also, a letter regarding the need for excellent record keeping and a recommendation that the client retain professional services to handle all payroll and employee forms.

6. Finally, several quotes from local in-home caregiving companies to show the hourly wage for in-home services in the geographic area where the services under the agreement are being rendered.

BURDEN ON CARETAKER

Personal-care agreements are important for the person receiving the care, but they are also important for the caregivers.

Individuals that take on long-term-care duties often see a decrease in earning potential and frequently have to cut into their own savings to provide for the person they are caring for.[4] Caregivers usually cannot afford to quit their nine-to-five job, but they may be forced to cut back their hours in order to care for an elderly parent.[5] These caregivers often put their own retirement at risk to care for a parent.

A 2009 national survey of caregivers showed that over half of the responding caregivers reported a medium to high level of burden.[6] A 2010 national survey of the full-time workforce also came to the conclusion that individuals who were employed full time and who also had caregiving responsibilities suffered from lower well-being than those without such responsibilities.[7]

---

4. Knox, *supra* note 3, at 1272 (citing Peggie R. Smith, *Elder Care, Gender, and Work: The Work-Family Issues of the 21st Century*, 25 BERKELEY J. EMP. & LAB. L. 351, 370–72 (2004)).

5. *Id.* (citing Paula Span, *FamilyCaregiving on Contract*, N.Y. TIMES NEW AGE BLOG (June 25, 2009, 1:03 PM), http://newoldage.blogs.nytimes.com/2009/06/25/caregiving-on -contract/ (quoting elder law lawyer Craig Reaves)).

6. Thomas P. Gallanis & Josephine Gittler, *Family Caregiving and the Law of Succession: A Proposal*, University of Iowa Legal Studies Research Paper Series Number 13-2, 762, 767 (2013). Extensive data about the characteristics of caregivers and care recipients is available from an in-depth survey of a nationally weighted sample of caregivers providing assistance to persons people aged 50 and or older conducted in 2009 by the National Alliance for Caregiving and the AARP, NAT'L ALLIANCE FOR CAREGIV- ING, CAREGIVING IN THE U.S. 2009: A FOCUSED LOOK AT THOSE CARING FOR THE 50+ (2009), in which surveyed caregivers were more likely to report a high level of burden if they were primary caregivers, they were older, they were in fair or poor health, they were not employed, they had lower incomes, or the care recipient lived with them, *id.*; the survey used an index to measure the burden of care based on the number of hours of care per week provided and the number of instrumental activities of daily living (IADLs) performed, *id.* at 109.

7. Gallanis & Gittler, *supra* note 6, at 767 (citing Dan Witters, *In U.S., Working Caregivers Face Wellbeing Challenges*, GALLUP WELLBEING (Dec. 8, 2010), http://www.gallup.com /poll/145115/working-caregivers-face-wellbeing-challenges.aspx). The survey, con- ducted by Gallup and Healthways, used an index consisting of six areas—life evaluation, emotional health, physical health, healthy behavior, work environment, and basic access to necessities—to measure overall well-being.

It is believed that caregiving has detrimental health and psychosocial consequences for caregivers. People frequently hear stories of the healthy wife who is taking care of her husband who is suffering from dementia. Often, when the husband finally passes, the wife's health takes a quick downturn and she passes soon after. Being a caregiver, especially for a loved one, takes a toll. Caregivers are more likely to suffer from poorer physical and mental health than non-caregivers.[8]

Because of this burden, the family lawyer (or the lawyer in the family) is going to see more and more caregivers who want to create personal-care contracts that specify that the caregiver will agree to help the elderly person for a set amount of time in exchange for an hourly wage for these services.[9]

After the death of the affected loved one, lack of a personal-care agreement often leads to an estate administration problem. Many states provide a legal basis for an uncompensated caregiver to file a claim against the estate. The decedent's creditors, provided they have an allowed claim, generally will be ranked ahead of the beneficiary when it comes to collecting on a claim.[10] If the family caregiver does not have a personal-care contract, the caregiver will have a hard time establishing a status as a creditor with an allowed claim. In fact, many states' dead man's statute, which makes any testimony showing that the decedent entered into an express oral contract inadmissible, will stop caregivers in their tracks if they do not have a written contract.[11] Even if caregivers are able to imply an oral contract existed, they are faced with the common-

---

8. Gallanis & Gittler, *supra* note 6, at 767 (citing Evercare & Nat'l Alliance for Caregiving, Caregivers in Decline: Findings from a National Survey 5–7, 11–25 (2006)); Family Caregiver Alliance, Fact Sheet: Caregiver Health (2006), *available at* http://www.caregiver.org/caregiver/jsp/print_friendly.jsp?nodeid=1822; Dan Witters, *In U.S., Caregivers' Emotional Health Often Suffers*, Gallup Wellbeing (May 27, 2011), http://www.gallup.com/poll/147815/caregivers-emotional-health-often-suffers.aspx; Dan Witters, *In U.S., Caregivers Suffer from Poorer Physical Health*, Gallup Wellbeing (Feb. 4, 2011), http://www.gallup.com/poll/145940/caregivers-suffer-poorer-physical -health.aspx.

9. Knox, *supra* note 3, at 1272 (citing Paula Span, *FamilyCaregiving on Contract*, N.Y. Times New Old Age Blog (June 25, 2009, 1:03 PM), http://newoldage.blogs.nytimes.com /2009/06/25/caregiving-on-contract/ (quoting elder law lawyer Craig Reaves)).

10. Gallanis & Gittler, *supra* note 6, at 770 (citing Unif. Probate Code § 3-805 (2011), 8 U.L.A. 240–42 (1998) (priority of probate claims)); § 3-807, 8 U.L.A. 256–58 (payment of probate claims); § 3-902, 8 U.L.A. 268–70 (abatement); § 6-102(b), 8 U.L.A. 241 (creditors' rights in non-probate transfers).

11. Gallanis & Gittler, *supra* note 6, at 770 (citing 1 McCormick on Evidence 276–79 (5th ed. 1999); Robin L. Beardsley, *Recent Development, Evidence—The Dead Man's Statute: State Legislatures and Courts Conflict*, 25 Am. J. Trial Advoc. 213 (2001)).

law presumption that the services were rendered gratuitously.[12] It is possible to rebut this presumption, but it is a difficult road.[13]

Some states are recognizing this problem and addressing the needs of the family caregiver. The Illinois Probate Act permits family members who live with and care for a "disabled person" to file a claim for reimbursement in probate court upon the disabled person's death.[14]

EMPLOYMENT TAXES

The Internal Revenue Service has special rules that apply specifically to workers (caregivers) who perform in-home services for elderly or disabled individuals. Because caregivers generally work in the homes of the elderly or disabled individuals and these individuals have the right to tell the caregivers what needs to be done, caregivers are usually treated as employees of the individual for whom they provide services.

If the caregiver employee is a family member, the employer may not be responsible for employment taxes. (Warning: Reread the first sentence of this paragraph. It *does not* say that employee is exempt from paying income taxes. Rather, it states in a much more limited way that the affected loved one is not responsible for their portion of employment taxes.) However, the employer still needs to report the caregiver's compensation on a W-2. (See Publication 926 Household Employers Tax Guide for information.)

If it is determined that caregivers are not employees, the caregiver is still required to report compensation as income on Form 1040.[15] Depending on the facts and circumstances, the nonemployee caregiver

---

12. Gallanis & Gittler, *supra* note 6, at 771 (citing Worley v. Worley, 388 So. 2d 502, 507 (Ala. 1980); Brown v. Brown, 524 A.2d 1184, 1187 (D.C. 1987); Stafford v. Stafford, 402 S.E.2d 71, 72 (Ga. Ct. App. 1991); *In re* Estate of Raketti, 340 N.W.2d 894, 901 (N.D. 1983)). In Louisiana, the presumption applies as long as a parent "[or] other ascendant[]" is not "in need." *See* LA. CIV. CODE ANN. art. 229 (2009); Succession of Francke, 52 So. 2d 855, 857 (La. 1951). In some states, the presumption relates to family members in the same household. *See, e.g.*, Riddle v. Edwards, No. S-9706, 2001 WL 34818270, at *2 (Alaska Oct. 10, 2001); Sullivan v. Delisa, 923 A.2d 760, 769–70 (Conn. App. Ct. 2007); Della Ratta v. Della Ratta, 927 So .2d 1055, 1059 (Fla. Dist. Ct. App. 2006); *In re* Estate of Keeven, 882 P.2d 457, 464 (Idaho Ct. App. 1994); Prickett v. Womersley, 905 N.E.2d 1008, 1012 (Ind. 2009).

13. *Id.*

14. *Id.* (citing 755 ILL. COMP. STAT. 5/18-1.1 (2011)).

15. *See* IRS, FAMILY CAREGIVERS AND SELF-EMPLOYMENT TAX (2010).

may have to pay self-employment tax.[16] Under a personal-care agreement, family caregivers do not owe self-employment tax on the payment for a family member unless they are in the business of providing care to others.[17]

> **Practice Pointer:**
>
> The determination of whether a family member caregiver is an employee is a fact-specific and complicated manner. If drafting a personal-care agreement in which the caregiver and the person receiving the care are related, lawyers need to be familiar with the state's laws on employment.

The Invisible Opponents: The Backstory of Cultural and Religious Tradition, Judicial Bias, Elder Abuse Statutes, and the State Medicaid Department

When someone provides a service for someone else, there is an expectation of compensation, but as mentioned above, when the same services are performed by a family member, the presumption is that the services were performed gratuitously.[18] Courts have historically held the presumption that when one family member provides a service for another

---

16. *See id.*
17. *See* IRS Form 1040; *see also Family Caregivers and Self-Employment Tax*, Internal Revenue Serv., http://www.irs.gov/Businesses/Small-Businesses-&-Self-Employed/Family-Caregivers-and-Self-Employment-Tax (last updated May 3, 2013).
18. Knox, *supra* note 3, at 1279 (citing Plowman v. King (*In re* Pauly's Estate), 156 N.W. 355, 356 (Iowa 1916) (explaining general presumption of services performed for member of same household not creating payment obligation); Andrews v. Div. of Med. Assistance, 861 N.E.2d 483, 486 (Mass. App. Ct. 2007) (indicating services given to family member presumed gratuitous); Ann Laquer Estin, *Love and Obligation: Family Law and the Romance of Economics*, 36 Wm. & Mary L. Rev. 989, 994–95 (discussing limitations to permitting compensation for interactions between family members); Jonathan S. Henes, Note, *Compensating Caregiving Relatives: Abandoning the Family Member Rule in Contracts*, 17 Cardozo L. Rev. 705, 705 (1996) (stating general rule of expected compensation for services and exception when services performed by family)). When services are performed for a family member, "naturally a question arises whether such services would have been rendered gratuitously . . . or whether a genuine transaction occurred with expectation of payment for value given and received," *Andrews*, 861 N.E.2d at 484. *But cf.* Northrup v. Brigham, 826 N.E.2d. 239, 243 (Mass. App. Ct. 2005) (refusing to apply gratuitous presumption despite romantic relationship between parties). Unlike other courts, no Massachusetts court has ever applied the presumption that unmarried cohabitants in a close relationship perform services for each other without expectation of remuneration, *id.*

family member, the person does so out of love and the services are considered gratuitous. Not only is there a historical prejudice against the adult child who is caring for an elderly parent, but in some states that prejudice is written in the administration rules that state. Lawyers are going to have to overcome the assumption that relatives perform services for each other out of love or mutual convenience.[19]

This can be quite a presumption to overcome, because the prejudice against contracts among relatives dates back to the 1800s, when it was assumed that relatives performed services for the mutual convenience of everyone in their household.[20] Not only do lawyers need to overcome these legal presumptions against familial contracts, there are also deep-rooted cultural beliefs about caregiving among family members.[21]

For example, there are strong cultural beliefs at play that suggest parents should receive reciprocal free care from their children because of the years they spend as uncompensated caregivers raising their children.[22]

---

19. Knox, *supra* note 3, 1279 (citing Harold C. Havighurst, *Services in the Home: A Study of Contract Concepts in Domestic Relations*, 41 YALE L.J. 386, 390 (1932) (describing courts' expectations of reciprocal services among family members)).

20. Knox, *supra* note 3, at 1279 (citing Jonathan S. Henes, Note, *Compensating Caregiving Relatives: Abandoning the Family Member Rule in Contracts*, 17 CARDOZO L. REV. 705, 706–09 (1996) (questioning utility of family-member rule in contemporary society)); *see also* Snyder v. Nixon, 176 N.W. 808, 809 (Iowa 1920) (describing reciprocity among family members for services, thus precluding recovery). When families lived in the same household, they could perform reciprocal services; however, due to increases in geographic mobility, family responsibility for eldercare has shifted, typically to the child who lives closest to an elderly parent. Joshua C. Tate, *Caregiving and the Case for Testamentary Freedom*, 42 U.C. DAVIS L. REV. 129, 165 (2008), at 175–76. *But see* Havighurst, *supra* note 19, at 390 (describing pre-1932 cases in which only one of many children cared for aging parent). Additionally, increases in the age at which women bear children may also affect distribution of eldercare, thus imposing greater responsibility on family members with no dependent children, *see id.*

21. Knox, *supra* note 3, at 1281 (citing Estin, *supra* note 18 (noting risks of simplifying family relationships to merely economic functions); Katie Wise, Note, *Caring for Our Parents in an Aging World: Sharing Public and Private Responsibility for the Elderly*, 5 N.Y.U. J. LEGIS. & PUB. POL'Y 563, 571 (2002) (describing filial responsibilities corresponding to positive family relationships)).

22. Knox, *supra* note 3, at 1281 (citing Estin, *supra* note 18, at 1045–46 (explaining how acts of love do not require reciprocation); Wise, *supra* note 21, at 567–71 (reviewing various theories for requiring children to care for aging parents); Rachel Emma Silverman, *Who Will Mind Mom? Check Her Contract*, POST-GAZETTE, Sept. 7, 2006 ("It's hard to put a dollar figure when you are doing something for your mom.")).

> **Practice Pointer: Not for Love and Affection**
>
> Practitioners need to actually build into the language of the personal-care agreement that the transfers made under this contract are not for love and affection, but rather they are for services rendered to the elder by the caretaker for fair market value.

Medicaid Issues with Personal Care Contracts

Seniors suffering from dementia who wish to qualify for state-paid nursing home care are required to spend down until they only have $2,000 in countable assets (this number varies from state to state).[23]

As mentioned in chapter 5, the state Medicaid agency is going to examine all major financial transactions that occurred during the five years prior to Medicaid application.[24] This is where the personal-care contract needs to be very precise in how it details the care being provided. The state Medicaid agency will be looking to see if the caregiver agreement is being used to allow the parent to simply gift assets to children and still apply for long-term care on the state's dime.[25]

State Medicaid agencies will generally look at two factors to determine whether a transfer of assets disqualifies the person receiving the care for Medicaid benefits:

1. the fair market value of the transaction
2. the intent behind the transaction[26]

---

23. Knox, *supra* note 3, at 1282 (citing 130 MASS. CODE REGS. 520.003 (2012) (listing $2,000 as maximum value of assets owned by individuals to receive Medicaid)). While there may be variations among states, assets counted toward the $2,000 limit generally include checking and savings account funds, stocks, bonds, retirement funds from which withdrawals may be made, and real estate. *See* ELLEN O'BRIEN, LONG-TERM CARE FIN. PROJECT, GEORGETOWN UNIV., MEDICAID'S COVERAGE OF NURSING HOME COSTS: ASSET SHELTER FOR THE WEALTHY OR ESSENTIAL SAFETY NET? 12 n.2 (2005). Exempt assets include a home, car, and burial funds, *id.*
24. Knox, *supra* note 3, at 1282 (citing 130 MASS. CODE REGS. 520.019(B) (explaining Medicaid agency looks at elder's transactions for full 60 months prior to application)). The Deficit Reduction Act, adopted in 2006, extended the look-back period from 36 to 60 months prior to when an elder applies for Medicaid long-term-care benefits. *See* Pub. L. No. 109-171, § 6011 (2006) (codified as amended at 42 U.S.C. § 1396p(c)(1)(B)(i) (2006)). Money that leaves an elder's estate in payment for goods or services will be regarded as "legitimately" reducing the elder's estate, Andrews v. Div. of Med. Assistance, 861 N.E.2d 483, 484 (Mass. App. Ct. 2007) (explaining why money may leave elder's estate legitimately).
25. *Id.*
26. Knox, *supra* note 3, at 1283.

Fair Market Value

The first thing a hearing officer or judge usually checks when evaluating a personal-care agreement is whether caregivers are being paid fair market value for their services.[27]

This is especially the case when the services are being performed by a family member. While services performed by relatives are often presumed to be gratuitous, the State Medicaid Manual states that "[r]elatives and family members legitimately can be paid for care they provide."[28] The State Medicaid Manual further explains that the Medicaid applicant is required to show that the funds transferred to the related caregiver and the services received were exchanged for fair market value.[29]

"Fair market value" is defined by the State Medicaid Manual as "an estimate of the value of an asset, if sold at the prevailing price at the time it was actually transferred."[30]

While that may sound simple enough, determining the prevailing price of eldercare services is not as easy as it sounds. Just about everyone, including hearing officers and judges, has a different opinion as to how to determine the prevailing price for caregivers. The authors always include two or three fee quotations from commercial in-home caregiving companies in their personal-care agreement binder. The fees charged by the family member caregiver under the personal-care agreement drafted by the authors' law firms are typically pegged at $2 to $3 per hour less than the commercial services.

---

27. *Id.* (citing Andrews v. Div. of Med. Assistance, 861 N.E.2d 483, 486 (Mass. App. Ct. 2007) (presuming transfers between relatives for care gratuitous, and thus less than fair market value)); *see also, e.g.*, Piers v. Bigney, No. CV07-0043, 2009 WL 6574639 (Mass. Super. Ct. Mar. 31, 2009) (questioning fair market value of agreement); 130 Mass. Code Regs. 520.019(F)(2) (2012) (determining eligibility for MassHealth benefits includes uncovering whether resources transferred for fair market value); Massachusetts Office of Medicaid Board of Hearings, Appeal 1001965, at 11 (Oct. 29, 2010) (unpublished hearing decision) (on file with the Massachusetts Office of Medicaid Board of Hearings) [hereinafter Massachusetts Medicaid Appeal 1001965] ("[This] case is essentially about whether Appellant received or intended to receive fair market value.").

28. Knox, *supra* note 3, at 1283 (citing Ctrs. for Medicare & Medicaid Servs., State Medicaid Manual § 3258.1(A)–(A)(1) (2001)) (stating elder may pay relative, but transfers for love alone not considered legitimate).

29. *Id.*

30. Knox, *supra* note 3, at 1283 (citing Ctrs. for Medicare & Medicaid Servs., *supra* note 28, § 3258.1(A)–(A)(1)) (defining fair market value); *see also* 130 Mass. Code Regs. 515.001 (2012) (giving MassHealth's nearly identical definition of fair market value).

Nonetheless, there is no legal formula as to how to determine a fair market hourly wage, or even who should make that determination.[31] AARP provides an estimate of how much home-health aides are paid in each state. In some states, this estimate might be sufficient to show that the transfers in question were made for fair market value.[32] However, some state Medicaid agencies pay their personal-care attendants a much lower hourly wage than private caregivers, and that may skew fair market value.[33] Lawyers should create an evidentiary record as to how they determined a fair rate to be incorporated into the contract.

After establishing the fair market rate, lawyers still may face questions about what services are included and, in the case of Alzheimer's disease, how wages would change with intensified care responsibilities as the disease progresses.[34]

Another issue to consider when calculating the fair market rate is any formal training that the caregiver may have. For example, a child

---

31. *Id.*
32. Knox, *supra* note 3, at 1284 (citing Massachusetts Medicaid Appeal 1001965, *supra* note 27, at 6, 10 (accepting as finding of fact $23 per hour as average rate as determined by AARP); *Long-Term Care Cost Calculator*, AARP (Oct. 2006), http://assets.aarp.org/external_sites /caregiving/options/your_options_calculator.html (providing calculator for care costs based on state and type of care)).
33. Knox, *supra* note 3, at 1284 (citing *Piers*, 2009 WL 6574639 (noting MassHealth pays $12 to $18 per hour for personal-care services); Massachusetts Medicaid Appeal 1001965, *supra* note 27, at 5–6 (describing MassHealth pay rate as $10.84 to $12 per hour for its personal-care attendants)).
34. Knox, *supra* note 3, at 1284 (citing Weitzel v. Dehner, No. 08-0627-D (Mass. Super. Ct. Dec. 30, 2008) (noting intensity of care that elder would require given she had Alzheimer's disease); Massachusetts Medicaid Appeal 1001965, *supra* note 27, at 10 (discussing elder's need for 24-hour care in determining whether elder received fair market value); Massachusetts Office of Medicaid Board of Hearings, Appeal 0818313, at 6 (May 12, 2009) (unpublished hearing decision) (on file with the Massachusetts Office of Medicaid Board of Hearings) [hereinafter Massachusetts Medicaid Appeal 0818313] (taking into account elder's medical conditions in determining fair market value)). In *Weitzel*, a caregiver's mother had Alzheimer's, and the judge found that the condition would have necessitated a level of care commensurate with a nursing home, *Weitzel*, No. 08-0627-D. According to a clinical social worker, a nursing home in the elder's area would have cost $4,000 per month, yet the daughter only received $2,500 per month, *id.* at 2. Even with this evidence, a hearing officer initially found the agreement invalid, and only later, when reviewed by a judge, were the transfers held to be intended for fair market value, *id.* at 4, 6. In another case, the hearing officer found that the elder, who was diagnosed with dementia, paid fair market value for services after taking into account the elder's need for 24-hour care, Massachusetts Medicaid Appeal 1001965, *supra* note 27, at 10, 12.

who is acting as her mother's caregiver and who just happens to be a nurse may have a higher fair market rate than her sister, who is a lawyer.[35]

Unfortunately, there is a great deal of uncertainty when it comes to determining fair market value.[36]

Intent

Once lawyers have provided an evidentiary basis to prove that the transfer of assets were for fair market value, they still must demonstrate that the transfer of assets was made for reasons other than to qualify for Medicaid or that the elder receiving the caregiving services intended to pay for the services.[37]

Simply providing verbal assurances that seniors were not considering applying for Medicaid when they transferred assets to the caregiver child is not sufficient proof that the assets were transferred for a reason other than to qualify for Medicaid.[38] It is important to recognize that anyone applying for nursing home Medicaid benefits is burdened by the presumption that any transfer of assets for less than fair market value is deemed to have been motivated by an intent to impoverish oneself to qualify for Medicaid benefits. While the presumption is rebuttable, those who sit in judgment of the evidence are the employees of the state Medicaid department who do not often rule in favor of the Medicaid applicant. The senior needs to have a written personal-care agreement and extensive supporting documentation.

However, even though the parties to the personal-care agreement may have anticipated being forced to use nursing home Medicaid when and if the senior's assets become exhausted, that does not preclude them

---

35. Knox, *supra* note 3, at 1285 (citing Forman v. Dehner, No. BRCV2009-01045, 2010 WL 2344934 (Mass. Super. Ct. Apr. 7, 2010) (pointing out daughter unlicensed as homemaker)). To support the claim that the caregiver agreement terms represented fair market value, the elder's daughter provided the court with a cost-of-care survey for homemaker services in Massachusetts, *id.* The judge highlighted that the survey was for average pay rates of licensed homemakers, and that there was no evidence the caregiver in the case was a licensed homemaker, thus making the cost-of-care survey inapplicable, *id.*

36. Knox, *supra* note 3, at 1285.

37. *Id.* at 1286.

38. *Id.* (citing STATE MEDICAID MANUAL § 3258.10(C)(2) (requiring "convincing evidence" about "specific purpose for which the asset was transferred")).

from giving "reliable proof" that the senior intended to receive valuable services in exchange for the transfer of assets.[39]

Hearing officers and judges will examine the senior's personal-care agreement, looking for reliable proof that the assets were exchanged for valuable services.[40] There is some disagreement as to how specific the written agreement must be,[41] but it is best to make the agreement as specific as possible.

In some states, it may be essential that the personal-care agreement be entered into prior to services being rendered.[42] In other states, those reviewing the contract will be looking for specifics such as how long the services will last, how many hours per week, what standards of services

---

39. Knox, *supra* note 3, at 1286 (citing Gauthier v. Dir. of the Office of Medicaid, 956 N.E.2d 1236, 1244–45 (Mass. App. Ct. 2011) (contemplating how parties could have intended fair exchange even when also planning to use state funds); Andrews v. Div. of Med. Assistance, 861 N.E.2d 483, 485 (Mass. App. Ct. 2007) (describing need to show elder's intent to pay for caregiving services)). In *Gauthier*, the court separated the analysis of whether the elder's purpose of transferring assets was to qualify for Medicaid from the analysis of whether the elder's intent was to pay a caregiver for services, 956 N.E.2d at 1243–44. According to *Gauthier*, the elder could have intended to make an equal exchange of assets for caregiving services even if he or she failed the purpose analysis, *id.* at 1244. In another case, however, the Massachusetts Appeals Court's foremost analysis focused on the elder's intent to pay her relatives for services, *Andrews*, 861 N.E.2d at 485–86. After finding that the elder lacked intent to pay her relatives for services, the court reasoned that the purpose of the transfer was to lower the elder's assets in order to qualify for MassHealth, *id.* at 487.
40. Knox, *supra* note 3, at 1286 (citing STATE MEDICAID MANUAL, *supra* note 38, § 3258.10(C)(1) (noting written arrangement may rebut presumption of less than fair market value for caregiving services)). The presumption that services provided for free at the time of rendering were intended to be provided without compensation, can be challenged, *id.* "[A]n individual can rebut this presumption with tangible evidence that is acceptable to the State. For example, you may require that a payback arrangement had been agreed to in writing at the time services were provided," *id.* § 3258.1(A)(1).
41. Knox, *supra* note 3, at 1286 (citing Weitzel v. Dehner, No. 08-0627-D (Mass. Super. Ct. Dec. 30, 2008) (using durable power of attorney as adequate demonstration of agreement to compensate daughter); *cf. Gauthier*, 956 N.E.2d at 1242 (listing multiple inadequacies with caregiver agreement)).
42. Knox, *supra* note 3, at 1286 (citing Treat v. Exec. Office of Health & Human Servs., 923 N.E.2d 1093 (Mass. App. Ct. 2010) (highlighting written documentation created after services rendered); *Andrews*, 861 N.E.2d at 486 (describing invoice for labor and supplies dated after services provided)). *But see Weitzel*, No. 08-0627-D (accepting agreement as valid when daughter provided caregiving for free prior to any formal agreement); 130 MASS. CODE REGS. 520.007(J)(4) (2012) (requiring enforceable contract only when transaction involves payment in exchange for services provided in future); Massachusetts Medicaid Appeal 0818313, *supra* note 34, at 6 (allowing daughter to perform services for mother gratuitously before payments for services began).

are being provided, and what, if any, provisions provide for a refund.[43] In some cases, those reviewing the contract may investigate whether the services mentioned in the agreement were actually the services that were performed.[44]

Thus, while a valid, written caregiver agreement is a necessity, it is difficult to find a universal standard for what must be included in the agreement.[45]

Avoiding the Hidden Traps of Nursing Home Contracts

Most of the nursing homes in the United States are owned by regional and/or national multiple-site corporations. Large corporations can afford to employ excellent legal counsel that has the benefit of focusing a practice exclusively within the long-term-care facility niche. Those lawyers know the law, the regulations, and the cases. The nursing home chains are keenly aware of what commonly causes them to lose money. Lawyers can be assured that nursing homes have demanded that their legal counsel draft nursing home contracts to put lawyers' clients at a disadvantage. When lawyers review a contract for a client, they are at a distinct disadvantage. The highly knowledgeable opponent drafted the contract to make sure that the nursing home was not going to lose

---

43. Knox, *supra* note 3, at 1287 (citing *Gauthier*, 956 N.E.2d at 1242) (listing grievances with lack of specificity in caregiver contract); *see also* Forman v. Dir. of Office of Medicaid, 944 N.E.2d 1081, 1087 (Mass. App. Ct. 2011) (criticizing contract for not quantifying number of hours per week caregiver would provide services); E.S. v. Div. of Med. Assistance & Health Servs., 990 A.2d 701, 704, 710 (N.J. Super. Ct. App. Div. 2010) (finding contract inadequate despite enumeration of hours, weeks, and years for caregiver services)). Specificity was insufficient for one caregiver contract because certain provisions stated that the caregiver agreement could not be transferred, assigned, or conveyed, and therefore it had no fair market value, *see E.S.*, 990 A.2d at 710.

44. Knox, *supra* note 3, at 1287 (citing *Gauthier*, 956 N.E.2d at 1242) (noting discrepancies between services provided to elder and services promised to elder in contract); *Forman*, 944 N.E.2d at 1086 (highlighting mismatch between services listed in contract and services provided citing)).

45. Knox, *supra* note 3, at 1287 (citing Massachusetts Office of Medicaid Board of Hearings, Appeal 0601673, at 3 (June 13, 2006) (unpublished hearing decision) (finding acceptable agreement prepared by lawyer with caregiver's duties and hours per week of care)). *Compare Gauthier*, 956 N.E.2d at 1242 (desiring specificity in contract regarding hours), *and Forman*, 944 N.E.2d at 1087 (requiring greater detail in contract regarding hours and duration), *with* Massachusetts Medicaid Appeal 0818313, *supra* note 34, at 6 (finding agreement providing basic monthly payments valid irrespective of lack of specificity about services).

money. Lawyers should take this into consideration so they won't look like the man rowing his boat out to attack the U.S. Seventh Fleet.

Recent studies reveal that nearly 70 percent of those 65 and older will eventually need some sort of long-term care assistance.[46] When a family reaches the point where it becomes necessary for an affected loved one to enter a nursing home, it is one of the most difficult decisions they will ever have to make. When Alzheimer's disease has progressed to the point where the affected loved one can no longer live alone, or when the primary caregiver can no longer provide the level or expertise of care that is necessary, a move to a nursing home is the next stop on the Alzheimer's care journey.

There are ways for lawyers to help clients through this difficult time. As always, having a plan and knowing the right questions to ask beforehand will allow lawyers to provide invaluable help to their clients.

Lawyers need to counsel their clients to visit several different nursing homes before narrowing down their choices. Within urban areas, there are companies that specialize in connecting prospective nursing facility residents with facilities. One nationwide organization is called A Place for Mom (www.aplaceformom.com). This type of organization is compensated by being paid a commission from the long-term-care facility. Lawyers should look for such a service within their jurisdiction. Because the organization is paid on commission, it is important for lawyers to understand that they may not have listing contracts with all facilities; therefore, one may not be shown the entire panorama of options. This statement is not meant to be critical, but rather to express the possible limitations of such services.

The Centers for Medicare and Medicaid Services rates nursing homes. The system is called the Nursing Home Compare. It includes ratings of nursing homes based on quality measurements, staffing ratios, and health inspections. The website is www.medicare.gov/NursingHomeCompare.

Once clients have found a few facilities that look like good options, they should visit each one several times, preferably at different times in the day and at least once during a meal.[47]

46. WILLIAM SIEBERS & ZACH HESSELBAUM, PAYING FOR LONG-TERM CARE IN ILLINOIS (2012) (citing U.S. Dep't of Health & Human Servs., *Planning for LTC*, www.longtermcare.gov /LTC/Main_Site/Planning/Index.aspx (last visited May 5, 2013)).
47. WILLIAM G. HAMMOND, RICK L. LAW, KAREN HAYS WEBER & MARY HELEN GAUTREAUX, THE ALZHEIMER'S LEGAL SURVIVAL GUIDE: ACTION GUIDE 42 (2009).

It is important to find a nursing home with an Alzheimer's special-care unit.[48] Alzheimer's sufferers have unique needs and will have a much better nursing home experience if the nursing home staff is capable of dealing with their needs. Staff in special-care units should take specialized training courses in order to be able to encourage the residents' independence and help them realize the maximum potential of their mental and physical abilities as their dementia progresses.[49]

Lawyers need to advise their clients that the special units often come at an added price. Some states have established guidelines for these units, but there are no federal guidelines.

Practice Pointer: Nursing Homes with Special Alzheimer's Units

Lawyers should advise clients to look for the following qualities from a nursing home with a special unit before agreeing to pay the higher rate:

- Does the facility confirm all incoming residents' Alzheimer's diagnosis?
- Is the staff aware of the progressive nature of Alzheimer's disease, and how do they address the expected changes in the mental and physical abilities of the residents?
- Are all of the employees in the special unit (the housekeepers, maintenance workers, etc.) given some training regarding Alzheimer's?
- Are the buildings and grounds designed for people suffering from Alzheimer's disease?
- Are the resident activities appropriate for people with Alzheimer's?

It is also important for lawyers to advise clients early on in the nursing home search that this type of care is expensive. Fees average around $45,000 a year nationwide, and can be as expensive as $100,000 or more. Most insurance plans do not cover this type of long-term care and neither does Medicare.

Fortunately, Medicaid is available for qualified individuals. Medicaid is a federally funded, state-administered medical assistance program that is explained in detail in chapter 5.

Nursing home contracts are supposed to include language informing the people signing the contract that they should consult with a lawyer. However, this language is usually going to be in small print buried in the contract. Lawyers need to encourage their clients to allow them

---

48. *Id.*
49. *Id.*

to review the contract with them. Many laypeople may not know or may be afraid to strike through parts of a contract that they don't agree with. Even though nursing home contracts should be reviewed by legal counsel, the majority of nursing home contracts are not brought to the attention of counsel unless or until a problem has arisen after admission and the contract has been signed.

There can be several potential traps in nursing home contract language. The best thing to do is to draw a line through the offending language. For example, many nursing home contracts will "request" that someone else sign along with the potential resident. When author Rick Law was in law school, his business law professor stated emphatically, "A cosigner is a fool with a pen in his hand." Those excellent lawyers who have drafted nursing home contracts have crafted many ways to comply with the law and yet attempt to turn family members into cosigners who are referred to as "responsible parties." When a layperson who is either an agent under a health-care power of attorney, caregiver under a personal-care agreement, or an honest and reliable child carrying the burden of decision making sees the words "responsible party," they do not perceive that to be synonymous with "cosigner."

The use of the words "responsible party" in this case leads to many people being deceived into becoming a cosigner for the affected loved one. The lawyer must explain to a family member that assuming the role of "responsible party" means that the person is assuming liability for any debts created by the resident. Under the Federal Nursing Home Reform Act,[50] nursing homes are not allowed to include responsible party language in their contracts anymore; nonetheless, it is almost omnipresent in those contracts that are brought into the authors' offices for review.

Practice Pointer:

Do not let a family member be a responsible party. Lawyers should have the potential residents sign the contract as long as they are still capable. If they are no longer capable, just have the family member sign as an agent or representative and make a big "X" through the responsible party's signature line (or put the resident's name as the responsible party) so that it is very obvious that the family member is not agreeing to be the responsible party.

---

50. 42 U.S.C. § 1396r(c)(5)(A)(ii) (2012).

Don't be afraid to have family members strike through portions of the contract that make them uncomfortable. If the nursing home has a problem with striking through provisions, then it may not be the right nursing home.

The Federal Nursing Home Reform Act requires that the nursing home assess each resident's functional capacity, but the resident is presumed to have the capacity to sign the contract unless the resident is the subject of a pending petition for an adjudication of disability.[51]

Depending on what stage of dementia the client is in, it may be necessary for the power of attorney or guardian to sign on the client's behalf. Practitioners need to keep in mind that nursing homes are prohibited from requiring a third-party guarantor.[52] One of the tough realities of long-term care, if the family of the affected loved one can afford to pay privately, is that the lawyer will have substantial negotiating power in modifying a nursing home contract. However, if the family is limited to finding what is referred to as a "Medicaid bed" in a long-term-care facility, the choices may be much more limited. In the current economic and health-care environment, state budgets are under extreme pressure and nursing home Medicaid often constitutes 50 percent of the state's Medicaid budget. Many states are drastically restricting nursing home Medicaid reimbursement rates, which is causing the number of Medicaid beds available to be very restricted. Lawyers working with families in this circumstance will have much less negotiating flexibility.

Another trap is the assignment of the resident's Social Security check even when the resident is paying privately for care. Often the nursing home will try to have the elder or the power of attorney sign documentation stating that the Social Security check is to go directly to the nursing home. This is unnecessary if the elder is paying privately, and the client should not sign over their rights to the check. On the other hand, when the affected person's nursing home care is being paid by the state nursing home Medicaid benefit, that person may be required to assign the check to the care facility.

---

51. 42 U.S.C. § 1396r(b)(3) (2012).
52. *Id.* §§ 1395i-3(c)(5)(A)(ii), 1396r(c)(5)(A)(ii); 42 C.F.R. § 483.12(d)(2) (2003).

> **Practice Pointer: VA Aid & Attendance Benefits and Nursing Home Medicaid**
>
> When dealing with those who have Alzheimer's, at some point it is most likely that they are going to need assisted living and/or nursing home care. When that elder is a veteran, lawyers should have them consider Veterans Affairs (VA) benefits, as well as Medicaid.
>
> Every elder needs to be evaluated on a case-by-case basis to determine the best planning options. Elders who are veterans may have additional benefits available to them that are not available to the general population. In some states there are specific veterans nursing homes and other state-provided long-term-care benefits. Nationally, the VA special monthly pension is similar to Medicaid in that it is an asset- and income-needs-based benefit. In other words, a veteran must have very limited assets and income and be burdened by substantial recurring medical expenditures to be able to qualify for the special monthly pension. This benefit is referred to as the "VA Aid & Attendance Benefit." Unfortunately, many veterans have engaged in self-impoverishment tactics to qualify themselves for this benefit. Due to the five-year look-back for nursing home Medicaid benefits, it is foolish for an aging veteran to transfer assets to attempt to qualify for VA benefits.
>
> The VA Aid & Attendance benefit has a limited shelf life. The special monthly pension can provide sufficient funds to assist a veteran who is receiving in-home or assisted-living care. However, eventually the cost of nursing home care is almost always going to outpace the VA pension benefit.

Arbitration Clauses: The Bane of the Litigator and Clients

One of the methods currently being used by nursing home contract drafting lawyers to cut nursing home losses from litigation is to include binding arbitration clauses within the standard form contract. As lawyers review any contract, they should be on alert for the presence of such clauses. Nursing homes are raising arbitration clauses as a defense, even within the context of wrongful death actions and personal injury suits. Arbitration provisions have been found by federal courts to be valid under the Federal Arbitration Act[53] because it was determined that the

---

53. 9 U.S.C. § 1-16 (2008).

contract involved interstate commerce and therefore was enforceable.[54] The U.S. Supreme Court has found for nursing homes and against families in a recent case involving nursing home arbitration contracts.[55]

The authors recommend that their clients limit the grant of authority to their agents under a power of attorney for financial matters and/or power of attorney for health-care decision making so that the agent does not have authority to agree to dispute resolution by arbitration. Lawyers should check the case law within their jurisdiction to determine how best to draft a response to standard form clauses that require dispute resolution by arbitration.

Residents' Rights

The Federal Nursing Home Reform Act lays out the rights of the residents.[56] Under the federal act, a nursing home facility is required to protect and promote the rights of each resident, including, but not limited to the following rights:

1. The resident has the right to exercise rights as a resident of the facility and as a citizen or resident of the United States.[57] This means the resident is free to make financial and medical decisions.

2. The resident has the right to be free of interference, coercion, discrimination, and reprisal from the facility in exercising those rights.[58]

3. In the case of a resident adjudged incompetent under the laws of a state by a court of competent jurisdiction, the rights of the resident are exercised by the person appointed under state law to act on the resident's behalf.[59]

4. In the case of a resident who has not been adjudged incompetent by the state court, any legal-surrogate designated in accordance with state law may exercise the resident's rights to the extent provided by state law.[60]

---

54. *See* Rainbow Health Care Ctr., Inc. v. Crutcher, No. 07-CV-194-JHP, U.S. Dist. LEXIS 6705, at *18 (D. Okla. 2008).
55. *See* Marmet Health Care Ctr. Inc. v. Brown, 132 S. Ct. 1201 (2012).
56. 42 C.F.R. § 483.10 (2012).
57. *Id.* § 483.10(a)(1).
58. *Id.* § 483.10(a)(2).
59. *Id.* § 483.10(a)(3).
60. *Id.* § 483.10(a)(4).

The act also states the following:

1. The facility must inform the resident both orally and in writing in a language that the resident understands of the resident's rights and all rules and regulations governing resident conduct and responsibilities during the stay in the facility.[61]

2. The resident or legal representative has the right upon an oral or written request to access all records pertaining to the resident, including current clinical records within 24 hours (excluding weekends and holidays); and after receipt of records for inspection, to purchase at a cost not to exceed the community standard photocopies of the records or any portions of them upon request and two working days advance notice to the facility.[62]

3. The resident has the right to be fully informed in language that the resident can understand of total health status, including but not limited to, medical condition.[63]

4. The resident has the right to refuse treatment, to refuse to participate in experimental research, and to formulate an advance directive.[64]

5. The facility also must inform residents that are entitled to Medicaid benefits, in writing, at the time of admission to the nursing facility or when the resident becomes eligible for Medicaid of the items and services that are included in nursing facility services under the state plan and for which the resident may not be charged; those other items and services that the facility offers and for which the resident may be charged, and the amount of charges for those services; and inform each resident when changes are made to the items and services specified above.[65]

61. *Id.* § 483.10(b)(1).
62. *Id.* § 483.10(b)(2)(i).
63. *Id.* § 483.10(b)(3).
64. *Id.* § 483.10(b)(4).
65. *Id.* § 483.10(b)(5).

Practice Pointer:

Residents are entitled to manage their personal finances and choose their health-care providers. Elders should not sign a contract that requires the resident to deposit personal funds with the facility.

The nursing home must keep residents informed of any plan of care and any changes in that plan and must allow the residents to be an active participant in their own health-care plan. This includes allowing residents to refuse treatment. The fact that people are residents of a nursing home doesn't mean they lose their rights.

Nursing homes must assess a resident's needs every 12 months and create a health-care plan appropriate to the needs of the particular resident.[66]

Practice Pointer: Participate in the Health-Care Plan

Lawyers are entitled to be present with clients/residents (or the resident's representative if the resident no longer has capacity to make health-care decisions) to ensure that the resident's best interests are served by the health-care plan.

Patient Transfers/Discharges

Although each state has its own rules regarding transfers and discharges, if the facility accepts Medicaid and/or Medicare, it is bound by the federal rules.

A nursing home may only transfer or discharge a patient under federal law if it is

- necessary for the resident's welfare and the resident's needs cannot be met in the facility;
- appropriate because the resident's health has improved sufficiently so the resident no longer needs the services provided by the facility;
- the safety of individuals in the facility is endangered;

---

66. *Id.* § 483(d)(3).

- the health of individuals in the facility would otherwise be endangered;
- the resident has failed, after reasonable and appropriate notice, to pay for (or to have paid under Medicare or Medicaid) a stay at the facility (or a resident who becomes eligible for Medicaid after admission to a facility, the facility may charge a resident only allowable charges under Medicaid); or
- the facility ceases to operate.[67]

Facilities must give notice to the resident and resident's representative and the notice must provide the following:

- the reasons for the transfer and discharge
- the effective date of the transfer or discharge
- where the resident will be transferred or discharged to
- a statement informing the resident the he/she has the right to appeal the action to the state
- the name, address, and telephone number for the state's long-term-care ombudsman[68]

The facility is required to provide 30 days' notice from the effective date of the transfer or discharge except for emergency situations.[69]

 Case Study ———————————————————

Difficult Discharge

A client of one of the authors had early-onset Alzheimer's, which means that he was affected by Alzheimer's before the age of 65. He became incapacitated at the age of 46, and during the next six years until he died, he was moved from one nursing home to another 16 times. Some Alzheimer's sufferers exhibit rage, anger, and aggression. It is very common for Alzheimer's facilities to discharge a resident if they have difficulty with that resident.

This client was young and strong and a threat to nursing home staff. If a client poses a threat to an employee or another resident, the nursing home doesn't have to give a 30-day notice. Staff will call the family and say, "Come and get your loved one within the next 24 hours!"

The above case study demonstrates why it is so important to find a facility that knows how to deal with residents with Alzheimer's dis-

---

67. *Id.* § 483.12(a)(2).
68. *Id.* § 483.12(a)(6).
69. *Id.* § 483.12(a)(5).

ease. Sometimes the staff can actually minimize the rage by being more agreeable with the resident and by diverting their attention to something else.

Check the applicable specific services being provided for the care recipient:			
	Help with dressing		Training for substitute/additional Caregiver
	Help with bathing		Supervision to prevent care recipient from harming himself
	Help with ambulating		Supervision to prevent care recipient from harming others
	Help with toileting		Providing a protective environment for cognitive impairment
	Help with incontinence		Providing restraint or direction if care recipient is uncooperative
	Medication reminders		Physical Therapy
	Help with feeding		Administration of medications
	Providing meals		Placement of Catheters
	Homemaker Services		Changing sterile dressings
	Supervision to prevent wandering		
	Transportation or transportation assistance		

 **Expert View**

The Hope of Vanquishing Alzheimer's Disease

Harry Johns is president and CEO of the Alzheimer's Association.

Q: Let's start with a common misperception: that Alzheimer's is not a fatal disease.

A: Most people still do not realize the basics of Alzheimer's. Alzheimer's disease is progressive, degenerative, and ultimately fatal. Unfortunately, laypeople still think about the disease as "a little bit of memory loss." I talk to people all the time, all over the country. Many times, when I say that Alzheimer's disease is progressive, degenerative, and fatal, people respond, "Alzheimer's disease isn't fatal!" Well-educated people in high positions will argue back at me, "You don't die of Alzheimer's disease!"

Q: Do you often see denial when early symptoms appear?

A: Denial is a really powerful evolutionary protection. If we simply accept all the terrible things that go on in the world every day and don't operate on some level of denial, we would all cease to function. Denial helps us to deal with everyday life. Unfortunately, denial as related to Alzheimer's disease leads to many bad outcomes.

Q: What are the earliest signs of Alzheimer's?

A: Memory loss is often the first sign that others recognize and attribute to Alzheimer's disease. Here are the 10 early warning signs:

- memory loss that disrupts daily life
- challenges in planning or solving problems
- difficulty completing familiar tasks at home, at work, or at leisure
- confusion with time or place
- trouble understanding visual images and spatial relationships
- new problems with words in speaking or reading
- misplacing things and losing the ability to retrace steps
- decreased or poor judgment
- withdrawal from work or social activities
- changes in mood and personality

Q: Does it always start with memory loss?

A: There really is a general lack of knowledge throughout our society about the progression of this fatal disease. Most people believe that

Alzheimer's disease always starts with memory loss, but it doesn't. My mom had the disease. The first thing that she admitted to was not being able to balance her checkbook. All through her life, every week she had balanced her checkbook to the penny. She just could not do it anymore. That is what is called the loss of "executive function." This is very important for lawyers to consider when they are doing planning for senior clients.

Q: What is the family doctor's role in all of this?

A: I want lawyers to know that medical doctors do not want to give their patients the diagnosis of Alzheimer's disease. Attorneys need to know that, so that they realize they are encountering people in their offices who have not been diagnosed by their physicians as having dementia, but they are definitely cognitively impaired. I am sure that raises a host of ethical issues. But the attorney needs to know that clients are going to tell them that they are cognitively okay even when they are well past the point of being okay.

In fairness to the doctors, there are those on the positive side of the bell curve who are doing exactly the right thing. Unfortunately, many doctors do not want to give the diagnosis because it is terrible. They do not want to be the one who tells the individual or the person's family that their loved one has a diagnosis of an incurable disease.

The medical profession faced a similar situation in the 1960s. Back then, there were really no effective cures for cancer. Based on numerous studies at the time, 90 percent–plus of all doctors admitted that they did not tell patients with cancer that they had cancer. Today, we are in the same situation with Alzheimer's disease. The drugs that we have available to treat those with Alzheimer's disease do not work well enough to cure the disease. In addition, they don't work long enough for sufficient numbers of people for doctors to feel that they have an effective tool to aid their patients. Nonetheless, it is important that people do get diagnosed early, because the drugs that we do have now work sufficiently well for some people to substantially lengthen and improve their functional lives.

Returning to the issues of the early signs of Alzheimer's disease: Memory loss is the most frequent first sign recognized by the family as a sign of dementia, but there are other changes too. Behavioral changes often occur first. People may either withdraw from others or they may become more aggressive. Look for personality differences in a person as a possible sign of the beginnings of Alzheimer's disease. The problem is compounded by the fact that many people affected by Alzheimer's recognize the changes within themselves and then actively work to hide what is going on from others.

Q: What resources are available to patients and families?

A: The Alzheimer's Association has resources that can help lawyers to know more about helping their clients deal with Alzheimer's disease. Attorneys can make a direct referral to the Alzheimer's Association or go to www.alz.org. There is a helpline available 24 hours a day, 365 days a year, at (800) 272-3900. Via the helpline, the Alzheimer's Association has highly trained social workers available to counsel attorneys as well as others about the disease. In addition, the Alzheimer's Association website has a host of resources available to everyone.

The Alzheimer's Association has a program called Trial Match™, which is set up for matching people to clinical trials that are very specific to a person's circumstances, locale, and the availability of the trials, and also the kind of care they're already getting. The Alzheimer's Association is available to help by telephone, and in person in communities across the country.

The Alzheimer's Association offers various intervention programs that can make a difference in a person's functional life. Many of these intervention programs provide as much assistance to people as what some of the drugs can do. We have programs that help caregivers, as well as programs that help individuals who have this disease stay engaged—the kinds of things that keep them active, the kinds of things that don't have them withdraw in the way they otherwise would. We know that if people stay engaged and don't withdraw as much and do those kinds of things, it can improve their functional lives on a comparable level to what some of the drugs can do.

Q: What are your hopes for the future?

A: The future for the Alzheimer's Association would be that Alzheimer's disease is vanquished and we are out of business in just a few years. But, most likely, we will continue to exist, because there is a need for additional research, and a continual evolution of the types of drugs that will be available. There will be a need for guidance to assist patients and families on the pathway of care. Modern medicine has conquered many diseases, and we can certainly hope that the same happens with Alzheimer's disease. That would be the ideal.

GLOSSARY

A

acute-care condition—a diagnosis that a person can get well from. Medicare generally covers acute-care conditions. The opposite of chronic care.

advance directives—written documents, such as the living will, power of attorney for health care, power of attorney for property, and the do not resuscitate order (DNR), that set forth health decisions to be made once people can no longer make these decisions for themselves.

Alzheimer's disease—a degenerative brain disease of undetermined cause that is the most common form of dementia, usually starting in late middle age or in old age, that results in memory loss, impaired thinking, disorientation, and changes in personality and mood. The Alzheimer's Association labels the disease as degenerative, progressive, and fatal.

Alzheimer's journey—individuals with Alzheimer's often progress through this trajectory:

- memory loss ignored
- memory loss masked/denied
- unsafe alone
- aid needed
- assisted living required
- nursing home required
- hospice care required/death

The **family of a loved one with Alzheimer's** often progresses through a **complementary trajectory** that may have some of these components:

- memory loss ignored
- memory loss masked/denied/facilitated
- memory loss assistance needed by loved one, but hidden from "outsiders"

arbitration clause—one of the methods used by nursing home lawyers to cut nursing home losses from litigation is to include binding arbitration clauses within the standard form contract. Nursing homes are raising arbitration clauses as a defense, even within the context of wrongful death actions and personal injury suits.

assisted-living facility—nursing home or other type of facility for people who cannot live alone because they have chronic-care conditions, such as Alzheimer's disease.

B

beneficiary—one for whose benefit a trust is created.

C

capacity—generally defined as the mental ability to perceive and appreciate relevant facts and make rational decisions.

capacity worksheet—a checklist of sorts aimed at helping lawyers assess their clients and determine whether or not the client has diminished capacity.

care managers—licensed clinical professionals, usually with advanced degrees, with extensive knowledge of health care, aging, and different issues that affect people with disabilities. They are often nurses, social workers, and licensed clinical counselors.

caregiver child—child taking care of a parent with diminished capacity.

charitable pooled trust or **d4C trust**—an irrevocable gift that provides both a lifetime income from premium investment options and an unprecedented charitable tax deduction.

chronic-care conditions—a condition, such as Alzheimer's disease, that is not going to improve. The opposite of acute care.

citations to discover assets—a broad, pre-complaint discovery tool designed to "level the playing field" for guardians and representatives of people who may not understand or be able to articulate what happened to their assets. This is a defense against financial exploitation. Citations to discover assets allow one to obtain discovery without having to file suit and without having to plead facts requisite to survive a motion to dismiss.

citations to recover assets—a procedural mechanism that is a defense against financial exploitation, but it does not typically create any substantive legal rights. One must plead cognizable legal theories such as incapacity or undue influence, coercion, and duress. Undue influence, coercion, and duress are very often pleaded in the alternative. Unlike citations to discover assets, citations to recover assets are subject to dispositive motions.

cognitive impairments—mental impairments associated with confusion, forgetfulness, and other memory issues.

colicky dementia—a form of dementia in which the individual is unpredictable, inconsolable, and has disproportionate behavior reactions to the reality of the individual's environment, inner health, and caretaking. The individual exhibits a chronic state of anxiety, panic, and circular thinking that lasts for periods exceeding three hours a day, more than three days a week, for more than three weeks.

community spouse—for purposes of this book, the term "community spouse" as defined by nursing home Medicaid regulations is a spouse that continues to live in a personal residence within the community while married to a person who has been institutionalized in a nursing home.

contractual capacity—level of capacity required for the execution of inter vivos trusts, deeds, and nondurable powers of attorney. Contractual capacity is defined as the ability to comprehend and understand the terms and effect of the contract.

countable assets—assets that count toward the state determined maximum for Medicaid purposes. These include bank accounts, certificates of deposits, money market accounts, stocks, mutual funds, bonds, retirement accounts, pensions, second cars, second or vacation homes, and any other items that can be valued and turned into cash.

custodial care—assistance with preparing meals, bathing, grooming, toileting, and other activities of normal daily life. Medicaid does not pay for custodial care.

D

d4A or self-settled trust—a special-needs trust funded with property belonging to the beneficiary and/or beneficiary's spouse, such as a direct inheritance, recovery in a personal injury lawsuit, or a gift.

d4B or Miller trust—a trust in which a person has assigned the right to receive social security and pension payments, in order to avoid having too much income to qualify for benefits like Medicaid.

d4C trust or **charitable pooled trust**—an irrevocable gift that provides both a lifetime income from premium investment options and an unprecedented charitable tax deduction.

dementia—a form of mental disorder resulting from degeneration of the brain. For purposes of this book, dementia includes degeneration of the brain caused by Alzheimer's disease, Parkinson's disease, and as many as 70 other causes. Dementia does not refer to traumatic brain injury.

death is imminent—in medical terms, an imminent death means a determination made by the attending physician according to accepted medical standards that death will occur in a relatively short period of time, even if life-sustaining treatment is initiated or continued. The "relatively short period of time" is defined as six months. One becomes qualified for hospice if death is imminent.

Dependency and Indemnity Compensation (DIC) Benefits—unmarried spouses, dependent children, and parents of veterans can all potentially be eligible for the wide variety of Veterans Affairs benefits.

diminished capacity—when a person's ability to communicate, to comprehend and assess information, and to make reasoned decisions is lessened.

disability—when, for purposes of this book, a person is unable to manage his or her person or estate due to mental deterioration or physical incapacity.

disability panel—when drafting estate planning documents such as a revocable living trust, one option is to offer the client a disability panel for the determination of sufficient incapacity to trigger the removal of the trustee. This panel often includes family members and one attending physician. They often empower a majority to rule in the decision making, but some clients may be more comfortable with a unanimous decision.

disinheritance—the act by which the owner of an estate deprives a presumptive beneficiary of the right to inherit.

do not resuscitate (DNR) order—instructs health-care professionals not to perform cardiopulmonary resuscitation if a person's heart stops or if the person stops breathing. DNRs are signed by a doctor and put in the individual's medical chart. The DNR is the only advance directive that is also a doctor's order or a physician's order for medical care.

E

exempt—for purposes of this book, refers to assets of an individual that are not counted toward the determination of eligibility for means-tested public benefits.

F

fiduciary relationship—fiduciary relationships exist as a matter of law in certain relationships, such as lawyer-client. However, a fiduciary relationship can also be found as a matter of fact. Courts consider the following factors:

- degree of kinship between the parties;
- disparity in age
- disparity in health

- disparity in mental conditions
- disparity in education and/or business sophistication
- degree of trust placed in the dominant party
- degree of dependence or reliance placed in the dominant party

Once lawyers have a fiduciary duty by fact patterns, they can argue undue influence in a financial exploitation situation.

15-minute reset—a way to detect memory issues such as dementia. Often, people with excellent social skills (still common in women in their 80s and 90s) are able to hold a conversation that includes all the correct words and head nods. However, after around 13 or 14 minutes they will start the conversation over again, almost as if they were playing a tape.

financial exploitation—the act of taking advantage of a person suffering from dementia for financial gain. Financial exploitation is overwhelmingly committed by people related to the victim or in a position of trust.

five-year look-back period—when a person applies for Medicaid benefits, the state agency will look at all gifts and transfers made in the last five years. Gifts and transfers may not be made simply to be eligible for Medicaid benefits. The burden of proof is on the recipient to prove that the gifts or transfers were *not* improper.

forensic accounting—a specialty practice area of accounting that applies accounting techniques to solve legal issues. Often used to investigate and document financial fraud.

fraudulent conveyance—a transfer of property that is made to swindle, hinder, or delay a creditor, or to put property beyond a creditor's reach.

G

geriatric care manager—a person with special training in the area of elder care trained—for purposes of a personal-care agreement—to conduct a survey of the physical environment within the home and an inventory of all resources available to an individual.

guardian—someone appointed by the court to serve as a representative of a person with a legal disability—for purposes of this book, Alzheimer's disease.

guardian ad litem—often referred to as "the eyes and ears of the court." Before the temporary guardianship hearing is held, the court appoints a guardian ad litem to visit the person with alleged disabilities, make a determination and report back to the court as to whether emergency relief is necessary and reasonable under the circumstances.

356 | Alzheimer's and the Law

guardian of the estate—person responsible for the care, management, and investment of the estate. In some states, a guardian of the estate is referred to as a conservatorship and may do the following for the ward:

- make financial decisions
- enter into contracts
- estate planning
- file lawsuits
- sell real estate
- apply for government benefits

guardian of the person—someone who assists the ward in the development of maximum self-reliance and independence and may do the following:

- make medical decisions
- oversee the residential placement of the ward (with court approval)
- ensure that the ward receives proper professional services
- release medical records and information

guardianship—a legal relationship that is established and monitored by state courts under state laws. It is a mechanism for empowering someone (the guardian) to act on behalf of an incapacitated individual (the ward).

grantor—a person who makes a transfer of property by deed or writing.

grantor trust—a trust established by an agreement that is not a will. Trustmaker retains sufficient control as defined by the Internal Revenue Code (I.R.C. §§ 671–679) of the property entrusted, realizing taxes on income from the property.

H

hospice care is a team approach to caring for an individual in the final stages of a terminal illness, such as Alzheimer's. The goal of hospice care is to provide comfort, reassurance, and support for the dying patient and family and friends.

hospital insurance—see Medicare coverage.

I

inpatient—a key term for Medicare eligibility. Medicare helps pay for inpatient care in the hospital or skilled-nursing facilities following a hospital stay. The patient must be "admitted" and not merely "under observation." Typically requires a 72-hour hospital stay.

institutionalized spouse—as defined by nursing home Medicaid regulations, an individual who

- requires care in a medical institution such as a nursing home; and
- is married to a person who resides in the community at least one day of the month.

inter vivos trust—a trust that becomes effective during the lifetime of the trustmaker/settlor/grantor and provides access to the trust corpus according to the terms of the trust. Often called a living trust or revocable living trust.

irrevocable trust—a type of trust that, as a general rule, cannot be revoked or changed after it has been signed; or a revocable trust that by its design becomes irrevocable after the trustmaker dies.

L

life-sustaining treatment—any medical treatment, procedure, or intervention that in the judgment of the attending physician, when applied to a patient with a qualifying condition, would not be effective to remove the qualifying condition or would serve only to prolong the dying process. Those procedures can include, but are not limited to, assisted ventilation, renal dialysis, surgical procedures, blood transfusions and the administration of drugs, antibiotics, and artificial nutrition and hydration.

limited guardian—a guardian who has been appointed by the court to exercise the legal rights and powers specifically designated by court order entered after the court has found that the ward lacks the capacity to do some, but not all, of the tasks necessary to care for his or her person or property, or after the ward has voluntarily petitioned for appointment of a limited guardian. A limited guardian is appointed by taking away certain rights of an individual and giving certain rights.

living will—a document (advance directive) that only takes effect when two doctors certify in writing that the creator of the living will is irreversibly ill or critically injured and near death.

long-term care options—a variety of services that include medical and nonmedical care for people who have a chronic illness or disability. Long-term care helps meet health or personal needs. Most long-term care is to assist people with support services, such as activities of daily living like dressing, bathing, and using the bathroom. Long-term care can be provided at home, in the community, in assisted-living facilities, or in nursing homes. A person may need long-term care at any age.

Look-back period—see five-year look-back period.

M

Medicaid—a program typically administered by the individual states, with funding from both the federal government and individual states. Medicaid is a means-tested health-care benefit program. To have medical expenses paid, applicants typically must meet impoverishment guidelines, which include both income and asset limitations.

Medicaid bed—many assisted-living facilities have a certain amount of beds set aside for Medicaid recipients. Many states are drastically restricting nursing home Medicaid reimbursement rates, which is causing the number of Medicaid beds available to be very restricted.

Medicaid trusts—a term used to describe a trust created for the purpose of protecting assets from being treated as available for spend down on health-care services. The grantor/trustmaker makes a gift of assets to the trust with the express purpose of qualifying for Medicaid. The history of Medicaid trusts has been a continual assault by federal and state governments to eliminate the ability of individuals to use trusts as asset protection devices while qualifying for nursing home Medicaid benefits.

Medicare—a non-means-tested federal health-care program that provides benefits primarily to U.S. citizens who are over 65, blind, and/or permanently disabled. Medicare was not created to pay for 100 percent of an individual's health-care expenses. For those individuals who are over 65, blind, and/or permanently disabled, and also have insufficient income and assets to pay deductibles, it is possible to be "dual eligible" for both Medicare and Medicaid. Medicare is supposed to pay for acute care, assuming the person needing the care is placed as an inpatient.

Medicare coverage—hospital insurance, medical insurance, Medicare advantage plans, and Medicare prescription drug plans, all with their own eligibility requirements.

hospital insurance (Part A)—most people age 65 or older who are citizens or permanent residents of the United States are eligible for free Medicare hospital insurance.

Part A helps pay for inpatient care in a hospital or skilled-nursing facility (following a hospital stay), some home health care, and hospice care.

medical insurance (Part B)—anyone who is eligible for free Medicare hospital insurance (Part A) can enroll in Medicare medical insurance (Part B) by paying a monthly premium. An individual who is not eligible for free hospital insurance can buy medical insurance, without having to buy hospital insurance, if 65 or older and:

- a U.S. citizen; or
- a lawfully admitted noncitizen who has lived in the United States for at least five years.
- Part B helps pay for doctors' services and many other medical services and supplies that are not covered by hospital insurance.

Medicare Advantage Plans (Part C)—individuals who have Medicare Parts A and B can join a Medicare Advantage Plan. Medicare Advantage Plans are offered by private companies and approved by Medicare. Medicare Advantage Plans generally cover many of the same benefits that a Medigap policy would cover, such as extra days in the hospital after using the number of days that Medicare covers.

Part C plans are available in many areas. People with Medicare Parts A and B can choose to receive all of their health-care services through one of these provider organizations under Part C.

Medicare Prescription Drug Plans (Part D)—anyone who has Medicare hospital insurance (Part A), medical insurance (Part B) or a Medicare Advantage Plan (Part C) is eligible for prescription drug coverage (Part D). Joining a Medicare prescription drug plan is voluntary and requires an additional monthly premium for the coverage. Some beneficiaries with higher incomes will pay a higher monthly Part D premium.

Part D helps pay for medications doctors prescribe for treatment.

mental incapacity—an absence of mental capacity in which one is unable to properly control one's assets and/or one's health-care decision making.

Miller or **d4B trust**—a trust in which a person has assigned the right to receive social security and pension payments in order to avoid having too much income to qualify for benefits like Medicaid.

Mini Mental State Examination (MMSE)—commonly used test to detect memory issues. It can be used by clinicians to help diagnose dementia and to assess its progression and severity.

minimum monthly marital needs allowance (MMMNA)—the amount of monthly income that the state Medicaid agency calculates the community spouse needs to survive. For example, the MMMNA in Illinois is $2,739 per month.

N

non-payback special-needs trust—any special-needs trust that is not a payback trust—primarily because it was created by a third party that has no legal obligation of support for the beneficiary.

non-spouse, third-party trustor/settlor/trustmaker/grantor—when the person who creates a trust or provides funding for a trust is not the beneficiary or the spouse of the beneficiary.

non-service-connected disability pension—a benefit for veterans or their surviving spouses with low incomes who have permanent and total disabilities when that disability is *not* related to military service. This is often referred to as a "special monthly pension" (or sometimes an "improved pension").

P

payback special-needs trust—sometimes referred to as a stand-alone trust, because each trust is individually drafted and will be received separately by the government. These trusts must be for the benefit of an individual under 65 years of age; the beneficiary must have disabilities as defined in 42 U.S.C. § 1382c(a)(3); the trust must be established by a parent, grandparent, legal guardian or court; and at the beneficiary's death, any residual funds are first used to pay back the state for Medical assistance received.

pay down—see spend down.

personal-care agreement—for purposes of this book, an agreement in which a person contracts to care for an individual with dementia. It is critical to affirmatively state within the agreement that the transfers made under the contract are not for love and affection, but rather for services rendered to the elder by the caretaker for fair market value.

Physician Orders for Life-Sustaining Treatment (POLST) Programs—provide a platform for end-of-life conversations between doctors and patients and a uniform way to document the wishes regarding those decisions so the patient's desires are understood and properly prioritized.

plenary guardianships—a person who has been appointed by the court to exercise all delegable legal rights and powers of the ward after the court has found that the ward lacks the capacity to perform all of the tasks necessary to care for his or her person or property. This is the main type of guardianships and consists of guardians of the person and guardians of the estate.

pooled trust—a trust established and administered by a nonprofit organization, which creates separate accounts for each beneficiary of the trust, but who also pools the assets of these separate accounts for the purposes of investment and management of funds. Funds deposited in the pooled trust are to be used for the sole benefit of an individual with special needs. The purpose of the trust is to supplement and not supplant any governmental benefits available to the individual with disabilities.

power of attorney—documents that allow a family member or trusted friend to have legal authority to carry out the wishes of people suffering from Alzheimer's once they are no longer able to speak or act for themselves. They can be for financial matters or health-care decisions or for property.

> parties to **power of attorney**—the person granting the authority by signing the documents is referred to as the principal, and the person being granted the authority is the agent or attorney of fact. This person stands in for the principal and is authorized to take almost any action for the principal so long as that action is included in the powers of attorney document.

public benefits—when individuals and families experience crises such as job loss, illness, disability, or divorce, they may face the prospect of falling into poverty (or becoming poorer) and losing health insurance coverage. There are two principal categories of public benefit programs—those that provide benefits regardless of income and those that limit assistance to people with low or modest incomes.

- The first category of programs includes the major social insurance programs such as Social Security, unemployment insurance, and Medicare.
- Programs in the second category are often referred to as "means-tested" programs. Means-tested programs play a large role in reducing the extent and severity of poverty and providing health care to low-income Americans. Some 11 million low-income U.S. citizens are lifted above the poverty line by means-tested benefits, and more than 55 million receive health insurance from the means-tested medical programs, Medicaid and State Children's Health Insurance Program. Most of these people would otherwise be uninsured.
- For purposes of this book, U.S. citizens who are affected by Alzheimer's disease and other dementias will most typically confront issues of eligibility for nursing home Medicaid benefits. The average senior citizen does not have sufficient savings or other assets to privately pay for one year of either assisted-living or nursing home care. Over 60 percent of the costs of nursing home care in the United States is paid by Medicaid.

Q

qualifying conditions (living will)—the conditions that trigger a living will to come into effect. They typically trigger a doctor to speak to a family member about making an end-life decision or cause an attending physician to say no more life treatment or to make a referral to hospice.

R

responsible party—for purposes of a nursing home contract, signing as a responsible party means assuming liability for any debts created by the resident. Under the federal Nursing Home Reform Act, nursing homes are not allowed to include responsible-party language in their contracts anymore; but the term is almost always included anyway.

revocable trust—a type of trust that can be revoked or changed at any time.

ruse entry—a form of scam in which the perpetrator pretends to be someone that the victim would allow into the house, such as a city water department worker.

S

self-settled or d4A trust—a special-needs trust funded with property belonging to the beneficiary and/or beneficiary's spouse, such as a direct inheritance, recovery in a personal injury lawsuit, or a gift.

sequencing—the act of putting things, people, and events in their proper order. People with Alzheimer's typically have trouble with sequencing.

short-term guardian—a guardian appointed to take over the guardian's duties each time the guardian is unavailable or unable to carry out those duties. A short-term guardian may be appointed in writing, without court approval.

special monthly pension—see non-service-connected disability pension.

special-needs trust—a type of irrevocable trust designed to benefit an individual who has a disability by allowing the retention and use of funds that can be used for the sole benefit of the individual and still qualify for means-tested public benefits, such as Supplemental Security Income and Medicaid. Use of the funds in a special-needs trust are limited to supplementing, but not supplanting, any benefits provided by governmental programs for people with disabilities.

spend-down requirement—a situation wherein a person must first use excess assets (as defined by Medicaid regulations) to privately pay for medical bills, prior to becoming eligible for nursing home Medicaid coverage.

spoofing—a financial scam in which perpetrators change their caller ID or e-mail address in an effort to appear to be someone legitimate, such as the victim's bank or credit card company.

stand-alone special-needs trust—established while the trustmaker is alive to make the trust available so that others may choose to deposit assets for the well-being of the person with special needs. For example, a parent creates an estate plan with a stand-alone special-needs trust for the benefit of a child. The parent informs the child's grandparents or other relatives of the availability of the trust to receive funds from those individuals or their estate plans.

substituted judgment standard—used to determine how the ward would have made a decision based on the ward's previously expressed preferences and make decisions in accordance with the preferences of the ward.

successor agent—term used for agents next in line behind the primary agent, usually used when dealing with advance directives. If the primary agent is not available, a successor agent may be called upon.

Supplemental-needs trust—see special-needs trust.

surrogate decision maker—a court-appointed decision maker for an incapacitated person, generally authorized to make health-care decisions for the patient. This is not a guardian.

T

temporary guardian—there are certain circumstances (including a guardian's death, incapacity, or resignation) in which the court may appoint a temporary guardian. For a temporary guardian to be appointed, it must be deemed necessary for the immediate welfare and protection of the person with alleged disabilities or estate on such notice and subject to such conditions as the court may prescribe. A temporary guardian has all of the powers and duties of a guardian of the person or of the estate that are specifically enumerated by court order.

testamentary capacity—the ability (also defined as being of sound mind and memory) to appreciate the following elements in relation to each other:

1. understanding of the nature of the act of making a will
2. general understanding of the nature and extent of the property
3. general recognition of those people who are the natural objects of the bounty
4. understanding of a distribution scheme.

testamentary special-needs trust—a trust that is created through a testamentary document, most often a will. A special-needs trust is a trust set up for someone with special needs in order to provide for that person's care and well-being. Therefore, a testamentary special-needs trust is a trust created by a will for the benefit of a person with special needs.

testamentary trust—a legal and fiduciary relationship created through explicit instructions in a deceased's will. A testamentary trust goes into effect upon an individual's death and is commonly used when someone wants to leave assets to a beneficiary but wishes to control the time, place, and manner of the distribution. Testamentary trusts are typically irrevocable.

testamentary will—a legal document that is used to transfer the probate estate to beneficiaries after the death of the testator.

third-party special-needs trusts—a special-needs trust that holds only property that did not belong to the beneficiary, the spouse, or any other person legally responsible for the beneficiary, before going into the trust.

totten trust—also referred to as a "payable on death account," a trust in which the settlor places money into an account that will become payable to the named beneficiary upon the death of the settlor.

transferred assets—the transfer of something of value from one person, place, or situation to another.

trapped inside the will—for purposes of this book, a trust that is created within a testamentary document such as a will and is not an independent, freestanding trust.

V

vulnerability—there is no legal standard for vulnerability, but vulnerable individuals are more likely to make poor financial decisions and are prime targets for scam artists and criminals.

W

ward—the subject of the guardianship, sometimes referred to as the conservatee.

wrongful resuscitation—the act of resuscitating a person against that person's wishes. These wishes are usually detailed in an advance directive.

INDEX

AARP, 334
ABA. *See* American Bar
    Association (ABA)
Abduction, 29–30, 269–270
Abuse, elder, 209–210, 320–321
Acute care, 186, 187, 188–189
Administrative expenses, special-
    needs trusts, 161
Adult children, conflicts among,
    237–238. *See also* Caregiver
    children
Adult children with disabilities,
    special-needs trusts for,
    169–174
Adult day care, 10–11

Adult Guardianship and
    Protective Proceedings
    Jurisdiction Act (2007),
    268–270
Advance directives, 53–150
    agent choice, 85–86
    Alzheimer's disease context,
        57–60
    definition of, 61
    do not resuscitate orders,
        55–56, 84–85
    federal laws, 61
    importance of, 53–60
    living wills, 60–68, 71–72
    online products, 59–60

Advance directives, *continued*
Physician Orders for Life-
Sustaining Treatment
programs and, 87
power of attorney, 68–83
ramifications of not having,
54–57
state laws, 61–68, 89–143
Advocates, 56
Agents
choosing, 85–86
definitions, 68
dissolution of marriage as
grounds for revocation in
California, 65
health-care agencies as, 75–76
New York law, 79
successor agents, 59, 76
Aging process, 297–301
Alabama
advance directives, 90–91
guardianships and
conservatorships, 268
Alaska
advance directives, 92
guardianships and
conservatorships, 268
Alcohol abuse, 286
Alzheimer's Association
family support program, 227
resource availability, 350
Safe Return program, 9
statistics, 18–19
Alzheimer's Caregiver Institute,
15–17
Alzheimer's disease
advance directives, 53–150
definition of, 1–2

ethical issues when dealing with
clients with, 25–50
financial exploitation, 283–314
government benefits, 185–224
guardianships and
conservatorships, 229–277
journey of, 4–18, 316–317
living situation of those living
with, 8
nursing home contracts,
337–347
personal-care agreements,
315–337
questions lawyers must address,
2, 58–59
signs of, 2–3, 5–6, 8–9, 225–227,
300–301, 348–349
special-needs trusts (SNTs),
151–181
statistics, 17, 18–20
young onset, 174
American Bar Association (ABA)
Commission on Law and Aging,
25–26, 34, 70
Formal Ethics Opinion 96-404,
28–29, 31
Model Rules of Professional
Conduct (*See* Model Rules of
Professional Conduct)
American Medical Association, 8
American Psychological
Association, 25–26, 34
Antibiotics, 74
Arbitration clauses, 342–343
Arizona
advance directives, 92–93
guardianships and
conservatorships, 268

Arkansas
  advance directives, 94
  guardianships and
    conservatorships, 268
Aschenbrenner, Cherie, 292–293,
  294, 296, 301, 309
*Assessment of Older Adults with
  Diminished Capacity*, 34–38,
  46–47
Assets. *See also* Transferred assets
  changes in ownership and
    power of attorney, 83
  citations to discover, 303–305
  citations to recover, 305–307
  Medicaid eligibility, 199–208
Assisted living, 11–13, 188
Attestation clause, 81
Attorney-client privilege, 29
Attorneys. *See also* Capacity
    evaluation; Client-lawyer
    relationship
  financial exploitation, 290,
    292, 302
  importance of consulting with
    before Medicaid spend down
    process, 203–205, 207
  questions to address about
    disease, 2, 58–59
Attorney's fees, 204–205

"Badland Decisions," 162
Banks, 241
Behavior, changes in, 225–226
Beneficiary designations, power of
    attorney, 82
"Best interests" hearing, 270–273
Bookkeeping services, 325
Brain, aging process, 297–301

Bryson, Dean, 36–37
Bypass estate planning, 166–167

California
  advance directives, 63–65,
    94–95
  divorce actions brought by
    guardians and conservators
    on behalf of ward, 275
  guardianships and
    conservatorships, 247–248,
    261–262, 275
  Medicaid, 216–217
  Medigap policies, 194
  power of attorney, 77
Caller ID, 294–295
Capacity
  guardianship and, 235–236
  levels of, 21, 58
  power of attorney
    requirements, 69
Capacity evaluation
  abbreviations, 47
  challenges, 21–23
  client interview script, 48–50
  client-lawyer relationship and,
    26–34
  common mistakes, 278–281
  conclusion codes, 47
  estate planning issues,
    298–299
  example of, 23–24
  orientation questions,
    232–234
  before power of attorney
    creation, 286–287
  speaking to client alone, 303
  worksheet for, 35–38

Caregiver children
    court's presumption that
        services performed by are
        gratuitous, 330–332
    personal-care agreements,
        319–321
    Rule 1.14 issues, 33–34
Caregivers. *See also* Personal-care
    agreements
    burdens on, 197–198, 327–329
    employment taxes, 212,
        329–330
    tips for, 147–150
    wages, 324, 333–335
Care managers, 211, 232, 237
*Center for Special Needs Trust
    Administration, Inc. v. Olson*,
    162–163
Centers for Medicare and
    Medicaid Services (CMS),
    56, 338
Charitable pooled trusts, 154, 155,
    160–163
Charities, solicitations by, 3
Church members, financial
    exploitation by, 301–302
Citations to discover assets,
    303–305
Citations to recover assets,
    305–307
Civil liberties, 254–255
Client-lawyer relationship
    client with diminished capacity,
        26–39
    communication, 39–40
    confidentiality of information,
        40–42
    conflicts of interest, 42–46

Clinical assessments, 234
Clinical trials, 350
Coercion, 306
Cognitive impairments, 26, 227
"Colicky dementia," 315–316
Colorado
    advance directives, 96–97
    guardianships and
        conservatorships, 268
Comfort care, 145
Communication, client-lawyer,
    39–40
Community spouse resource
    allocation (CSRA), 201, 206
Community spouses, 164,
    200–202, 205–206
Confabulation, 21–22
Confidentiality of information,
    40–42
Conflict, family, 237–238
Conflicts of interest, 42–46
Connecticut
    advance directives, 98
    divorce actions brought by
        guardians and conservators
        on behalf of ward,
        276–277
    guardianships and
        conservatorships, 268,
        276–277
Conservatorships. *See*
    Guardianships and
    conservatorships
Contested guardianships and
    conservatorships,
    252–258, 260
Continuous care, 145
Contractors, drive-by, 295–296

Contracts. *See also* Personal-care
agreements
among relatives, 331
assisted living, 13
caregivers, 209–212,
318–319
in-home care, 318–319
nursing homes, 337–342
Contractual capacity, 47, 58
Corporate guardian of the
estate, 241
Countable assets, Medicaid,
199–200
Court-appointed guardians,
232, 268
*Cruzan v. Director of Missouri
Department of Health*, 84
CSRA (community spouse
resource allocation),
201, 206
Cultural issues, 331
Custodial care, 10, 189

Dead man's statutes, 328–329
Death, 15–18
"Death is imminent," 71, 72, 73
Debt collection scavengers, 296
Deficit Reduction Act (2005),
200, 204
Dehydration, 146
Delaware
advance directives, 98–99
guardianships and
conservatorships, 268
Delusions, 9, 33–34
Dementia
"colicky," 315–316
definition of, 1

Dependency and Indemnity
Compensation (DIC),
222–224
D4A (self-settled) trusts, 157–158,
160, 161, 169
D4B (Miller) trusts, 160
D4C (pooled) trusts, 154, 155,
160–163
DIC (Dependency and Indemnity
Compensation), 222–224
Dignity for client trust, 156
Diminished capacity, 5–6, 26–39.
See also Capacity evaluation
Disability, assessment for
guardianship, 233–235
Disability panels, 298–299
Disability pensions, veterans non-
service-connected, 219–224
Disclosure, avoiding
inappropriate, 32–34
Disinheritance, 166–167
Dissolution of marriage, 65,
270–277
District of Columbia
advance directives, 100
guardianships and
conservatorships, 268
Division of assets, 205–207
Divorce, 65, 270–277
DNRs (do not resuscitate orders),
55–56, 84–85
Doctors. *See* Physicians
Documentation, 235, 320–321,
326–327
Do not resuscitate orders (DNRs),
55–56, 84–85
Drews, In re Marriage of, 270–272
Drive-by contractors, 295–296

Drug abuse, 286
Durable power of attorney, 61, 68, 80–81
Duress, 306
Duty of loyalty, 45

Eighth Circuit Court, pooled trusts, 163
Elder abuse, 209–210, 320–321
Elder-law attorneys. *See* Attorneys
Electronic advance directives, 65
Emergencies, temporary guardianship in, 242–246, 248–249, 253
Emergency medical services, 11–12
Emotional abuse, 285–286
Employer-employee relationship, 318
Employment taxes, 212, 329–330
Escape clauses, 13
Estate plans and planning. *See also* Capacity evaluation
bypass estate planning, 166–167
declining representation, 25–26
drafting, 298–299
examination after Alzheimer's diagnosis, 235, 280
guardianships and, 237
Ethical issues. *See* Model Rules of Professional Conduct
Exempt assets, Medicaid, 199–203, 205–206
Expert testimony, 256–258
Exploitation. *See* Financial exploitation

Fair market value, 333–335
Falling, 9

Family members, 29–30, 330–332
Federal Arbitration Act, 342–343
Federal law
advance directives, 61, 75
special-needs trusts, 157–158
Federal Nursing Home Reform Act, 340–341, 343–345
Feeding tubes, 73
Felony, 310–311
Fiduciary relationships, 307–309
15-minute reset test, 6
Financial decisions, power of attorney for, 68, 80–83
Financial exploitation, 283–314
abuse of power of attorney for, 285, 286–288
by attorneys, 290, 302
defenses against, 303–311
drive-by contractors, 295–296
during economic hardship, 288–289
emotional abuse and, 285–286
examples of, 229–231
forensic accounting, 291–292
"grandma scam," 293–294
by guardians, 290–291
infomercials, 3
lotteries, 3–4, 294
online scams, 288
by police officers, 289
prosecution difficulties, 312–314
ruse entry scam, 295
"sex for signatures," 284–285
spoofing, 294–295
by strangers, 292–293
thief's justifications for, 285

vulnerability of elderly people, 297–301

"wolf in sheep's clothing," 301–303

Financial issues, burden on caregiver spouses, 197–199

Finkel, Sanford, 36–37, 278–281

Five Wishes, 70

Five-year look-back period, 207–208

Florida

advance directives, 65–66, 100–101

divorce actions brought by guardians and conservators on behalf of ward, 273–274

guardianships and conservatorships, 248–249, 262–265, 273–274

Medicaid, 215–216

Medigap policies, 194

power of attorney, 77–78

Flynn, Amy, 285, 286

Forensic accounting, 291–292

Form 1040, 212, 329

Fraud, 306–307

Fraudulent conveyance, 162

Georgia

advance directives, 102

Geriatric care managers, 149, 211, 323

Gifts and gifting

of agent with power of attorney, 83

interest in home, 89–90

and Medicaid eligibility, 207–209

Gift tax, 208–209

Golbert, Charles, 286, 290, 302, 305, 307–308

Government benefits, 185–224

Medicaid (*See* Medicaid)

Medicare (*See* Medicare)

Veterans Affairs (VA) benefits, 219–224, 342

"Grandma scam," 293–294

"Granny snatching" cases, 269–270

Grantors, 155

Grantor trusts, 173

Guardian, defined, 231. *See also* Guardianships and conservatorships

Guardian ad litem, 242–246, 252

Guardian of person, 239–240, 258–259

Guardian of the estate, 240–241, 259–260

Guardianships and conservatorships, 229–277

appointment of guardian, 249–258

contested, 252–258, 260

court appointment, 232, 268

disability requirement, 233–235

divorce actions on behalf of ward, 270–277

family conflict, 237–238

guardian defined, 232

importance of, 229–231

mental capacity, 235–236

monitoring of, 290–291

purpose of, 231–232

reporting requirements, 258–260

Guardianships and
conservatorships, *continued*
state law, 232, 247–249,
261–268, 270–277
state terminology
differences, 232
substituted judgment standard,
236–237
termination or removal of
guardian, 260–268
types of, 238–246
uniform law governing,
268–270
Guilt, 285, 314

Hallucinations, 9
Hawaii
advance directives, 102
guardianships and
conservatorships, 268
Health-care agencies, power of
attorney, 75–76
Health-care plans, nursing home
residents, 345
Health-care power of attorney. *See*
Power of attorney for health
care
Health care proxy (New York),
79–80. *See also* Power of
attorney for health care
Health issues, of caregivers, 328
Hearings
contested guardianship,
254–258, 260
divorce actions brought by
guardians and conservators
on behalf of ward, 270–273
Helpline, 350

Higgason, In re Marriage of, 275
Home-based care, 10, 182–184,
186, 318–319
Home-health aids, 334
Home health care, 188, 190
Homes, gifting interest in, 89–90
Hospice care, 15–18, 144–146,
190–191
Hospital insurance. *See* Medicare
Huey, Jo, 15–17, 147–150

Idaho
advance directives, 102–103
guardianships and
conservatorships, 268
Illinois
advance directives, 62–63, 104
citations to discover assets,
304–305
contested guardianship,
254–257
D4C (pooled) trust ban,
162, 163
disability definition, 235
divorce actions brought by
guardians and conservators
on behalf of ward, 270–273
elder abuse law, 209–210,
320–321
financial exploitation of elderly
person, 310–311
guardianships and
conservatorships, 238, 268,
270–273
Medicaid, 212–215
Medigap policies, 194
minimum monthly marital
needs allowance, 201

power of attorney, 75–77
qualifying conditions definition,
  71–72
surrogate decision makers, 55, 59
terminal illness definition, 70–71
Illinois Probate Act, 255, 304, 329
Illinois State Bar Association, code
  of ethics, 7–8
Immediate power of attorney,
  80–81
Imminent death, 71, 72, 73
Incapacity. *See also* Capacity
  evaluation
  citations to recover assets, 306
  definition of, 52
  estate planning issues, 298–299
Income limitations
  Medicaid, 198, 201–202, 214,
    215–216
  veterans non-service-connected
    disability pensions, 221–222
Indiana
  advance directives, 104–105
  guardianships and
    conservatorships, 268
Infections, 16, 149
Infomercials, 3
Informed consent, 45–46
In-home care, 10, 182–184, 186,
  318–319
Inpatient care, 188
Institutionalized spouse, 164,
  200–201, 205–206
Intent, transfer of assets and
  Medicaid eligibility, 335–337
Internal Revenue Services (IRS),
  212, 329–330
Inter vivos trusts, 58, 82, 167

Iowa
  advance directives, 106
  guardianships and
    conservatorships, 268
Irrevocable trusts, 158, 159, 207

Jacobson, Shay, 229, 285,
  300–301, 315–316
Johns, Harry, 348–350
Joint representation, 42–46
Joint tenancies, power to server, 82

Kansas
  advance directives, 106
Karbin v. Karbin, 271, 272–273
Kentucky
  advance directives, 106–107
  guardianships and
    conservatorships, 268

Law, Rick, 30, 53, 340
Letters
  declining representation, 25–26
  follow-up after meetings, 38
Liens, Medicaid, 200
Life-sustaining treatment, 55–56,
  71, 73–74, 86
Limited guardianship, 246, 248
Live at Home Technologies,
  182–184
Living situations, 8
Living wills, 60–68
  defined terms in, 60
  federal law regulating, 61
  purpose of, 60
  qualifying conditions, 71–72
  state law regulating, 61, 62–68
  Terri Schiavo case, 60–61

Long-term care, 38, 197–199. *See also* Nursing homes
Long-term care insurance, 186
Look-back period, 207–208
Lotteries, 3–4, 294
Louisiana
advance directives, 108
Luster v. Luster, 276–277

Mail, financial exploitation scams, 292–293
Maine
advance directives, 108–109
guardianships and conservatorships, 269
Mainzer v. Avril, 274
Malpractice, 167
Maryland
advance directives, 110
guardianships and conservatorships, 269
Massachusetts
advance directives, 110–111
guardianships and conservatorships, 269
McRae v. McRae, 274
Medicaid
asset spend down strategies, 203–209
caregiver contracts and, 209–212, 320–321, 322, 325–327, 332–337
coverage, 197
custodial services, 10
eligibility, 199–212, 320–321, 322, 325–327, 332–337
Medicare vs., 187–188

misunderstandings about, 195–197
nursing home coverage, 15
power of attorney, 80
purpose of, 197
state examples, 212–219
state implementation, 195–196, 197
stigma of, 196
transfer-of-assets period-of-ineligibility rules, 158
unallowable special-needs trusts, 167
VA benefit asset limitation test and, 222
Medicaid bed, 341
Medicaid trusts, 158–159, 160–163
Medi-Cal (California), 216–217
Medical reports, 258
Medicare
Alzheimer's disease coverage limitations, 185–187
benefits, 190–192
coverage, 187–188, 189
custodial services, lack of coverage for, 10, 189
deductibles, coinsurance, and copayments, 191, 193–194
eligibility, 187, 189–190
hospice care guidelines, 15, 144–146
Medicaid vs., 187–188
Medigap policies, 193–194
Part A, 189–191
Part B, 191
Part C (Medicare Advantage Plans), 192

Part D (prescription drug coverage), 192–193
purpose of, 188
Medicare Advantage Plans, 192
Medicare Catastrophic Coverage Act (MCCA), 205
Medigap policies, 193–194
Memory loss, 4–8, 21–22, 317–318
Mental capacity. *See* Capacity
Mental health facilities, admittance by guardian, 240
Mental incapacity. *See* Incapacity
Michigan
advance directives, 112
Miller trusts, 160
Mini Mental State Examination (MMSE), 23, 287, 301
Minimum monthly marital needs allowance (MMMNA), 201–203
Minnesota
advance directives, 112–113
guardianships and conservatorships, 269
Mississippi
advance directives, 114
guardianships and conservatorships, 269
Missouri
advance directives, 114–115
guardianships and conservatorships, 269
MMMNA (minimum monthly marital needs allowance), 201–203
MMSE (Mini Mental State Examination), 23, 287, 301

Model Rules of Professional Conduct
Rule 1.4, 39–40
Rule 1.6, 40–42
Rule 1.7, 42–46
Rule 1.14, 26–39
Mohrmann v. Kob, 274–275
MoneyPak, 293–294
Monitoring technology, for remote in-home care, 182–184
Montana
advance directives, 116
guardianships and conservatorships, 269
Mosey, Sara, 36–37

Nadkarni, Nishad "Nick," 21–24, 28, 33–34, 36–37
National Hospice Association Guidelines, 15
Nebraska
advance directives, 116–117
guardianships and conservatorships, 269
Needs assessments, 323
Net worth limitations, veterans non-service-connected disability pensions, 221–222
Nevada
advance directives, 118
guardianships and conservatorships, 269
New Hampshire
advance directives, 118–119
New Jersey
advance directives, 120
guardianships and conservatorships, 269

New Mexico
  advance directives, 120
  guardianships and
    conservatorships, 269
New York
  advance directives, 67–68,
    120–121
  divorce actions brought by
    guardians and conservators
    on behalf of ward,
    274–275
  guardianships and
    conservatorships, 249,
    265–267, 269, 274–275
  Medicaid, 218–219
  Medigap policies, 194
  power of attorney, 79–80
Non-allowable transfers, 204,
  208, 210
Non-payback special-needs trusts,
  156, 164
Non-service-connected
  disability pensions,
  219–224
Non-spouse, third-party special-
  needs trusts, 156, 165, 167,
  172–174
North Carolina
  advance directives, 122
North Dakota
  advance directives, 122–123
  guardianships and
    conservatorships, 269
Notice
  contested guardianship
    hearings, 255
  nursing home transfers and
    discharges, 346

Nursing homes
  with Alzheimer's special-care
    units, 339, 346–347
  choosing, 13–15, 338–339
  contracts, 337–342
  cost of, 14–15, 339
  fear of, 309–310
  health-care plans, 345
  Medicare's lack of coverage,
    186–187
  residents' rights, 343–345
  Social Security check
    assignment to, 341
  transfers and discharges,
    345–347

Ohio
  advance directives, 124
  guardianships and
    conservatorships, 269
Oklahoma
  advance directives, 124–125
  guardianships and
    conservatorships, 269
Omnibus Budget Reconciliation
  Act of 1993 (OBRA 93),
  157–158, 168–169
Online advance directives, 59–60
Online financial scams, 288
Oral contracts, 328–329
Oregon
  advance directives, 126–127
  guardianships and
    conservatorships, 269
Orientation questions, 233–234

Parkinson's disease, 73–74
Payback special-needs trusts, 156

Pay down requirement, 203–209

Peck, Kerry, 233

Pennsylvania
advance directives, 128
guardianships and
conservatorships, 269

Pensions, veterans non-service-
connected disability, 219–224

Personal-care agreements
court's presumption that
services performed by family
members are gratuitous,
330–332
drafting after care has started,
321–322, 336
drafting tips, 211–212, 323–327
employment taxes, 212, 330
importance of, 209–211,
320–321
lack of, 328–329
Medicaid eligibility and, 320–321,
322, 325–327, 332–337

Personal-care attendants, 334

Peterson, Carolyn, 144–146

Petitions
for adjudication of disability
and appointment of guardian,
250–252
for termination of guardian,
260–261

Physician Orders for Life-
Sustaining Treatment
(POLST) programs, 87

Physicians
Alzheimer's disease diagnosis,
349–350
capacity evaluation, 298–299
patient privilege, 7–8

Physician testimony, 257–258

A Place for Mom, 338

Plenary guardianship, 239–241

Pneumonia, 16

Police officers, 289, 301, 309

POLST (Physician Orders for
Life-Sustaining Treatment)
programs, 87

POMS (Program Operations
Manual Systems), 158

Pooled Advocate Trust, In re, 162

Pooled (D4C) trusts, 154, 155,
160–163

Power of attorney for health care,
68–83
agent appointment, 85–86
drafting, 69–75
guardianship vs., 232
importance and purpose of, 68
mental capacity
requirements, 69
questions to ask before
granting, 68–69
revocation of, 76–77, 78
state law, 75–80

Power of attorney for property
abuse of for financial
exploitation, 285, 286–288
adult children as, 209–210
agent appointment, 85–86
drafting, 80–83
guardianship vs., 232
importance and purpose of, 68
mental capacity
requirements, 69
questions to ask before
granting, 68–69

Prenuptial agreements, 201

Prescription drug coverage,
Medicare, 192–193
Priests, financial exploitation
by, 302
Principal agents, 59, 65, 68, 76
Program Operations Manual
Systems (POMS), 158
Property, power of attorney for.
See Power of attorney for
property
Protective orders, 254
Public benefits. *See* Government
benefits

Qualifying conditions, 71–72
Questioning technique, 279

Real estate tax collection
scavengers, 296–297
Reporting requirements,
guardianships and
conservatorships, 258–260
Representation, declining, 25–26
Residence, principal place of,
200–203
Residential facilities, guardian's
placement of ward in, 252
Respite care, 10, 145
Responsible party, in nursing
home contracts, 340
Revocable trusts, 158, 159
Rhode Island
advance directives, 128–129
Ruse entry, 295

Safety, 8–9, 11–12
Samis v. Samis, 275–276
Schiavo, Terri, 60–61

Self-employment tax, 212, 330
Self-settled special-needs trusts,
157–158, 160, 161, 169
Sepsis, 16, 149
Sequencing, 301
"Sex for signatures" scam,
284–285
Short-term guardianship,
241–242, 260–261
Short-term memory, 301
Skilled nursing care, 188, 189,
190, 203
SNTs. *See* Special-needs trusts
(SNTs)
Social Security Administration
(SSA), Program Operations
Manual Systems (POMS), 158
Social Security checks,
assignment to nursing
home, 341
South Carolina
advance directives, 130
guardianships and
conservatorships, 269
South Dakota
advance directives, 130–131
guardianships and
conservatorships, 269
pooled trusts, 162–163
Special monthly pension, veterans,
219–221, 342
Special-needs trusts (SNTs),
151–181
administrative expenses, 161
for adult children with
disabilities, 169–174
case study, 152–154
common mistakes, 167–169, 175

D4A trusts, 160
drafting challenges, 155–157
goal of, 151
law governing, 157–159
Miller trusts, 160
payback vs. non-payback
  trusts, 156
revocable vs. irrevocable
  trusts, 159
for spouse, 164–169, 176–181
testamentary trusts, 164–167
third-party, 172–174
transfer of assets from inter
  vivos trust, 167
Spend down requirement,
  203–209
Spoofing, 294–295
Spousal special-needs trusts,
  164–169, 176–181
Springing power of attorney, 80–81
Stand-alone special-needs
  trust, 170
State law
  advance directives, 61–68,
    89–143
  dead man's statutes, 328–329
  guardianships, 232, 247–249,
    261–268, 270–277
  Medicaid, 195–196, 197,
    212–219
  Medigap policies, 194
  power of attorney, 75–80
Statutory power of attorney,
  70, 211
Strangers, financial exploitation
  by, 292–293
Substituted judgment standard,
  236–237

Successor agents, 59, 76
Supplemental needs trusts. *See*
  Special-needs trusts (SNTs)
Surrogate decision makers, 54–55,
  59, 77–78, 240

Taxes
  employment, 212, 329–330
  gift, 208–209
Taylor, Shelley E., 297–298
Technology, for remote in-home
  care, 182–184
Telephone, financial exploitation
  scams, 292, 293–295
Temporary guardianship,
  248–249, 252, 261,
  264–265
Tennessee
  advance directives, 132
  guardianships and
    conservatorships, 269
Terminal illness, 70–71, 72
Termination or removal of
  guardian, 260–268
Testamentary capacity, 35–36, 58,
  279–280
Testamentary special-needs trusts,
  164–169
Testamentary trusts, 58
Testamentary wills, 58
Texas
  advance directives, 132–133
Thies, William, 225–227
Third Circuit Court of Appeals,
  pooled trusts, 163
Third-party special-needs trusts,
  156, 165, 167, 172–174
Totten trust, 83

Transferred assets
  federal statute, 158
  five-year look-back, 207–208
  non-allowable, 204, 208, 210
  personal-care contracts and,
    320–321, 335–337
  special-needs trusts and,
    158, 165
"Trapped inside the will," 165, 170
Trusts, power of attorney, 82–83.
  See also Special-needs trusts
  (SNTs)

Undue influence, 306, 308
Uniform Adult Guardianship
  and Protective Proceedings
  Jurisdiction Act (2007),
  268–270
Uniform Health-Care Decisions
  Act, 142–143
Utah
  advance directives, 134
  guardianships and
  conservatorships, 269

Vaughn v. Guardianship, 273–274
Vermont
  advance directives, 134–135
  divorce actions brought by
    guardians and conservators
    on behalf of ward, 275–276
  guardianships and
    conservatorships, 269,
    275–276

Veterans Affairs (VA) benefits,
  219–224, 342
Virginia
  advance directives, 136
  guardianships and
    conservatorships, 269
Voirin, Linda, 299–300, 303, 309,
  310, 312–314
Vulnerability, determination of,
  297–301

Wages, of caregivers, 324,
  333–335
Wandering, 8–9, 11
Ward, defined, 231. *See also*
  Guardianships and
  conservatorships
Washington
  advance directives, 136–137
  guardianships and
    conservatorships, 269
Weight loss, 16, 146
West Virginia
  advance directives, 138–139
  guardianships and
    conservatorships, 269
Wisconsin
  advance directives, 140–141
"Wolf in sheep's clothing,"
  financial exploitation by,
  301–303
Wrongful resuscitation, 55–56
Wyoming
  advance directives, 142